Victory Dances

The Story of Fred Berk,
a Modern Day Jewish Dancing Master

by Judith Brin Ingber

To Talla,

Who understands so well how to live with beauty — and helps people to absorb art in life

Best,
Judy
December, 1985

© Judith Brin Ingber
   1985

Published by the Israel Dance Library, 26, Bialik St., Tel Aviv, Israel

American Distribution by Emmett Publishing
2861 Burnham Boulevard, Minneapolis, Minnesota 55416

ISBN 0-934682-11-9

CONTENTS

FOREWORD. 5
ACKNOWLEDGEMENTS. 6
CHAPTER ONE: FRED AS HE WAS. 8
CHAPTER TWO: VIENNA. 14
CHAPTER THREE: SWITZERLAND. 30
CHAPTER FOUR: ENGLAND. 34
CHAPTER FIVE: CUBA. 37
CHAPTER SIX: AMERICA 44
CHAPTER SEVEN: OPTIMISM 48
CHAPTER EIGHT: RECONSTRUCTIONISM 51
CHAPTER NINE: AMERICAN DANCE AT THE Y. 54
CHAPTER TEN: RECONSTRUCTION AND DANCERS. . .58
CHAPTER ELEVEN: THE JEWISH DANCE GUILD. 61
CHAPTER TWELVE: SEEING AMERICA. 65
CHAPTER THIRTEEN: EUROPE .68
CHAPTER FOURTEEN: ISRAEL .71
CHAPTER FIFTEEN: STAGE FOR DANCERS. 75
CHAPTER SIXTEEN: ANOTHER START. 79
CHAPTER SEVENTEEN: THE "MERRY-GO-ROUNDERS" 83
CHAPTER EIGHTEEN: ISRAEL AND HEBRAICA 86
CHAPTER NINETEEN: CATASTROPHE 90
CHAPTER TWENTY: LABANOTATION. 93
CHAPTER TWENTY-ONE: CAMP BLUE STAR 96
CHAPTER TWENTY-TWO: THE ISRAEL DANCE FESTIVALS. 97
CHAPTER TWENTY-THREE: BERK'S ISRAEL. 100
FOOTNOTES. 108
LIST OF WORKS BY FRED BERK 114

Dedicated to my sons, Shai and Noah and also Claudia V.

FOREWARD

by Anna Sokolow

I remember meeting Fred Berk in New York and in Israel. He was one of the first artists I knew who was deeply interested in Israeli folk dancing. His dedication will always be remembered.

Fred had been on a quest. Not content with a mere superficial or "tourist" knowledge of folk dance, he delved into the roots and meanings of the dances of Jews from all over the world. He not only realized the importance of their preservation but he worked with tremendous energy, depth and integrity to transmit them to others.

Fred was extremely active in Israel in the world of folk dance. He traveled throughout the country wherever folk dances were performed and also visited the Israeli villages of the different ethnic groups. In that way he saw and learned dances from the many parts of the world where Jews have lived. Fred was also closely associated with the pioneers of dance in Israel: Gertrud Kraus, Sara Levi-Tanai and Gurit Kadman, to name a few.

In the United States, he was very active in presenting Israeli folk dance. He brought Israeli dance to New York, an environment which hardly knew of its existence. We are very lucky to have this extremely important book which tells Fred's story. It will speak not only to dancers, but to all people, as Fred Berk did, reminding us of our international roots. In gathering folk dances from all over the world, he has reminded us of joy in life — a common language, a language shared by all people who are interested in art and culture. Recognizing the importance of passing on folk traditions, he dedicated his life to finding, preserving, teaching, and performing these dances.

ACKNOWLEDGEMENTS

Without the ongoing and sympathetic support of Dr. Riv-Ellen Prell including her outright donation of office space to write in, this book would not have been completed. I also wish to acknowledge Dr. Dawn Lille Horwitz's initial help in New York, Giora Manor's continuing aid throughout the years culminating with the publication of this manuscript in Israel eight years from its beginning, the constant support of my husband Jerome and the patience of Shai and Noah when I went off to the library to work on "Dod Fred's story." Others through the years who offered invaluable advice, information and expertise include Ruth Brin, Selma Jeanne Cohen, Ruth Goodman, Ayalah Goren, Dr. Bert Horwitz, Toni Helstein, Ruth Lert, Bernard Liebhaber, Gertrude Lippincott, Sylvia Rosen, Steven W. Siegel, Celida Villalon, Leland Windreich, and Sybil Zimmerman.

Fred Berk's story would not have been complete without the interviews and materials generously given me. My thanks go to Dov Alton, Vyts Beliajus, Bonnie Bird, Bruce Bloch, Yardena Cohen, Miriam Cole, Ralph Davis, Katya Delakova, Elsa Dublon, Jeff Duncan, Ya'acov Eden, Judith Eisenstein, Howard Epstein, Laurie Freedman Myers, Helen Garbutt, Ruth Goodman, Art and Ayalah Goren, Gary Harris, Mary Hinkson, Doris Hering, Shalom and Devorah Hermon, Dr. Bert Horwitz, Claudia Vall Kauffman, Steffi Kay, Shula Bat-Ari Kivel, Herb Kummel, Sara Levi-Tanai, Paula Levine, Sophie Maslow, Sima Mittman, Joyce Dorfman Mollov, Meredith Monk, Esther Nelson, Alwin Nikolais, Genevieve Oswald, Herman Popkin, Doris Ebener Rudko, Bessie Schönberg, Steven W. Siegel, Marcia B. Siegel, Anna Sokolow, Walter Sorrell, Manon Souriou, Paul Spong, Carolyn Strauss, Yemmy Strum, Rivka Sturman, Livia Drapkin Vanaver, Lucy Venable, Ann Wilson Wangh and Ernestine Weiss.

I am grateful, too, for the encouragement of the following editors who published excerpts of this biography as it was in progress: Dianne Woodruff, editor of Congress on Research in Dance's *Dance Research Journal* (The Vienna Years, Spring, 1981); Adam Lahm, editor of *Arabesque* (Sept., 1983), Giora Manor, editor of the *Israel Dance Annual* (1983 issue), George Dorris, editor of *Dance Chronicle* (Summer, 1984).

The primary illustrations for this book were given to me by Fred Berk and Katya Delakova. Other photos came from the Bernard Liebhaber collection and that of Livia Drapkin Vanaver. Kind permission to reproduce materials was given to me by the Dance Notation Bureau which published Fred Berk's *Holiday in Israel*, notated by Lucy Venable, in 1977; William Como, editor of *Dance Magazine*, and Steven W. Siegel, archivist of the 92nd St. Y.

Herman Popkin of Camp Blue Star and the Nikolais-Louis Foundation were also generous in loaning material.

As several persons appearing in these pages emigrated from one country to

another, they changed their names or the spelling thereof. Thus Fritz (Friedrich) Berger became Fred Berk and Claudia Vall-Kauffmann became Kauffman. Hence the variation in spelling in different chapters of the book.

CHAPTER ONE:
FRED AS HE WAS

The first time I met Fred Berk I was in my last year at Sarah Lawrence College. It was May, only a week before graduation in 1967. I was one of three students appointed to drive into Manhattan to pick him up and bring him back to teach in the dance department. On Friday mornings, Bessie Schönberg, the director of the college dance department, invited special guest teachers. Fred Berk was the last for the year. I knew his name from the small, neatly framed advertisement which had appeared for years in *Dance Magazine*: "Fred Berk, Director of the Jewish Dance Department, 92nd Street Y, New York City." It had always aroused my curiosity, but now I was not sure I liked the idea of such a guest for our last class. Like other students in the dance department, I hoped for a career in dance after graduation and I resented giving up precious class time for folk dance and not a technique class.

Berk lived in an apartment house on the East side near the 92nd St. Y. Adinah Margolis (an MA candidate in dance who had been Berk's assistant at the 92nd St. Y) went in to get him. When she returned with him and his accompanist I was taken aback. Berk was slight in build like a dancer, it was true, but he was totally bald and seemed relatively old and he wore a heavy orthopedic boot on one foot. He limped toward the car, leaning on his cane. Schönberg also had a pronounced limp but none of us attached any importance to it. She had been one of the legendary dancers in Martha Graham's first company and knew how to teach our bodies to move and our minds to think deeply about and create dance.

Berk and his accompanist moved into the back seat beside me. Without any small talk Berk leaned close and asked, "Have you heard any radio reports today?" Like Schönberg, he spoke English with a German acccent. For a minute I was surprised but then I realized he meant had I heard news of Israel. King Hussein was warmongering, President Nassser had closed the Tiran Straits and Egyptian troops were amassing on the Israeli border. We talked about Israel and her crisis on the 25-minute return trip to Sarah Lawrence in Bronxville.

Talk of war was ill-matched to the serenity and look of the Sarah Lawrence campus with everything in full bloom: the yellow forsythia, the pink and white dogwood trees and the purple wisteria on the arbor over the walk-way to Reisinger were particularly beautiful. We guided Mr. Berk to the basement dance studio in the performing arts complex of Reisinger designed by the modernist architect Le Corbusier. The dance studio was an odd triangular shape for a studio, the widest wall covered in mirrors with curtains waiting on either side to be closed as a backdrop for intimate studio performances. The wooden floor was springy as it must be for dancers and was highly glossed, favoring the bare feet of modern dancers.

Once in the dance studio where Schonberg awaited Berk, we hurried through

into the dressing room to change into our leotards and tights for the session on Israeli folk dance. I supposed it would be the usual horas which I knew from bar mitzvah celebrations.

Berk had entered the studio slowly, stepping down into the room with deliberation. He seemed to bow when Schönberg introduced him to the class. Perching on one of the tall stools, his accordionist standing beside him, he explained in spare terms the elements of the dances he would teach and introduced the variety of rhythms and movement patterns in quick succession. Soon we were circling, jumping and stomping until we reeled with the joy and excitement he built in us. We followed him as if we'd always known how to folk dance and preferred it above all else, as if we had never lost the communal feeling and group identity defined by generation after generation of townfolk dancing together at holidays and festivities. Despite the differences in our backrounds and geographic origins, we felt bound together in a way no technique class had given us.

He taught simply, but it was the simplicity of a master. There were no extra words, extra movements or padded time. I felt transformed by his lesson. My dancing seemed to expand me, to enlarge my relation with my classmates in a new way, to share in a communal joy. And it tied me to my people in Israel at a perilous time in a way I had rarely experienced.

During the following week, war broke out in the Middle East and I started my first job in Manhattan: assistant to the editor of *Dance Magazine*, the most important dance publication in the country under the skillful editorship of Lydia Joel. At the *Dance Magazine* office which was right off Broadway on 47th Street I met countless dancers, read countless stories on all aspects of dance and marveled at innumerable piles of dance photos. Slowly I acquired a more all-inclusive perspective on dance than I had before — anything a choreographer or a community called dance was as legitimate as the classics for the pages of the magazine. Folk dance took on new meaning for me when Joel chose the Yugoslavian Kolo dancers' photo for the cover of the first magazine I worked on.

To my surprise, Fred Berk telephoned me one day. Could we meet to discuss something? Later I learned that the request for a personal meeting to discuss a project was his trademark. He never did business over the phone and rarely by correspondence. He came to the office at lunchtime and we walked over to Jimmy's on 8th Avenue, a dark, quiet tavern. I was embarrassed passing peepshows and sleazy magazine shops, but Berk took no notice having already started to tell me the point of his visit. He had brought a manuscript on the recreational aspects of folk dance. Would I help him to rewrite the article and did I think *Dance Magazine* could use it? Other articles by Berk had appeared in the magazine before; I looked over the carefully typed article. His writing style was ponderous, almost halting, so different from the spirit of his dance class.

He asked if I were dancing. I looked at the menu as I sheepishly replied I did not have money for classes. To change the subject, I told him about the dance concerts I was able to see as a staff member of *Dance Magazine*. I went almost every night and sometimes twice on the weekends to see touring companies, loft perfomances of avant-garde dancers, concerts at Judson church in Greenwich Village, and dancers in sneakers at the old Yiddish Theatre, the Anderson on the Lower East Side. On the way back to the office Berk asked if I would like to come to his Wednesday night open session where both experienced and new folk dancers were welcome. "It's not far from where you live. You could be a scholarship student," he simply said. He understood how terribly I missed actually dancing and he seemed to understand my financial plight.

I accepted his offer eagerly.

The next Wednesday I walked to the 92nd St. YMHA, the fabled institution where so much of American modern dance had been premiered and performed over the years. It was a magic name in the New York dance world. I peeked in on the theatre on the main floor where a few weeks before the entire dance world had turned out for Louis Falco's company premiere. The house around the stage was richly paneled in dark wood and the names of Maimonides, Mozart and Moses circled the walls in gold letters near the ceiling as if to spread some kind of magic aura of the past over the proceedings.

Upstairs, in the large studio where Berk always taught, a crowd of perhaps 100 people milled about. They were all ages and sizes, wearing an assortment of footgear — Balkan dancing shoes, ballet slippers, and boots — and costumes — from leotards to shorts to slacks. Perched on a stool before a microphone at a long table on which a phonograph and a stack of records waited, Berk suggested starting with dances which everyone knew. Then he divided the class into long lines which changed into half circles and then the dancers joined hands making arches with dancers passing underneath until more and more intricate figures evolved following his constant directions in the clear, concise manner of talking he had. I marveled at the simplicity and strength of his instruction, at the joy and willingness of the class to try whatever he suggested.

At subsequent classes, Berk spoke about other dance teachers and dancers. He mentioned Gertrud Kràus, his first dance teacher from Vienna who had moved and worked in Israel. At another session, Hadassa Badoch demonstrated Yemenite-Jewish dance movements, something I had never seen before, with such a beautiful gliding yet angular quality. I was surprised by the combinations of rhythms and steps that she presented. I continued to dance at these Wednesday night sessions for the two years I worked in New York.

When the winter session started, Berk asked me also to attend the Tuesday evening rehearsals of his performing group, *Hebraica*. Adinah Margolis was staging "Around the Well," a new dance of hers. It was clear that the group was "amateur" and I would not be paid, but that was not important to me. I was rankled when Berk said "amateur", as I had always thought of this classification as somewhat deprecating, alluding to dance as a hobby of inferior quality. But I discovered in Berk's Tuesday sessions that the quality and seriousness and excitement were as high as those I knew in professional classes. It was rather the reasons for participating and the outcome which were different — the individual dancer found expression within the group, and that was unique. Some of the dancers were Wednesday night regulars. Most were high school students and many had grown up, so to speak, dancing at the Y. Some had been students of Berk whereas others worked with modern dancers in the Y dance department. The atmosphere was workmanlike. Rehearsals went like clockwork, beginning and ending exactly on time. In between there were no wasted moments. Berk was superbly prepared and filled each rehearsal with performance skills, choreographic elements, dance technique and humanism — all essential for a dancer's development.

During the dress rehearsal for the winter performance Berk and Gary Harris, the rotund lighting designer for the 92nd St. Y theatre, wore headphones and talked to each other. Sometimes Harris was in the wings and sometimes in the lighting booth; Berk was seated dead center in the best seat in the house. They spoke softly, the professionals that they were, in a telegraphic, abbreviated form of communication. They seemed to be in perfect rapport; there were no histrionics as the performance approached. Berk was steady, quiet and controlling and he demanded full-out expression. "A dress rehearsal is for you, not for your costumes," he said.

Regretfully I left the 92nd St. Y and New York dance, but I was happy to marry

and move to Israel with my husband in 1972. I knew Berk brought American youth on summer tours to study Israeli folk dance. Berk invited me to attend some of the remarkable workshops he had arranged with Israeli folk dance creators like Moshiko, Yaacov Levy, and Rivka Sturman; the next summer, he asked me to teach some classes for his touring youth. He was always business-like; he paid me handsomely by Israeli standards and he paid immediately, in the tradition of performers who are paid as soon as a concert ends.

One day in 1974 he invited me to a sidewalk cafe overlooking the Mediterranean Sea. The sun was setting as we sipped "Eiskaffee," a wonderful Israeli summer drink of iced coffee and ice cream served in a tall glass. He said he had decided to retire in Israel and had bought an apartment across from the Yarkon River in Tel Aviv, only a few blocks from where Jerome, my husband, and I lived.

Being neighbors changed our relationship. We saw each other often, and it was not restricted to dance situations. Jerome took him through the industrial area of Tel Aviv far to the south to get his license plates; we helped him carry boxes of his favorite operas and books from the post office when his household goods began to arrive from New York. On the phone he would ask for the "super," (slang for building caretaker or apartment superintendent) when he needed Jerome to come with his electric drill to make holes in the concrete walls to hang pictures. The two men joked in Yiddish. Berk loved to cook for us: wonderful meat stews, chicken soups, and pungent salads.

Berk particularly enjoyed the beach at Caesarea. There, where the Mediterranean had carved out a kind of cove, the Romans long ago had built a walled city, their capital in honor of Caesar. Pillars and columns with fluting and scrolls could still be found in the sands. South of the cove was the reconstructed Roman amphitheatre. Empty during the day, at night sometimes the amphitheatre was crowded with audiences to see the Israel Festival and hear Theodorakis, the Berlin opera, the Israel Philharmonic, or the London Festival Ballet with Rudolf Nureyev. Fred was a regular at Caesarea for concerts, too.

We picnicked during the quiet afternoons and did not leave until sunset. That was when the breakers took on a more menacing quality, sending spume swirling over the rocks. In the 1940's Caesarea was one of the landfalls for the illegal refugee boats from Europe.

But we never spoke of history. Once, driving back to Tel Aviv from Caesarea, Fred took a wrong turn and we found ourselves in an elegant neighborhood of beach houses and villas.

"Where are we?" I asked.

"In Yenevelt!" he said laughing.

"Yenevelt?"

"No place!" said Fred. "That's what Yenevelt means in Yiddish!"

Friday at four we gathered at Gurit Kadman's home for a special Shabbat-eve that usually included cherry and plum tortes, apple strudels and peach cakes. She was a dancer and had spearheaded the development of Israeli folk dance and the national folk dance festivals at Kibbutz Dalia, which had become a culural pilgrimage for both Israelis and visitors. With Shulamit Kadman, one of the first doctors in Israel, she had emigrated to then Palestine from Germany with Leo Kadman, her husband, in 1920. Fred had met Gurit on his first tour of Israel in 1949; I was introduced to the household in 1972.

The Kadman garden was the scene of many celebrations: Fred's realization of his dream to live in Zion, the end of the Yom Kippur War in 1973, and the birth of my first son. The war had isolated us from both Europe and America. There had been no mail delivery for weeks; even news of the war and our soldier friends and relatives were rare.

We had just waited and prayed. The few men appearing on the streets of Tel Aviv were mostly too old or too young to fight. Few foreigners had remained in the country. One late afternoon, I remember, Berk and I walked slowly along Yermiyahu Street near his apartment. Because of the blackout, the deepening dusk seemed darker and more foreboding than in the past, and we scanned the skies for bombers. Berk was upset because a visiting Jewish dancer who had been working with the Batsheva Dance Company had returned to the United States. He felt that the morale of the company had suffered with her departure. "Solidarity is important," he said. To Fred, a dance company was an organic unit and so was the Jewish people.

When my son Shai was born, we celebrated many times over. Our friend Shulamit poured pear brandy for all of us to toast his arrival on January 25: it wasn't only Shai's birthday, it was also Fred's. From the first moment they had a special rapport. Who would guess he had never had his own baby? He could calm Shai and entertain him. Fred was the first to help me spoonfeed Shai.

When my husband and I decided to return to America after five years in Israel, Fred asked no probing questions. He simply said. "Let's make sure you have a repertoire of Israeli folk dances to teach in America." He laboriously climbed the four flights of stairs to our apartment every morning until he had taught me 10 Israeli folk dances, helping me to document each one in a special notebook. Learning a folk dance to teach it was something very different from dancing it. He set up the formula: the title of the dance he wrote in his big, black, block letters at the top of the page. Each dance had a form which he enumerated by letter, there was a description of the tempi, sometimes he notated the melody, the accompanying music, plus an explanation of who made the dance and any special circumstances surrounding it. He chose the dances and each one was a classic of Israeli folk dance repertoire.

Baby Shai sat under the dining table as I rehearsed and Fred hummed or sang the tunes in his full resonant voice. Occasionally Fred would hold him on his lap, gently beating the little baby fingers with his on the table.

When he taught me the couple dance by Rivka Sturman, "Dodi Li," ("My Beloved") his most favorite dance, he got up without his cane and danced it with me. He glided beside me, his strong arm holding me and guiding me forward. We danced in unison and it was exhilarating. Unlike our walks on the street, there was no trace of a limp or hesitation. I was dancing with an experienced partner and a dancer.

As summer and fall passed, we would meet in the garden on the Yarkon River, the eucalyptus trees shading his apartment from view. He received news clippings from the *New York Times* of dance performances in New York and he always shared them with me. He showed me his articles for *Hora Magazine*, which he had published in New York three times yearly, on all aspects of Israeli folk dance. "My English always sounds so German," he would say ruefully. I corrected some of the articles and listened as he told me about plans for his newest book, *Machol Ha Am: Dance of the Jewish People*, (published in 1978). I could see his powers at work: a manila file folder of photographs got thicker and thicker with more and more precious examples of Jewish dance. I shared his excitement when he located the first concert program of the Jewish dancer Baruch Agadati from 1917. He coaxed Israeli dance directors Gurit Kadman and Sara Levi-Tanai to give him photos from their own collections.

During the summer his own first teacher and dance director, Gertrud Kraus, fell ill. She had been a modern dancer in Vienna and given Berk his first performance and choreographic experience 45 years earlier. Every day he drove to the hospital to visit her. Usually I went, too, with Shai. First Fred watched the baby in the garden of the hospital while I went upstairs, and then he went upstairs. Each time he would bring

Kraus the German *Stern* magazine and occasionally dark chocolates. He was very devoted.

One day by the river he told me he was feeling poorly. "My insomnia is worse and I feel washed out. One of my former students is a nurse at the Rambam Hospital in Haifa and has arranged an examination for me there." He didn't refer to the appointment again, but I knew what day he was to go. By 8 in the evening I was alarmed not to have heard from him. Finally, he answered my phoning. "I can't talk now," he said abruptly and suddenly started weeping.

Speaking with forced composure I heard him say that he had incurable cancer.

Berk made plans to leave Israel before us. He came to dinner and sat stiffly at the end of the table, so unlike his manner just a few mornings before, teaching me folk dance. "Judy," he asked, "would you consider writing my biography? You're coming back to America, too. We could talk by phone and you could visit me in New York and I'll come to Minneapolis. You could talk to some of my students and colleagues. You already know everyone in Israel. Would you do it?"

I realized I knew nothing about him, really. Where was his family? How had he survived the Holocaust? When had he come to New York? Had he performed in New York as well as Vienna? It was so peculiar to feel so close and yet to know so little about his life.

"I'll show you all my programs, my books, my letters. I consider myself a collector of Jewish dance more than anything else."

And so I began to inquire about his life and the story of *Victory Dances* unfolded, the story of the Jewish dancer par excellence.

Jewish dancing masters have an honored and venerable tradition beginning in ancient time. The Levites of the Temple would dance in front of the Jews gathered for celebrations, urging them to celebrate God in joy by participating in dance, such as at the Succot Holiday, when the Levites peformed for the masses juggling flaming torches on the steps and dancing.

Rabbis, too, in later times set the tone at weddings, often dancing first to show the participants how to celebrate in a Jewish way — to dance in order to fulfill the commandment of insuring the happiness of the bride and groom. This Jewish decree was refined during the Medieval and Renaissance periods in Europe when the Jewish dancing master, a specialized role in the community, taught dances in the special communal *Tanzhaus* or dance halls where Jewish wedding receptions were held. The dancing master, in the role of master of ceremonies, called the *Bachdan*, kept the joy at its peak and helped to preserve the special character and solidarity of the Jewish community intact by teaching and leading the dances, often travelling from community to community to perform his task.

By the 19th century the Chassids, in their courts, took dance as their most ecstatic way to celebrate God and life. The Chassids danced their way through the year at many different holiday celebrations, in prayer and at rites such as the *Bar Mitzva* and weddings. As Fred Berk's own life unfolded he lived out the classic roles of the Jewish dancing master and the righteous Chassid. He performed and taught as he went from place to place, in Europe, in Cuba, throughout the United States, in Israel and even in South America, gathering Jews and enhancing not only their joy, love and knowledge of Jewish culture, training the young as well as the old, Jews and non-Jews, thus bringing together people through celebration of life in Jewish dance.

CHAPTER TWO: VIENNA

In Vienna in 1911, Jacob and Henrietta (Blau) Berger lived in the "II.-District", on 14, Jartenstrasse or Untere Augartenstrasse. The district lay between the Danube River and the Donaukanal and was a major commercial area as well as the Jewish quarter. Jacob operated a small dairy farm his parents had started years before right inside the city. Jacob was an ambitious man, quick-tempered, violent on occasion. He dressed like a dandy and was especially proud when his second child was a son. Friedrich Berger was born on January 25, 1911.

During the years of the First World War, while most of the city was starving, farmers brought the Berger family bread, eggs and vegetables in exchange for the dung from their stables which they needed to fertilize their fields. Neighbors came in and out of the little dairy shop, school boys came early in the morning to deliver the milk and various work hands helped with the 30 cows and 52 horses in the adjoining stable and barn.

"I remember we had goats, pigeons and cats who gathered under the enormous tree in the yard. I liked to feed the cats. In the evenings I would walk outside and bang the side of a tin bowl filled with milk, making a noise. Five or six cats would jump down from the barn and come running. What I really paid special attention to were the goats. There was one I especially loved. It was a horrible day when I looked out from the balcony and saw that goat being slaughtered.

"My special place for fantasies was the basement of our house. I would go downstairs with a candle and play alone behind the barrels and huge troughs for washing laundry. Doing the wash was a three-day event which included pumping water from the pump in the yard, boiling it in huge vats and troughs from the basement. When everything was washed and rinsed, the clothes were hauled up into the attic to be hung and dried. Besides the basement, I loved playing between the hanging clothes in the attic. Special dishes for the Passover holiday, used ony once a year, were packed in large barrels and stored beyond the clothes lines in the attic. The barrels made wonderful props for my stories, too."

When Fritz was five Franz Joseph, emperor of the Hapsburg Empire, died. All households ceremoniously hung black flags from their balconies. The end of World War I. radically changed the map of Europe and the Hapsburgs, who had ruled for 700 years, were banished even from Austria itself after their empire disintegrated.

Fritz noticed that his family took in boarders, a refugee family who spoke Yiddish. "There was a little boy my age. Although we could not understand each other, we played together in the stables and the hayloft. He dressed differently from me, too, and had the traditional uncut forelocks, *peyot*. One day he said he wished he were more like me, without *peyot*. Well, I went into the house, got scissors and cut one off. Then he

got scared and ran to his mother. This was the one time in my life when my father's beating was justified.

"That family was the first I ever knew to leave for America. They left with only a bundle on their back. I remember thinking how poor the mother was and how sad she looked. Of course I didn't realise how lucky she was to leave at that time. Who was to dream what would befall us all later?"

The Berger family spoke only German. Despite their cows and hayloft, their environment was a cosmopolitan city. Like their Jewish neighbors, the Bergers looked down on non-Viennese gentiles and non-Viennese Jews. Yiddish speaking Jews began pouring into Vienna after World War I., escaping not only the harsh effects of the war, but also the pogroms in Russia.

"When I was thirteen or so, someone from school took me to the Viennese Zionist youth group, Blau-Weiss. I was fascinated by the principles of sharing amongst the youths. We took a Sunday hiking trip and everyone brought a lunch. There were some really poor children on the outing, with nothing to eat. We made a big pile of all the lunches and then divided the food. To share like this I though was just wonderful! I was so happy that I told my mother about it the first thing at home. She, however, was horrified. What if I had eaten *traif!* (non-kosher food). I was never allowed to participate again."

There was an indifference in the Berger household to the Zionist ferment within the Jewish circles of Vienna. Herzl and his dreams for a free Jewish society in Palestine meant nothing to them. The very areas that were to become so important and so meaningful to Fritz in later life — sensitive treatment of children, Zionism and the arts — had utterly no place in the Berger home.

"My father went to an Orthodox synagogue, a small little *shiel* (the Viennese dialect for a small synagogue) in the neighborhood. I was the dutiful son and sat next to him every Saturday during the almost day-long prayers. My mother, on the other hand, was raised in the impressive large Conservative synagogue. Even as a married woman she continued to worship there. She was not independent of my father, it was only due to her parents' influence that he agreed to let her continue. Only occasionally was I allowed to fetch her and my sister.

"I was struck by the dignity of the place. The women sat upstairs without any screens separating them from the men, like in my father's *shiel*. The rabbi was a statuesque, charismatic man, the Chief Rabbi of Vienna. I also remember a choral group singing upstairs, accompanying the cantor, so different from the chaotic din of loud men praying on their own at my father's synagogue."

Fritz's father continued to mismanage money. He had extravagant hobbies, expensive horses and elegant clothes and he kept up family appearances by forcing the children to drive with him in his beautiful buggy with his thoroughbred horses, despite mother's protests.

"He ate so much he couldn't bend down to tie his shoes. My sister and I would have to perform that task for him. Three or four times a day he would send me down to the tavern to get him draft beer in a big jug.

"Creditors would come more and more often to the house and I lost all respect for my father. He would lock himself in his room for days and wouldn't even talk to my mother.

"At first I was too young to have chores, but when we started to lose all our money, I helped out. At 15 my sister had to start working because there wasn't even money for her dresses. I suppose this was in 1924.

"When the time for my *Bar Mitzvah* came, the family was very proud. At

thirteen, a Jewish boy takes on full religious responsibilities and my family was expecting fine things. Never mind that I had been studying Hebrew and it had been a tortuous experience. I was terrified to have to stand before all the adults and say my prayers and read from the Torah. I was to begin by reciting a speech. As I came to the word 'Grandmother,' honoring her, I stopped and just sat down. I simply forgot everything I was supposed to say and escaped by returning to my family pew. I began to weep. People thought I was crying for my grandmother, who was in fact mortally sick.

"We slowly lost everything we owned but a few horses. My sister, who was four years older than I, went to work in a factory in order to help cover our living expenses. The house we lived in and the dairy were taken away by the creditors." Fritz's mother maintained her rigid schedule of cleaning the house and locking up the main salon to be perfectly tidy for guests. She always looked immaculate and lady-like in her long dresses, impeccably stylish. Unlike other Orthodox Jewish women she wore no wig, but groomed her long hair after the Viennese fashion.

"My father started a moving business with the few horses he could keep. In the summers we used to move people to their country homes or to rented holiday apartments near the spas. We had a big cart with horses. In the autumn, we would move the vacationers back home. All this moving back and forth was a great joy for me. Each journey was a whole day's work. I would sit with the coachman. Sometimes, he would sleep and let me hold the reins on the way home. The horses found their way by instinct, but I had the feeling I was doing something very important.

"Traveling had always enchanted me. Watching the trains go by, I would conjure up the most magical of destinations. My favorite thing was to travel to my aunt. She had a wonderful home at the spa of Baden bei Wien. I spent the summers there. She was the sister of my mother and had no children of her own.

"Life with my aunt was so different. She would listen to me. I would tell her stories or show her my stamp collection and we would take walks in the evening. She was the only close person I had, the very closest person to me. She was so very warm and understanding.

"Baden bei Wien had a summer theater presenting all the famous operettas and light plays of the season. I saw every summer performance as my aunt's little escort. It opened a new world for me, which fascinates me today as much as it did in my childhood. When I returned to Vienna I searched for ways to continue to go to the theater.

"Sometimes the public school I attended organized field trips to the opera or theatre, and I would be in heaven. Of course I wanted a closer look at the actors and actresses who made the plays come to life. I started to stand near the stage door after performances. There was always a group of young people at the stage-door waiting and I got to know them.

"It was a little circle of friends that had nothing to do with my family, my neighborhood, my school or my Jewishness. That little group, waiting to see the stars of the opera or theatre, all spoke the same language. We shared something deep and beautiful — the communication of the arts. As a result our personal ties were very special, too.

"All were autograph seekers, so I became one, too. I saw fans at the stage door with autograph albums, flowers and programs so I, too, began to present flowers. I suppose I overdid the passion, but the theatre brought me to the best thing I knew — even a group of friends, and later a club where I tried my hand at acting.

"I was part of a fan club for the actress Else Wohlgemuth. She was my passion for two years. I remember we would take any opportunity to celebrate her, including

marking *der Göttlichen* ("The Divine") birthday. I collected over sixty photos of her, each one autographed. In real life she was married to a count and lived across the park from the theatre. Once, I succeeded in opening her carriage door after a performance, and then I raced through the park, beating her horses to the other side. I managed to open the door for her a second time. It made me perfectly happy.

"This all seemed to be a dream world, the world of the theatre, and I never presumed to think I would be able to enter it.

"My school work became more and more difficult for me. Nobody listened to me at school or at home. I gave up trying to do my homework and closed out everything but the stolen outings to join my friends at the stage door. I got terrible grades, but still I found no way to study. It seems I could not learn anything from a book. I was expelled from school.

"To make matters worse, my father constantly yelled at me and then he would end up beating me. Finally, I remember my father screamed, 'You cannot spend your days at home anymore. You're fourteen and a half years old and it is time you start working. I will find you work as a furrier or a goldsmith's apprentice, whichever allows you time off for the Sabbath.' When he could get no response from me, he took his cane and beat me until it broke."

Lilacs bloomed when Fritz began his apprenticeship to Josef Hochbaum, a jeweller, on April 19, 1926. "My duties were cleaning the shop, washing windows, preparing the materials needed during the day, shopping for everything the work required, building a fire in the potbellied stove in winters. When I was not working as the goldsmith's glorified servant, I sat at the workbench on a low stool, melting, filing, polishing and preparing the metals for the master's hand."

During Fritz's first year of apprenticeship, eighty-five workers were shot to death during a street demonstration in Vienna, followed by a general strike throughout the city. It took military force to break the strike.

For five long years Fritz walked five flights up to the workshop several times a day. The goldsmith rarely talked to him, only when something was needed. Fritz was terribly bored and hated the work. Since he showed no interest, he was given nothing to do with the silver or gold, although he was obligated to attend a vocational school once a week. During the years of apprenticeship, Fritz made only one ring (with the help of the goldsmith) in order to pass his final examination.

"I began work at seven in the morning. Since my boss was a very stingy man, he rationed the kindling and firewood for the whole week. Whether I had enough by the end of the week was of no interest to him. He only wanted the place warm when he arrived at eight. My only escape was running errands. I was never paid any streetcar fare, so I would visit customers on foot. The goldsmith had no idea how long it took to walk from place to place, so I combined my errands with trips to stage doors throughout the theatre district."

Young Fritz would walk the Ringstrasse, the main circular artery separating the old inner city of Vienna from the outer districts. The boulevard had replaced the fortifications of the old town surrounding a vast complex of public buildings and private dwellings.[1] The Ringstrasse became a symbolic focus of the dominant liberal culture — schools to educate the elite of a free people, the centers of constitutional government and the museums and theatres to bring higher culture to all.[2] Walking along the Ringstrasse one could pass the Opera House, the twin Museums of Art History and Nature, the Parliament, the City Hall, the Burgtheater and the University.

Further from the Imperial Palace, the Opera and the Burgtheater, Fritz would have found a simpler building with three concert halls, the Konzerthaussaal. Here the

big orchestras performed and sometimes the great solo dancers also appeared. As he walked, Fritz's autograph book was always under his arm, even when juggling sacks of coal, metals, wood and the morning newspaper.

Inside his autograph book were clippings and newspaper photos of actors and actresses carefully pasted onto the pages, so Fritz could correctly identify the personalities if he chanced to see them on the street. "Once I saw Anna Pavlova drive by in a hansom carriage. She was such a teeny, pale woman with a sad face, that I was surprised. The carriage stopped and she got out to look in the window of an antique shop. I rushed over to her and that is how I got here autograph."

Another lucky incident happened during one of his walks. "When the dancer Ida Rubinstein was in Vienna performing a work by Maurice Ravel, I saw them leaving the opera house after a rehearsal. Of course I got autographs for my book from both of them."

On Fritz's walks through the city, he would often sneak into rehearsals. "I remember seeing Friedrich Schiller's "Mary, Queen of Scots" with my idol, Else Wohlgemuth at the Burgtheater, maybe even fifty times. One always knew in advance when rehearsals took place and who would be acting. I would only go to see her rehearsals. Our group at the stage door exchanged news and gossip about the different performers. Every little detail about their lives was important to us. Sometimes we would even bribe their chauffeur with brandy, wine or cigarettes to tell us where our favorite actress had been and with whom she had dined."

Fritz's beloved Burgtheater was a special place. The foyer itself was magnificent, with two enormous staircases, one originally for the Hapsburg Court and the other for the public. They were lined with marble and wood, hanging crystal chandeliers casting a shimmering light on statues of famous actors along the ascent. The lavish staircases were joined by a curving gallery with an outside balcony, allowing the audience to promenade, beautifully dressed, during intermission. They could gaze at the ceiling paintings and panels painted by Gustav Klimt.[3] Who would dream that the youth who stole time to stand by the stage door would one day make his own debut inside?

The longer Fritz worked for the goldsmith, stooping over his workbench, the more round-shouldered he became. His mother became upset by his posture and sent him to a doctor. Gymnastics or some kind of exercise was recommended to Fritz as a cure.

"My sister, who usually had nothing to say to me, knew about a school of rhythm-gymnastics run by a dancer named Gertrud Kraus. On my walks through the city I began to notice Kraus' name on billboards and kiosks." A Kraus performance outdoors in one of the city parks (with pantomimist Cilly Wang[4]) appealed to Fritz and he went to watch.

"I was very impressed by her solos with their eerie and evocative quality. During the intermission, I went backstage as I was used to, to soak in the atmosphere and perhaps even to see Gertrud Kraus. Instead, I met her mother who asked what I wanted. Quite spontaneously I said, 'To study with Kraus.' Her mother gave me the studio address and instructed me to go there the following Saturday afternoon.

"Despite my family's strict Sabbath observance (no traveling and no activity except prayer and study until sundown), the Saturday following the concert, I went. A spiral staircase wound up to the studio and I saw Kraus standing at the top wearing a kind of sarong. She seemed like a vision. I was awed, and stood there dumbly looking up, feeling even worse than my usual tongue-tied self. Even so, Kraus invited me to her classes.

"I went there every Saturday afternoon to dance. Once, maybe after half a year

of study, Kraus suddenly said: 'Class, turn around. Watch Fritz and do the exercise exactly his way. That is what I want.' It was the first time I ever heard praise! She was not aware of what she had done to me. Her words gave me the biggest encouragement I had yet experienced. As a matter of fact, I later learned, as a teacher you never know how your words affect your students. Kraus moved me!"

In interviews with Fritz during the last three years of his life he returned many times to descriptions of his early classes with Kraus. "I think what first impressed me generally in Kraus' class was her music. I had very little exposure to music before that. I remember at five or so my mother did take me to hear "Carmen" at the Volksoper and she explained to me that someone would be shot in the last act. I spent the whole time waiting for that death and have no recollection of the music. Certainly I had no exposure to classical music in my home. Kraus would accompany all of her own exercises and improvisations dashing to the piano from the studio floor in front of the dancers, where she would demonstrate. She provided all accompaniment during the 3 or 4-hour long class, matching the artistry of her dance images with musical interpretations from her own background. She was a trained pianist who had appeared in solo concerts of music. Her tempo and selections uncovered something in me while I danced. I was deeply moved by classical music, my soul soaring with the musical phrases.

"Modern dance was altogether new in its approach, its philosophy and its technique. Kraus' approach was unlike that of the other Viennese dancers who tried to make their students into carbon copies of their particular styles. Gertrud encouraged us to choreograph and to be conscious of form, despite training us to be emotional. The trend was to express oneself and when we danced, it was all-consuming."

Other students of Kraus have spoken of her uniqueness in encouraging personal expression and choreography. Mia Slavenska in *Dance Magazine*[5] stated that she divided her time studying with Egorova, Preobrajenska and Kschessinskaya in Paris and Gertrud Kraus in Vienna. "With Kraus, I discovered endless possibilities for expression and creative freedom in dance... she encouraged my first attempts at choreography." At that time other Viennese modern dancers moved in the waltzy, lyric style of the Wiesenthal sisters or the grotesque comic manner of Cilly Wang or Gertrud Bodenwieser's movement classes at the Vienna Academy, while Kraus offered something different.

Fritz attempted to define its uniqueness. "I was thrilled with the combination of the emotional and the physical in the movement of my body. Conquering gravity and moving through space was a total thrill, an emotional burst throughout my whole being. We would dance a variety of different ideas on themes sometimes having to do with night and whispering or loneliness, sometimes Biblical, sometimes social, against war and dictators. Gertrud in particular, but all of us, thought we were universal artists, belonging to the world and creating for the world. As students we were more aware of our Austrian folk songs and dances than of our own religious backgrounds.

"Of course, I had heard about Kraus's triumphs in Munich at the International Dance Congress the year before (1930)." He started to study with Kraus the following year, when he was age 20 and Kraus 28.

Gertrud was a graduate of the piano-department of the State Academy of the Arts and in order to earn money accompanied the modern dance classes of professor Gertrud Bodenwieser, the head of the department at the Academy. Bodenwieser used to ask her students to prepare and show dance studies of their own to the class. One day Kraus surprised everybody by getting up from her piano stool and performing a dance composition she had prepared, though she was not a student and had never took dance classes. She became a student of Bodenwieser.

As a youngster she had been a medal winning athlete and she maintained her physical prowess as well as her musical talents. But Bodenwieser and she had disagreements over Kraus' dance composition ideas. Kraus walked out of her class and began choreographing by herself. In 1926 she gave her first solo dance concert in Vienna and by 1930 had taken a group of dancers to the International Dance Congress. "Ballet company directors as well as modern choreographers and teachers from all over Europe arived in Munich for 7 days to see and to be seen."[6] Ted Shawn had come from the U.S. to perform at the congress.

Mary Wigman's "Monument to the Dead," was supposed to be the main event of the Munich Congress, but it was presented only as a 'work in progress.' Gertrud Kraus received much critical acclaim for her group piece, "Songs of the Ghetto."

The critic Fred Hildebrand of the *Berliner Tageblatt* wrote in his review of the "Songs of the Ghetto" that "my heart was filled with joy, so beautiful was their (Kraus' dancers) sorrowful dream and their trust in God."[7] . . .the dance was not based on pure personal fantasy; the traditional elements of Hassidic dance added poignancy. . ."

Another critic called it "The most ambitious event and one of the greatest of modern and ballet. Over 1,400 including Rudolf von Laban and Mary Wigman from Germany, Gertrud Kraus from Vienna, Gret Palucca from Dresden, Valerie Kratina from the Dalcroze School at Hellerau [took part].[8]

When Fritz joined Kraus' school he knew she had won acclaim for her "Songs of the Ghetto" but he didn't relate to the Jewish subject matter of the suite. Studying with an acclaimed choreographer was inspiring and he was happy to see so much dance. Perhaps one day he, too, could perform.

Fritz did not know that his fascination with the physical and emotional elements of movement were distilled in the dances of the Chassidim, a mystical sect started by eastern European Jews in the eighteenth century. Here was a Jewish approach to dance expressionism that would give direction to his whole career at a much later time. Once, while dancing at an open air performance with Kraus, "something happened to me which I still cannot explain. While dancing outside, seeing the stars and the sky, the trees with their shadows, and feeling the stillness of the night, all this transported me into a different world. It was as if I was united with the universe, a kind of very religious feeling, exhilarating. I felt that this must be the essence of dance."

For this young man who had never been articulate or able to express his feelings, dance provided an ecstatic outlet and a beautiful way to channel his own hidden talents. That it enabled him to focus his own religious feelings was also a surprise. He was like an unidentified Chassid — the Chassid who needed no learned intermediary to reach God or his fellow man, the Chassid who could dance in ecstasy — combining the physical and the spiritual in all that he did.

Rabbi Zalman, a famous Chassidic sage, said that divine sparks emit from God, and man converts them back into the spiritual through prayer and dance. Dance is one of the processes for transforming physicality into spirituality.[9]

"Kraus encouraged us to choreograph, to bring in new dance studies to class. I remember my first suite of dances was "The Marseillaise," the second a Russian dance which drew on everyone's interest in the Russian Revolution and the third was about 'a capitalist'. I played the central figure, exploiting the two workers, struggling with them. Of course, the workers triumphed in the end and I was beaten — one of our hopes at that time.

"We decided that the two workers should be in red and I in black. Because there was no money, I had no idea how I would get a costume. So I asked my mother. By then she knew I danced seriously, but she forbade that my father should know. 'Don't

we have a black flag somewhere in the attic?' she asked. 'In 1916, when Kaiser Franz Josef died, every house was required to hang a black flag out of the window.' Well, 15 years later I went up to the attic and found the flag, nicely rolled and wrapped, never having been used since. I took it to the seamstress next door. I was so skinny that she made me a pair of pants, a cummerbund, and a loose Russian shirt from the flag. The performance came and on stage, when I bent down, the pants split. Not on a seam, but the rotting material itself tore. That was the end of my 'Capitalist Dance.' "

One of the dancers in his "workers piece" was a trim young woman with intense eyes and a ready laugh named Claudia Vall. Her parents wanted her to learn ballet and music. They provided well for her. She had had a governess from a very young age who, as she grew, accompanied her to all her lessons. Her father owned a brick and tile factory in Zagreb, Yugoslavia, so he could afford the best for his youngest daughter. By the time she was 16 she was an accomplished musician and dancer. Her parents wanted her to attend a kind of finishing school after high school, so they sent both Claudia and the governess off to Vienna.

"Although I stayed at the school they'd chosen for me, I went to auditions and was accepted to study at the State Academy for Music and Performing Arts (Akademie für Musik und Darstellend Kunst,where Fritz also studied in 1933). I spent the mornings studying music and dance and the afternoons studying acting, anatomy and drawing. At first you could have seen in me what my parents wished for: a conforming little girl in a black uniform and white apron; but in the competitive and lively atmosphere of the arts school, I changed. I auditioned and was accepted for a Max Reinhardt production, "The Miracle." Imagine the contrast of my governess delivering me to the stage door and me walking onto the stage to play a drunken whore under Reinhardt's direction!"

During this period, Claudia attended a dance concert of Gertrud Kraus. She was so impressed with Kraus' expressionist style that she decided to study modern dance with her. Claudia remained in Vienna three years, and during that time studied and performed with Kraus. She also got to know Fritz Berger, Katya Delakova, Elsa Scharf, Otto Werberg and other dancers in Kraus' school and company. They were an adoring group whom Gertrud had gathered — adoring of her and of each other.

The friendships were intense and deep, for they spent hours together rehearsing Kraus's dances and studying with her. "These were entrancing hours. The atmosphere was one where you completely forgot yourself and only worked on what Kraus wanted." The dancers also worked together on their own dances, and performed in each other's etudes. These were intense statements about their political, spiritual and emotional beliefs, worked out in dances.

Fritz asked Claudia to dance in his trio etude about the plight of the workers, as he saw them, in the hands of money hungry employers. His outlook was so different from hers! She was struck by the thin shy young man who, she found out, worked as an apprentice to a goldsmith and secretly took dance lessons, despite his parents' stern disapproval of him and his desires. She thought of all the love and encouragement she'd always been given to study the arts.

Their friendship was cemented during performance. That's when dancers really depend upon each other, especially in the face of the ever critical director and audience. This dependency and aid, the natural elements of relations built in a performing troupe, later would help save Claudia's and Fritz's lives.

Kraus brought in other dancers and artists to stimulate her troupe. Perhaps it was 1932, when she invited Rudolf Laban's assistant Fritz Klingenbeck to speak about dance notation. Laban by then had founded a whole system of dance analysis. Later it would have a startling effect on Berk's career, but at this point he remembered learning

some of the elementary facts of Labanotation.

Kraus herself had worked a bit with Laban. A description of her work is found in Giora Manor's 1978 biography, *The Life and Dance of Gertrud Kraus*.[10] "Austria in the late 1920s was torn by violent struggles between Socialists and the Nationalist parties, who demanded a fusion (*Anschluss*) of the republic with its German neighbor. Both camps commanded semi-military organizations. The Socialist movement was active not only in politics but built vast housing projects for the workers and maintained various cultural and educational institutions. Gertrud became involved in these activities and was one of Laban's assistants when he organized the annual Trade Unions' Parade in which dozens of dance groups participated."

Choreographers became adept at handling masses of people on stage. Operas such as "Aida" were given as tourist attractions in annual outdoor performances, coupled with pageants based on Austrian history staged in front of City Hall on the Ringstrasse. "Once, I remember, Gertrud choreographed the 'Blue Danube Waltz.' In Vienna, the Danube River makes a grand curve and she took that as her motif. She had maybe one hundred and fifty young girls coming into a stadium using the same step, holding up a long silky blue scarf that fluttered and curved in the breeze. People were yelling and screaming, it was so beautiful.

"Rival political parties would sponsor pageants in different areas of the city. We'd do our choruses of movement for any party that would hire us, really. I remember Gertrud did a Russian Easter scene for the Communists in which Manon Erfourt, Mia Slavenska and I danced. Another pageant I remember was in honor of the fallen soldiers of World War I. Gertrud choreographed it on five platforms and we began crawling up through the levels with gas masks on our heads. I was so nearsighted I could not see when to begin according to the visual cue I'd been given. I remember being pushed upwards by the young woman next to me."

Fritz's happiest year was when he was fired by the goldsmith. "I had completed four years as his apprentice and one year with full pay. I joined Kraus's professional dance classes in the mornings. During my apprenticeship to the goldsmith, I had found ways to attend more and more theatre and music concerts. Every few weeks I would manage to hear the Vienna Philharmonic. I could only afford standing-room, which meant arriving three to four hours before the box office opened. Everyone in line knew each other, however, and it was great fun to talk about what we would see or hear. If I was in line for the theatre, we would gossip about the actors.

"I was lucky enough to get into the claque at the Deutsches Volkstheater. We did not get paid, but at least we did not have to wait in line for standing-room tickets. Before the theatre opened its doors, we were allowed in free of charge. We would select a good place in the standing-room section, and follow the instructions of the claque-chief. Most of the main theatres had someone in this role to lead the applause. He was paid by the star to applaud when she or he entered or concluded their famous speeches or even simply bowed. The claque-chief would give us the signal and then we would start yelling 'bravo' and madly applauding. We even threw flowers. Although everyone in the audience knew about the claque, especially at the opera, it was all accepted for the sake of the stars and the atmosphere."

The year that Fritz concluded his apprenticeship, 1931, marked his entry into backstage life. Instead of waiting at the stage door or applauding the theatre stars, he actually began to participate. Somehow he found out about plays and revues at the Volksoper, then briefly renamed the Schauspielhaus.

"My first experience lasted about two months as an extra, playing the role of a coolie in a big pageant about China, "Brülle China." At the dress rehearsal I was handed

yellow make-up and a coolie hat. Afterwards, I carefully watched how everyone removed their make-up and I figured I was doing the same thing. On my way home I could not understand why everyone was staring at me. Only at home did I discover that I was still streaked with yellow make-up. I did not know that one removes make-up with cold cream.

"Next I was in a revue, 'Quer durch Wien,' [Across Vienna], dancing as a member of a football team. Then Anna May Wong came from Hollywood and I found out she was to star in a revue also at the same theatre. Six young men who could sing and dance were needed. I was the only one picked from the revue even though I had never studied singing! We had to sing and do social dancing with Wong. This was my luckiest, happiest year. I was on the stage and nothing could stop me!"

Ominous evidence of anti-Semitism was growing daily. In Vienna, the Jews felt their non-acceptance in many spheres. It had always been a simple fact of Viennese life, and somehow the Jews coped. Who paid any notice to a flyer such as the one circulated by the Nazi Workers' Party as early as 1928? The State Opera announced a premiere of "Johnny spielt auf" by the Austrian composer Ernst Krenek who was half Jewish. His opera depicted the life a a black musician in the U.S. The Nazi flyer stated "this decadent theme about the Jews and the Negroes degrades our glorious State opera. All anti-Semites are invited to the protest rally on January 13, 1928. Jews are not allowed to attend."

Fritz was invited to join the Kraus dance company in 1931. "What an experience! The two years that I worked with Gertrud opened me up. She gave me confidence, a new direction and the beginnings of my real identity. None of us dancers who were Jewish were aware of our backgrounds. We all considered ourselves well assimilated into the city life and we thought that that was good. Nevertheless, Gertrud would challenge us often with themes from our heritage, Jewish themes."

Kraus's first solo dance tour to Haifa, Jerusalem, Tel Aviv and Cairo in April of 1931 "was very impresive for us," recalled Fritz. "She was consumed by the rhythms and sights of those exotic places and they influenced us all. She choreographed "The Yemenite Boy" for four women and me as the Yemenite. She dressed me in the materials and cloth she had bought in the Jerusalem *shuk* (market). This dance introduced me for the first time to the concept of Oriental Jews (Jews from Arab countries) and their very wiry, delicate movements. Of course, these were sifted through Gertrud's own perceptions and choreography. Later on, I also danced in her previously staged 'Songs of the Ghetto.'

"Gertrud choreographed 'The Chassidic Wedding,' with herself as the bride and I as her groom. This was not only a starring role, but it was also something deeply emotional for me, the first taste of an element of Jewish life that really appealed to me. I also remember her 'Miriam's Dance.' I was one of four youths dressed like slaves. On stage, we performed on several levels. Gertrud was on a big platform in the center, with steps leading down to the other levels. The men joined her for a triumphal dance — we had big discs in our hands and she held a tambourine creating a very effective tableau.

"I also remember her 'Wailing Wall.' This was the most moving dance experience of my life. During the rehearsal Gertrud stretched a sheet across the studio space. She said it represented the western wall of the ancient Temple of Solomon, still standing today in the heart of Jerusalem. Traditionally Jews have taken their prayers and hopes there, crying to God to hear them, hence, the name Wailing Wall. She placed our heads and hands in certain positions as if we were peering over the wall; she sculpted us, using images of Chassidim praying. I had the feeling she was hewing us from stone from some deep place in her heart."

In the foreword to his book, The *Chasidic [sic] Dance* (p. ix), Fritz wrote, "This dance awakened in me untapped feelings of Jewish identification. I never before realized the presence of these emotions... only when I came to the United States in 1941 during the Holocaust did these dormant feelings crystallize into a deep ongoing commitment to Jewish dance."

Also during the time that Fritz was a Kraus company dancer she choreographed for the Vilner Truppe, Yiddish actors from Vilna, Poland, who toured Vienna. "She involved me in the group and I remember participating in a few shows with the Yiddish troupe. It was run on a cooperative basis. I became totally engrossed for several reasons, but perhaps primarily because it was the first time that I was in an Eastern European Jewish environment. In any other context but the theatre I would have reacted to these Jewish actors as any other Viennese Jew would — with scorn and probably derogatory remarks.

"Gertrud choreographed and staged the movements for me, another man and four women. I loved going in the evening to the theatre and making-up for my part. That thrilled me, even though those in the troupe were so poor, and their style so tragic, one of pathos and extended emotion.

"I had heard Yiddish before, but understood very little of the language. I became very friendly with one of the actresses who told me the first stories I ever heard about pogroms in Russia. Her stories were from her personal experience. She told me of the Cossacks who rode into her village and mercilessly slaughtered the Jews. I heard about the incredible difficulty of starting over as refugees in a new place. Never did I dream there was a portent in all this for me, too. I would sit with this actress in her dressing room enraptured, before we went on stage.

"I do not remember what plays we did or what I danced, but the atmosphere was terrifically meaningful to me. The theatre was in the Jewish section of Vienna, next to an amusement park. My pittance of a salary bought me only a frankfurter in the park after each performance, but I could not have been happier."

Dance had brought Fritz self-esteem, friends and a public who cared about what he thought and what he danced. With another Kraus dancer, Otto Werberg, Fritz produced some dance concerts. Their first concert was given at the Urania Hall in Vienna on November 8, 1932. The dancer Grete Bock performed with them accompanied by a violin and flute. They would rent a small hall, often a beer hall with a little stage at the back — something like an off-off Broadway theatre. There were also three Volkshochschulen of the Socialist parties. In these theatre-halls, lectures and cultural programs were held for the members. One, the Urania, was centrally located in Vienna and the other two in the suburbs. Fritz would pay a token fee, and although there was no curtain in front of the stage, causing some rearrangement of dances, he had no worry about advertising and filling the house. Fritz only rarely thought of the remote big theatres. Even dancers of renown could only rent a big theatre for matinee performances because all the theatres had their own evening programs.

Fritz's father began to take notice. "All the years that I had been studying and the two years performing with Gertrud I was terrified that my father would find out. I finally found the courage to tell him there was a course in dance history and music at the State Academy that I wanted to take on Saturdays. My father asked if I had to ride the trolley to get to the academy. When I answered in the affirmative, knowing full well this broke the ban on travel during the Sabbath, my father yelled, 'Well, just don't get off on our street, where neighbors might see.' "

On another occasion the senior Berger heard from a friend in the synagogue one Sabbath that his son's name was advertised on a billboard. "He came home and asked

me if I danced in public."

"Yes," I said.

"Do you make money?" asked my father.

"Yes," I said nervously.

'Then it's all right with me."

Fritz took heart as his successes in dance continued and he decided to open his own studio, a first floor conventional-looking dance studio in a district near the Ringstrasse, the "VI. Bezirk" (District) on Mariahilferstrasse. Many young people came for exercise and fitness as well as dancing lessons. His dancing partner, Claudia Vall Kauffmann, even remembers studying tap with him. Fritz was able to build up his studio so successfully, that he could afford to help his parents financially as their business continued to fail.

Fritz rushed from studio to concert halls to friends amidst the old elegance of the former Hapsburg capital. People sought his company. He was lean and handsome, with a quick sense of humor, a far cry from the lonely, subdued, misunderstood child of the Berger household.

Neither Fritz nor his friends paid much attention to the artists' changed position in Germany. Nevertheless, the Nazi's attitude towards creativity began to have its chilling effects. A suite from Paul Hindemith's new opera, "Mathis der Maler," premiered in 1934 at the Berlin Philharmonic even though the Nazis criticized the composer in the press as a "degenerate artist." Their power and criticism led to the dismissal of the conductor after the premiere. Josef Goebbels, Minister of Propaganda, denounced as "decadent, perverse and destructive," anyone who deviated from the cultural party lines of the Nazis.[11]

In Vienna an international dance competition was announced for June 1934. A French journal, *Archives Internationale de la Danse Revue,* reporting on the Viennese competition stated that the "object was to discover new talents." There were divisions for solo works and company pieces; each entrant was allocated fifteen minutes to perform. The winners of each day continued until the fifth day when finalists were selected for the winning Gala performance. That evening the Mayor of Vienna would award a gold medal, a silver medal and five bronze medals.

The jury was international, including Americans, Poles, Hungarians and Japanese (Dr. Wolfgang Born's "Le Concourse International de Danse a Vienne" article on the competition in the July 15th, 1934 edition of the French journal). Fritz was at first too intimidated even to consider entering the competition. His childhood inferiority complex seemed to overwhelm him. But his friends and dance colleagues urged him to compete. The opportunity of performing in such an illustrious setting finally won Fritz over. In addition to performing, he knew there were three prizes of 1,000 Shillings each offered by the Ministy of Public Education of Austria, as well as a prize for soloists by the honored dancer Grete Wiesenthal and commemorative medals by the International Archive of Dance and the City of Vienna.

He chose three solo dances that he had created during his apprenticeship to Gertrud Kraus. "Argentinian Dance Song," was a light, joyful dance with spectacular backfalls and attitude turns. "Chorale," to César Franck's music was Fritz's mystical impression of Catholic ritual in a cathedral. "The Tyrant," was his own social statement about Hitler, although he made what he considered a more universal statement by using the image of Pharoah.

On the fifth day of the competition, Fritz was still in the running. He began the day quaking, the tension of the competition threatening his composure and stage presence. At the end of the day, posted amongst the winning names of the competition

was that of Fritz Berger, bronze medal winner. Of all the seven medal winners — gold, silver and bronze — he was the only Viennese chosen. The rest were from Czechoslovakia, Poland, Sweden and Latvia. Newspaper critics praised the winners.

Fritz veritably flew into the world of established Viennese dance. One of the famous and beloved dance soloists from the Vienna Opera, Hedy Pfundmayr, came backstage after one of his performances. Fritz knew her from the opera, especially her role as Potiphar's wife in the "Legend of Joseph." She asked to see him at her home. He was flabbergasted. What did she want with him?

When they met, Pfundmayr explained she wanted to expand her own solo performance repertoire. She had already learned Austrian folk dances from a folklore specialist and now she wanted folk steps from another country. Although she had grown up in the Vienna Opera Ballet corps, she was anxious to learn about dance in a broader way. Perhaps Fritz could teach her the hora for a solo she wanted to do, called "A Girl from Palestine". He gladly taught her the hora in exchange for her teaching him the Austrian Ländler, a gliding, waltz-like partnered dance, which later, when Fritz performed in Cuba and the U.S.A., became part of his repertoire. Perhaps the hora and the Ländler both reflected different facets of his identity, while he had to move from country to country.

Pfundmayr took Fritz under her wing; she got him into a few movies, including a film version of the opera, "Prince Igor." By now, however, the Nazi influence had seeped into Viennese life and affected Fritz's work. "We had to state in our contract if we were Jewish. Sometimes we were excluded from new films and films with Jewish dancers or actors were simply banned from showing in Germany."

The prestigious Burgtheater occasionally needed dancers and pantomimists in special capacities. The arrangement was that the Opera would supply performers for each play. The opera dancers had entered the government supported institution as children, passed strenuous examinations and study, and only joined the company as young men and women. Both the Opera and the Burgtheater provided for their actors, dancers and singers for life. There were hardly any Jews amongst these permanent performers.

Through Hedy Pfundmayr, Fritz was recommended as a substitute dancer and pantomimist for the Burgtheater. "I thought it was a dream. I had long ago left the stage door and stopped collecting photographs and autographs, but the Burgtheater still remained a kind of holy shrine for me. As I walked to my dressing room, entering through the stage door for the first time, passing the name plates on all the doors, I remembered the dreams and yearnings of my younger days. I was sure I had arrived in heaven.

"Word got around that I was to appear at the Burgtheater. My family, my old friends and my neighborhood took notice of me. I felt so accomplished! Suddenly, for all those in my old neighborhood, I was somebody."

In 1936, Fritz was called by an agent to stage and perform Austrian dances at the Austrian Embassy in the Hague. There was to be a gala celebration and the best of Austrian dance and song was to provide the entertainment. He was asked to arrange waltzes and traditional Ländlers for himself and two dancers. Part of the payment was a round trip airplane ticket. "What excitement! I could not decide which was the greater thrill, an invitation to perform at the Austrian Embassy in Holland, or my first chance for airplane travel. I did not dare tell my parents beforehand, but when I arrrived, I sent a telegram explaining that I had flown to Amsterdam! It was a glorious evening, and the day after the grandiose Embassy party, we were to fly back. But the weather was so bad we were grounded for seven hours, and when we took off we reached only as far as

Dresden, Germany. There we were given a choice of staying until the next day to try flying again, or traveling that night by train through Germany to Vienna. I opted for the train. Hitler was firmly in power and I had no desire to stay in Germany.

"I received the shock of my life on the road from the airport to the train station. On the bus and outside, everywhere I saw signs forbidding the Jews to enter — I got sick, it was so unbelievable. Sure, I had read about the restrictions in newspapers and felt anti-Semitism myself. But somehow we had always managed. Vienna, after all, was home. I had grown up with comments like that of the husband of Hedy Pfundmayr 'of course we know you are Jewish, but my wife loves your work.' Quota systems governed how many Jews could learn at the university or work in many areas. Government jobs were almost impossible to attain. Still, I was not prepared for what I saw with my own eyes in Germany.

"When I got home, I told my family, but they belittled my report and told me nothing could happen to us in Vienna."

His friend Claudia ahd written to him from Italy. He knew she'd left Gertrud Kraus to study in Berlin with Vera Skoronel and Gret Palucca, but had been bothered by the atmosphere there and returned to Zagreb. But in Yugoslavia she missed other performers so badly that she went to Salzburg where she met Angela Sartorio[12] and Lisa Czobel,[13] who had both danced with Kurt Jooss. They convinced Claudia to dance professionally with them in Italy.

In the winter of 1937 Claudia and the Italian company performed in Vienna. After the concert in the Grosse Konzerthalle, they sat together and Fritz was introduced to Angela Sartorio.

"I was so happy, and I could see he was happy, too. He had changed so, now that he was staging dances, teaching, performing and touring full time. He laughed with some irony when he mentioned his parents. He was helping to support them with his earnings in dance."

In Florence, Claudia lived in a little pensione, in a small room. "All I remember is that there was a place for my tap shoes, ballet shoes, an accordion and a phonograph. The other very sedate tenants thought I was a circus performer! On my evening off I can remember taking my gramophone out onto the pergola (a big upstairs balcony) to practice. Sometimes I pretended I was Ginger Rogers. It made me laugh and think of Fritz in his own dance studio in Vienna. We had such fun together because he taught us tap in the style of Astaire." Astaire's movie with Ginger Rogers, "Swing Time" had come out in 1936. They all saw "Swing Time" and "Flying Down to Rio." They practically memorized every step in "Top Hat." Out on the pergola she imagined all kinds of scenes out of Fred Astaire movies. She danced as if wearing long elegant gowns. A man who also lived in the pensione enjoyed the pergola rehearsals, too. He would come out in the evening and start cranking up Claudia's gramophone so she would not have to interrupt her dancing. Gradually, the petite dancer and the elegant, tall man began to converse between her dances. She learned he was from Northern Germany, had studied medicine in Italy and was now a practicing doctor in a Florentine hospital.

Eventually he invited her to dinner. "That was particularly pleasurable, as I mainly ate persimmons for dinner. I loved them, but also I could not afford much else. I ate a very big breakfast and that was supplemented by fruit for dinner."

Once she injured her knee and the doctor found out about it, when the usual evening balcony rehearsals did not take place. He decided to treat her himself in the pensione, with a new therapy machine he lugged home from the hospital. "It gave a special light and he showed me how to direct it, to heal my knee."

The dance company was short of men, so Claudia wrote to Fritz and asked him

to join the company for a tour of Italy, France and Switerland. Would he like to come to Florence? This was not his first invitation to dance in Italy. He had come first at the invitation of Trudy Goth,[14] also a former student of Gertrud's. Goth had returned to her native Italy in the early 1930's to create a modern dance company. She had worked on occasion as an impresario for other performers and because she came from a wealthy family she could entertain artists of international standing in high style.

Fritz accepted a position to dance in the Goth group more because he wanted to see Italy than to perform with her. He considered her creations pedestrian and dry, but the positive side was that she allowed him to insert his own solos into the program. He soon discovered that Italian audiences responded to the humor of his dances and he began to love performing for them.

He also loved walking along the streets of the Italian towns they passed through. The siena and terra cotta colors of the buildings reminded him of all the Italian opera sets he'd seen as a boy during the stolen magic hours at the Vienna opera rehearsals. Now it was no stage set. It was a real, vibrant Italian street scene. He loved eating in the outdoor cafes, strolling past the small shops and watching the way men greeted each other with vigorous embraces and affectionate back slaps right on the street. He enjoyed watching the brightly colored knit dresses of the Italian women which moved so fetchingly as they walked. The Mediterranean atmosphere was such a contrast to Vienna! Temperamentally he felt very much at home.

He was happy to accept the Balletto's invitation. It was all the more enticing because he would dance with Claudia again. She was so happy and bubbly on their first walk through Florence. She put her arm around him and exclaimed, "Oh Fritz, come meet the man I'm going to marry!'" Upstairs in the pensione's biggest suite, she introduced Fritz to the doctor, someone his complete opposite. George Kauffmann was tall and elegantly dressed. Whereas Fritz was talkative and had a twinkle in his eye, Kauffmann was pensive. He would have preferred to devote himself to reading books and listening to fine music rather than to social exchanges or working with groups, like Fritz. But the two men struck it off. They enjoyed talking to each other. And they both adored Claudia.

Fritz stayed to dance in Florence only for a brief time. The proposed tour through Europe had to be postponed and Fritz couldn't stay on. He returned to Vienna.

Despite growing unemployment and anti-Semitism, Fritz continued to work. He was developing a following of students at his own school and received many dance jobs in the suburbs of Vienna in variety programs and musicals. Frequently, the dances he choreographed had folk flavor, including tangos. Ländlers, the Viennese waltz, polkas and mazurkas. Not only were these dances a part of the modern dancer's repertoire, the folk dances provided ready identification and enjoyment for the audiences. This was quite unlike the work of American modern dancers who prided themselves in originality of both movement and theme. Martha Graham's "Primitive Mysteries," for example, or Doris Humphrey's "New Dance," stood apart from the American folk dance motifs and represented something entirely new in American theatre dance.

Fritz's first chance to work specifically with youth came in 1937 when the program director of the Socialist Workers Organization invited him to teach a class for teenagers. They were to come twice a week from many different sections of Vienna in order to learn to dance and also to develop a short production that would include Austrian folk dances. Fritz had over fifty students at each session and the eight couples selected for the production became his very devoted followers. He staged the "Annen-Polka" to Johann Strauss' music and whenever they performed it, it had to be repeated three times by demand of the audience. Fritz realized that the dance served as

a recreational outlet for the youngsters and the technical requirements were less important than the feelings of joy and comradeship in dance. Stressing these, he was still able to get fine results. This method of working with untrained performers served Fritz years later in developing some very fine programs in America.

Hitler invaded Austria on Friday, March 11, 1938. "I remember I was at the grocery store at noon and heard the news. I ran home to alert my parents and said it was all over for us Jews. They said, 'don't be silly. They have lived with him in Germany since 1933. It will not be that bad.' How hopelessly wrong they were! People were so frightened they committed suicide, others found ways to smuggle themselves across the borders. In the first days of the *Anschluss* no one realized what a thorough job the Nazis had done in paralyzing the Jews.

"The landlord of my dance studio told me I could not teach there any more, but if I wanted to rehearse he would let me. But what would I rehearse for, I wondered? No one would hire me. The pianist, who had played for me for years, in the studio and in performances, was seemingly a very close friend. However, he told me he did not dare to continue working for a Jew. Someone might report him. Whatever Jewish pupils I had gave up their studies, frightened to go out. The Gentile students would not go to a Jewish teacher. All contracts for my performances were cancelled. The sudden realization that we were paralyzed in our professional life and our personal life was terrifying. One was left alone, without friends, fearful anyone and everyone would turn you in. My summer plans to go to Paris and study with the famous Russian ballet teacher Olga Preobrajenska went with all my dreams. The Italian festival performance fell through. We feared for our lives. In every building, every office and every street you felt totally in danger. In our own building there was one Gentile family with seven children. As soon as Hitler marched in, we found out that all three of the boys had been in the Nazi underground. They immediately started looking for my sister, whom they considered argumentative. Anyone could turn in a suspect. She had married and moved out of the house and had her own glove-making enterprise. Later, she was arrested and taken away to a concentration camp.

"The very same week Hitler took over, I got a call from the director of the youth group of the Socialist Workers Organization. He told me it did not make any difference who I was, 'our youngsters love you and we want you to continue.' I told him I was too afraid to travel in the streets. The director said he would send five or six teenage boys to accompany me to the dance sessions. They came, we walked together, they surrounded me on the street or on the trolley.

"The youth group met in the back room of a suburban beer hall. I was taken to the back door and taught the class, but then it began to dawn on me how serious were the difficulties for the group. My 'guards' had to travel all the way back into the city at night with me and then return on a long trolley ride to their homes. The second time I taught, one of the owners came to the teenagers and I heard them whispering and saw the frightened faces of the youths. When I got home, I called the director and said I could not come any more. Everyone would have gotten into trouble.

"Out of the blue, I received a telegram offering me a job in Switzerland. I could receive legal working papers for nine months! I asked no questions, not about salary, not about who I was to dance with, nor where we were to go. I accepted! I left with one suitcase filled with costumes and music. My parents still clung to the outdated faith that all would be well and we would soon meet again in happier times."

CHAPTER THREE: SWITZERLAND

The little troupe Fritz joined performed political satire in basement cafes.[15] Between World War I and World War II, a very popular form of theatre developed, known as the "Kleinkunstbühnen," or the 'little theaters'. Four or five performers, plus a pianist in the manner of Brecht and Weill, would often make up their own skits and jokes, perform folk dances and entertain. In Zurich, Fritz was hired into a show like this which then toured the German-speaking parts of Switzerland.

"We were all Jewish refugees; a very good looking singer, a pianist, a master of ceremonies who could introduce the numbers and tell jokes in 4 languages, an actor and me with a dance partner. After performances, the m.c. would pass a hat and whatever we received, we divided up.

"After 3 months of this, the singer came to us and explained she'd met a very rich man who wanted to star her in a revue with international acts. The impressario was to form a group of six girls and our singer would be the star. I should choreograph for them and there would also be a group of Arab tumblers and a French contortionist. So we traveled together and the show was very successful."

Fritz became very friendly with the show's contortionist. She performed in a dramatic way on the top of a table. A single spotlight shone on a small box on the table and somehow the surprised audience watched a young woman slink her way out of the tiny box.

Despite the fact that Fritz knew no French and the young woman knew no German they were always together. If they had something important to say to each other Fritz would yell for the master of ceremonies of the show to come over and translate. They all travelled together for months, performing in big theatres throughout Switzerland. The performers received a good salary and Fritz was very happy.

Suddenly a letter reached him from the foreigners' police. It stated that his legal work permit was revoked. He would have to leave immediately. In addition, it stated that a new law had been passed that all Austrians had to give up their passports at the German Embassy.

"I went to the German Embassy and the big picture of the Führer and all the men saluting *'Heil Hitler'* were enough to strike fear in anyone for months. I was afraid that anyway I wouldn't be issued a German passport. Without a passport I couldn't even travel home to Vienna. Well, I got a passport, but on the front there was a huge red "J" for *Jude* (Jew). It made the passport almost invalid anyway, because Jews did not get any visas. There was no recourse at any embassy I would turn to."

Somehow his predicament was communicated to his friend the French contortionist. She was outraged. "You'll go with me to Paris!"

"How will I get there?"

"The French still believe in the revolution, in *fraternité, egalité* and *liberté.* Hitler is a crazy one!"

The petite performer took the protesting Fritz to the French embassy in Zurich. When the officer asked to see his passport, Fritz handed him the new German document, his Nazi passport of the German Reich issued December 12, 1938. "We can't let you go to France, you might remain in our country," said the officer coldly.

"What are you saying," screamed the little performer. "You stand for France and that is my country. We represent freedom. You can't treat someone like that." She was screaming so loudly that the police threw them out.

Fritz remembered how indignant and shocked the little French performer had been. It seemed like a little pebble thrown against a giant brick building by a child, but this futile deed left him with a wonderful feeling, that some people could still act with humanity.

There was nothing further he could do. Anyway, the company disbanded when the beautiful star of the troupe got a visa to the Dominican Republic. Fritz asked where that was and she said she had no idea, but she was going. As long as there was someplace to go to, you went.

He packed his costumes and the music for his dances into his suitcase, said goodbye to his friends, and walked to the train station. It was packed with people milling in all diretions. He was in no hurry though, always way ahead of schedule, so he moved slowly through the crowd, threading his way between the trunks, packages and small children.

"Fritz!" he heard someone exclaim, and turned to see Claudia Vall and her tall husband, George, rushing towards him. They were changing trains from Florence on their way to the port to catch a ship.

"Where are you going?" It was the obvious question to ask, but he repeated it loudly because there was so much hubbub.

"We're going to Havana."

A year after Fritz had arrived in Florence, Benito Mussolini, the founder of Fascism, branded Jews as racially impure and blamed them for his failures in Ethiopia. He introduced racial measures in July, 1938. Amongst them was the new law that no Jew could practice medicine.[16] Claudia's husband had been practicing with an Italian doctor, but when the new edict was published he was forced into idleness. There was no way Kauffmann could continue.

Claudia and Kauffman decided to leave Italy for Switzerland. They were married in Zurich. And they tried to find a country that would allow them in.

"In Zurich we started combing the different foreign consuls to see who would give us a visa. I had my Yugoslavian passport, but George's German passport made it much more difficult. It seemed like a lark and an adventure at first, but then it began to seem impossible to get passage anywhere. Then we discovered that Cuba would take us in!

"We went back to our hotel to pack our belongings and I had a wire waiting for me from Trudy Goth. She had left Italy for Cuba and wired me to come to Havana because there was a job as a dancer for me there.

"Here's our Havana address." Claudia hurriedly scribbled the address on a piece of paper she found in her purse and pressed it into Fritz's hand. There was no time even to ask how she got the visa. He looked at the numbers and the words Havana, Cuba once again, before putting the paper in his pocket.

He continued on to his train. The steam rising above the tracks gave an eerie quality to his Swiss leave-taking. He'd never paid any attention to the man-made mist

before. Everything seemed so mechanical and unnatural — bursts of steam forced into our faces, even the clouds aren't where they're supposed to be.

When he reached home, he was surprised to see a letter waiting for him. It was from Dürer,[17] the concert manager who had originally gotten him out of Vienna for Switzerland. He was writing now from Amsterdam. "I want to get my sister out of Vienna. If you arrange a company of five dancers and include my sister, I'll get you a contract to tour night clubs and movie houses for three months in Holland."

Fritz jumped at the chance and began to think of a plot. He had no trouble hiring four dancers, but Dürer would arrange the legal papers for five. When the new company would disembark from the train, the sister could 'accidentally' fall from the last train step and turn her ankle so badly she wouldn't be able to perform. Fritz choreographed the dances for four dancers and himself, rehearsed in Vienna with his new troupe, and off they went as planned.

Everything seemed like an adventure to the young man. He didn't really believe that anything could happen to him. Who could dream that there would be a 'final solution' for his whole family, his neighborhood, his community.

On the third day of his legal stay in Holland, his visa was revoked. The Dutch too were wary of Jewish visitors from Hitler's Reich. He was allowed only to finish the week at the night club. However, he was supposed to buy all the train fares for his "troupe" to get to their respective homes in Belgium, Switzerland and Austria. The little money he had went for their tickets.

"I had room in a pensione that was very elegant. Each night I moved up one flight to a cheaper room. It was January and bitter cold. Finally I ended up in the unheated attic with absolutely no money. I was desperate and I didn't know what to do." The magnitude of the Nazi takeover became clearer and clearer to him. Unable to work in Vienna, and now forced out of Switzerland and Holland, he decided to try to leave Europe altogether. A dancer from Gertrud's group had settled in London, so Fritz wrote, inquiring whether he could visit. The reply came that if he could somehow secure passage to London, the family would feed him and he could always sleep on the floor.

Fritz went to the English consulate to ask what he needed to do to get a permit for a company of dancers. He was told that he had to have proof of contracts and actual engagements for work in both England and Holland as well as a round trip ticket from Amsterdam to London and back again. Without any of that, a temporary visa would not be issued to Britain. Although it seemed impossible, he set out to try.

He sold his only valuable possession, his grandfather's watch, and secured enough money for one ticket to London and back. Through another agent, who was a friend, he got false bookings and contracts that promised work in Holland in two months.

The remaining problem was how to secure a re-entry document from the Dutch authorities when they had already notified him that he was to leave Holland immediately? He decided to go to the foreigners' police in Amsterdam to talk to the officer in charge. Speaking as directly and simply as possible, Fritz outlined his plan to the officer. "You don't want me in Holland and I don't what to be here. I have a chance to go to England, but I need a re-entry permit from you. If you issue me the permit, I promise never to use it."

The Dutchman looked him straight in the eyes. "I'm so tired of stories and dramas. No one ever comes to me with a true story. You're the first, so I'll give you a re-entry permit but I'm also marking your passport with a little cross in the corner. This mark is our code making the permit invalid. If you should return to Holland, the border police seeing this code would not allow you to re-enter Holland. Instead, they would

send you straight to Germany."

The next day, Fritz returned to the British consul fortified with the re-entry permit to Holland, fake contracts and the round trip ticket. He received a 10 day visitor's visa to England.

The last entry in his German passport with the tell-tale "J" stamped on it, was the entry "Good for single journey on condition that the holder does not remain in the United Kingdom longer than the third week of February 1939 and does not enter any employment paid or unpaid." He left the Hague on January 23, 1939 and landed in London on January 25, 1939, his birthday.

CHAPTER FOUR: ENGLAND

Fritz found out about the Jewish London organization called Woburn House. He thought they would be able to help him find work and a place to live. The man there told him there was nothing they could do because he had a visitor's visa for 10 days in England.

The Woburn advisor took out five postcards and wrote in Fritz's name inquiring for home hospitality for a Jewish refugee. Then he gave Fritz the name of a solicitor who would do the work of applying for an extension of his visa free of charge.

Fritz tried to find work in London while he waited for replies to the postcards. He met different dancers but none had work and no one could offer assistance.

He returned to Woburn and was told that in fact someone had replied to his request, but the department worker told him it would be better to wait for a different reply. A woman had come to Woburn House in person to answer his inquiry but she looked as if she was in such difficult straits herself she most likely would be of no help.

Desperate, and with no other prospects, Fritz decided to take a train to Rotherfield in Sussex to the address of one Elizabeth Graham, the woman who had responded to the request of Woburn House. At the station, he was surprised to find a taxi waiting which took him to a charming house, belonging to Graham. She lived frugally but was served by a maid, a gardener and her driver. Fritz was her guest for four months. She was an unusual and generous sponsor, providing him with English lessons, securing him work as a private dance teacher and also sponsoring Fritz's parents whom she brought from Vienna and sheltered in London for the duration of the war. Elizabeth Graham had been a field nurse in World War I. Witnessing the brutalities of the Germans, she vowed to help someone escape them if ever the need should arise. Fritz and his family were the beneficiaries of Graham's generosity.

When he arrived, he was immediately ushered into the dining room where the table was set for tea. It gleamed with the silver service and silverware, and the plates of biscuits and dishes of jams and cream looked lovely. They ate silently, after exchanging the few words they knew of German and English. He was shown to his room upstairs which had a lovely view of the garden, trimmed and carefully arranged, and then the fields and rolling hills beyond.

At 9 in the evening he was called again and taken to the drawing room where he was served coffee while Miss Graham listened to the news on the wireless. He, too, was anxious to understand the news, but was terribly frustrated because of the limitations of his English. Slowly, as the weeks passed their ritual of listening to the broadcasts began to seem less foreign. The two occupants of the house began slowly to communicate with each other, Fritz using his hands and some pantomime, building on the English lessons

Miss Graham provided for him.

She was a benevolent but stern sponsor. She clearly believed in the good of work and tested Fritz's willingness by assigning him to aid the gardener in chopping trees in the orchard, fixing the fence or even moving furniture in the house. She kept him busy with little chores.

Once a week, he would find two pounds sterling under his napkin at breakfast, a very generous allowance. She refused any thanks and in a slightly embarrassed way would tell him he should take the train to visit his friends in London, go to see a movie or speak to the solicitor about his papers. As the months passed, Fritz realized with what understanding and empathy she viewed his situation.

Neither asked many questions of the other. Each sensed a need to respect each other and not to intrude. But Miss Graham was clever. She sent him to exercise every day in the garden. Somehow she learned he was a dancer, and if this were true, she said, he'd need his daily training.

That was a welcome addition to his schedule. He noticed the way that the grey skies and mist were an almost daily accompaniment to his exercise. At first it seemed gloomy, but later he ignored the somberness of it, as he did with tedious music for an uninteresting dance class. It was just something to endure, because daily class was one of those necessities.

Dance became a means to meet people, to exercise his new English, and even to bring him much needed money. Again, it was Miss Graham, who arranged a meeting with a well-to-do younger neighbor. Fritz was driven to the woman's estate for an interview, which passed satisfactorily enough for him to be hired as her children's dance teacher.

When the woman explained that she loved to dance at parties but that her husband did not, Fritz felt himself on dangerous footing.

"Would you accompany me and my friends next Saturday evening to a ball and be our partner? We would pay you for your services."

"Yes, Madame," came the reply, but inside Fritz felt like a gigolo, and he hated the whole idea. He went many times with the women to different estates in the surrounding area. They were always very correct, but he hated the idea that his beloved dance could be put to such a facile, disconnected use. And he hated being used.

Later in April, during Passover, the woman who had originally employed him invited him in to her home when the evening's entertainment was finished. She moved the servants out of the library, offered him some brandy and closing the door behind the servants, she turned to Fritz with imploring eyes.

"I beg you not to mention this to anyone. Not my husband, nor my children nor Miss Graham. I have been interested in helping you, in sustaining you, so that you can get to a better place to live. No one here knows I too am Jewish. Take this money and may it help you to make a new beginning for you."

Fritz undoubtedly appealed to the woman. He was very well mannered and polite, even if his language was very limited. Miss Graham had outfitted him in English tweeds at her tailor's, and the new clothes showed off his trim and fit figure. His face was compelling, at once boyish and mature, his dark eyes were ready to meet anyone's gaze, yet there was sensitivity in them as he watched his interlocutors. The incongruous element was his balding head. One wondered what his real age could be.

Once the women took Fritz to a movie house where they saw an American film. "I sat the whole time not understanding a word. We all got a good laugh, when they confided in me that they couldn't understand the 'American-English' either."

One morning, at breakfast at the end of April, Miss Graham told Fritz that she

had procured passage for him on the *R.M.S. Orbita* bound for Cuba. She had had to buy Fritz a roundtrip ticket, but it was of no importance. The important thing was that he would have safe passage to a country where he could make a new life. He should go immediately to the tailor and have a traveling suit made up. She would hear of no thanks.

THE NEW YORK TIMES, SUNDAY, DECEMBER 16, 1984

DANCE VIEW
by ANNA KISSELGOFF

Striking Records of An Art in Motion

Fred Berk dancing in the 1950's

CHAPTER FIVE: CUBA

Fritz probably arrived in Cuba on May 12, 1939, on what turned out to be the last ship from Europe that was permitted to discharge its passengers. The *St. Louis,* which reached Havana three days later, was forced to return to Hamburg, Germany with its 907 Jewish refugees, who met their death in Europe.[18] Cuba was in the throes of an economic depression because the price of sugar cane had slumped. The island had no other industry and Havana was inundated with cheap labor from neighboring Haiti where conditions were even worse and this, coupled with the influx of European immigrants created a difficult atmosphere.

Although three U.S. Jewish organizations and five Jewish-Cuban groups had opened offices in Havana to care for the refugees, the government sanctioned anti-Semitic and other repressive internal measures.

The port closed down after the landing of the *R.M.S. Orbita.* In fact, the newspaper had reported the port already closed for fear of Nazi submarines.

For most Europeans, the West Indies had always represented romance, mystery and perpetual warmth. Now, for many, it had become a place of refuge where they could wait for the precious visa that would permit them to emigrate to the United States to make a new life. Despite the sworn determination of the Nazis to wipe out the Jews, few countries offered them a haven and until Fritz's arrival, Cuba was one of them.

On board the *Orbita,* Fritz enjoyed the rare, timeless interlude that life on a ship offers. He arose at 6:00 every morning to exercise and practice tap dancing. On the third day, one of the Spaniards on board, who had fought in the Civil War on the Republican side (he had lost an arm in battle) and who was also fleeing to freedom, asked Fritz to teach him to tap dance. Through signs, Fritz managed to convey the idea that he would give him lessons in exchange for lesons in Spanish. By the end of the two-week voyage, Fritz had learned the Spanish for right *(dereche)* and left *(izquierda),* words essential to every dancer, and some other useful Spanish words and phrases, while the former soldier was able to do the time step.

Fritz thought about his friend Claudia Vall. He pictured her waving gaily to him as he disembarked.

He found himself perspiring heavily in his English "light-summer" suit under the tropical May sun when he stood on the Havana quay. But George and Claudia were nowhere in sight. After waiting a bit, he carried his luggage through a crooked street to a wide, open avenue lined with palm trees and cactus, wondrous plants to his European eyes. By dint of showing the Kauffmann's address to passersby and then bus passengers, he was able to reach their apartment. Claudia and George were astonished to see him. Earlier, the newspapers had reported that the port was closed. In the Kauffmann's

apartment they could hardly hear each other for all the excited questions and answers about where their friends were and what had happened to each of them.

Claudia explained that Havana was an active dance center. The Sociedad Pro-Arte Musical, an organization founded by wealthy patrons in 1918 to enrich the cultural life of the city,[20] brought in companies on tour and arranged concerts. In 1937, the organization had sponsored Ted Shawn, Yeichi Nimura and Lisan Kay,[21] while in 1938 the Ballet Caravan had presented a dazzling program. Later that year the advanced pupils of the Pro-Arte ballet school appeared in a program. From 1931-1938, the school was conducted by Nicolai Yavorsky, a former member of the Opera Privé de Paris. Among his students were the talented Alicia Martinez, her future husband, Fernando Alonso, and his brother, Alberto. The two young men were the children of Pro-Arte's president, Laura Rayneri de Alonso. But by the late 1930s the three well-trained dancers had left Cuba, Alberto to perform with the de Basil Ballet Russe while Alicia and Fernando danced in Broadway shows, and with Ballet Theatre.

The Pro-Arte building was constructed in 1928 on a site between old Havana and the Miramar, a stretch of shore where the wealthy Cubans lived to be near the city's fine clubs and beaches. Known as the Teatro Auditorium, the building housed impressive facilities: a library, a concert hall with a Steinway piano for small gatherings, a small hall for ballet classes, a theater with a seating capacity of 2,500, and offices. Claudia recalled,[22] "I came to Cuba as a legal member of a dance company connected to a new Mozart Opera Troupe. Trudy Goth arranged the job for me, but in fact, the Opera Troupe fell apart soon after I arrived. The dancers decided to perform with a soprano from the company and we toured the private clubs in Havana." From the other dancers she learned Spanish and English which were her fifth and sixth languages. "We did not suffer from changing to a new life because we became part of the artists' colony of Havana," she said.

Fritz could hardly wait to start rehearsing with Claudia. Of course they could make a program together, but where could they rehearse? He had brought costumes and music with him. When could they get started? Claudia laughed. He did not need to be so anxious — things were different in Havana. There was no hurry. People took their time to enjoy themselves. He must learn to adapt to the slow pace.

She and George took Fritz back to the port to friends who knew of a vacant two-room apartment. It was a building near the port, a deteriorated area of Havana where pimps, prostitutes and refugees were able to take advantage of cheap lodgings. Fritz was delighted that one window in his apartment faced the sea.

To be able to earn money he and Claudia rehearsed; Fritz advertised dance and exercise classes for women. Refugees were drawn to them for they had little to do but wait for a visa to America. The almost unbearable tension of waiting for news of family members in Europe and wondering what the future would bring could be broken with the promised benefits of exercise and art brought to them by Fritz's classes.

Fritz loved the tropics and the leisurely way of life, and he loved the informality of Havana. "It was still all so innocent. The Cubans I met would ask me why I left Europe and I'd say because I'm Jewish. What's that? they would ask me." He toyed with the idea of remaining in Cuba, although he found the heat taxing. *"Hace calor!"* was one of the first phrases he learned in Cuba, "It's so hot!" Claudia remembered that during rehearsals he often threw down the Russian Cossack fur hat he wore in one dance and raged, "It's too hot to dance!"

The team of Vall and Berger found acceptance almost at once. Within a month of Fritz's arrival, an agent friend of Claudia's booked them into the theatre of Pro-Arte Musical de Habana, although it was the end of the concert season. On June 19, 1939,

they presented their program[23] of duets to the music of Chopin, Graupner and Liszt and dances native to Russia, Croatia and Austria.

The dances reflected the themes of their Viennese modern dance training — love and empathy for people in dances with traditonal folk motifs and rhythms, as well as dances of social comment and dances of mood. "Danza de saltos y cabriolas," was a dance protesting war to Schumann's music. "Lucha de los elementos," to Chopin, was a dance of romance. To a different Chopin selection (all played by Thea Glusman on the piano) the couple danced a dance of love, "Romance de Amor" and "Rebelde," also to Chopin, representing barricades during the 1848 revolution. A dance inspired by a picture of Breughel, "Danza Campesina," was performed to music by Graupner. In the second half of the program Fritz and Claudia performed national dances of Russia, Poland and Croatia, the latter with costumes form Claudia's native Yugoslavia. They completed the program with two Austrian favorites, a Ländler to Schubert and a Viennese waltz to J. Strauss.

"I was not used to such an expressive audience, to such yelling and screaming for us," recalled Fritz later. "I was familiar, however, with the theatrics at the stage door from being in a paid claque as a youngster in Vienna. But this time, instead of being a fan, I was the star!" Fritz was referring to a scene the agent staged at the stage door: he sent the dancers outside in their make-up and dressing gowns, something considered taboo in Vienna, to sign autographs. "We were met with an uproar of cheering, and the waiting claque begged for our signatures. Then we dramatically departed."

A favourable review appeared in the *Havana Post,* the English newspaper. In her popular column, "Music Corner Review," Clotilde Pujo especially cited the dancers' "interpretation of the characterizations (which) were done with much knowledge, gusto and good team work. The costumes were picturesque."

In a few months Fritz was offered a job teaching at a music school. By constantly questioning his students, he was able to teach the fundamental dance classes in basic Spanish. He and Claudia were an accepted part of the artists' colony in Havana. "We worked in clubs all over the city," said Claudia. "It was a wonderful time. We weren't like the other refugees who were only dreaming of life in America."

December was the beginning of the high season in Havana. Despite the war in Europe, the races started and the Casino opened its doors; fashionable tourists from North and South America poured into the city from December until the Casino closed in March.

Claudia and Fritz added four new dances to their repertoire, a parody of a dance pastorale to music by Grainger, a Scotish dance, a Spanish dance to Albeniz and a Hungarian dance to Dvorák. These they performed at the Lyceum theatre on Dec. 6, 1939.

They also danced in the clubs, a string of elegant buildings facing the beach or La Concha. Most of the life of the city began after sundown, when the heat abated. In summer the people spent their days at the beaches; in winter, they paraded the streets and sat in the bodegas and cafes.[24]

The hotels favored by the wealthy visitors were the Nacional, the Sevilla and the Presidente, with the Nacional at the top of the list. A sign in English advertising "Claudia and Frederick" at the entrance to the Nacional is pictured in one of Claudia's scrapbooks. Their program included dances of different countries such as a Polish Mazurka, a Russian Trepak and the dancers' native Croatian and Austrian dances as well as their protest dances against war.[25]

The team was also featured at the Nacional's New Year's Eve celebration. According to the advance publicity for the evening's Festivities given in the *Havana*

Post: "The main ballroom of the Hotel Nacional will be fittingly decorated in gay silver and blue for the New Year's party to be held at the hotel Sunday night. A special New Year's Eve dinner has been arranged and two exremely talented dancers, Claudia and Frederick, will come with their theatrical interpretations of folk dances found in different countries." Claudia remembers that the electricity failed in the middle of the gala and the dancers found themselves on a pitch black stage.

She and Fritz also toured the island, sometimes performing with an orchestra and at other times accompanied by a pianist. Their programs were combinations of solos and duets based on folk motifs seen in Europe, but Fritz also performed his best known solos from Vienna which had won him the bronze medal five years before.

Tours in Cuba were not all successes, however. "I remember," Claudia recalls, "we were booked in Santiago de Cuba, on the other side of the island from Havana. When we got there, we found they had no orchestra to accompany us, as we had been promised. The stage was in terrible shape. Somehow we found a trumpeter and a violinist, who was also the village shoemaker. At one point I suddenly faced Fritz on stage during the perfomance and asked him 'Do you want me to follow the trumpeter or the violinist?' We both started laughing so hard we couldn't go on."

But in other ways life in Cuba continued to be pleasant. Fritz could not get enough of the street life: the fish peddlers and the sponge sellers, the gaiety, the smells and the movement. Rhythm seemed to be everywhere. There was always someone playing the bongos, maracas, guitars and throngs of people often danced down the streets. The most remarkable street dancing appeared during February, the month of Mardi Gras. The day before Lent, and even for some days afterward, especially on Sundays, long parades of *comparsas* and Havana's poor, decked out in garish and glorious costumes, danced the conga. Trucks drove slowly up and down the streets alternating advertisements for candidates from loud speakers with music to accompany the parade floats. Music and singing were everywhere.

"Suddenly people would start dancing the rhumba," he recalled. "I had never seen such a love of movement. The rhythms absolutely entranced me. After the daily spectacle of the Mardi Gras I decided to study Spanish dancing, but the teacher I found could not explain to me what to do. So, I just copied his movements, thrilled."

In the spring of 1941, Fritz saw his first version of the Russian ballet when the Original Ballet Russe de Monte Carlo under Colonel W. de Basil came to Havana. The company was on tour of Central and South America, under the Hurok Management. During the last week of their scheduled performances in Cuba, the dancers objected to being paid in local currency. Unable to reach an agreement with the management, the dances went on strike. In retaliation, Hurok cancelled further bookings. Consequently, the company was stranded in Havana from April through August.[26]

Fritz was fascinated by the ballet dancers. He was also delighted to meet many of them at the beach, which had become an informal rehearsal setting. Many of the dancers in the Original Ballet Russe, like Fritz, were displaced — their families were separated, their European and Russian home towns ravaged by war. Many travelled on so-called passports of the League of Nations, the Nansen passports issued to stateless refugees, not recognized by all countries. Consequently, many of the dancers were restricted in where they could travel. In conversation, most of them were concerned about the war in Europe and the certainty that soon the United States also would be embroiled. Nevertheless, when they began their exercises and acrobatics on the beach, they became playful and energetic.

It was about this time that Yavorsky, who had left the Pro-Arte ballet school in 1938 opened his own studio and started a small dance company. He asked Fritz to join

as a character dancer, an offer that pleased Fritz greatly. Another European dancer who was invited to join the company was Nina Verchinina who had been a favorite of Massine and a Laban pupil, a member of the stranded Ballet Russe troupe.

Fritz's own spirits were down because his dear friend and dance partner, Claudia and her husband had received the necessary visas to enter the United States. George no longer wanted to be known as Mr. Vall, he was after all a doctor and was eager to start practicing medicine and to build a real life for himself and his wife. America offered him everything that he wanted and there were certain to be dance opportunities for Claudia there. The Kauffmanns decided to leave for a more certain future and they promised to secure an affidavit for Fritz so he too could follow them.

Even with the opportunity to perform with a good dancer under Yavorsky, Fritz considered carefully what to do. An interesting season of dance lay ahead: Kurt Jooss' company was scheduled to perform in Havana and Martha Graham was expected in the winter. David Lichine, star of the Ballet Russe, was putting together a spectacular cabaret show, "Congo Pantera," for the Tropicana nightclub.[27]

Fritz decided to sign up with Yavorsky's company for six weeks; by then he hoped to have his visa. He would then go and join the Kauffmanns in America where surely there would be a more secure future for work, too. He discussed his situation with the Cuban manager who had arranged his bookings for the last 18 months and the manager suggested that he change his name to something less Germanic. That couldn't hurt when he applied for his visa; perhaps a name like Friedrich Berger would evoke asociations with the Nazis now that America was close to war with Germany. Fritz came up with a simpler name, Fred Berk, and he used it first when he applied to the American consulate for legal papers to enter the United States.

Luckily, Geroge soon received a place to train in Colorado Springs with job security in medicine, which meant that he could write to the consulate in Havana to sponsor Fritz. With proof that there was a family in America who could provide for him till he found work, Fritz was granted a visa. He would have barely enough time to complete his contract with Yavorsky before it expired.

One spring day like any other in Havana, he went to rehearsal, and then visited the beach. He felt the joy of knowing something new was in store and soon he would trade the tropics for something different. The next morning, however, he awoke with horrible pains in his right leg and uncontrollable shivers. Nevertheless, he dressed and limped out of his apartment to go to rehearsal. He was able to reach the bus stop but could not board the bus, the pain of reaching for the first high step was unbearable. Alarmed, he managed to return to his apartment where he crawled into bed.

Fritz called upon one of his neighbors, a Latvian refugee doctor. The old man concocted a crude traction device using a weighted tea kettle tied to Fritz's foot, letting the kettle dangle over the end of the bed. He instructed the feverish Fritz to continue to lie in bed for many days. Fritz could do nothing else. Day and night he suffered from severe muscle spasm and pain in his hip.

When no one had seen or heard from him for several days, a former student came to his apartment. Shocked by his condition, she informed the Joint Distribution Committee, an organization aiding Jewish refugees which sent a Cuban doctor with a social worker. Thinking that Fritz was one of the German-speaking refugees who did not understand Spanish, the doctor told the social worker the results of his examination: an acute septic arthritis of the hip resulting from an infection, which was destroying the hip joint.[28] He held out little hope for recuperation.

"My Spanish was fluent and I had no problems understanding the dire situation I was in," Fred recalled some years later. "I was terrified, but what could I do? I was put

into a very crowded hospital with only one nurse and one orderly for our entire floor. My room was a ward with eight patients and only one of us could move — a young boy who hopped on one leg to get around. The poor boy did favors for all the rest of us because there was no one else to help us. There was also little food, and there was never enough fresh water in the stifling, smelling rooms. Antibiotics were not available at that time in Cuba. On Fridays the Joint Distribution committee sent me some chicken for the Sabbath. I split it eight ways and we all felt it was a holiday."

Friends brought Fritz his first dance books in English. "One was about Serge Diaghilev and the other about Anna Pavlova. I spent the several weeks in the hospital reading the books over and over with the help of a dictionary. Not only did I learn the details of the two artists' lives, but my English improved also."

Fritz read the German-American newspaper as he lay in bed. Ads proliferated proclaiming products sold by recent immigrants. A small ad for a dance studio in New York attracted Fritz's atttention and he read carefully. The teacher, Katya Delakova, was a friend from Europe! She had survived! He noted the address and eagerly wrote her inquiring about her story. Maybe they could meet if he could gain entry to the U.S., if he could get back into performing shape, if he could become active and dance again.

They had first danced in each other's compositions under Gertrud Kraus' tutelage in Vienna. Delakova had gone to Yugoslavia, married there, and divorced. Twice she invited Fritz to dance with her. He loved to travel, and seeing a country so rich in folk dance excited him immensely. They socialized little during their rigorous road tours, but he had wonderful memories of their work together. Eagerly he waited for her reply from America, wondering what had befallen her.

Delakova wrote back but gave no details. Later Fritz was to learn that Delakova's journalist father had waited too long in Vienna covering political events. She had returned from Yugoslavia to try to convince her parents to go to join an uncle in America. She arrived too late — one uncle was already in Buchenwald, a Nazi concentration camp. Her father was arrested, but her sister managed to flee by foot over the mountains to get to France. Somehow her father was miraculously released from jail, coinciding with the arrival of the precious and very rare visa to America. Delakova stayed in Vienna on her Yugoslavian passport to try to free her uncle from the camp, visiting him with food packages and clothing, but after a year she gave up and joined her parents and sister in America.

'She was in a stupor, numbed by her experiences. She wanted to ignore her feelings, to push away all the facts and memories. She joined an assembly line in a factory, making dolls. Holding so many miniature lifeless limbs in her hands hour after hour, she slowly began to yearn for a creative experience. She realized she wanted to transform her feelings for the Jewish people into dance. She contacted the Jewish Welfare Board and met Janet Weissman who believed in her work and became her personal representative. Delakova was sent to perform for Jewish women's groups, including Hadassah gatherings, and the Y in Patterson, New Jersey.

There, by chance, she shared a program with Benjamin Zemach. He, too, was making dances on Jewish themes and she was moved to work with him further. She joined his group and became his partner.

Delakova answered Fritz's letter and wrote about her work with Zemach. Together they were trying to develop a whole Jewish cultural center. Fritz should try to come!

"I left the hospital on crutches. I would treat myself to swimming and lying in the hot sand on the beach. I got very friendly with David Lichine, Michael Panaieff and Tatiana Riabouchinska[29] who were amongst the Ballet Russe dancers also frequenting

the beach. They encouraged me constantly and told me I could be back dancing in a few months. They were right, but it took a full year.

"My visa to the U.S. had expired while I was hospitalized and I had no idea how I could pass the physical examination at the consulate. To be taken into America you had to be in good shape (no one with physical handicaps was allowed in). Well, once I got into the embassy I put my crutches down and somehow, clinging to the walls and sort of leaning, as if nonchalant, the examiner didn't even notice my condition. I got a new visa." Three years after escaping Vienna, he was able to enter the United States.

CHAPTER SIX: AMERICA

His first night in the United States, in June of 1941, was spent at the Lafayette Street Shelter run by the Hebrew Immigrant Aid Society in New York City. They took him in as he had no family to go to. Many times since Berk has returned to the building — ironically, it has become Joseph Papp's famous Off-Broadway Public Theatre.

"I had a very strange impression of America that first evening. I was so concerned about not knowing English and there, on New York City's lower East side everyone seemed to speak Yiddish — the people on the street, the policeman, the waitress."

Berk did not stay in New York; he journeyed by train to Colorado to his friends, Claudia and George Kauffman. He was impressed with the easy-going manner of the Americans and their matter-of-fact ways. In the dining car on the train he simply pointed to something on the menu — a triple decker sandwich. With his English, how could he know what that was? When the huge sandwich was served, he tried politely to eat with knife and fork. "Who could eat with their hands with my upbringing? Then I noticed how other people were eating, so I too abandoned my silverware and just started chomping."

Even though Berk still suffered from his arthritis, he received injections and therapy for his hip through his friend, Dr. Kauffman. Gingerly he began to dance. He was thrilled when he was taken to a square dancing party by friends of the Kauffmans. "But I couldn't undertstand the square dance caller. I thought that as he was talking, he was teaching us the formations. The second time the music was repeated I again did what I had seen, but I could not understand what was happening! I was constantly in the wrong place, messing up the squares. I did not understand that the caller improvised everything he said."

Gradually, his leg improved and he and Claudia were able to resume performing. They even got bookings at luncheons through the square dancer caller. Then the couple went to the famous choreographer/teacher Hanya Holm. Originally German, she had come to New York in the 1930s to open the official Mary Wigman Studio, and then had become independent. In the summer of 1941 she, too, had come to Colorado to start a summer school of dance at Colorado College (this developed into a yearly summer school of great importance to dance). Holm was very thoughtful and kind to the dance team of Vall and Berk, giving them advice on where they could perform and making suggestions about their work.

All that fall and early winter they performed in hotels and private clubs as they did in Cuba. At Christmas time they got a night club booking in Denver. The audience was full of soldiers who would whistle and jeer. Suddenly it seemed to the young German doctor that it was totally inappropriate for his wife to be performing in such an

atmosphere.

On January 9th and 10th, 1942 they performed at the 26th Annual Convention of the Colorado Society of Engineers. "We had an agent who got us bookings. Usually they were good, but as the war progressed there were less and less conventions and hotel work. He booked us into a nightclub in Denver and that was the last straw for my George. In Cuba he had been Mr. Vall, the husband of the dancer, but now he was a doctor beginning a new career. At the Catholic hospital they didn't approve of his dancing wife."

Until that moment, they had all planned to move to California. Claudia had visited Los Angeles and she knew that there was only one modern dance company there, that of Lester Horton. She had seen an agent with her photos from Europe and Cuba who told her "I wouldn't go across the street to see something like that." She knew the only way that she and Berk could dance again was in hotels as a ballroom exhibition team. For that they would need new costumes, and permission from George to continue as they had.

In Colorado Springs they had all lived together in a little house. That is, George would stay the weeknights at the hospital while he interned to learn American medical ways, and they would all be together on the weekends. "We all got on fabulously well. We were friends, and we had all been refugees, we shared everything we had. At first it was wonderful."

Ironically, when Dr. George Kauffman got work in Los Angeles, he decided he didn't want to bring Fred. "It was a terrible thing. I didn't know how to present it to Fred. I needed his approval so badly, and now I was faced with the situation of telling him we couldn't work together any more. But Fred was an extremely practical man, with his feet firmly on the ground. He understood it all. It was clear the modern dance opportunities for Fred were in New York, not in Los Angeles. He was able to repay all the money we had loaned him to the last penny, working in New York."

Berk left for Manhattan and the Kauffmans for Los Angeles. Claudia tried to form a class in character dances at Lester Horton's studio. He was interested, but his dancers weren't. It was very usual to teach character classes in modern schools in Europe, but Claudia didn't have one student at Horton's. So she went back to the ballet, to teach and to study. Without Fred close by and his brotherly concern as well as artistic expertise, Claudia performed no more.

Berk borrowed some money from his friends and hopped a bus to New York City, traveling for three days and nights. He was elated when he arrived, his first stop in the big city: a Bond's on Broadway clothing store. He bought a new camel hair coat and hat, outfitting himself in high style. He bought a pair of shoes and a new suit. He hadn't been outfitted since Miss Graham's shopping spree when first he arrived in England. He found a small room to rent and looked up his friend Katya.

She invited him to dance at Benjamin Zemach's. Berk joined the group almost immediately, dancing every morning with six or seven others in rehearsals and class. Zemach quickly recognized his creative abilities and asked him to do two Chassidic dances for an upcoming studio performance. Berk called one "Shabbat" and the other "Scenes from a Chassidic Village".

"In neither did I have to move very much for I still had to pamper my hip." He was effective, nonetheless, and one could catch glimpses of the turns and gliding that were so characteristic and effective in his work. His flair for arranging groups was also an aid in Zemach's concerts. In the following months he performed with Zemach's group at Carnegie Hall, Town Hall, and the Mecca Temple, (known today as City Center).

Delakova remembers that Berk danced Abel and Zemach, Cain, while she danced

Cain's wife. They also did a Chassidic suite together. Despite dance work on Jewish themes, Zemach's approach was too removed from their concerns. The couple finally decided they really wished to develop their own repertoire.

"We thought when we started dancing the Tcherkessia — a simple four steps back and front which was a common folk motif in Eastern European dance — that we could awaken people to Jewish things. But we were also interested in folk dances of many peoples and wanted to create a program that would show the strength of the common man." As the duo worked they realized there was nothing innately Jewish in the Tcherkessia steps. They needed something more special and identifiable in their quest for Jewish expression. What was it that would help them speak to their new audiences and speak for their own souls?, they asked themselves.

To pay his living expenses, Berk got bookings in night clubs. The two created a tango which was a vignette of a jealous man and his femme fatale, and an Apache dance which became their big hits. "We also did ballroom dances with leaps and swirls. We took the salon and folk dances we knew from Europe and used them in many situations, for entertainment and as a way to formulate our serious dance ideas. It was to be only our beginning, until we could get some money," said Delakova.

Nightclub performing was a real trial for Berk. Not only the one-night stands bothered him, but the boredom between acts wore him down. He disliked the accepted practice of going out into the audience and doing ballroom dances with the patrons. But all this brought them much needed funds.

The couple applied for dance jobs in New York's Yiddish theatres. It was strenuous work for little pay, but they did not have to travel or work in the club atmosphere. They worked in both the National Theatre and the Clinton on Second Avenue.

"For a weekend of nine performances we might make $80.00. On Friday we gave one performance, we did three on Saturday and five on Sunday! We would always be part of a variety program which included soap opera type skits, singers, a movie, us and a finale with all the performers. We would never rehearse the finale beforehand. The director would call us together about an hour before the curtain and tell us in what order to walk on. The audience was always delighted because the program reminded them of their home country. Their homesickness for a world that was disappearing must have been very acute.

"Usually it was very amateurish, but occasionally we would meet some of the great Yiddish actors and we would experience something of their artistry and the tradition of the acting families.

"I tried to explain all the new happenings in my life by letter to my angel in England. Miss Graham's reply was that judging from the way I was corresponding with her, I was forgetting all the correct English I had learned in Britain."

As summer approached they began to think about leaving the humid city. Delakova knew someone at a resort, Maud's Summery, in the Catskill Mountains. They were given room and board for dancing in ten weeks of performances as well as programs during the Jewish High Holidays in September. Most of the clientele spoke only Russian and Yiddish. They loved the combination programs of an evening's entertainment which included a singer, a musician plus the Berk/Delakova duo. Each night of the week featured a different type of programming such as folk dance on Tuesdays, "serious" concert dancing on Fridays and a variety entertainment on Saturdays. Again, the two stretched their outlook of dance even further, using their ideas to entertain the well-to-do families who wished to while away the summer evenings with pleasant dance.

The two worked very hard all summer and Berk realized between rehearsals and performances that he was more and more drawn to Delakova. He loved her very much. He was ecstatic. "I want to marry Katya," he wrote to Claudia Kauffman in California.

"For a while I was jealous of Katya (Delakova), of course. After Fred left, she got to dance with him.

"He sent me a letter from the Catskills that they were dancing together. 'The moon was shining,' he wrote, 'and it was the happiest summer of my life.' He was deeply in love with Katya and he wrote me soon after that they had decided to marry. "Actually without performing together, our friendship continued to grow. I was finally free of his criticism and that waiting for his approval and praise. From year to year I felt a freedom between us grow. He never had approval, real, deep approval, in his character. One wanted to be around him for other things."

The couple realized they had met many families during the summer with children who could perhaps be convinced to come to dance classes. They decided to scout New York City for an apartment that would be big enough to include a dance studio and living space. During the war years housing was almost impossible to find, for so many workers had come to provide manpower to fuel the nation's war production. In 1942, apparently once luxurious and inordinately large apartments were not the sort needed by the new workers. Delakova's mother searched, too, for housing and discovered a very large ground floor apartment on Riverside and 72nd Street overlooking the Hudson River. It was a dream! Katya's parents and the new couple would all live together, a caring family such as Fred had never known.

Besides, in a main floor apartment, the dancers would disturb no one below — neighbors would not complain of overhead dancing. There was room for a studio and dressing rooms as well as a costume storage-room, plus two and a half baths, a grand living room facing the river and a bedroom for Katya's parents and one for themselves plus an ample kitchen. They brought forty folding chairs in case they would present lectures and small performances in their studio space. The landlord even promised them three months free rent if they repainted the apartment. Ready, they opened their first dance school.

CHAPTER SEVEN: OPTIMISM

Berk left Europe on the eve of the Holocaust. He arrived in the United States a few months before the country entered World War II in 1941. America would change and Fred Berk had a hand in shaping the changes of American Jewish life in its cultural aspects. The quiet, relatively unknown Viennese modern dancer was transformed into an authoritative, creative man who played a part in the focusing of American Jewish change. Berk was amongst those who came from Europe and brought a spark that ignited in America despite a difference in language, tempo of life, and an entirely different milieu.

Berk maintained his humanitarian, apolitical stand in America, but the themes of his dances and the format of his first concert in New York really reflected his beliefs. With his dance partner, Katya Delakova, he presented "Make Way for Tomorrow", on Janaury 23, 1944 at the Times Hall Theater on West 44th Street exactly four years (less two days) after he escaped from Nazi Europe.

Berk and Delakova interlaced American folk dances about pioneers settling the frontier, (sung by James Phillips), with dances of Jewish pioneers working the land near Jerusalem. The combination of American folk music with Jewish folk music and the ideas of pioneers blended together in a kind of wonderful community of common goals and optimism. The program also included folk dances from Yugoslavia, Austria, Russia and America.

The simple program note expresssed their outlook. "We speak to you of little things in the daily life of man — not suffering and pain of peoples, for no fear can be felt unless experienced and we want no pity but, rather, understanding. We speak to you of humor, heroism and love of different peoples — to speak until the different and the strange become your brother." Berk communicated great warmth in his dances with Delakova and his optimism was totally believable.

Unlike the technically oriented modern dancers of America, Berk and his partner stressed their individual personalities and their emotions, whether joyful or serious, giddy or fervent. Berk's medium build — he was 5'8" — seemed to change with the qualities the different characters and stories his dances required. He could seem dominating and imposing or light and witty, depending on the various characters he portrayed.

"It came out of us, it was so alive," Delakova remembered. No one told the dancers what to show on stage. It was their good fortune to have been trained in the European expressionist dance. This provided them with form for creating dances of conviction, that spoke in a foreign, yet totally comprehensible manner to their American audiences.

Particularly appealing was Berk's smooth, gliding manner in the lyric Austrian Ländlers, waltz-like folk dances. He loved to turn, and his jumps were vigorous and

buoyant. Not a technically flashy dancer, he nonetheless had a manly cariage and spun easily and joyously. He had learned to partner in the old manner. Berk shrugged off discussion and soliloquies about the war, about Europe, about his own family. Never open about his own personal life, he maintained a kind of personal aloofness. But his humor and his encouragement made him attractive and beloved by his students and the other dancers around him. But his well-guarded privacy also made a kind of gulf, distancing him from even those closest to him. At first he didn't understand his own need for privacy. He believed his father's explanation, that his stupidity and his unsuccessful relations with others proved that he was worthless. He retreated further into his own imagination, until dance brought him out, and made him articulate. "Even though I always remained an island, to keep myself away from exploitation and commercialism, many times I was yelled at and I always said to myself I would be doing something else if I wanted something different. I would have been in business if I wanted money; I would have been a speaker if I wanted to talk." He wanted to dance.

Dance was his outlet and his joy. Once at Town Hall during a concert he danced the role of a prophet from the Bible, while a choral group accompanied him. There was one spotlight that shone on him. Suddenly he felt an emotional bursting, as if he was dancing in the sun and he could reach out and take off. He understood in a flash the image of Elijah taking off in a chariot of fire. His power as a performer and teacher came from his inner conviction, not from explanations.

"And what could we do with our memories of Europe? We didn't do anything, we didn't speak about Europe. We were guilty of surviving, and we couldn't make sense out of our survival, so we danced."

Other survivors were dancing, too, which seemed at first like an inappropriate response. Thousands of miles away from where Berk and Delakova were performing, a whole new dance experience was taking place, which would later become a pivot, a central part of Fred's professional life. While the war was raging in Europe and the Far East, the small Jewish *yishuv* (community) in Palestine, numbering no more than 600,000 people, continued to build its life in all its aspects, including culture, the arts — and dance.

Gertrud Kraus, Fred's former teacher and many other artists from Europe, who had settled in Eretz Israel before the War, were teaching, creating and performing. Gertrud's close friend, Gert Kauffmann, a dance teacher who immigrated to Palestine in 1920, was perhaps the first one to realize that there was a need for a new, Israeli folk dance:

In 1944 Gertrud often listened as Gert Kauffmann talked about a new plan for dance in Palestine. There must be something that could express the determination of the *yishuv* — the community of Jews living where they always had belonged in their ancient homeland. Dance was needed to help fortify the kibbutzim, help to bring the Jews a sense of joy at being back on the land, a sense of common cause with all the other kibbutzim and collectives and villages and Jerusalem, Haifa and Tel Aviv. Somehow there needed to be a knitting together of the *yishuv,* to show their solidarity to the world. Surely dance could do that.

Maybe the time to show such a thing was at *Hag Hashavuot,* when the book of Ruth is traditionally read. Kibbutz Dalia in the hills of Ephraim had invited her to make a dance about the Story of Ruth. Maybe she would gather other dancers, too, invite them to show their dances, teach each other, and talk about how to make a new folk dance.

Not everyone was convinced she was right. For example, Yardena Cohen in Haifa was against the idea because she said there was no way to create a folk dance. She

herself was making dances for kibbutzim in the north as part of specific pageants.

"But you're using folk materials in your dance, and you've included wonderful instruments, colorful straw baskets and an ancient air in your work. It shows something of the old and of the new and it will take hold. You are making that new dance."

Yardena argued, "but it's not a folk dance." Finally, she relented and agreed to come to Dalia with her musicians. Her group danced the simple dance she devised to an ancient Sephardic Jewish melody from Spain. Yardena called it "Mahol Ovadia" or Ovadia's dance, named after her accompanist. Her copper hair shone in the sun as she danced barefoot outside urging her dancers to be precise. The modern dance training she'd had in Europe helped her to clarify what she wanted, but it was not Western. It was indeed something new and yet old and Middle Eastern.

Gert invited Sara Levi-Tanai to bring to Dalia a group of dancers from Kibbutz Ramat Hakovesh. Sara worked as a kindergarten teacher. But she had a burning desire to set Bialik's poetry to music and to dance it. Bialik's words were so inspiring. But maybe she would take the words of "Song of Songs" as an inspiration. She was carried away by the memory of her mother singing Yemenite songs and of the vision of a strong desert people renewing their life. Dance was her vehicle.

Gert convinced her, too, to come to Dalia.

And she persuaded Rivka Sturman from Kibbutz Ein Harod to come. Sturman, originally from Germany, like Gert, brought a group of teenagers with her to dance her new dance "The Goren". Goren, meaning the threshing floor where the sheaves of wheat are threshed by an ox pulling a kind of sled over the wheat, before it is flung into the wind to separate the grain from the chaff.

Lea Bergstein had a dance she created for the spring holiday, the *Hag Ha'omer,* at Kibbutz Ramat Yohanan. She, too, agreed to journey to Dalia with her dancers to show it and teach it. Gert also convinced the administration of Kibbutz Dalia to prepared a natural amphitheatre, so that an audience could watch the dancers.

An overriding problem for the gathering was the British-imposed curfew. No one was allowed to be on the roads from sunset to sunrise. How would the audience be able to leave after the performance? Gert decided that the dancers would simply have to dance until dawn. The program was to be 12 hours long!

Miraculously it became a huge success. The audience stayed all night. The Dalia Festival gave an impetus to the development of Israeli folk dance, just as Gert had planned.

The audience came on a pilgrimage and left renewed and inspired by what they saw: the youth of Israel dancing on the land with a new rhythm and a new gusto, affirming their life despite the tragedies in Europe and World War II and the pending threat of the neighboring Arabs.

CHAPTER EIGHT: RECONSTRUCTIONISM

With the keen eye of new comers and outsiders, Katya Delakova and Fred Berk sized up their varied audiences. They evolved a manner of work that fit their talents and brought succes to their aims in helping to reconstruct Jewish life in the U.S. in the '40's. Through their work they contributed to the renaissance of Jewish cultural life in America.

Berk and Delakova's programming attested to their wide appeal. They could attract and hold the attention of Yiddish speaking audiences, college students, women's Zionist groups, performing in theatres, at rallies as well as religious gatherings. These varied audiences were all excited by the same message: an empathy with the displaced Jews, who were otherwise very remote from the American experience; dances that made the reality of Israel a vivid element of Judaism, a portrayal of Judaism in dance as a multi-faceted civilization.

They performed in theatres ranging from Carnegie Hall for the Hapoel Hamizrachi Council; the 92nd St. YM and YWHA Adult School of Jewish studies in concerts on Jewish theme; programs for the Brooklyn Jewish Center Intra-League Festival of Hebrew Arts, as well as folk dance programs at the American Museum of Natural History. There were also programs at the Jewish Theological Seminary of America plus programs for youth groups including Habonim or the Labor Zionist Youth Festival. They performed repeatedly for the Manhattan Zionist Club and the Society for the Advancement of Judaism, the synagogue started by Dr. Mordecai Kaplan.

In general, these audiences were part of the prosperous American Jewry. Many had left the old teeming Orthodox neighborhoods and gone on to the new "second settlement" neighborhoods and the suburbs. Sociologists point out that it was here that patterns of future American Jewish life were developing. Many audience members, children of immigrants who had deserted Judaism[30] were thrilled by the programs of Berk and Delakova.

The rise of the Jewish Community Center movement in the 1940's coincided with Delakova and Berk's growing popularity. The JCC movement had previously worked to "Americanize" new Jewish immigrants, teaching English, hygiene and skills. With the terrible realization of what was happening to Jewish communities all over Europe, JCC Centers in America began to search for programs to make Jewish identity in America more viable. The Jewish Welfare Board, the national organization for Jewish Community Centers and YM-YWHA's (Young Men-Young Women's Hebrew Association), formed a lecture bureau to supply artists, lecturers and cultural programs to centers all over the country.

The Young Men's and Young Women's Hebrew Associations had begun as a kind of educational and social center for German Jewish youth in the mid-19th century, first

in Baltimore. As immigration expanded, the YMHA's concerns were barely distinguishable from the aims of settlement houses, but as the Jewish population became more prosperous and more Americanized, the Y realized there could be a focus on Jewishness, rather than religious observances. There could be a common Jewish element in a variety of activities — religious, political, cultural, intellectual, philanthropic. This new kind of community, it was hoped, would replace the dying European Orthodoxy. Judaism would be maintained in a new form adapted to America.[31]

Mordecai Kaplan, a professor and rabbi at the Jewish Theological Seminary (rabbinical seminary for the Conservative Jewish Movement), saw this as an opportunity to revive and strengthen American Judaism. In his book *Judaism as a Civilization* he argued for the re-establishment of central Jewish communites in America but with new dimensions. These dimensions included developing the creative individuality of artists in order to nourish religious expression of the Jews. Kaplan was an agitator. He acted as a leavening agent within both Reform and Conservative Judaism, far beyond the numbers affiliated with them or with Kaplan's movement, the Reconstructionists.[32]

In the 1920's, 30's and 40's Mordecai Kaplan taught at the Jewish Theological Seminary. His students were fascinated by his synthesis of Zionism, religion and the arts with other Jewish interests combining together to form "a Jewish civilization." In the Conservative movement in particular his influence was felt.[33]

The ideas of Reconstructionism complemented Berk and Delakova's work. They worked in institutions inspired by the Reconstructions, like the Lecture Bureau of the governing board of Jewish centers. Kaplan was also influential in the programing at the 92nd St. Y and Jewish summer camps.[34] Delakova was known to the director of the Jewish Welfare Board's Lecture Bureau, Janet Weissman. Since Weissman was looking for ways to expand programming beyond the conventional Jewish book reviews and historical lectures, she asked Delakova and her new partner Berk to audition. In that way they might become an approved attrraction for the Bureau's listing to all Jewish Community Centers throughout America.

Weissman invited the couple to perform for an audience of social workers in New Jersey. She went with the dancers to judge the show for herself and to watch the reaction of the audience. What she saw was a repertoire that brought to life Biblical figures, legends, and scenes from Eastern European Jewish life. There were also dances about Zion, "Hora," and "Chalutzim (the Pioneers)" which were the two dances in the repertoire to become trademarks for Delakova and Berk.

Weissman decided not only to book the dancers, but also to promote them in earnest. Delakova and Berk began immediate extensive touring of the East Coast. She also booked them into Hillel houses on many college campuses and under the auspices of the Jewish Welfare Board they performed about forty concerts a year. Berk remembered a performance at Madison Square Garden in New York City where the dancers received a terrific reception: "Although our 'Halutzim' was done in silence, the driving rhythm of each section repesented different work movements of the pioneers such as clearing, planting and reforesting the land of Israel. The technicians at Madison Square Garden placed microphones underneath the wooden stage floor. The rhythmic crescendos at the end of each of the five sections, with our feet tapping on the floor with incresing rapidity, never failed to bring down the house. "

The dancers offered their teaching services in many Jewish Community Centers around New York City and thereby increased their exposure.

If educational material was needed to go along with the performance the team would write up the information and the Jewish Welfare Board would publish it. In this way their first books, *The Dances of Palestine* and *Jewish Folk Dance Book*, were

published. Delakova and Berk also developed the first gramaphone records for Jewish folk dance music as a result of encouragement from the JWB.

Prior to the JWB's interest in Delakova and Berk, Jewish dance had been sponsored by other organizations. Since 1936, the Hebrew Arts Committee under Kaplan's inspiration at the Jewish Theological Seminary had sponsored a dance group, "Rikkud Ami", or "Dance of My People". The group was directed by Corinne Chochem. She produced concerts, wrote dance booklets on Jewish holidays, and performed on a nationwide television broadcast over WABC held at Madison Square Garden in 1942.

From this beginning, the Hebrew Arts Committee became more and more of a force in Jewish arts, partly because of a gifted rabbinical student at JTS named Moshe Davis.[35] He saw a connection between the arts, Judaism and the spontaneous growth of a Jewish youth movement, the establishment of Hebrew camps and the growing number of educators and laymen interested in Hebrew. All these were encouraging reasons to develop a strong Hebrew Arts Committee. The aims of the committee were to serve Jews who spoke Hebrew, as well as those who did not, through the arts. These aims were to be "transmitters of moods and of feelings, by which Judaism may be brought to our people with clarity, conviction and form."[36]

There were high calibre artists involved, such as Leonard Bernstein, and many fine goals were achieved. The committee hoped that artists would embrace Jewish themes in the Hebrew language. "In the dance, as well as in graphic and plastic arts, the themes are based on Hebrew sources." This was broadly interpreted to include Biblical and legendary themes as well as modern Hebrew language themes.[37]

The Hebrew Arts Committee itself had subdivisions including theatre, a Jewish literary organization and music groups. The committee urged the establishing of a Hebrew Arts School in New York, which was realized. Katya Delakova and Fred Berk were to become a part of those dreams. Their work with the Hebrew Arts Committee coincided with their work at the 92nd St. Y, famous as a showcase for American modern dance as well as a place for arts and letters and Jewish thought.

Berk and Delakova had auditioned to be presented on the Y stage in 1942. If they were successful, they would be members of an elite professional group of dancers who were chosen to appear in a new dance program at no cost to themselves. They would be presented to the growing New York dance audience by one of the city's most prestigious cultural institutions.

The 92nd St. Y stands on the southeast corner of Lexington Avenue and 92nd Street. It is an unassuming brick 3-story building, flush with the sidewalk, on a block of unassuming buildings. There seem to be more families and small children on the street than in some of the more commercial blocks to the south. It was started in 1874 by a group of wealthy Jewish businessmen who wanted to help Americanize the new Jewish immigrants from eastern Europe.

CHAPTER NINE:
AMERICAN DANCE AT THE Y.

In 1934 Fritz had successfully tried for dance acceptance in Vienna at a time when, in America, modern dance was struggling for its own acceptance.

Bennington College in Vermont began its Summer School for Dance in June, 1934. There fundamental technique was taught by Martha Hill, with two-week courses each taught by Martha Graham, Hanya Holm, Doris Humphrey and Charles Weidman. Two, sometimes three technique courses were taught simultaneously and naturally there were many conflicts of theory and opinion.

Humphrey and Holm were figures of American modern dance who touched Fred most when he was forced into a new world. At the same time, another key personality in his future, Dr. William Kolodney, began dance programs at the 92nd St. Y. Since 1934, the program at the 92nd St. Y had become less geared to social adjustment of Jewish immigrants, when Kolodney joined the organization as Director of Education. During his nearly 40 years in that position, he created provocative programming in many areas, which became landmarks in the cultural and artistic life of the city. His poetry programs contributed to the development of American letters and his dance programs were at the heart of modern dance development in the U.S.

Under Kolodney, the 92nd St. Y's importance in dance grew and his endeavours were primarily towards young dancers and choreographers. A series of audition-winner concerts began in 1942 to give dancers a chance to perform in the theatre at the Y. Some of the dancers who started their careers at the Y went on to dominate the dance scene in America for many years to come.

Among the dancers and choreographers who were given a chance to perform at the Y in 1942 were Sybil Shearer, Eleanor King, Valerie Bettis, Nina Fonaroff, Agnes de Mille, Carmen de Lavallade, Geoffrey Holder and Helen Tamiris, Gertrude Lippincott, Iris Mabry, Yuriko, Middi Garth, Pearl Primus, and Paul Draper.[38]

During the war years, modern dance had somehow maintained itself through the drive of individual dancers, although some institutional help was offered during the summer months. Bennington College in Vermont provided a stage, personnel, audience and a stimulating environment. But in 1941, Hanya Holm left Bennington in order to establish her own center of dance in Colorado Springs. Another important summer performance site was the Jacob's Pillow Dance Festival in the Berkshires, established by Ted Shawn. However, during the regular dance seasons, everyone scrambled for survival. For example, Graham received commissions, notably from Elizabeth Sprague Coolidge, and even managed a Broadway season in 1944 when she created the crowning dance of her Americana pieces: "Appalachian Spring." Many choreographers were interested in American themes.

Doris Humphrey continued to create her own choreography, but was always

interested in the development of other choreographers. In 1940, she and her partner, Charles Weidman came up with an alternative to the usual modern dance circuit of touring, Broadway concert appearances and occasional excursions into Broadway choreography. They founded the 16th Street Theatre, an ingenious place with a small bank of seats and folding screens in lieu of scenery. Their Sunday night performances, according to one critic, "hatched some of the finest works in contemporary dance.[39]

For the dancers working outside a company framework, the Forties provided a new solution which soon became a way of artistic life for all styles of dance: performing at the 92nd St. Y. In 1942 Kolodney gathered a committee of teachers and dance personalities to choose the participants in the dance-concerts of the Y. At one time, the committee included Martha Hill, Besie Schönberg, and Jerome Robbins.[40]

An article in *Dance Magazine* indicates how the dance concerts at the 92nd St. Y were creating careers. "Only a year before, Janet Collins had arrived in New York virtually unknown. It is not inaccurate to say she became a star overnight. It took, in fact, several days before the Sunday papers came out with notices of her first official New York appearance. On the basis of only two solos during a performance at the 92nd St. Y she was acclaimed 'as the most highly gifted newcomer in many a season,' 'The most exciting dancer in a long time. . .'"[41]

Walter Terry, the dance critic of the *New York Herald Tribune*, described Kolodney's system for auditions: "All dancers struggle. Even the famous ones find it difficult to finance tours and New York recitals. The young dancers are at the bottom of the heap, for when, where and how do they have an opportunity to present their wares to the public? The YMHA has realized the plight of these young Americans and has hit upon a way of helping them. For six seasons, the YMHA's Dance Theatre series has presented first-rate dance attractions in the modern comfortable and well-equipped Kaufmann theatre at 92nd St. . . This year, the series director, William Kolodney, and the dance teachers' advisory committee held auditions and from these six young artists were chosen to appear at the Kaufmann Auditorium under the sponsorship of the Y. Expenses were paid, dancers took no financial risk and yet, they had an opportunity to appear professionally in a recognized dance center before an attentive audience; this aid to American dance may be on a small scale, but it is a start in the direction of fostering and cherishing an important native art. Certainly, all young dancers will look to the YMHA as a source of encouragement and perhaps Mr. Kolodney will find that his interest in the younger generation of American dancers will be responsible for the launching of one or more distinguished careers."[42]

The years proved Terry to be right. Careers were made at the Y and they were also maintained there. For one, Kolodney had a very low-cost policy for use of the theatre for those who were not part of the auditioning process.

The maximum fee to use the house in 1939 was $75, which covered the cost of printing tickets and programs, the stage crew, ushers, box office attendants, and other technical aspects of the concert. Relative to other theatres or renting a Broadway house, the low fee made the 92nd St. Y one of the most active venues for dance in New York City. "No man before or since, went to such lengths to rent the Y stage for recitals and workshops at ridiculously low fees to such early pioneers as Martha Graham, Charles Weidman, Doris Humphrey, Pauline Koner and others."[43]

Kolodney also saw to it that the performance aspect of dance was backed by a strong educational component. He was not a patron of one particular dance outlook or style. What he wanted was quality and the highest artistry. He created a dance center that was not only welcoming and practical for as many dancers as possible but also challenging. Kolodney wanted to develop audiences for dance as well as dancers.

Martha Graham was the first Education Director in Dance at the 92nd St. Y. A few years later Doris Humphrey took over, succeeded by Hanya Holm, Elsa Findley, and Bonnie Bird. The offerings in dance were as impressive as those in the best college dance departments: lectures in dance history and theory and lessons in a variety of styles and techniques. Over the years they included Dalcroze, Humphrey-Weidman, Graham, improvisation and ballet.

In 1944, Doris Humphrey began her "Dance Making Class for Choreographers" at the Y, which was designed for professional choreographers and dancers and became the basis for her book, *The Art of Making Dances*. In addition to a special children's department in the dance education department, there were classes for dance teachers, professionals, young adults and many other categories of students.

Lecture-demonstrations were presented by Louis Horst, with members of the Martha Graham Concert Group (April 1, 1939); Dance Fundamentals and the significance of space in dance by Hanya Holm and company (December 14, 1941); discussions and demonstrations of dance as a social force by Walter Terry and demonstrations by well-known dancers (1951-1952); "Contemporary Music for the Dance" by Ted Shawn and Jesse Meeker; Jerome Robbins and Morton Gould; Valerie Bettis and Bernard Segal (December 15, 1947); workshops on the "Use of Poetry for the Dance" by John Malcolm Brinning (1948); and open interviews conducted by Walter Terry with leading dancers who talked about their approaches to creating dance: George Balanchine, Jerome Robbins, Doris Humphrey, Helen Tamiris and Agnes de Mille.

Kolodney was as interested in developing Jewish dance as in dance in general: educationally, through performance and audience development.

Kolodney had also encouraged Jewish dance programming since he arrived at the 92nd St. Y. In 1937, the Russian Jewish dancer, Benjamin Zemach and his group performed with Max Helfmann's choir. Zemach had performed in Russia and created dances on Chassidic and Eastern European Jewish life. He maintained this interest in America and gathered other dancers around him, including Katya Delakova, Aquiba Kiok, Sadia Gerard, Freda Dova, Leon Rubin, Ben Weiss, Rae Andors, Eva Meyer and Lillian Weinberg.[44]

Dance also was offered in the Adult School of Jewish Studies at the YMHA. On February 28, 1942, Corrine Chochem and the "Rikkud-Ami" Dance Group presented a concert with dancers Goldie Fogel, Sylvia Fiacre, Ruth Shul, Natalie Bonner, Hilda Gelbart, Dorothy Gellis, Evelyn Dlugacz and Evelyn Hersh.

In October 1942 Fred Berk and Katya Delakova applied to the audition series of the Y. They stated they had made concert tours throughout Yugoslavia, Rumania, and Austria in 1936. After their reunion in New York they had performed in Rochester, New York, in a "Palestine Night" (June 7, 1942) and the Zionist Convention at the Hotel New Yorker on October 14, 1942. In fact, Berk had been in the U.S. only one year. Kolodney's reply to their proposal was as follows:

Dear Mr. Berger:[45]

Thank you for filling out the form requesting an audition to appear on the concert of five dancers to be given by the Dance Theater of the YMHA on Sunday afternoon, 14 February at 3:30.

I have set your audition for 11:50 a.m. on Sunday, December 13. You will be allowed 15 minutes, including changes, in which to present two dances. You will also be

expected to present two more, if requested.

The stage will have a dark blue velvet backdrop and two dark blue velvet legs, allowing for two entrances on each side. The lighting will be straight with no special effects. You will also have the use of a Steinway concert grand piano and an electric phonograph with a loud speaker attachment.

You will be expected to do your dances in costume.

If you are accepted, you will be expected to give another audition of your repertoire on Sunday, January 24. The purpose of this second audition is to select from your repertoire the numbers for the final program on February 14, when you will be allowed 15 minutes in which to present your part of the program.

The artist's fee for appearing on the program for a quarter of an hour is $35.

Kolodney presented Berk and Delakova many times, along with many others.

CHAPTER TEN: RECONSTRUCTION AND DANCERS

After their first presentations at the Y, Delakova taught Jewish dance at a unique summer camp for Jewish youth, called the Brandeis Camp. Berk worked nearby at the Jewish resort, Maud's Summery. He taught large groups of vacationers who had no special abilities nor a flair for dance. Although he was able to perfect teaching methods for large groups who thought they had no interest in folk dance, he hungered for something more. This he found on his visits to Delakova. She taught youths who were starved for self expression and for the kind of direction and meaning offered to them at the special camp.

Brandeis Camp was started by Shlomo Bardin, a pioneer educator in both Palestine and America, who was moved to experiment with the summer camp idea. He drew on two different sources: the Israeli *kvutzah* or group where not only cooperative ideals prevail, but there is also high regard for study; and the Danish Folk High School, an institution which had successfully trained young adults for community leadership within a peiod of a few months.

Bardin was an inspired leader who searched for new ways to give youth a new sense of Judaism. This coincided with the thinking of a number of Jewish organizations such as the Zionist Organization of America, Hadassah, B'nai Brith, the Centers, which thought the young Jewish leadership was "quite inadequate." Without Jewish information and leadership training, their national programs could only be conducted on a somewhat adolescent level.[46] Bardin's staff was talented and included Max Helfmann, the musician, Moshe Davis, a young rabbi; Katya Delakova and many others.

Dance became a key way to reach the young people at the camp. Partly it was because of the dramatic style of Delakoya. She was aided in her enticing work by the innovative musician Max Helfmann. They used dance to enhance the quality of Jewish life expounded at Brandeis as a celebration and ritual. "We allowed the personality of the campers to grow in all ways. We consciously wanted to help our students beyond the technique of dance," said Katya Delakova, recalling this period.

The theorists had written that: "The average young American is an avid dancer. Dancing is the core of his social life. That it should, therefore, play a conspicuous part in the camp program was quite natural. But how could it be given a specifically Jewish character? It was felt that it would be worthwhile to experiment with folk dancing of the type that prevailed in Israel... It was sufficient that the camper was reminded of Israel, something that he had come to recognize as positive and creative in character. He saw in its history, in its achievements and in its triumphs, an answer to the questions which had so badgered him. Were the Jews a parasitic people? No, look at Israel. Were they cowardly? No, look at Israel. Were they enterprising? Of course, look at Israel... Folk dancing became the norm, while social dancing was regarded as a challenge to the

camp's special character... By relating Jewish symbols and ritual practices to a dynamic Jewish culture, the opportunity was presented to invest the Jewish youth with new meaning."[47]

Two young men at the time, Herman M. Popkin and Herb Kummel, later spoke about what dance at Brandeis meant to them. Popkin, a camper with Delakova, said that his classes with her had been his first experience of Jewish folk dancing. Of course it was not called "Israeli", because this was before the state of Israel was founded. Through the dance, he was able to change his whole attitude to Zionism.[48]

Herb Kummel was another youth reached by the dance. He had grown up at the Brooklyn Jewish Center (a synagogue) where Richard Tucker was the cantor and Moss Hart did theatre programming. Although it was clear that there was Jewish cultural expression at the center, Kummel never dreamed of the possibilities of his own self-expression of Jewish themes through art. He went to Brandeis Camp and met Delakova and Berk.

"Berk often visited the Brandeis Camp, knew the campers, danced with us in our general sessions, offered ideas and participated in some of the informal planning,"[49] said Kummel.

Kummel discovered that there was a way to combine his love for Israel with dance. He was surprised to realize that one need have no synagogue or outwardly religious affiliation to make the conection work.

That summer, Moshe Davis spoke often with both Delakova and Berk. Davis decided to involve them with the Hebrew Arts Committee. When they all returned to New York City, Davis surmised that the dancers would need a place to continue gatherings on Jewish dance themes. He rembered that the gymnasium at the Jewish Theological Seminary was often available and made the necessary arrangements to have Delakova and Berk teach in the gymnasium.

After their own morning rehearsals with a pianist from 9:00 to 1:00, their children's classes in the afternoon, they taught at the JTS in the evenings. As Davis had predicted, the Delakova and Berk classes were most remarkable. Their students were teachers in Jewish education, teachers at the JTS, dancers interested in Jewish themes, rabbinical students of JTS and young rabbis. Dance was to assume special meaning for them all. "It swept us off our feet — this urge for Jewish expression. We felt we were building a new monument, building from the deep roots of our people," said Delakova, thinking back to 1943.

Delakova and Berk began teaching the student rabbis how to celebrate holidays and stage pageants using dance. "For without rabbis and philosophers, you cannot make a big movement and you cannot make real research on honest themes," said Delakova.

The dancers had found a way to use something in dance that grew from their own loss and the chaos they had experienced in Europe, with the freshness of American youth, and their need to express themselves with their Jewish experience. The dance leaders were bouyed up by the kindred souls in the Hebrew Arts committee and at the Jewish Theological Seminary.

Through the Hebrew Arts Committee there was a pooling of energy, a focusing of talents and an excitement that created new strength. There were countless meetings and debates among the Hebrew Arts Committee members. "We met many many evenings running. We would debate and argue about our art, both in general terms and in specific, individual relations to art. Some of us argued about the monetary worth of Jewish arts, could we ever make a profession out of Jewish arts? Others debated whether folk arts were as important as pure art. Some of us were tied to the folk arts. Every balladeer and folk singer was considered a Communist during this time and they

used their folk songs for political argument rather than artistic goals. We, however, wanted to use folk arts for something more sophisticated: to reshape a whole people in a new way. We were not quick to accept folk dance and folk music per se, but we could appreciate them for their sense of participation and commaraderie," said Judith Kaplan Eisenstein, one of the leaders of music in the Hebrew Arts committee.

The Eisensteins, Judith (the daughter of Mordecai Kaplan) and Ira (a young rabbi of the Reconstructionist movement) became friends of the dancers Delakova and Berk despite their unending debates. "Whatever renaissance of Jewish arts occurred, if you want to call it that, was kept alive by nerve and drive," said Judith Eisenstein. Through her, Berk became associated with Kaplan's ideas. For him it wasn't ideology, nor was it book-learning and studying as a disciple at the seminary. Berk's understanding of Kaplan's teachings about unifying Judaism through the arts was also not the result of committee activity. He sensed the vitality of Kaplan's ideas through the practical work with other gifted artists and thinkers. Class after class convinced Berk of the hunger young Jews felt for cultural expression. He began to see that there was a place for himself, and a role to help fulfill the young Jewish Americans through dance on his terms.

CHAPTER ELEVEN: THE JEWISH DANCE GUILD

In a short time Katya and Fred created three different groups of students at the Jewish Theological society. There was a regular folk dance group headed by Berk; there was a group for creating dances for pageants and for the holidays, such as *Lag B'Omer* and *Hag HaBikkurim*, directed by Katya Delakova; and together they directed a group of experienced dancers who were interested in the use of Jewish topics for dance performers: The Jewish Dance Guild. They searched for an artistic group experience that would create something unique for these young people. They wrote a newsletter about their activities and spent countless hours together rehearsing, creating, performing and even earning money together. Only five years before, Fred was a hunted young man who learned that dance was a means of physical survival, enabling him to cross borders to stay ahead of the Nazis. Now, in his new country, he was learning that dance was a means for emotional survival too.

One of the dance students at the Jewish Theological Seminary evening classes was a young woman refugee from Belgium, Shulamit Bat-Ari Kivel.[50] She had had dance training in Europe. For two years during the war she was hiding in the countryside in France. "I vowed to myself that if I lived, I would dance." Eventually, she reached New York, where she began to work and with her funds she paid for ballet and modern dance lessons. "But what I wanted to do was to dance about my Jewish experience." She searched until she found the Seminary classes.

"Katya and Fred's classes were terrifically satisfying and meaningful. I was not an observant Jew and neither were they, but we were looking for something Jewish, a way to express what we'd been through. We made dances that were relevant to Jewish themes.

"The combination of Katya and Fred's talents were extraordinary. Katya used to say that men were more serene and poetic and it was the women who were the earthy ones. She taught the more modern improvisational and dramatic aspects of the work. Fred seemed to have a lighter touch and he concentrated on folk movements rather than modern. Eight of us formed a semi-professional class. Then the directors created the Jewish Dance Guild, using all of us students. Fred and Katya had dreams for us, that we would all live together in a big old house in order to create and work.[51]

"They encouraged us to create our own dances and when we started performing together, the programs included some of our own dances. They helped us to find jobs, so we could sustain ourselves in order to work with the group. For quite a while we danced in their own studio and then we worked every day and moved to the 92nd St. Y for rehearsals. They were so complete and with such a total approach and lots of experience to draw on! Delakova and Berk were models, as teachers and as human beings.

"Fred's approval was terribly important. He had wonderful judgment and he could quickly see where you were 'going off' as a dancer. And he was very good at giving people confidence that they could and would dance; he had such a positive approach to people which allowed students to develop movement ideas in class.

"Once my father, a Hebraist, Zionist and teacher came to see a dance performance at the Society for the Advancement of Judaism. He reacted with, 'but that's not specifically Jewish. It's a human being on stage.' Perhaps to others it seemed indeed as if we were using modern dance technique and only our Chassidic pieces were ethnic in character. There was so little Jewish dance seen at the time that Fred and Katya were left to their own resources, which were primarily interpretative, and they developed a uniquely personal statement of their Jewish identity that came out of their own humanism."

Delakova and Berk were able to create a special social environment and bring Zionism to life through their dance. They saw this as a tool for inspiring youth to find real roots and a real identity. "The dance material that they gave us was simple enough to grasp quickly and exciting enough to entrance the audiences. We learned to perform. Wrapped around the whole dance experience was Israel and Judaism. They gave us a new place and it was very important for us. Even holidays took on a special taste after our work together. They were able to generate idealism for youth, equality and democracy and things spiritual. We were given roots and a kind of non-religious but heart-felt Zionism," said Herb Kummel.[52]

The dancers rehearsed together every morning — including technque class and later an opportunity to teach each other. "I remember that when Katya gave the class, Fred would take it with us," recalls the Guild dancer Joyce Dorfman Mollov. "We knew by then that he had difficulties with a sore hip and we were amazed how he could adapt the combinations and work them out with other parts of his body if his hip troubled him. We felt flattered that one of the directors 'studied' with us.

"We knew that they had to perform in nightclubs and go on tour in order to earn a livelihood with their art, sometimes having to lower their standards," continued Mollov. "One morning Katya had left $20 in her pocket in the dressing room, for she was going to buy a pair of shoes after the rehearsal. The money was stolen and she felt very badly about it. Fred comforted her and said, 'So we shall dance one more night and you will have that money again.' "

Berk and Delakova developed programs for the Hebrew Arts Committee on three different levels. It was the professional group for which they began to create choreography. "The Golem" was an example of their work. They took the Medieval Jewish legend about the Golem, which was a clay figure of a man created by the Rabbi of Prague, Rabbi Loew, the Maharal, to help his oppressed people. At the rabbi's command, the Golem would do good deeds to ease the plight of the poor Jews of Prague. In the legend, the Golem goes beserk and the rabbi returns him to dust. In the dance, Berk and Delakova reflected some of their European experiences by changing the ending to read "the final outcome is uncertain, for who can foretell the consequences once dark forces are awakened," as they wrote in the program notes. The dance was performed many times. An exciting performance for the group took place at Symphony Hall in Boston in the late fall of 1946, because the future prime minister of Israel, David Ben Gurion was present. "We had prepared a program with Max Helfmann's choir on the subject of *Hag Habikkurim* (spring harvest festival). Interwoven with the dance group and choir were numbers by Katya and Fred including their dramatically effective "Halutzim". We performed "The Golem" and also "Songs Come to Life," as well as "Hora", Mollov remembers.

"I noticed David Ben Gurion sitting in the first row as we danced. In his keynote speech, which came after our performance, he spoke about the young dancers and the expression on their faces as they placed the *Bikkurim* offering on the stage. He was moved and spoke about it. You can imagine the impact this acknowledgement had on us. I had only recently come from Winnipeg, Canada, in order to study Jewish dance — my own background was strongly 'shetl' Jewish living mixed with Zionism. The idea that I was in the same hall as Ben Gurion, a magic name in those heady, frantic days before the establishment of the Jewish state, was overwhelming. Here he was and I could see him and he me because of an artistic rendering made possible for me by the dynamic and skillful dance leadership of Delakova and Berk. . ."

During 1946, the Jewish Theological Seminary asked Berk to direct a pioneering television program honoring the *Tu Bishvat* holiday, a late winter holiday celebrating the planting of trees in Israel. Delakova and Berk agreed to do their two signature dances, "Hora", and "Halutzim" which fit very well to the theme of the holiday. The program was, as was the custom then, broadcast live. An inexperienced young rabbi was the moderator for the television program and he suddenly finished his concluding remarks, fourteen minutes before the program was to end. "Those were the worst stage moments of my life," said Berk laughing. "We had to improvise and invent dance on the spot to fill the gap, and each minute seemed like an hour."

By 1947, both Katya and Fred had joined the faculty of the dance department at the Y, which was by then directed by Doris Humphrey. They taught four mornings a week. They conducted a Jewish Dance Repertory Group, a course for dance leaders and another for Palestinian (Israeli) and Jewish folk dance. They added the Jewish Dance Guild to their programming at the Y. The company was first seen at the Chanukah Concert on December 9, 1947, and their dances were of several types, not just the story of Chanukah. Their program included "Songs Come to Life"; a new dance, presented as a sketch, "The Golem"; "Hora"; "Planting Trees"; and "Nameless Heroes". Later in the month, the group and their directors danced at the Y for the Manhattan Zionist Club. The dancers included Bat-Ari, Nachum Blackman, Joyce Dorfman, Efrem Weitzman, Jeanette Squire, Dina Entin, Lillian Fisher, Phyllis Grilikhnes, and Paula Levine.

By the spring of 1947, Delakova and Berk had created a new dance, "Hagadah, a Story of Spring."[53] Its message was that in spring the enslaved and hopeless arise. Their other new dance was "There is no Justice". The program note explained that the dance depicted a "tale of Chelm, a little town which lies hidden from all the world in the deep forests of Poland, inhabited by simple believing people. Some call them fools, and some call them wise men."

In all the Jewish dance program at the Y till then there had been reminiscences about Europe and European Jews, sometimes with a humorous component. Delakova and Berk did that, too, but they also dealt with subjects others had difficulty even facing: concentration camps, the Jewish dead and what they meant to American Jews. Their dance "The Deathless Voice" was inspired by a last letter from a friend dated September 1940 which stated: "There is nothing left. I escaped to the next town."[54]

A performance of the Jewish Dance Guild in December, 1947 included "Figures from Eastern Europe, Meditation" by Fred Berk. This stood out even in the framework of the general dance community, which was not much concerned with big themes and issues of identification and cultural renewal. In the *Dance Observer* of January, 1948 Nik Krevitsky commented in his review that "the *joie de vivre* was delightfully refreshing in a season of dance which seems to be preoccupied with psychoanalysis. . .

the dancers were extremely effective and dignified and... aquitted themselves admirably, giving promise of developing into a worthwhile addition to our folk dance groups. The directors as well as the participants deserve credit for the good taste which this first performance displayed."

On Jan. 28, 1948, the Jewish Dance Guild appeared in a series for "contemporary Jewish Art" in Patterson, New Jersey; they danced at the United Nations Festival (the dancers included Dina Entin, Lillian Fisher, Nachum Blackman, Salome Bat Ari, Paula Levine, Janet Squires and Efrem Weitzman.) On May 25, 1948, the Hebrew Arts Festival included Katya Delakova, Fred Berk and the Jewish Dance Guild performing at the Brooklyn Jewish Center. In addition to an original suite, "Songs Come to Life" to music by the contemporary Jewish composer Max Helfmann, a dance by one in the group, "Young Voices Arise," (Nachum Blackman-Shachar) was performed. The group wrote the program note which explained: "The Jewish Dance Guild is a cooperative group of young American men and women who have felt the need of expressing their Jewish heritage (customs, ceremonies, festivals and holidays of the Jewish people) through the medium of dance — both folk and modern interpretive dance."

The folk dance unit became more and more important to Berk. "It was my first experiment creating on my own." Until this period his wife had been the main voice and he was unsure of his own viewpoint and subjected his creativity to her definitions and manner of teaching. A dance Berk created at that time showed him that he could succeed. It was theatrical and within his context of Jewish art. "I wanted to evoke the spirit of Israel, a feeling of comaraderie amongst the dancers and also something specifically Jewish. At the time I did not know enough Hebrew to put a sentence together. I asked one of the rabbinical students who danced for me to run onto the stage yelling 'Mayim, Mayim', until we turned the word into a rhythmic chant and conveyed the feeling and the spirit of the precious discovery, rejuvenation and life itself in Israel."

In 1948, it seemed as though Berk had perfected a mold for teaching, performing and creating dances. The *Bulletin* of the educational activities of the 92nd St. Y states that "a Jewish dance repertory group rehearsed Tuesday, Wednesday, Thursday and Friday mornings for two hours."

He treated his dancers with a totally professional dance outlook and encouraged them to study other dance styles, too.

CHAPTER TWELVE: SEEING AMERICA

From the mid-1940s Delakova and Berk were moving not only in Jewish cultural circles, but in the core group of modern dance. They had become friends of Louis Horst, the musical director for Ruth St. Denis and then, from 1926 to 1948, for Martha Graham. Their friendship with Horst started when Katya took a choreography class with him at the Jean Erdman Studio. Horst believed that choreography was a craft to be learned as well as an art and he exercised a strong influence on modern dance in the U.S.

"For about three years, I was in his lecture demonstration group. I could see that he had a crystal clear vision and principles and could make a stance without being a dancer himself," recalled Delakova.

In fact, Horst was hardly dancerly. He was a tall, broad, a Whitmanesque[55] figure. He never danced himself, but sat at the piano to the side of the dance studio, as he presented his class with assignments. He delivered his criticism of the results from his piano-stool and those who listened to his comments would sometimes cringe. Berk comments Horst had a wry, dry sense of humor when talking with his friends, but could be brutal to his students. "I remember once, when I sat in on a class, he asked a student for an answer to a question. The student halted and didn't answer and this peeved Horst. He insisted on a reply. "I'm thinking," said the student. Horst retorted: "With what?"

Berk did not always agree with Horst, expecially with his dictum that students must always find new music to accompany their dances. "I thought he wielded too much power in the modern dance world and was too one sided: only dealing with variations on a theme. On our long rides in the country Katya and I would have debates on what I felt was his too cerebral approach to dance. I said, I could always tell one of his students on stage — first there would be the exposition of an idea and then it would be repeated in a different body part, say with a leg, an arm or the head. I didn't want to be a mathematician and this is what it seemed to me he demanded. Maybe that is one of the things that drew me so to folk dance in the United States. It was emotional and I could see youngsters dancing and enjoying it.

"But we always enjoyed eating in restaurants with him," said Berk. Horst had studied music in Vienna and the three felt a common bond.

On their cross-country college tours, Berk and Delakova were introduced to dancers working outside of New York City. The University of Wisconsin at Madison was one of their first college tours, arranged through the Hillel Organization. There they met Margaret H'Doubler, founder of the first collegiate dance department (in 1926) at the University of Wisconsin where she also created Orchesis, a movement of university dance companies.

Margaret H'Doubler had written that "the young must be prepared to live

creative, productive lives in the society that may wish to change. The language, customs, ethics — all must be learned in ways that will result in knowledges and skills and values that will contribute to a society of well-adjusted individuals who have discovered a way of life that is worth living." Her ideas may have sounded utopian to the two, who had left a ruined society, but H'Doubler's teaching was very convincing. Besides, Delakova and Berk had similar outlooks. They agreed with her when she said, "Art is the only medium man has for expressing and communicating values and meanings found in everyday living experiences — values that are sensed as the result of the contact of man's mind with reality."[56]

Delakova and Berk also met H'Doubler's first assistant, Louise Kloepper, who had been the first American to graduate from Mary Wigman's School in Germany.[57]

They all had lunch together. "For the first time in my life, I was hit by the energy that an older person can maintain. As long as one remains creative, it seemed to me, one is young. I was simply bowled over by H'Doubler's energy. She set a challenge to me unconsciously, that I've always kept in my mind," said Fred.

The concert given at the University of Wisconsin at Madison was reviewed by Chicago critic Ann Barzel, who wrote that "the packed house was so responsive that the audience became almost part of the performers... good dancers with God-given lyric movement and well-trained bodies perform with emotion, intellect and humor."[58] H'Doubler too wrote to them, that "it was because we felt artistic truth in your dance, that seeing you and seeing your dance gave us such a warm feeling towards you."

In 1946, before their tour to the south, Delakova and Berk were officially married on October 1st in New Jersey. They began their tour in Atlanta and Berk was shocked at his first sight of divided trains, with sections set aside for blacks. He was horrified to see they were not permitted to drink from the white fountains or use white bathrooms. he was very disillusioned and had a hard time believing he was still in America.

Delakova and Berk came to Black Mountain College, the unorthodox liberal arts college in North Carolina. "It struck us like a kibbutz, with its communal atmosphere. We were accepted as total artists and not specifically as Jewish dancers," recalled Berk. "I remember that Ben Shahn was there at the time and he showed us his paintings. The limitations of performing with my deteriorating hip condition were more and more oppressive and I welcomed the wider definition of myself as an artist and not just a dancer." A placard advertising their "diversified program of modern dance" set the ticket prices at $3.00, $2.65, and $1.55.

During the summer of 1947, Berk returned to Hanya Holm's Summer Center in Colorado. He had first danced with Holm when he was a newcomer to the United States in 1941. On this second trip, he and Delakova came to the summer center as performing artists. Their common European modern dance outlook drew them to Holm. She began working with them and created "The Triad", a trio for herself with Berk and Delakova. It depicted the conflicts a woman faces between her lover and her child. Berk was the man, Holm the mother and Delakova the daughter.

Berk remembers that he had great difficulty "counting" his moves. "It seemed so arbitrary. I remember standing in the wings with Alwin Nikolais, her assistant at the time. It was before one of the dress rehearsals and I started complaining about my difficulty in counting steps. He said in his usual humorous manner, 'why don't you just add up all the counts and divide by four.'"

During the summer course Berk got to know Harry Bernstein (who later directed the Dance Department at Adelphi College) and Glen Tetley, as well as Nikolais. "The whole atmosphere in class was vibrant, during rehearsals or even in the exchanges at

meals and on breaks. Maybe it was due to the high altitude. I understood what mountain-top existence meant at the conclusion of each performance. I thought I'd die for lack of air!

"I rember Hanya's son, Katya and myself trekking one morning up into the mountains. We left so early, that the sun was just rising as we neared the peak. My mule instinctively slowed down — the sight of all the dawn colors awash in the sky made me silent. I was struck by the physical struggle of the climb upward and I felt it reflected something of my own symbolic climb in life. Nature could be stunning and fresh, with no ugliness or suffering. I had no reason to lament my hip infirmity. In spite of so many obstacles I knew I could still win. I thought to myself: victory dances — life is a fantastic victory."

CHAPTER THIRTEEN: EUROPE

Three years after the end of W.W.II, in the summer of 1948, Delakova and Berk decided to tour Europe with their programs. Their audiences were not in the theatre halls of Vienna or Munich, they were in the "displaced persons camps" in Europe — all those who were still waiting to build a new life, to find a country and a home after the devasting experiences of death camps and escaping the war machine. "We both wanted to do something for our people. We had come to certain conclusions about what made life worthwhile and we wanted to share them. Also, we felt so guilty that we survived the Holocaust. I'm not sure how we came upon the idea of dancing for the survivors of the death-camps. But we found out that the Joint Distribution Committee[59] had set up an entertainment department that sponsored programs in the DP camps. We had to pay our fare to and from Europe, but the Joint would pay all our expenses there, as long as we could offer entertainment with Jewish content.

"Once the European tour through the DP camps was arranged, I decided to stop for one week in London, so Katya could meet my parents and Miss Graham. I thought to bring to them some foods they had not eaten for a long time. With special care I watched the package in our cabin as we crossed the ocean on the *Queen Elizabeth*. As we arrived and were ready for the custom inspection, I was shocked to discover the package with all the wonderful delicacies was gone. Missing were all the beautiful things I so much wanted to bring. How the thief found out it was food, I will never know.

"It was a very touching experience to meet my parents after nine difficult years. We also went to see Miss Graham. Again, she refused to hear any words of thanks which I tried to express to her. But she actually saved my life!

"From London we went to Paris. After the plane ride our first meal should have been breakfast. I tried to order *café au lait* and rolls in my meager French. I couldn't understand what everyone was trying to explain: there simply was no coffee, nor bread or milk. Everything was rationed. Coming from America, it was our first adjustment and shock."

In Paris someone from the main office of the Joint took the dancers on their first day to see an orphanage. Despite the fact the children were without family because of the war, Berk found it was lovely. The children were taught to decorate their home, even though they had hardly anything to work with. They had taken cut-outs from the newspaper and pasted them on the walls as if to recover the creative aspects of life which they had lost during the war.

"We traveled to Munich, where we were given a driver and a van and assurances that every displaced persons' camp would have a record player, so we packed our records and costumes and set out. In the first DP camp we found that there was no record player — it had been sold for money. I was so distressed to see the profiteers

within the camps, selling what was meant for the good of the whole place.

"In general, the tour was a devastating experience for me. You ask yourself why were you spared such an experience? I had an American passport and it only served to underline my sense of guilt.

"Those we saw in the camps were just passing time. We saw them, sick, helpless, not knowing where to go or how to get there. I drew on this for my dance 'The Long Wait', which was accompanied only by the ticking of a metronome."

The tour took Berk and Delakova from Paris to Italy for a month, Vienna, Bad Gastein and Salzburg and they spent another month in Germany before returning to Paris.

In a little Austrian mountain village they performed at a childrens' camp, ironically called Buchenwald (after the concentration camp). For them, Berk and Delakova performed dances from their existing repertoire but also taught folk dances. One of the officials of the Joint wrote about one of their performances in Italy: "It took place in the beautiful Villa Cavalletti and was based on the traditional theme of *Hag HaBikkurim* (Festival of the First Fruits). There was a group of some 15 girls and boys who participated and who had been hastily but skillfully trained by Berk and Delakova for the occasion... the people, young and old alike, were for a while taken into a higher atmosphere by the art of the dancers and the familiar Jewish themes, so close to their hearts and so rich in nostalgia."

Berk returned to Vienna, the city of his birth. "From Italy, we traveled by train to Austria, passing first through the English occupied zone, and then the train stopped at the border of the Russian zone, in an open field next to the beautiful mountain of Semmering. The Russian searched the train and looked at our papers. As they saw we were Americans they simply said '*raus!*' (get out) Taking our luggage, they threw it through the window and as we got off, the train pulled out. We were sitting on top of our suitcases at 5 in the morning surrounded by a chilly mist, not knowing what to do next. Suddenly, a truck with British soldiers appeared. They explained to us that from time to time the Russians expelled Americans from trains, without provocation. The British took us to their headquarters where we spent the day. At midnight they hid us in a truck, covered us with blankets and smuggled us into Vienna."

Berk found the city of his youth and its surroundings still beautiful. "I just wished it had no people in it. I could never stop looking into faces, wondering whose death they were guilty of. My beloved aunt and my sister had been killed. I thought I would only allow children in the city.

"I went back and saw my old Jewish neighborhood, the streets where I grew up." The houses stood in their old places, but all the people he used to know were gone. "There was no one left. Except a man from a family I knew, working in his upholstery shop, as of old. I walked in and he started to sob — he told me of what happened to all the people in the neighborhood, how he had assumed I, too, was dead. He had nowhere to go after the war, so he came back.

"Even before the war, my private feelings for Judaism weren't positive. My impression of my father's Judaism was negative and I had experienced anti-Semitism in Vienna. I had lacked an understanding of even the most basic dreams of Zionism, that a new country could offer an entirely free and different approach to Jewish life.

"Despite all this, I took some pleasure in seeing Vienna again, for one has roots that can't be pulled out of one's soul, no matter what.

" 'What makes life worth living?' I kept asking myself. I tried to build an honest love, a fascination and a dedication to a new kind of Judaism, but my guilt-feelings never went away. As the years passed and more and more wars came to Israel and I

stayed on in America, where I had become so estabished, it seemed to get more definite. But I knew, in a way, I had become my own Zionist organization. Eventually, I affected so many young people, influenced so many to visit Israel or to actually settle there, I know I lead many youths to think differently about their Judaism. I'm positive that all this grew out of my very wrong, negative upbringing. It made me want a change for the youth of today. These feelings came not from lectures, books or study, but from life itself, of going through the DP camps, of reflecting relentlessly on those killed and the luck that seemed to be with me always."

CHAPTER FOURTEEN: ISRAEL

One year after their tour of the Displaced Persons Camps of Euope, when Israel was hardly 12 months old, Berk and Delakova decided to tour the new state.

They set up a performance schedule that included nine kibbutzim, some already established for several years by earlier pioneers, some newly founded on the borders and in the Negev.[60] They also visited the cities and met friends and colleagues from Europe, such as Gertrud Kraus and Elsa Sharf, as well as new acquaintances in Israel's dance life. Gurit Kadman (formerly Gert Kauffman), was one of these personalities. A few months before the Berks' arrival in Israel, Kadman had organized the second of what became several historical folk dance festivals at Kibbutz Dalia where she presented original Israeli dances by creators such as Sara Levi-Tanai, Rivka Sturman and Yardena Cohen. She introduced Berk and Delakova to them and the new aspects of Israeli dance.

"Seing the reality of Israel shook me up," said Berk. "This was a terrifically positive experience — a symbol of new life for Jews, and an incredible contrast to the horrible state we'd found the Jewish people in, when we saw the DP camps, just one year before. Nothing stood in a Jew's way in Israel — we stepped off the plane and the porter was Jewish, as were the bus driver, the policeman, the farmers, the landlords, the professionals. It was inspiring."

The kibbutz environment Berk and Delakova discovered was unlike anything they'd ever experienced. Every blade of grass they saw on the kibbutz was tended like a child, so precious was the new greenery in the Israeli landscape recently coaxed from the desert. At the first kibbutz they visited, Revivim, Berk noticed every little plant in the field was covered by paper protectors to keep the sand from burying it. Nothing seemed to be taken for granted. He heard about the first child, just born on the kibbutz and sensed the communal pride when a kibbutz member (not the father of the new-born) told him, "*We* just had our first daugher."

The Jewish dancing team found the kibbutz audiences to be extremely receptive, attentive to all aspects of their dances. Berk also loved the kibbutz audiences for sitting around after the performances to talk about what they'd seen, even criticizing the ideas and the themes of the dances, which was very stimulating to the performers. At Kibbutz Alonim, in the north, Berk said the children seemed to be everywhere, especially during rehearsals. The first Hebrew word he remembers hearing from them was *karachat*, "baldy" in English. Berk had started to go bald as a young man and was used to designing a variety of hats and wigs which he wore when performing. During the performance he heard the children whispering amongst themselves, "But where's the bald one?"

Berk and Delakova were the first American performers to go as far south as Eilat on the Red Sea. They'd been invited to an army post there by a high ranking army

officer who'd seen a kibbutz performance. They related the story of their performance there in the *Reconstructionist Magazine*.[61] "We left Beersheeva, the last outpost of water and civilization in a command car with a driver and two armed soldiers. We were advised that we would find in the desert neither a piano nor electrical current to play the phonograph. So we quickly decided on Moshe, a young talented musician from kibbutz Hulata, who played the flute exquisitely. He arranged our music for his instrument... here and there we saw a herd of camels, the ever present sand and rocks sometimes revealing lonely antelope or strange birds... the ride from Beersheva took us about 12 hours (nowadays it can be done in half that time). Here the Gulf of Aqaba spread before us, the Red Sea wonderfully cleansing... our senses occupied with the heat and the sternness of the Biblical desert.... In the afternoon the 'recreation committee' started to worry about our stage. They brought tabletops from the mess hall – about 12 of them – huge wooden plates which were nailed together... we waited till 9 at night when two jeeps would provide lights for the 'stage'... we discovered it was already too dark to make up and since there was no light for Moshe to read his music by, we sent for three petrol lamps....The audience of about 400 were newcomers from Morocco with long beards. They began to frighten us a little with their restlessness, we must confess. To tell the truth, they did not know what to expect either.... The flute came out of the night like a charm; all those bearded faces became as delicate as velvet....

"The program lasted about an hour. There were three Hassidic themes, some Horas, a work dance narrated by Moshe who also led the soldiers in some group singing. When it was over, we went down to the Red Sea for a swim. And long into the night we could hear the soldiers singing in their tents. They were singing Hassidic melodies" (an irony of immigration to Israel which mixed Jews from all countries of the world).

Berk was nourished by his first trip to Israel. He gathered manifold impressions of the people and the countryside which inspired him and his work. He drew on an image of a Druze village they drove past in the night for his dance "Lila." He remembers the stillness of the night and the vision of the Druze women sitting, clad in black, on steps leading up the mountain in the moonlight. He was inextricably bound to the new country and returned in 1955, 1959, 1968 and after that, every year. On each visit he learned the newest of the Israeli folk dances to teach in America and he increased his involvement in the dance-life of Israel as the length of his stays increased.

Although Berk had such a positive response to Israel, when he returned to New York he affirmed his intentions to work outside of Israel. He felt stimulated and excited to teach and create for American Jewry. New York was home and he resolved to continue in this new-found home, but his wife's focus shifted dramatically to Israel. They honored their commitments to perform and teach, and their public image was still strong.

Doris Hering in *Twenty Five Years of American Dance*[62] writes that "their programs are now a fascinating combination of old and new." Another important chronicler of dance, Louis Horst, described the team in a complimentary end-of-the-season review in his *Dance Observer*. Commenting on the Delakova-Berk and Company concert given March 25, 1950 at the YM-YWHA he said, "These two well-known artists have built up an enviable reputation for their excellent choreographic interpretation based on Biblical and Jewish folklore. But with this concert, a special interest was aroused, due to the fact that they were for the first time showing works that explored a new field, namely, the modern American dance. ...Berk was completely successful as a choreographer of 'Timely Ballads (of Organized women in an Organized World)', three very clever satiric sketches of urban America, excellently danced and 'put over' with

biting humor... of the folkloric portion of the program, the finest was Berk's powerful 'Meditation on the Sabbath'...."

Despite the successes, the tensions between Fred and Katya were evident to their friends. Claudia Kauffman came for a visit from California and went to several different dance schools with Katya to study dance curricula. "Had their relationship not been so strained, I might have had a good time."[63]

Berk and Delakova appeared nonetheless as partners in a new Manhattan venture, Cafe Habibi, a nightclub on Broadway and 46th St. Big-name Israeli entertainers appeared there and the public lined up around the block. But by the second year, the management had to begin to use American entertainers to keep the programs filled and the Americans that appeared were those from the Jewish Welfare Board's lecture lists, still considered an exclusive group. Berk and Delakova were amongst these.

"We had a five week contract with a five week option. I think we were supposed to do three shows on Saturday," said Berk. "The floor was concrete and as I think back now, this must have damaged my already weakened hip very badly. Because I wanted a break from performing on my sore leg, we struck on an idea. Sunday afternoons we decided to teach folk dancing. It worked out so well that the management agreed to give us a percentage of the gate because so many came to participate. We taught horas, Tcherkessia and the dances being done in Israel that we had seen on our tour." Fred and Katya began to cancel some of their joint activities. They made no more presentations at the Y after the completion of their teaching duties in the dance department.

Meetings with the Hebrew Arts Comittee continued. Judith Kaplan Eisenstein recalls the time when the two couples were close. "We had to battle for arts, for Jewish education and for our own ideas. We also battled about our relationship to Israel.[64] We were a group of friends who were considering moving to Israel to live there. We would meet in each other's houses and talk for hours and hours. Ira and I felt the Israelis only wanted the top artistic personalities, which we weren't, although some of us were musicians and some dancers. Berk said that Israel wanted a Martha Graham, not himself or Delakova. Besides, he was tired of moving from city to city and country to country. He wanted to dig in. There was friction on this point with Katya, for she wanted to move to Israel. Berk felt that Jewish arts were not encouraged in Israel and that there was a more creative atmosphere in the United States," said Eisenstein. The evenings would end in strained silences.

Still, during the summer of 1950 Katya and Fred traveled together to a large camp in North Carolina called Blue Star, situated where the Blue Ridge and Smoky Mountain Ridge meet. Harry, Ben and Herman Popkin were co-owners of the co-ed camp for Jewish youth. Herman had met Fred and Katya at Brandeis camp and wanted them to bring their expertise to the camp he was in charge of. Despite opposition from his brothers and parents, who thought camping was for sports and vigorous out-door life[65] the dance team of Berk and Delakova came and established a program which included an Israeli performing group that toured to the Asheville Folk Dance and Music Festival and Hendersonville, N.C. All the campers participated in a Dalia Festival modeled on the festival in Israel[66]; Berk and Delakova instilled love of Jewish culture in the camp, not only of recreational dance. The campers could see the meaning and excitement of Jewish dance in the *Shavuot* holiday festivities which usually occurred during camp. The holiday would be celebrated with dance and pageantry, as would the Sabbath and *Havdalah*, the concluding ritual of the Sabbath, separating the holy day from the work-days of the week.

Berk and Delakova were enthusiastic about their charges and the new program. Berk cajoled the 14 year old boys into participating in dance through their counselor, a

tall winsome fellow adored by the boys. The counselor was round-shouldered and stooped, so Berk decided to give him some help and call the sessions body-building lessons. "I made the lessons very strenuous and gradually I would introduce rhythms and different quality movements, until the boys were dancing. They all became very enthusiastic."

Tensions between Katya and Fred built, and when Judith Kaplan Eisenstein and her husband took a summer trip and visited them, the couple was hardly on speaking terms.

Back in New York Berk threw himself into all kinds of activity. He did not want to recognize the growing estrangement from his wife.

THE BROOKLYN MUSEUM

announces

STAGE FOR DANCERS

Season 1951—52

STAGE FOR DANCERS is a series of eight dance recitals devoted to forms and developments in the modern dance. The series will be presented on the third Wednesday evening of each month from October to May in the Auditorium of the Brooklyn High School for Homemaking, 901 Classon Ave., Brooklyn at 8:30 P.M. Subscription admitting one to each of the eight recitals, $3.60 (Inc. Tax). Discount of 10% to Museum Members.

TENTATIVE PROGRAM FOR THE SEASON

OCT. 17   LOUIS HORST, LECTURE DEMONSTRATION
NOV. 14   RONNE AUL, PEARL LANG, KATHERINE LITZ
DEC. 19   MERCE CUNNINGHAM, JEAN HOULOOSE, BARTON MUMAW
JAN. 16   DONALD McKAYLE, DANIEL NAGRIN, MIRIAM PANDOR
FEB. 20   DELAKOVA-BERK, MYRA KINCH, JUDITH MARTIN
MAR. 19   RUTH CURRIER, RENA GLUCK, STUART HODES, GLENN TETLEY
APR. 23   DANCE DEPARTMENT OF SCHOOL OF PERFORMING ARTS, LECTURE DEMONSTRATION
MAY 21   CAROL BARKO, VIRGINIA COPELAND, ANDREY GOLUB, ALWIN NIKOLAIS and the HENRY STREET PLAYHOUSE DANCE COMPANY

Hanna T. Rose, Curator of Education   Fred Berk, Coordinator of Dance Programs

For subscription, please fill out attached form and mail to the Education Division, Brooklyn Museum, Eastern Parkway, Brooklyn 17, New York

CHAPTER FIFTEEN: STAGE FOR DANCERS

When Fred Berk was not on tour or performing himself, he would go to concerts, usually at the 92nd St. Y. Occasionally he'd see the few concerts organized and supported by his touring partner from the 1930's, Trudy Goth, but he did not view this period as particularly creative years for dance in America.

Dancers had to find their way back into dance after World War II and they also had to cope with less work by the pioneering modern dance figures.[67] By 1949, Doris Humphrey had stopped performing. Hanya Holm was working on Broadway, which many considered a cop-out. Those who were rebellious, such as Alwin Nikolais, Merce Cunningham, Eric Hawkins, Donald McKayle, Geoffrey Holder and Paul Taylor declared themselves opposed to what they came from, but their counter-reaction took time to take effect. The start of the '50s was that in-between time, when dance was less creative in its modern vein.[68] Graham was shifting into her Greek period.

Modern dancers had few accepted outlets for performing. It was a vicious circle, for without regular performance it became very difficult to develop one's craft. By the 1950's there was a change even in the respected theatre for modern dance at the Y. "During the thirties and to a large degree the forties, the Y harbored the bulk of modern dance performances. Each new recital brought intense reaction, excitement, and new audiences to see the radical new movement as it developed through its gifted disciples. During the fifties the intensity has slackened."[69] Berk began to give this problem of lack of performance space serious thought. Where could young dancers really get a start? Perhaps Berk's memories of his bronze-medal days in Vienna stimulated his imagination. He remembered the framework of many independent dancers showing dances together, of contests suppporting young dancers sponsored by the municipality of Vienna. He intuitively understood that something needed to be done to help young dancers.

"I went to a program at the 92nd St. Y and I congratulated the dancer afterwards. He said, 'for what? I'll owe money for three years.' "

This triggered an idea. Berk would try to create a place for young dancer/choreographers to show their work without having to find the funds to rent a hall and pay production costs. Berk and Delakova had often performed at the sculpture garden of the Brooklyn Museum in ethnic dance programs. Despite the fact that the big New York newspaper critics would not cover dance events outside of Manhattan and that a 20 minute subway ride to the museum was required, Berk was not deterred.

He went to the program director of the museum, Hannah Rose. Over lunch they talked. "It's not enough to run a children's modern dance class here. I'd like to suggest a modern dance series in the sculpture court. You could build a new audience and the informal atmosphere with the skylight and the little stage in the corner wouldn't be

threatening to either audiences new to dance or to new choreographer/performers. I'm so tired of the dance audiences that are like a kind of family gathering — the dancers perform just for other dancers."

Ms. Rose took the idea to the board of the museum, which had been partial to dance before. In 1937 there had been a Federal Dance Theatre under the WPA in the sculpture court. Nadia Chilkovsky, Jane Dudley and Sophie Maslow were among those who had shown dances there. The board accepted the new idea and even donated $75.00 per concert to cover expenses. Berk was made artistic director and producer of the series. Rose introduced every program and thought up the title, "Stage for Dancers."

"Stage for Dancers" was to become a vital vehicle for presenting scores of dancers in its three year's existence. During the 1950 season, the dancers appeared on the small stage in the sculpture court. There was no proscenium, no curtain, no wings and no magic of stage lighting. The Saturday afternoon audience, mostly of children and parents, became more and more fascinated and less and less noisy as the programs by Lucas Hoving, Alwin Nikolais and his Henry St. Playhouse Dance Company, Delakova and Berk and eight other performers danced their way through the first season.

Each dancer received $20 for participating in approximatley 20 minutes of dance. Berk combined known and unknown dancers so that three would share a program. "My idea was that there should be variety, abstract and realistic dances on the same program, and dancers from different schools of thought. It was a very diplomatic matter. I would never audition the dancers. They all knew they would be paid an honorarium — they were free of having to rent a theatre and to produce a whole evening. I usually just said to each dancer, 'look, you do your share and then just go,' and somehow it worked out."

Berk asked Jack Farris, a Weidman dancer, to be the stage manager and he was paid $15 for his work. Berk considered his work, "a labor of love," and he never took a salary for himself.

Dance Magazine wrote that Berk's programs have "a healthy air of adventure and discovery." To create his successful programs and to find the performers, Berk traipsed through New York dance studios looking for new dancers. "I went into every basement and attic studio I could find looking for dancers. At Helen Tamiris' studio I saw Daniel Nagrin. He told me he had a solo, so I said: fine."

He knew Glen Tetley from Hanya Holm's summer course and convinced him to choreograph what became one of his first works.[70]

Another outlet for dances were the classes of dance composition taught in such schools as the New Dance Group, the High School of Performing Arts, the then new dance department at Juilliard School and by Louis Horst. Berk turned to all the teachers — Horst, Doris Humphrey, Doris Rudko, Martha Hill, Juana de Laban, Hanya Holm — and asked for suggestions. He would freely mix performers from the different schools and styles such as Graham, Humphrey and Holm to fine effect.

In a way, he assembled the loners who probably could not have produced a whole program. Alwin Nikolais remembered the period as a time when "it was simply necessary to continue so that something new could eventually happen. Fred was making the possibility of continuity a reality.

"He was concerned about dance in a very generous way. He knew if he kept a broad selection in each program there would be a greater range of support. Besides his artistic vision, he was an excellent administrator."

Berk and Nikolais agreed there would be simultaneous programming in Brooklyn and at the Henry Street Playhouse, directed by Alwin Nikolais. On Monday, October 16, 1950, they jointly directed a program at the small theatre in the lower East Side

settlement house that was to become Nikolais' home base (from 1949-1970 Nikolais directed the Henry St. Playhouse). Donald McKayle presented his "Exodus," and "Sweet Song" and Lucas Hoving performed four of his own works including "A Very Modest Young Man." Rena Gluck showed two of her dances. These dances were only the first to be presented at Henry St. under the "Stage for Dancers" sponsorship.

"A series devoted to forms and developments in the contemporary dance," was what Berk and Nikolais termed their endeavor. On March 18, 1950 Nikolais presented his humorous "Fable of the Donkey," and "Extrados," performed by his company which included Gladys Bailin, Phyllis Lamhut, Bruce King, Murray Louis and others. On April 19, the program included works by Jean Erdman, Berk, Nikolais and Donald McKayle. The following autumn the Henry St. Theatre presented Berk's choreography "Timely Ballads," and "American Suite" performed by Delakova and Berk with a group of dancers drawn from the performers on the "Stage for Dancers" series (including Jack Moore, Miriam Cole, Doris Ebener and Mary Hinkson).

As Berk and his advisor Hannah Rose worked out the details during the first season, it became increasingly clear that the series in Brooklyn could not continue at the museum because there was no proper stage. Just down the street from the museum was the Brooklyn High School for Homemaking with a good sized stage and curtains, lighting equipment and dressing rooms. The series was moved to the high school.

By the begining of the second season there was important press coverage. *Dance Magazine* described the new season in general and Berk in particular.[71] "If the New York concert stage can seriously be regarded as a dancer's idea of paradise, then it is safe to make an analogy between five people and the eye of the needle as described in the Koran: Joseph Mann, Trudy Goth, Fred Berk, Hazel Muller and William Kolodney... They rank in the superlative and the reason for this can be read both in and between the lines of the concert calendar of this issue. Without exception none of them depend upon concert management of dancers as a livelihood, all are engaged in broader professional careers, from which any time and personal effort subtracted toward the promotion of concert dance usually returns them a reward more spiritual and moral than negotiable. Why do they do it?

"They know the situation of dancers who can get nowhere without $5,000-10,000 in the bank to pay for a Broadway house and union designer, stagehands, electricians, unable to win critical attention outside Manhattan without means to buy professional concert performance in New York City.

"Berk brought the "Stage for Dancers" into being in 1950. He was and is a dancer for whom there have always been more bookings than he and his partner Katya Delakova have been able to cope with. In the 10 years he's lived in America, the Austrian born Mr. Berk has viewed with no little astonishment and finally with ire, the spectacle of capable dancers practicing their craft in studios year after year while audiences went to the movies or sat at home.

" 'I got bored with seeing the dancers sit around their studios and I decided something must be done to get them on stage. Let those who wish to tire themselves out trying for Broadway houses; we'll use any stage we can get and if audiences can't come to us, we'll go to them...'

The opener for the Brooklyn Museum series in the second season was Louis Horst with a lecture-demonstration. Despite philosophical debates between the two men, Berk knew how important it was for audiences to hear Horst. "I just told him it's been years since New York audiences had heard him. There's a whole new audience and a whole new generation of dancers that need to hear him." Matt Turney and Mary Hinkson were among the dancers who demonstrated for Horst. Other programs included dances by

Pearl Lang, Katherine Litz, Donald McKayle, Daniel Nagrin, Judith Martin, Ruth Currier, Stuart Hodes, Glen Tetley and Alwin Nikolais.[72]

Berk arranged an unusual conclusion to his "Stage for Dancers" season by preparing a gala performance on May 12, 1951 at the 92nd St. Y. The dancers he chose included Miriam Cole, Katya Delakova, Mary Hinkson, Gloria Newmann and Jack Moore in their own choreography and that of Ronnie Aul, Fred Berk and Alwin Nikolais. The review in the *Dance Observer*[73] stated, "The Festival of the Stage for Dancers Repertory Company concluded their season with a program well worth a celebration."

By the third season, performances under the auspices of the "Stage for Dancers" were held in Manhattan at the Henry St. Playhouse, at the Masters' Institute on Riverside Drive and at Cooper Union. The Brooklyn series also continued. By now dancers and dance audiences were quite willing to travel to Brooklyn. The *Dance Observer* noted in a review of the February 20, 1952 program that "Mr. McKayle's work ("Saturday's Child") was enough to justify the trip to Brooklyn; and if it was more remarkable for its suggestion of tremendous potentialities than for its immediate achievement, it was nonetheless remarkable for that."[74]

During the third season Pearl Lang and Doris Hering presented a lecture-demonstration, in innovative format. Lang danced her "Moonsung" and "Windsung" and then Hering, the *Dance Magazine* critic, presented an analytic discussion of the choreography. The conclusion was a repetition of the two dances. "The fact that they were even more enjoyable after withstanding the ordeal of being reborn is proof enough of Miss Lang's ability as a choreographer and power as a dancer," concluded a review.[75]

Berk brought this succesful lecture-demonstration to Manhattan.

"We presented it at the Cooper Union which had an extremely long and narrow stage. There would be no room for a group to join hands and make a circle. Any dance would have to be restaged to fit the peculiar dimensions of the space." At the back of the stage stood four pillars with curtains hanging between them. To exit or enter, the dancer had to brush the curtains aside. As Lang's rehearsal progressed she got flustered with the constant whipping aside of the curtains. She asked if they couldn't be nailed back. The superintendent started yelling, 'are you crazy? This is a landmark building and it can't be defaced in any way!' "

Berk racked his brains for a solution when Lang threatened to cancel the performance. If only he could find some sand bags to hold the curtains ajar! It was already 6:30 in the evening. Suddenly he rushed off.

A few minutes later he returned with 20-pound bags of sugar from the nearby grocery store. They weighted the curtains open and the performance went on as scheduled.

During the last season of "Stage for Dancers" Berk presented dance students of Brooklyn college, the High School of Performing Arts, Sarah Lawrence College, and the production workshop group and students from Alwin Nikolais' Playhouse company. Berk's interest in creating opportunities for young dancers was very evident in his choice of performers for his last season.

CHAPTER SIXTEEN: ANOTHER START

Album pictures of Katya and Fred[76] on tour through the South and West in February, 1951 do not show any of the mounting tension between them. They had agreed to finish their performance obligations and they carried out all their contractual agreements. In addition to appearing together in "Stage for Dancers" in Brooklyn, they toured to Lake Lure, Mt. Mitchell and the Cherokee Reservation in North Carolina; Okefinokee area in Georgia; St. Augustine, Florida; Columbia, South Carolina; Las Vegas, Nevada; Los Angeles, Santa Susana and San Francisco, California; San Antonio, Texas; New Orleans, Louisiana and cities within the Smoky Mountain area.

But privately, everything had broken down between them and Katya decided to leave Berk for a new life in Israel. Berk rented a loft for himself. There was no hot water in his new living quarters, but there were many steps he had to climb to reach the studio, which taxed his hip unmercifully.

To his students, he was still the dynamic, effervescent figure. And oddly, this period which was so deeply painful personally, coincided with some of his most fruitful projects. Berk met an Israeli from Kibbutz Negba named Simcha Levine who had been sent by the Jewish Agency as a cultural representative to America to work with youth. "He invited me and about fifty young people to a 'training farm' of the Hashomer Hatzair youth movement outside New York City, a place for preparing young people for life in Israel. There I discovered that during the day there were lectures and work in the fields, but in the evenings we started to dance and would continue almost throughout the nights. Simcha had them dancing in a way I had never seen before. Most of the dances we knew as Jewish folk dancing in America were choreographed to Chassidic melodies. Folk dance records did not exist and a good accordianist was rarely available, so the accompaniment was singing while dancing. Some of the 'American Jewish dances', as they were referred to, incorporated some of the 'Swing' of American square dancing, too. Among these which had their origin in America were 'Dundai' and 'Ari Ara.'[77]

Simcha — called Sashka 'by everyone — had them involved in an infectious exhilarating atmosphere that seemed to put all the youth into a trance. They couldn't stop. I realized what an impact folk dance can have on young people who are motivated to experience something powerful and meaningful — in other words, finding their own identity expressed in dance. I decided to try my hand using folk dance in this way."

Levine was also the organizer of the first dance festival for Israel in New York which featured several Jewish youth groups dancing different Israeli Folk dances. "The First Israeli Folk Dance Festival and Contest" was dedicated to the Jewish National Fund Golden Jubilee at Hunter College near Park Avenue at 69th St. on Sunday, January 13, 1952. Levine needed more dances on the program and he asked Fred and

Katya to fill in.

Nine months later, on November 28, 1952 they got their official Mexican divorce.

"Levine saw my dance 'Hashahar' and said that as he was no dancer like myself, could I perhaps advise him about next year's festival? I told him straight away that I didn't like the idea of a contest. It's true that one group would win and they would be in heaven, but all the rest would feel terrible and that hardly seemed a way to direct a program honoring Israel."

Berk learned that a new organization, the Zionist Youth Foundation, was going to take over the festival and that Levine was going back to Israel. Berk was interviewed as a candidate for the post of festival director. Rather than setting each youth group against each other, he said, he would create careful stagings, so each group would artistically yield to the next, presenting each other, building towards a finale, which would be a true climax and celebration with all the groups on stage together. Berk was of course familiar with the effects of mass rallies of dancers from his performances in Europe. All his previous experiences in dance seemed to fall into place in staging the festivals, which became a yearly tradition. He got the job.

Berk's opposition to the whole concept of a competition ties in with his view of folk dancing as a medium for friendly contact among dancers. Human warmth was no less important for him than success. "Folk dancing stands for doing things together, being almost a family. There's a certain friendliness involved," he would say, "and I really look at this Festival as an educational project." In the midst of his loneliness he was working to find ways to promote togetherness.

One of the dancers from the first Festival Berk worked with was Dov Alton. He taught Alton and his partner Sara Levi-Tanai's "El Ginat Egoz" with its intricate Yemenite rhythms and Yardena Cohen's "HaYain Ve HaGat". Berk loaned the young couple costumes and offered advice and encouragement on how to set up tours and organize performances. The dancers joined him in his classes at the 92nd St. Y. Berk had been teaching high school students ballroom dancing on Sundays. His boss, Kolodney, wanted him to try to inject "something special, something Jewish",[78] but the youngsters weren't interested in anything Berk had to offer. He needed a different context for the Israeli dance. He wanted energy and excitement like the groups Levine worked with had.

Kolodney and Berk discussed the problem and came up with a new idea: Berk joined the staff of the dance department and on Wednesday evenings would conduct a class unlike any dance class advertised in the Y bulletin.

One wouldn't have to register for a whole term. The students could pay each time they came and the evenings would be called "Open Sessions," combining a learning experience with entertainment.

Dov Alton and others who had worked with Fred came eagerly. The Wednesday night sessions were open to all levels of dancers, whether experienced or beginners. They began at 8:15 and lasted until 11:00 p.m. Members paid .50, and non-members $.75. The sessions were called: "Jewish Folk Dancing; Wednesdays' participants will learn some of the old traditional, some of the Arabic and Yemenite dances, Jewish folk dances which were created in this country and the newest Israeli dances. Accompaniment will be an accordion and the songs will be taught."[79]

Berk established a format for the open session which became his trademark for teaching Israeli folk dance: he would begin with a warm-up of a few basic steps which appeared in the Israeli folk dances he would later teach. These elements included the Tcherkessia steps, the Debka step, the Mayim-Mayim step, the Yemenite step, and

everyone would execute them standing in place. Then Berk would play with the accents and dynamics of the steps. "After all, if everything is done legato, you can fall asleep or if everything is big and forte, you can get a headache. You must have shading." After 15 minutes there would be progressive hand-clapping on different steps and it became challenging for all the dancers to keep the different rhythms and movements straight. "Then we'd take the steps in different directions such as forward, backwards, sideways, maintaining the rhythmic clapping. You'd start to see the faces aglow and you'd know that victory dances — such was the success and beauty in the accomplishment.

"I wanted even beginners to understand the elements of folk dance and how these could be manipulated by the folk dance creators. I never looked at the feet of the dancers, but always their faces. If I saw them smiling, I knew I had reached the first plateau and if they were interested I knew this could be developed into something new.

"The warm-ups are like practicing scales," he'd say, "which serve many purposes. It is important to warm up and to key into dance."

"Sometimes he'd use rhythm exercises playfully like in a game or like answering questions. He'd use the drum, which was his way of participating physically and it gave the feeling of the Israeli environment — and the dancers would respond and answer to the rhythms he drummed. He wouldn't use terms and names of things which he said could be intimidating. He made things simple, enjoyable and uncluttered in his teaching, a rare thing," says Ruth Goodman, a former student who is at present the head of the Jewish Dance Department at the Y.

Enrollment in the Open Sesions on Wednesday nights climbed to over 100. Berk decided to add other classes during the week, at beginner and advanced levels, as well as a leadership training course in teaching folk dance. All the rich activity at the Y in Israeli and Jewish dance fell under the title of the Israeli Folk Dance Program, directed by Fred Berk.

The leadership training course got special attention. He involved the American Zionist Youth Foundation (AYZF) in sponsoring the leadership classes at the Y. Carolyn Strauss remembers the atmosphere of learning Israeli folk dances in the early 1950's in New York. She was a member of Young Judea, a Jewish youth groups, in the Long Island region. "We had meetings, but then mostly did Israeli folk dances. I especially remember "Mayim-Mayim," "Hine Ma Tov," "Bo Dodi," "Dodi Li," "El Ginat Egoz," and an endurance debka dance with quick squats that got faster and faster.

"As I went from my own Temple group to the larger regional group, the people became more interesting and the dances more varied. What I loved was the Israeli spirit; we all wanted to learn Hebrew and go to Israel. Although in my family we had never been observant in the least, I went to services and tried to keep kosher.

"The new dances I learned in the regional meetings were more complex, more of modern, fighting Israel, "Shir HaPalmach," "Roe Ve'roa," "Ken Yovdu," line dances as well as circle and couple dances. We all played the Israeli recorder and we danced at any occasion, especially at the week-end retreats in the country and conventions.

"Generally, one leader would teach a dance for the newcomers. The leaders, I recall, either had all been to Israel and had come back to train Jewish youth, or they were just waiting until they were old enough to get there. They all danced at the Y; the fervor was high, although there was criticism of some of the other Zionist youth groups. Competition was a real thing; what we all seemed to be competing about was who had the greatest spirit."

She participated in the Israel Dance Festival, which was directed by Berk, and she remembers being awed by the dances of the other groups. "In fact, Hashomer Hatzair, which we thought was communist, nearly tore the stage apart with their

dancing. Ours looked tame in comparison, gentle and bloodless. And we had given it everything we had! Endless discussions followed whether you had to be a political radical to have real feelings. As for me, I had no idea what communism really was. All I knew was that I had to keep much of my Young Judea activity secret from my father, who was convinced they were trying to 'indoctrinate' me. I kept on folk dancing, avidly went to the Y for the open sessions, and also to Greenwich Village to international folk dance meetings. I loved the Israeli dances best — no group but those Jewish youth groups at the Y could muster such spirit."

One needs tools in order to do any kind of work. In the case of dance, the tools belong first of all to the teacher. They are necessary in order to convey art. What is it that a teacher needs in the way of tools to teach Israeli folk dance? Berk gave this question much thought and he was inspired and clever in coming up with many answers during the years 1952-1980. He understood the need for proper music as well as ways to explain the steps of Israeli folk dance. Without these, Israeli folk dance outside of Israel could never become available. Someone far from Israel, who had never seen Israeli folk dance nor heard Hebrew, would have the potential for it, nonetheless. Through recordings which were supervised and produced by Berk, the necessary music became available. His records were the first professionally recorded selection of Israeli folk music played by excellent musicians, with instructions written by Berk, describing the dances.

He would begin his first class with a Biblical quote and ask the students to interpret it in dance. "Fantastic things happened. I would get youth from the different Jewish youth organizations like Habonim, Hashomer Hatzair, Masada, Bnai Akiva, who would come to the Y on scholarships paid by the Zionist Youth Organization. They had never thought in dance terms before, but they came up with interesting solutions. I might have them work with props, too. To be effective, for example, I would emphasize that in a shepherd's dance with staves the first thing that happens should not be that the staves get put on the ground, but used in the dance. At the end of the sessions following a final demonstration, I would give the dancers a certificate."

CHAPTER SEVENTEEN:
THE MERRY-GO-ROUNDERS

In addition to teaching, organizing the Israel Dance Festival and performing himself, Berk was facing a new kind of deadline on February 1, 1953: the premier of the Merry-Go-Rouners. This was to be a revolutionary kind of professional dance company which Doris Humphrey, director of the Y Dance Department, Bonnie Bird and Fred Berk had created for audiences of children. Their first program included a humorous dance, "The Fable of a Donkey" by Alwin Nikolais; "The Goops," a dance about popular ill-mannered cartoon creatures by Eva Desca and Fred Berk's newest dance, "Holiday in Israel."[80]

But Fred, suffering from arthritis, was discouraged. The dancers seemed unable to express the exotic rhythms from the various Jewish communties of Israel and his painful hip prevented him from demonstrating what he wanted: power in the stomps and elation in the jumps. How could he convey his conception by explanation alone? Even the music seemed lifeless, except when he sat next to the pianist, Bea Rainer and drummed out the rhythm.

Sitting in the darkened theatre beside Doris Humphrey, he tried to express his anguish. "If only I could show them!" he said, and then suddenly his voice broke and tears welled up in his eyes.

Humphrey herself suffered from arthritis which terminated her own performing career. "Fred," she said, "you *will* be able to coach them to do what you want, you *will* find the words. If you can choreograph a folk dance like this, you have a whole new direction in life. Now go, sit over there by the piano, sing and drum your rhythms. Put your feelings into your voice. Drum the dancers into the movement you want!"

Berk limped down the aisle. He slid onto the bench beside the accompanist. Singing and drumming with his hands rhythmically, he sparked the dancers. Their stomps became harder and their leaps higher and better defined. The dancers became more flirtatious and they radiated excitement. He knew then that he could make them ready for the premiere.

The dancers were trained in modern dance, many fresh from Juilliard's dance department. The idea was decidedly experimental: to form a company of trained dancers to perform only for children. Fred Berk loved the idea. Not only was the company a vehicle for his chroeography, he saw it as a means to help dancers. Times were difficult for young performers in the 1950s and they needed moral and practical supports for their art. The company provided a professional experience through which they could see their art in a new way. They were not asked to execute difficult technical feats, but to muster speed, color, emotions, accents and movements for a very critical audience.

Who is as discriminating as children? Who instinctively understood more about

sincerity and truth? Why shouldn't children be exposed to the best dancers? The highest quality? Not only Humphrey and Berk believed whole heartedly in the project but Alwin Nikolais and several other remarkable dancers of the period too.

Lucy Venable, one of the dancers in the original "Holiday in Israel" recalls that Berk's work methods were hard. As a pleasant but firm task master at rehearsals, he was always punctual and used his time to the fullest, arriving with a clear plan. Dancers worked well for him.

"Fred would not tour when we Merry-Go-Rounders went to Long Island or Brooklyn or New Jersey, but at the Y-performances I remember him sitting next to the accompanist, singing and in the last section, he would beat the drum."

Jeff Duncan, the first male dancer in the Merry-Go-Rounders company, says he was a typical modern dancer until he met Fred Berk. "I did not want to do anything but a narrow range of movements. I thought I knew what modern dance was made of and I certainly did not want to do any folk dance. I was arrogant, but during the rehearsals I began to like the movements very much. I became very involved. Berk encouraged me and taught me many performance tools. He was one of those very few who cared about their art. He and Doris Humphrey were both like that and it made for a very sympathetic and strong directorship. Berk was also involved in the direction of the dance company, though Bonnie Bird managed the day-to-day struggles and saw to the publicity, engagements and costumes. Berk convinced Nikolais to donate 'The Fable of the Donkey' for the premiere program."

Indeed, at the company's first performance the children sat enraptured. *Life* magazine sent a photographer and the published pictures attested to the wondrous effects the dancers and their dances had. The reviews in *Dance Magazine* and Dance Observer were equally enthusiastic.

In the issue following the performance, *Dance Observer* reported that "the adult repertory company charmed their audience with an afternoon of chatter, singing and dancing... the youngsters participated in the activities.,.. so that a frequent adult problem was which to watch — the dancers or the audience. The children began by clapping and singing to make the curtain rise and reveal the merry-go-round, a colorful affair of ribbons and hobby horses revolved by the dancers. Being assured that this magic vehicle would take them to wonderful places, they were easily led into the scene of 'The Donkey', danced by Murray Louis... Fred Berk's 'Holiday in Israel' was a happy choice for the only pure movement piece on the program. Especially exciting to the children was the dimming of the stage lights at the end of the *hora* which left just the dancers' torches to illuminate their figures as they apparently danced into the night."

Talking with Gary Harris, who designed the lighting for "Holiday in Israel," one gets a clearer sense of Berk's theatrical effectiveness, on of the reasons the dance itself was so appealing. Harris often collaborated with Berk at the YMHA and in many festival productions at the Felt Forum, Carnegie Hall and Lincoln Center.

"What Berk actually did at the end of 'Holiday in Israel' while the dancers perform the *hora* as if around a campfire, was an adaptation of a common European practice: shadow patterns. These have only recently become popular in the United States. By putting a single spotlight with a clear bulb down-stage, it is possible to get a 'wash' all over the sky. By dancing in front of this, the performers become enormous projected shadows, all over the back cloth. At the end of the *hora,* the dances returned to the stage in a solemn manner, in a very stately classic atmosphere. As the tempo picked up, the dancers became more and more celebrative. Then, as night wore on, the spotlight came up, casting huge shadows.

"When the audience cannot separate the technical aspects from the dance itself, you know something is working right in the theatre. I asked some people whom I knew to be particularly concerned with technical aspects of the theatre about their reactions, and they were puzzled: what effect was I talking about? What it really meant was, that the ending of the dance worked so well because the huge, whirling shadows were an extension of the spirit of the dance itself. Compressed into this closing sequence lasting only a few seconds, was a tiny microcosm of Berk's European training, his feeling for the spiritual, his wish to make the dancers look larger than life, his love for the Jewish meaning in the togetherness of the *hora*. Any artistic moment that really works can be examined from all angles. This last moment in the *hora* is such a climactic moment."

Despite his success as a teacher and choreographer, Berk still considered himself primarily a performer; indeed it was not until Febraury 23, 1953, that he was forced to change his mind. He performed that night at a rally honoring Israel at the Brooklyn Museum. The pain in his hip during his two solos was so excruciating he realized he had to give up performing.

On his way home from the rally, he worried about what he would do instead. By the time he entered his apartment and lay down on his bed, he had collected his thoughts. He would choreograph more for others and think about creating a Jewish dance group at the Y, concentrate on teaching and the Merry-Go-Rounders.

By 1954, Merry-Go-Rounders were presenting concerts to audiences of hundreds of children. For the December 12, 1954 program, Berk created a new dance, "Tyrolean Wedding."

But he wanted to use more Jewish dance themes. He noticed a trend in the few years since the establishment of Israel, that modern dancers no longer created dances with Jewish themes as they had in the 1940's. Israeli dancers filled the need, especially the Israeli dance theatre Inbal. On February 28, 1954, Berk produced the first program on Jewish themes with Israeli dancers Naomi Aleskovsky, Rena Gluck, Dina Navam-Tzelet who happened to be in New York at that time and his dance "Holiday in Israel" performed by the Merry-Go-Rounders. He decided to form "Ariel Dancers" to rehearse other new pieces of his own. The *New York Times* noted that he had collected a fine group, some of whom were dancers with Martha Graham. Dan Wagoner — an independent choreographer who today directs his own company and who was in the Graham company during this period — recalls Fred's mode of work. Still shy in his command of English, he preferred personal meetings. "He came all the way to my apartment," Wagoner said, "to ask me to join his company. Dancers would go to Fred because he knew what he was about. Martha didn't work for us all the time and he offered an interesting experience." The "Ariel" dancers included Yemima Ben-Gal, Don Boiteau, Bruce Carlisle, Joan Parmer, Joan Feder, Dick Fitzgerald, Ellida Kauffman (Gera), Gene McDonald and Sheldon Ossosky.

His hip was by now so painful he arranged a trip to California so that George Kauffman could recommend treatment. Besides the psychological rest of being with his dearest old friends, he received cortisone shots which seemed to help him. On his return to New York he moved in with another Viennese to cut his costs and to be closer to the Y.

CHAPTER EIGHTEEN:
ISRAEL AND HEBRAICA

Berk felt so much better that he began to plan another trip to Europe and Israel. First he went alone to Dover and London, to visit his parents and to Rotherfield to see his respected Miss Graham. She would never hear of financial repayment from him, despite her own dwindling reserves. He would send her extravagant food packages at Christmas time every year. In Israel he stayed with Gertrud Kraus.

Gertrud's basement apartment on Frug Street was only a block from the main pedestrian thoroughfare of Tel Aviv, Dizengoff Street, lined with outdoor cafes and shops. Berk sat with Gertrud in her favorite Ditza cafe, listening to well-known as well as young artists who came over to speak to her. Berk also visited his friend Gurit Kadman. Gertrud and Gurit were both important catalysts in the development of dance in Israel, the former in stage-dance and the latter in ethnic and folk dance. In their company, Fred felt and absorbed the excitement of the new culture they were helping to build.[81]

Gurit introduced him to an important group of folk dancers in Israel, the folk dance committee of the Histadrut. Through the Histadrut, (General Federation of Labor) a system for training Israeli folk dancers was established throughout the country. Festivals and companies were also created and run through the committee, which had budgets and personnel to aid the dancers. Berk went to a meeting at the Histadrut building in Tel Aviv. There he met Rivka Sturman, Shalom Hermon and Tirtsa Hodes; they made him into a kind of unofficial liaison in America for them. Because of his position at the Y, he could disseminate information on Israeli folk dance in New York and across America, facilitated further by his role as director of the yearly Israel Dance Festival in New York City, his teaching throughout the U.S., his production of Israeli folk dance records (accompanied by printed dance instructions) and his summer teaching at the Blue Star Camp. Throughout the years, Berk sponsored workshops for the members of the committee (and many others) on their individual trips to America.

During his summer trip in 1955, Berk traveled the Israeli countryside in search of dances, Yardena Cohen remembers. In a *Viltis* magazine article, Berk stated that he was able to bring back the newly created folk dances and to include them in his teaching repertoire.[82] He chose dances from several that the Israeli creators showed him. He learned and brought back to his students at the Y those he liked. The new ones he picked often became hits with the Israeli public, the true test of a good folk dance. Rivka Sturman recalled that she would show him her dances and often "he already knew the dances when we met. Surely I was glad and proud that he chose to teach my dances in New York."[83] "Harmonika" was one of the first of Sturman's dances that Berk chose and it not only proved to be popular in Israel and America, but also became one of the most widely loved Israeli folk dances in international dance circles.

"Harmonika" and Vicky Cohen's debkas, which he taught at the Wednesday open sessions at the Y, were to become two of Berk's all-time favorite Israeli folk dances.

"I took folk dances," he explained, "which I liked and which had a certain quality, a good flow from one section to another. I always tried to bring the creators to my own workshops in New York, but if I couldn't do that, I would learn the dances myself. Sometimes I'd take 15 dances back and sometimes only two. When I saw a dance I liked, first I'd write it out in longhand, describing all the parts as best as I could. At night, I would try to reconstruct it; then I'd go and watch the dance again and try to compare it to my notes. I learned with my eyes instead of with my feet. I also learned that the fewer words I wrote down, the better." He later took up the serious study of Labanotation, which helped him to create a record of the dances for himself and also to be precise in his teaching.

After returning from his trip to Israel in 1955, he kept trying to think of new forms to express his ideas. He talked with Dr. Kolodney and the conversation resulted in the formation of a new dance company at the Y, "Hebraica."

Kolodney gave him $2,000 to start the new company with, plus a closet for *schmates* (i.e., rags and old clothes, Berk's affectionate Yiddish term for costumes), his drums and records. "I never had a desk anywhere, just my closet," he recalled. Berk decided it should be a company of six couples. He would rehearse them once a week for two hours and create suites of new dances portraying Israeli holidays and scenes. With the development of the new company, Berk's domain at the Y became the "Jewish Dance Department."

Hebraica became the high point of the Y Jewish Dance Department program. The dancers were drawn from the best students in Berk's classes. "They were amateurs and dance was their hobby. They would come once a week for three-hour rehearsals. I believed that for each performance they needed to be highly motivated. I never had more than 10 or 12 performances a year and I always made each one important to the teenagers. Otherwise, dancing would become a kind of job or habit, and then there would be the danger of losing the spark and enthusiasm." The six couples of Hebraica always performed to sold-out houses.

All fall Berk worked with his favorite dancers, some also from other Y dance companies. He choreographed his ideas in suite form, offering many scenes in the folk flavor: "From A Fishing Village," "The Market Place," with a fruit vendor and other merchant figures, "The Vineyard," "The Desert," and by Chanukah the dancers were ready for their first performance, to which family members were invited. Some of the Hebraica dancers were those close to Berk: Dov Alton, Aryeh Cooper, Karen Geiger, Jan Goldin, Chifra Holt, Gila Melamedoff, Dov's former partner, Joan Parmer, as well as Manon Souriau and Nancy Stevens. Beatrice Rainer played the piano, as she did for the Merry-Go-Rounders.

Berk said, "I always envisioned the structure of the suite before the beginning of rehearsals. I knew if it would include a boys' dance, couples, girls' and a finale, or whatever. I would usually chose a theatrical prop that would be used throughout the suite, such as a fishing net. The boys brought it out, in another section the girls coiled it up and it became a rope over which the boys did a debka. In the finale in which all the 12 dancers participated, I used many variations of movement with the net."

Other suites that were especially successful included one about a market place, another about the desert, a suite about the different ethnic influences on culture, etc.

The idea of the fruit-vendor figure in the market suite was an image remembered from Berk's first trip to Israel. "I was intrigued by a man with a flat metal tray. He would throw it up onto his head and when it was empty he held it like a fan. It struck

me as very theatrical at the time." He rarely used poetry for inspiration. However, in "Voices from the Land," Chaim Bialik's poems helped him to create four very evocative dances: "Memories" (about refugees), "Desert," "Night," and "Hope."

"It's an awful lot of effort for us mortals to do everything with spirit, but that's what Fred wanted, even in rehearsal." Gary Harris, the lighting designer said, talking about Fred's work. " 'You have the responsibility to inspire people when anyone is watching,' he always said. Another important aspect of his work was his 'cleanliness.' If an idea was muddy or unclear, particularly if the kids came up with an idea, he'd try to find a way to simplify it. His vision always became very clear."

Livia Drapkin, who danced in Hebraica for 5 years, said that Berk "taught us how to be responsible. He taught us exactly what goes into rehearsals. Through Berk I understood what movement quality meant, what projection and dynamics were. I also realized how important it was for an audience to feel that you give yourself to them. He called our Tuesday evening gatherings 'rehearsals,' but we called them parties. You could feel Fred's motivation and his spirit was so infectious. He made us want to dance and that brought the group together. We usually started rehearsals in October and by Chanukah (in December) we always were a cohesive group. All in all he was a very loving but also a very strict director, otherwise he could never have pulled together a group of 12 teenagers."

Yet another explanation of Berk's manner with the youthful dancers was offered by Harris. "What gave him authority, was his command of his profession. He was an authority without being an authoritarian. He also had very great style and what he encouraged in the teenagers was their own style."

On the day of a performance the dancers and technical staff would gather at 8 in the morning. First there would be a general run-through of the show for Harris, the technical director, to set the light cues. Then there would be a dress rehearsal (in costume), a 15 minute break and then two performances at 3:30 and 5:00. Berk stressed that backstage preparation was as important as on-stage performance. Everyone pressed their own costumes and helped each other during costume changes. Some of the dances required the utmost discipline backstage. The dances about the different ethnic groups in Israel, for example, needed precise coordination, as each section had two different couples changing costumes for the next entrance. The finale had dancers in Russian, Chassidic, Arab and Yemenite costumes on stage all at once.

Many professional dancers received their first training from Berk in Hebraica. Any dancer Berk thought could become a performer, he encouraged to study dance seriously. The dance community took Hebraica seriously and the critics covered the concerts, publishing reviews in the different New York dance journals. A review in *Dance News* stated that: "The Hebraica Dancers are young, and attractive to watch. Fred Berk, the choreographer and director, wisely avoids pushing his nonprofessional dancers beyond their capability, but capitalizes on their youthful vitality and the zip inherent in the most basic steps of Israeli dance."

The winter of 1955 was a busy period for him. Berk was simultaneously rehearsing his Ariel company for a performance in February titled "From Many Lands" and planning the March performance of Hebraica for the Purim Holiday. He added new dances for Hebraica: "Chassidic Motif", "Scenes from a Settlement" and "Impressions", as well as the perennial showstopper "Holiday in Israel." He arrived at a format for his Hebraica programs which became routine: a narrator would introduce the children to simple movements related to the dance scenes which would follow, till everyone would dance in their seats. The accompanist would teach the audience simple holiday songs. While the narrator and musician were addressing the audience in front of the curtain

between the dances, the dancers had time for their costume changes and the program could run without any intermissions. Although the dances were designed for children, the parents enjoyed the programs as well.

CHAPTER NINETEEN: CATASTROPHE

From the outside everything seemed to be going beautifully. But Fred's hip got worse. Having to decide what transportation to take on his way to work, he chose the subway. Although it was less direct than the bus, he didn't have to climb the steep steps in front of everyone. Besides, on the subway no one stared at his unsteady gait or noticed whether he sat or stood. Subway passengers paid little attention to each other. On the bus, stony eyes seemed to track each clumsy step he took. At other times eyes had stared at him with rapt attention when he was performing in theaters in Vienna, Belgrade, Zurich, Amsterdam, Havana or New York. That kind of attention he liked. Like love, it pushed one to do better, even to accomplish feats unattainable in the dance studio. Then, every move was met by the spectators with attention and joy. He remembered how easily and fully his movements could capture the audience.

Holding on to the overhead strap, he outlined the upcoming rehearsal in his mind. He was interrupted when the train lurched, coming to a sudden stop. A stab of pain in his hip spread upward through his torso and down into his leg. He forced himself to get out and started to climb to the street. At the top he reached into his coat for his folded handkerchief to dry his brow and bald head. Sweating again, he thought wryly, without having done even one dance phrase!

At the corner of 86th Street and Lexington he looked at his wristwatch. There'd be time for something to eat at the little *Konditorei*, a German restaurant and pastry shop he liked. The dark green plants and the gay carved wooden toys in the window beckoned. He entered and without thinking asked in German for a *Linzertorte*. The waitress in her little pinafore and cap almost curtsied and said *"Bitte, Herr Doktor."* as she handed him the cake.

He abandoned his reveries and involuntarily pulled himself up, as if he were dancing a new role on stage. Doctor! In German, everyone has to have a title. His costume was correct: starched and ironed shirt, dark pants properly creased and a fat briefcase. With his bald head and framed glasses, he looked distinguished and serious. His usual poker face composure had returned. *"Herr Doktor,"* he mused. His father would have liked that!

Approaching the Y he glided his right leg forward so not even a trace of a limp was evident. At exactly 8:00 p.m. he opened the door to the small upstairs studio. He looked at his troupe and emphatically said, "Dancers, let us begin!"

His energy never lagged. It was partly fed by the enthusiasm of his dancers. He traced step after step, pattern after pattern for the circling dancers. He demonstrated what he wanted — his torso twisting to the right bringing attention not to his stepping left foot, but to the vigor and strength he wanted portrayed. His dancers watched him with real pleasure.

Staging a new entrance for the dancers he thought up ways to run for the center, for partners to meet, like some magical road-builder who knew the traffic patterns and interchanges so well there never were accidents.

Punctually at 10:00 he stopped, spoke about the next rehearsal and thanked them. He exuded confidence and strength; of course they would be ready for their winter performance. He smiled at one of the yongsters new to the amateur folk dancing group. "Not to worry," he said in his positive manner.

Not to worry, he kept saying over and over as he waited in the men's room. When he was sure the dancers had all left, he slowly, painfully started toward the stairs. The fatigue he had been ignoring and the pain overtook him. His shoulders stooped.

He saw Dr. William Kolodney, director of the Y, his faithful patron, coming up the stairs. Pulling himself back to his usual assured appearance, he forced a smile.

From the top of the stairs, he asked, "Are you sure there are no funds for costumes?" He raised his arm quizzically, crooking at the elbow and cocked his head, as if he were a Chassidic *rebbe* arguing with God. They both laughed. "Well, I'll take it up with my board," answered Kolodney.

That night, Berk could not sleep nor rest. The burning pain in his hip disrupted everything. Whether he lay on the couch, tried stretching out his leg slowly rotating it in the joint in some exercise he had been given by therapists over the years whether he read, or even took some codeine, he could not ease the throbbing and the aching. He could hardly manage the simplest, most ordinary steps and he could not be sitting, nor lying. What a state for someone who had trained for such physical control. To be without ease of movement was like being a violinst without his violin. Or, he thought, he was a mechanic who had lost all his tools. What could he do?

Resigned, he knew the answer — he should call a doctor in the morning.

He thought of all the doctors he had seen, first in Havana in 1941, then in Colorado, Los Angeles, New York. Somehow they had gotten him through bad episodes with his leg. He was not asking to perform now, he was simply seeking to find a way to execute the simplest motions. He searched through his desk drawer and found the name of a Viennese doctor who had once been recommended to him.

In the morning, he called for an appointment.

Berk cancelled no classses and no rehearsals. He willed himself to continue, although he began to depend on good students to actually demonstrate the dance movements he wanted in class. The Hebraica group rehearsed with their usual excitement. The Ariel repertory dance company, as well as his classes at the Y, continued as if all were usual. He told no one.

On the appointed day, he arrived punctiliously for his meeting with the orthopedic surgeon. After the examination he was told the hip joint should be fused. "We thereby could eliminate all pain," said the doctor with a small triumphant smile.

Have movements simply fused out of my being?, Fred thought to himself. He could not formulate any reaction, so he said nothing, just like when he was a child, and let the medical explanation wash over him. "I will think about it and call you back," he said seemingly emotionless.

Instead, he tried another doctor. Another waiting room, another examination, another wait. "Replace the hip joint," came the verdict. "How often have you done this operation?" asked Berk, knowing full well the great risks of pioneering surgery. He remembered Doris Humphrey's difficulties after hers. He shuddered inside, knowing he could never agree to that surgical solution. "Well, I will consider it and call you back," he told the doctor.

He took a quick trip to California during the winter holiday in 1956 to see

George and Claudia. This time he found no relief.

Finally, back in New York, he found a young doctor with a new suggestion: simply scrape the acetabulum or cup-shaped cavity in the hipbone into which the thighbone fits. In that way there would be no more calcium deposits and bone spurs to impede the hip movement, explained the doctor. It would be a clean and simple surgical method to correct the impediments to his motion. True, his right leg might be up to ¾ of an inch shorter, but a higher heel on his shoe could correct the difference and it would hardly be noticeable. The young doctor seemed assured and confident.

Berk agreed and they scheduled the surgery as soon as possible. It came as quite a surprise to his colleagues and students. No one had suspected a problem.

Lying on the operating table he found himself thinking in German when the anesthetist asked him to count to ten. As he struggled to wake up after surgery, incredible pain gripped him. Everything was immobile. A cast, the doctor had said, but up to my chest? He drifted back to a drugged, confused sleep.

The nurse seemed to hover over him and be on all sides of the bed as he fought the waves of nausea caused by the pain. The doctor came. Berk focused on the young man's face. Although he lay with his head on the pillow he felt bolt upright, yet the doctor looked down on him. All those steady elements — right, left, up and down, forward and backward — those directions he knew so well from dancing on stage and teaching were tricking him.

"I believe in telling my patients the truth. Your bones were very brittle. During surgery your thighbone fractured in many places. We could not finish the operation. We were unable to reconstruct the hip joint but we have removed the damaged bone. Your leg is now five inches shorter than the left. It looks now like you will never be able to walk again."

He was too stunned to say anything.

The nurse tried to straighten his pillow for him. He looked at her. "It's a pity," she said.

Suddenly he felt anger rising over the pain, anger at her stupidity, at her inability to help. God spare him from pity. He despised it in himself or from others. He had seen it when he was growing up in Vienna. His parents, his neighbordhood had pity for the Jews escaping Russia and the pogroms. But he noticed one odd thing about pity: you did not have to understand. You did not have to do anything but pity. Did pity change anything? Help anyone get jobs? "Pity about the poor chap's plight," the English immigration officer had said, but did that help him stay in England when the Nazis were waiting to deport him to be killed in an extermination camp? "Pity he won't walk," said the Spanish doctor in Cuba, but had that helped him?

Pity was despicable. He did not want anything to do with it. He would find a way.

CHAPTER TWENTY: LABANOTATION

The sudden ending of a dancing career is a trauma. It's not only the end of work, but seemingly the end of life itself, because one's real existence has been on stage. All one's energies, thoughts and plans were focused on the stage. When dancers can no longer perform, they are cut off from the instant recognition of their accomplishments. The audience responds when something witty, something grand, something enchanting or something troubling is presented by the dancer. The audience-response is food for the dancer, intensive beyond anything imaginable in regular exchange between people. And if you are accustomed to such a heightened response by hundreds of spectators daily, weekly, monthly and yearly, you suddenly are cut off from the sap of your life: recognition of who and what you are.

The dancer is often one of the few who have complete and continuous recall of himself or herself as a child, as a youth as well as an adult. Fred could remember how it felt to perform for audiences of all kinds of temperament and nationality. He recalled his emotions when leaping and turning. A leap on stage isn't just one movement — it is all kinds of remembered joy.

When Berk leapt, people watched. It was his half smile of success, and victory in life. He remembered jumping on the stage of the Vienna Opera, and jumping out of Hitler's grasp. His leap was a jump of joy because others, too, survived, and Israel was triumphant. He leapt when he was reunited with friends and the leap itself was a celebration of the fact that still, despite injury, he could jump. He was dancing a victory dance.

There was to be no more. No dancing, not even walking

Fred wouldn't eat and he wouldn't see anyone; he instructed the nurses he wanted no visitors and no phone calls. Stubble grew on his cheeks, but he only turned and looked at the wall when the nurses came in.

A physical therapist was sent in to work with him. She picked up his chart and said, "Are you Fred Berk, the dancer?" She recognized him as himself and not as an immobile patient. He turned to look at her and she smiled at him and said, "I'm a dancer, too. Let's work together to discover what's possible." Every day she came to work with him, every day she encouraged him. He said to himself, "I could kill myself or go on. I decided to go on."

He allowed visitors. One was his favorite Israeli folk dance creator Rivka Sturman who was visiting New York. She rushed in with a big bouquet of flowers. Fred promptly informed her that a fellow Israeli dance artist, Rachel Nadav, was on another floor, recuperating from surgery. He insisted that the bouquet be brought to Rachel. Rivka finally agreed to compromise by dividing the bouquet in half.[83]

After ten weeks his body cast was removed. His therapist coaxed him onto his

feet. Even with no hip joint to speak of, he was able to thrust his leg forward enought to propel himself into a step. He worked and worked and worked to be upright and mobile.

While Berk was still in the hospital, Rabbi Lelyvelt, the director of the B'nai Brith Hillel Foundation came and asked if he could direct a big pageant at Ebbets Field. Berk consulted with the dancers from his group and they encouraged him to accept. *Dance Magazine* published a picture of dancers rehearsing in Berk's room at the Hospital for Joint Diseases, preparing for the "Music Under the Stars" June 19, 1957 performance. Berk managed an Olympic feat: he staged three dances for 60 dancers from his hospital room.

Although the dancers were paid a fee by the sponsoring organization, the America Israel Cultural Foundation, none of them accepted the money. It was turned over to Berk, to help him with his medical costs.

When he came out of the hospital in May, he was $2,000 in debt. But this didn't bother him too much. A much bigger shock was seeing the shoe he had to wear with its enormous five inch heel and sole. Miraculously, he willed himself to walk on his own feet with only the help of a cane.

Berk went to California and while he rested at the Kauffman's he began slowly to exercise.

He pondered how he would succeed in teaching if he couldn't actually demonstrate the movements for his students?

Every once in a while, a modest, very personal article by Berk began to appear in small dance publications. In an article about Laban terminology for the folk dancer[84] he urged dancers to widen their horizons. He noted that "Folk dancing is usually learned by imitating a teacher who is in the center of a studio demonstrating. A good teacher will teach in sections. . ." A better procedure, is, however, possible, and he argued for it on the basis of his own experience.

"For the last 35 years I have been involved in teaching folk dance. In 1957 I underwent hip surgery which left one leg shorter than the other and the desperation of having to give up dancing. During the period of recuperation, I came across a book of Labanotation and had a renewed interest in this theory. A new world opened to me.

"Suddenly I was able to see movements in front of me and slowly I learned to verbalize them. Using Laban's terminology made it possible for me to continue to teach. I also became aware that by using Laban in teaching, students not only learn a dance mechanically but learn to understand all the elements of dance.

"While I was in my cast, I would read the Laban book; I didn't have enough knowledge to really understand all that was written, but the terminology appealed to me. It seemed to me this was a very clear way to analyze dance. I decided to learn more and called on my dance colleague, Lucy Venable. We knew each other from Merry-Go-Rounders and she was an able Laban notator.

"The first year teaching after my operation I couldn't demonstrate anything, I couldn't move at all. But students came and they paid me. For what? I wondered. I'd never been particularly articulate about dance nor did I ever intellectualize about it. When one performs one never has to articulate thoughts and feelings, one just has to dance them. Slowly, however, I realized I had something others don't. Even without actually moving myself, I could open up dancers and students to their dormant feelings. I could involve them in dance in a joyous way even after years of training with teachers who might have harped don't do this or don't do that.

"Laban's terminology gave me a way to analyze and see movement without actually doing it. It helped me to explain and I could teach without dancing movements

because the terminoloy was so clear. I also found the clarity made my students aware of the elements of dance. Until my failed leg surgery I acted like any other dance teacher, standing in front and indicating or using an assistant to demonstrate. With my sickness, I had time to digest what Laban was after. I became very clear and precise in my instructions.

"Folk dancers aren't trained in a broad dance sense. When they instruct or try to write down the folk dances they are usually not clear nor communicative because they use their own terminology and symbols.

"Laban also makes you very precise about movements, rhythm, directions and levels. There is no way to make mistakes with this clear system."

Lucy Venable recalls that Berk began to write down the folk dances he taught in Labanotation and then he collected dances from others. "Out of all this experience he got the idea of making a little book for dancers with simple Labanotation. We did "Ten Folk Dances in Labanotation" together and it was pulished by M. Witmark and Sons. It has had two printings since. Probably we only made $50 per printing in royalties, but we did not do it for the money. Many have used it in teaching and many more have learned and enjoyed the dances.

"Berk's objective was to keep the instructions simple, to notate only the step patterns and to describe the arm positions and movements in words, so readers would not find the notation too complicated. I learned a lot from him about keeping notation material simple and direct," said Venable.

"Since that had gone well, our next venture, again instigated by Fred, was "Dances from Israel." This was published by the Dance Notation Bureau, and it too had two printings. The choice of dances and basic notation was done by Fred: my part was always to check the notation with the movement and the text and to do the copy work and layout." As Berk and Venable met and talked, Berk also saw a need for developing a Labanotation correspondence course for folk dancers. The Dance Notation Bureau had such courses for those interested in modern dance or ballet, but the examples would have been too specialized for folk dancers. "He prepared two series of lessons. The Dance Notation Bureau still has these courses in print. The latest project, although not initiated by Berk, was checked by him. The Dance Notation Bureau published his famous "Holiday in Israel" in book form in 1978.[85]

Many dancers learned of notation and Labanotation first through Berk's folk dance courses. Notes from a workshop for teachers attended by Anne Wilson **Wangh**[86] at the end of the 1950's indicate the kind of material Berk used. At the first class he explained the importance of clarity. "Be clear about everything, even the characterization of the dance and explain how it relates to a nation. You don't have to be a professional musician or dancer to understand Laban, it is so logical."

Through Labanotation Fred found the necessary confidence to continue in his work. He had to conquer many fears, not the least being that of his appearance. He thought it was very incongruous for a dance teacher to appear in class limping on a cane, so he eventually trained himself to enter the classroom without it. He always sat on a high stool and directed the class only with his voice and enthusiasm, totally in command through the clarity he gained through Labanotation.

"Fred always used to say: you are teaching people, not material. That means you must meet their enthusiasm and eagerness and explain to them even the simplest of things. After all, that's what teaching is about. Not getting annoyed and not getting bored with the material," recalled Shulamit Kivel, another Israeli folk dance teacher. "Even when you have to teach *Zemer Atik* for the 500th time, for your students it is still a new experience."

CHAPTER TWENTY-ONE: CAMP BLUE STAR

Apart from Berk's department at the Y, he had another outlet that served to promote Israeli folk dance throughout America. This was his involvement at Camp Blue Star, situated in the midst of the Blue Ridge Mountains, in North Carolina. Berk worked there for 18 years. By 1956, before his surgery, he was teaching Israeli folk dancing and staging pageants for 700 campers, integrating dance into the regular summer activities.

He took a few summers off and then began directing a special program of leadership training in Israeli folk dance. Just as in his work at the Y, eh developed a special format, which influenced teachers and folk dancers from literally all over the country. He ran two different courses, each a week long, for 150 participants.

Usually the harvest holiday of *Shavuot* happened during camp time and Berk would create a special feeling of celebration through dance.

The Sabbath too would be celebrated in an outdoor Temple and the closing ceremony of *havdallah* would often include dancing. There was a spirituality and a sense of closeness in folk dancing at Blue Star that went beyond the mechanics of classes and programs.

During the course, the trainee folk dance teachers would be assigned practice sessions in which they had to teach the Blue Star campers. After the practice class, Fred would evaluate their work. He also taught "elements of choreography" as well as two daily classes of new Israeli dances. There were also optional classes in modern dance, singing and other subjects. In the evenings he'd run lectures on modern day Israel or dance in the Bible. On the last evening of the week there would be an open demonstration of Israeli dance for neighboring camps and members of Bue Star.

At Blue Star today there is a large building to house the folk dance workshops called the Fred Berk Dance Pavilion, an open air structure with a huge dance floor. The camp director, Herman Popkin, described Berk's years at the camp: "He was like a Chassidic Rabbi with a dedicated following. We know that at Blue Star, either in the camps or in the workshops, he brought his love for Israel through dance to many people, young and old."

CHAPTER TWENTY-TWO: ISRAEL DANCE FESTIVALS

In a characteristically self-effacing remark, Berk said once that "I'm not an expert in anything, but I have ideas. It was my idea to develop the Israel Dance Festival and it has become a part of the Jewish community in New York City." Berk became an expert at presenting a production with no speeches and no announcements. The program of dances (performed by many different youth organizations) built on tension and excitement to a huge finale with all participants on stage.

Few American trained modern dancers, if any, would have been able to cope with the huge numbers of performers involved, let alone conceive of the necessary vision of pageantry and overall structure. Berk was familiar with the effects of mass rallies of dancers from his performances at political rallies and Jewish organizations in Gertrud Kraus' company in Vienna. All his previous experiences in dance fell into place in staging the productions in New York.

The annual Israel Festival was at first held at Hunter College, then moved to Carnegie Hall in 1962, to the Felt Forum in 1970 and four years later to the Philharmonic Hall at Lincoln Center.

"From the moment they streamed into the area from all directions — hundreds of them in their bright costumes, singing and clapping — one's spirits rose. They were young, vital, joyous... perhaps the most exhilarating moment came at the end of the evening when all the dancers massed for 'Hatikva', broke into spontaneous dancing for the sheer joy of it."[87]

Berk was especially pleased with the four festivals held at the Felt Forum, because of its arena stage and how it lent itself so beautifully to the shifting of groups and the finale. But, unfortunately, the union requirements made it impossible to hold the Festival at the Forum and another venue had to be found.

"Once, at the Felt Forum," recalled Berk, "there was a great commercial show set up for the Monday following our festival and we didn't have any crossovers backstage or onstage because of all kinds of platforms. For me it was heaven; I used all the different levels and staged the dances in the various areas and it added greatly to the drama of the production. We rented a hotel near the Felt Forum for all the youth groups to gather and there were so many, we had to rehearse from 5 in the morning in order to get done in time for the afternoon performance. Had I had any hair, I would have lost it then, there was such tension. There were 14 groups and each one had 20 minutes on stage, with a break before the two shows. It was like a huge fiesta for all the teenagers."

Berk's assistant for the Festival was Ruth Goodman, who later took over many of the projects he started.

"An artist has to be someone who can always see something new. Fred could do

that and his wonder and excitement spread to the kids. That was his artistry. For the 10 years in which I was involved in the Festival the format remained the same, but there were always new kids, new parents and new audiences and therefore we felt there was no need to change it."

Over the years Berk developed a nucleus of professional staff for the Festivals. These were the experienced sound and lighting technician, Gary Harris; a professional costumer, Hattie Wiener, and a professional musician to handle all arrangements and conducting. The first conductor was Elyakum Shapiro, who became an assistant to Leonard Bernstein, and later several top Israeli musicians, including Dov Seltzer, Gil Aldema, Amitay Ne'eman and for seven years Shai Burstein (who also made many recordings of folk music with Berk).

At the first meeting of the group leaders of youth groups in late fall, Berk would tell them what theme had been picked for the Festival. These were of necessity large topics, such as "Israel", because the dances were generally based on broad themes such as the Sabbath or harvest, and joy. "We changed the theme from year to year."

The dance leaders of the youth groups would go back to their groups in the New York area and select the best dancers for the Festival, even though Berk stressed the educational rather than the competitive aspects of the Festival.

They taught and rehearsed their one dance each and then would show the results to Berk, who would suggest improvements before the general rehearsals of all the groups.

After seeing all the dances the youth groups planned to perform, Berk helped to improve the staging. In time for the "Transition Rehearsal" Berk devised the order of the groups' appearances, incorporated them in his overall thematic idea and created a good balance of stronger and weaker groups. "Here is where his artistry and expertise truly shone," said Ruth Goodman.

"He made the transitions so that there never would be a dead spot on stage. As one group arrived at the end-position, the next group would already be in its opening position. This dovetailing gave the performance a polished, clean look. During rehearsals while one group performed, all the kids not active in that dance would sit, grouped on the sidelines of the stage, watching and learning, not stashed away someplace backstage. Everyone would be part of the action all the time, which gave a sort of Israeli flavor to the whole event. In the dances involving all the groups at once, everyone moved to a different place on stage, which created a wonderful effect. A 'bridge' from the last piece to the finale would be carefully constructed by Fred."

The finale was a crescendo, with arms raised in unison in a "V" overhead. There would always be a spontaneous hora afterwards — it couldn't be helped. It was the essence of the spirit Berk carefully built up through the year-long rehearsals.

An interview in *Keeping Posted*, a publication of the Union of American Hebrew Congregations (April, 1974), illustrates Berk's unusual commitment and vision and how it functioned in the Festivals:

"I had serious misgivings about doing the 1974 Festival following the Yom Kippur War. I'd been in Israel during the war. The very idea of a *dance festival* at such a time struck me as being completely inappropriate. The casualties were so high, the tragedy so great! But one day I came across a line of Yiddish poetry, by M. Warshawski, which, freely translated is: "If I am beaten by the whole world — *davka* (in spite of) I will go out and dance!' That *davka,* necessarily, in spite of everything, we Jews must go on! The theme of our New York festival in 1974 was the Jewish holiday, because in these holidays our past, present, and future [is contained]...

The most complete comment on Berk's work with the Israel Festival was offered

by his technical director, Gary Harris. "If you're not busy working for the next generation, it's a dead end. A lot of people make monuments for themselves, but Fred built a monument for the kids."

CHAPTER TWENTY-THREE: BERK'S ISRAEL

In 1968 Berk was given his first official post with the American Zionist Youth Foundation (AZYF). Until 1968 he had maintained a free lance relationship with the organization, directing their Israel Folk Dance Festival held in spring, in honor of Israel's Independence Day. He preferred working in this manner and at the Y. He, too, was paid by project. He never wanted to run a dance studio for commercial purposes. He might have made more money that way, but he loathed worrying about over-head, up-keep and what to do with the studio in summer, when he preferred to travel. Berk was a sort of island unto himself business-wise, preferring to stick to his special projects and not to concern himself with any kind of commercial venture.

At the AZYF Berk initiated the publication of Jewish dance books. Some of the books he edited himself, in others different writers participated. Also under the auspices of AZYF's Israel Folk Dance Program, he organized a group study tour of folk dancers to Israel. For six weeks the participants would take part in an intensive program of dance instruction by Israeli folk dance choreographers, as well as in classes of dance theory and dance techniques, see performances of Israeli dance companies and perform themselves. Touring Israel and spending time on a kibbutz were included in this unique trip masterminded by Fred.

"In 1968 I arrived exactly on the day the Dalia Folk Dance Festival was held; and since one of the purposes of my trip was to see this festival for the first time, I went directly from the airport to the amphitheatre at Dalia. I stayed there for two days and was able to see the performances and general dancing, an experience I will never forget," said Fred. It was the last of the Dalia Festivals. 60,000 people attended and 3,000 dancers performed.

Shalom Hermon, a central figure in the folk dance movement in Israel, remembered that at the last of the Dalia Festivals (in 1968) "Berk's legs gave him so much trouble, I didn't think he would be able to manage all the steps in the outdoor amphitheatre built into the hillside. But he climbed them all, every one, and he said, 'you see? In Israel I am revived and rejuvenated!' So I told him he would have to move here to be cured."

Berk began all his projects simply enough with total love and dedication to Israeli folk dance. He wanted many more in America to understand this love, so he created a dance publication, *Hora*. In the first issue, (Fall, 1968) he wrote that the publication would "disseminate news concerning Israeli dance activities in America and Israel and provide dance enthusiasts with a comprehension of the history and development of Jewish dance." Every issue carried reports about Israeli folk dance festivals. In the Fall 1978 issue (11:1) the cover of the first festival program in America was reproduced. He wanted to report on all the Israeli fok dance activity in the U.S.,

Canada and other countries. By the late 1960's there were workshops, festivals, competitions, study groups, camps, holiday and Independence Day celebrations all over the continent.

He printed features highlighting Israeli folk dance creators, interviews and reprints of articles from journals Berk felt should be known to the readers of *Hora*. In the articles sometimes carrying his by-line, but more often not, one can trace changes in his own attitudes towards the Israeli folk dance movement.

One of the most remarkable developments documented in *Hora* is Berk's changing feelings about authenticity in folk dance and the use of a people's roots and traditional ethnic dances in performance. There is a marked difference between folk dance and ethnic dance, the latter developed for generations to a highly specialized style. The case of Israeli folk dance is very special, as there were no generation upon generation to develop a long history of dance in Israel: the Jewish pioneers since the turn of the century, aided by individuals who were interested in folklore and dances that would reflect their national heritage had 'to manufacture' Israeli folk dance for themselves. It was certainly based on the ethnic aspects of Jewish life and referred to the ancient lore from the Bible, when the people had been free in their own land. But Berk stressed again and again in *Hora* articles that Israeli folk dance was a choreographed phenomenon, created, taught, and spread by a core of ardent Israeli dancers.

After the great waves of immigrants from Asia and North Africa arrived in Israel soon after independence, the folk dance creators turned their attention more and more to the ethnic heritage brought by these new Israelis. Gurit Kadman was one of the first ones who recognised the importance of the ethnic basis for the further development of Israeli folk dance, which, due to an historical anomaly, had first acquired the contemporary superstructure and only later its ethnic underpinning.

Berk originally thought that ethnic style and authenticity was not one of the goals of Israeli folk dance. "Folk dancing is an exciting recreation and relaxation." But a disturbing intrusion in this healthy activity "is that many folk dance teachers insist on emphasizing the idea of everything being authentic. Of course, a dance should be taught the way it was originally done, but the participants should not be forced into movements and stylizations they cannot execute..."[88]

Berk addressed himself to the very real problem of authenticity, which he stated was "the knowledge and understanding of peoples, their religion, philosophy, habits and customs — in short, their complete way of life. Many dancers have been able to absorb the subtleties and characteristic movements... only because they have devoted many years to the study of one nation, usually living there, too."

He relates his experience in the early 1950's which colored his opinion that it was impossible for folk dancers to absorb special ethnic styles and he came to the conclusion that the study of the ethnic roots of Israeli folk dance was unnecessary for the Israeli folk dancer.

"A while ago I prepared a Yugoslav dance sequence of a performance at the Museum of Natural History (in New York City)," he wrote. "The group consisted of nine professional dances and one native of Yugoslavia. After the performance, the comments of the audience were mainly about the Yugoslav dancer — his grace, his style, and how differently he moved from the rest of us. The important fact is that we were all professional dancers and he was not. Even though he had trained us for many months in the minute details of his country's dance — and although we applied ourselves very hard to the task — all we achieved was a superficial imitation of his authentic dancing. This again shows that it is almost impossible to acquire an authentic flavor in dance by just

imitating steps."

Berk states the purpose of folk dance as far as he is concerned: if people are allowed to move freely within the given dance patterns, they will feel the freedom and joy which are, after all, the purpose of any and all folk dancing. "...The freer the participants feel, the more emotional joy they will derive from the dance... they will forget the stress and strain of everyday living and they will let go completely. This is as it should be."

However, after the 25th Israel Folk Dance Festival in 1976 in New York, Berk reflected on working with amateur folk dancers in performance.[89] By then he had trained, directed, staged and choreographed countless dances, performances and dancers. Although he still stressed the freedom of the performer, "the amateur performer brings no technique to his performance, but he does bring a tremendous enthusiasm and spirit which is sometimes lacking in the professional performer."

Israeli folk dance has gained a wide following in international folk dance circles and amongst Jewish youth. "For me, personally, the involvement, the discipline and the identification of young people is the most important and rewarding" aspect of folk dance. As before, Berk says that the dancer must learn to project "the freedom of dance on stage," but the important aspects of a performance are "that the dancers are motivated by their themes; what is overwhelming to an audience is the projection of their youth, their spirits... each dancer is involved intellectually and physically in Israeli folk dance which talks about the Jewish people, about Israel, about the Bible, about persecution and survival, about habits and customs, and about hope and peace."[90] He became more and more involved in the search for authentic Jewish folk dance.

He involved his students — the teenagers who accompanied him on summer trips to Israel — in his search for Jewish dance amongst communities of Jews from outside Israel, not only the Israeli folk dance of the modern state.

Berk continued to bring groups of youth on AZYF tours every summer. From this program of bringing folk dance students to Israel the idea of a course in folk dance at university level developed. "We were able to organize a course at the Hebrew University of Jerusalem in 1972, 1973 and 1974 in which Berk taught "The Basis of Israeli Folk Dance," and it was very well received, states Hermon.

Berk spoke to Hermon and his many other friends about his desire to settle finally in Israel. He explained he would be able to do this when he would retire from his job at the Y and receive social security cheques which would provide for him. But he feared, there would be next to nothing for him to do in Israel. "I suggested to him that he create an archive on Jewish ethnic dance for the Histadrut department of folk dance and he loved the idea," Hermon said.

For several years he had a charming vacation home in upstate New York at Woodstock, which he sold to buy an apartment in Tel Aviv near the Yarkon River. When he retired from New York he lived for more than half of the year in Tel Aviv. During his annual sojourn in Israel he still searched for new dances to bring back to New York.

"This is something very different from the dances created by Israelis such as Moshiko, Shelomo Bechar, etc. Berk thought that just because they were Israelis themselves did not mean that their creations were Israeli folk dances. He stimulated dance creators in Israel, too, especially with the recordings he would bring with him, with their good rhythm and the clear and correct instructions he wrote about how to do the different dances. In my opinion, they were better than any we produced in Israel. Berk confronted head-on the many Israelis who had settled in America and continued to

create dances which they called 'Israeli.' The purity of the 'Israeli character' was at stake and he found the dances that were made in the U.S. unacceptable," said Rivka Sturman, the veteran creator.

Another side of the burgeoning 'Israeli folk dance industry' in America that Berk detested, was its commercial aspect. In 1973 he wrote that "books, records, articles were made in order to fill the need of the tremendous popularity of Israeli folk dance in America..."[91] The fact that so many folk dance creators kept turning out records to go with their newly created dances in America, bothered him very much. He didn't accept their insistence on copyright and the payment of royalties they demanded.

In Israel Berk began to go to modern dance concerts again. It had been years since he had attended modern dance concerts — he thought he wouldn't be able to tell any more what dancers wanted to dance about or what they had to say. Once so involved in the modernism of dance, he thought it would have bypassed him in its newest forms.

Allida Gera, an American dancer who had been in his repertory company in the '50's and was living in Israel took him to a Bat Dor dance performance. He told Allida that the lobby surprised him, a kind of old-time splendor with mirrors and staircases on both sides, a small kiosk with coffee, cakes and sweets to one side. The foyer to the theatre actually doubles as a dance studio and the mirrors are there for the students in class as much as to reflect the well dressed audience. Batsheva de Rothschild, one time benefactress of Martha Graham and now of Bat Dor, could be seen in the foyer in her short fur jacket, standing quietly to the side of the crowd. Fred maneuvered the steep stairs carefully with his cane, stowing it under his seat on the floor in an abrupt, defiant way. Together they watched the concert; they might have seen one of Robert Cohan's or Paul Sanasardo's works or a new piece for the company by Lar Lubovitch or Charles Czarny.

"But where is the Jewishness or the Israeli character?" Fred lamented. Certainly the dancers are well trained, but he missed an expression of the place and times of Israel in the 1970s. He found himself quite capable of comment and criticism.

Another American dancer who had performed in his "Holiday in Israel" with the Merry-Go-Rounders in New York now performed in the Batsheva Company. He went to see Laurie Freedman in Graham's "Diversion of Angels," and again he was pleased to see beautifully trained dancers. But it was Inbal Dance Theatre that fascinated him and continually held his attention. Sara Levi-Tanai's ideas in dance excited him because her dances seemed to be filled with living images from the Bible, of desert life and of Israel in beautiful costumes, sounds and movement — textures using the Yemenite-Jewish dance. The dancers evoked in him what he loved most about theatre — the all encompassing world of a special creation. He had seen Inbal on their first tours to America in the late 1950s, and had asked Sara Levi-Tanai and her dancers, such as Margalit Oved, to teach at the Y whenever possible.

Giora Manor, the dance critic for Tel Aviv's daily newspaper *Al Hamishmar,* and biographer of Gertrud Kraus, often invited Berk to go with him to the theatre. "What I loved about going to any theatre performance with him, was his incredible enthusiasm, his 'ahh!' which he uttered in a very Jewish way, while inhaling. In a way he was an unspoiled innocent and there was always some element of wonder that he brought to every performance, in spite of his professionalism. He was a rather private person, but it was wonderful to talk to him. He was a wonderful audience because he reacted to what you said, even though he was not given to formulating abstract ideas himself."

His appetite for seeing performances seemed to increase simultaneously with his growing insomnia. He had a great desire to do things. His eyes took on a stabbing,

piercing quality, though he had surprising patience for daily routine chores like floor exercises, swimming, shopping, working in the archive, writing or visiting friends.

In the summer of 1977 he felt poorly, however, and he confided in a friend that he had little energy left to make the necessary preparations for the winter Festival in New York he was to direct and to continue with the folk dance workshops he taught in Tel Aviv. He thought about discontinuing his teaching commitments in New York. It was not his hip so much, as a terrible, overall fatigue. Eventually, he consulted a doctor who sent him to a specialist.

He was told he had inoperable abdominal cancer. The only course of action open to him was to return to the doctors when his pains became unbearable. As if in a trance, he kept on working. Despite his fatigue, he organized the Festival in New York and even went to teach at Camp Blue Star in 1978. Finally, he visited his friends the Kauffmans, who encouraged him to see yet another doctor in California. There he was prescribed radiation, hormone treatments and operations which left him exhausted, but his cancer was seemingly arrested.

Berk's doctor was encouraging and gave him a positive attitude: "We won't cancel anything. Just continue with work." Faced with a hopeless situation that could overcome even the most determined, Berk's indefatigable spirit egged him on. In the midst of his illness he embarked on a new project. The dancer turned director, choreographer, producer and folk dance teacher looked at his vast collection of articles, books, pictures and mementos amassed over the years. Even the New York City Public Library's Dance Collection at Lincoln Center could offer no bibliography or special listing of the works on Jewish dance. He decided that he would compile such a bibliography.

He went to Genevieve Oswald, the Curator of the Dance Collection of the Library and Museum of the Performing Arts at Lincoln Center with his new project. She knew and respected Berk's work and was delighted with his proposal. Oswald said, "Berk has a profound understanding of all kinds of dance and a very special understanding of Jewish and Israeli dance. It is a very articulate understanding. His powers of organization are excellent and for this reason I suggested he should start compiling an index of all the citations on Jewish dance from our 10-volume catalogue."

It was not an easy task to read every entry in the fat volumes and to make notes and then begin to catalogue them. When he was in New York he was often at the Dance Collection to do his research. He had a special shelf allocated to his accumulating index cards. It wasn't easy to decide what to include and where to draw the boundaries of his list. Oswald, after one of their innumerable discussions, said: "Jewish influence in folk dance, in the dance of the Renaissance, in the use of dramatic material indigenous to Jewish life has been a rich and vital part of the whole history of dance. But we wondered whether to include anyone in dance who's Jewish in the bibliography? What would be Berk's guide? Certainly we decided to include all social and folk dance in Israel and all prominent dancers who are Israeli, all dances on Jewish themes — life, concept, the Bible — no matter who did them. Basically, we decided that we would keep looking into the problem of defining what is Jewish dance."

To this end, Berk wrote letters of inquiry to some of the well known contempory Jewish dancers to elicit their opinions.

Despite surgery and chemotherapy, Berk continued his travels, his writing and also special programs on Jewish dance at the Y in New York. In 1977 a flyer advertised that "after five months in Israel Berk will teach new dances by Sturman." In 1978 he visited Israel again and in the spring went to Bucharest, Romania and Kiev before returning for more hospital treatment in America in June. Then he left for Los

Angeles to see the Kauffmans and spent the summer in Israel.

The following year, in 1979, he presented a special lecture at the Y on Israeli folk dance illustrated by films and shared a lecture with Anna Sokolow on dance in Israel. A spring reunion with dancers from the years of the "Wednesday open session" particularly pleased him. He taught dances together with Ruth Goodman and Danny Uziel, choosing those created during the first years of Israeli independence.

Jesting about his physical condition, he wrote to friends that "the medical treatments are terrific for me. I think in a few months I will be able to do my great number again, 'The Dying Swan,' but believe me, it will be more dying than swan."[92]

What particularly pleased him were plans in Israel to create a "Stage for Dancers" at the Tel Aviv Museum. The idea of encouraging young choreographers in Israel using the format Berk invented in the '50s in New York was brought to the attention of the museum and the Israel Dance Library by Yemmy Strum, a Berk dancer from New York now settled in Israel. The Israelis reacted positively to the "new outlet for talent." In the *Jerusalem Post,* Dora Sowden wrote: "Thirty-three dancers and 11 choreographers participated at the Recanati Auditorium of the Tel Aviv Museum in the first 'Stage for Dancers,' based on a model originated by Fred Berk in New York... and the first programme of seven solos and four group works was chosen from 30 applications. The chosen items were certainly worth seeing — and there was an audience for them: The hall was full."

Berk's appetite for travel took him to Germany and Austria and back to Israel in the late spring and summer. He had no regrets about leaving Vienna. He used money from a small pension owed him by the Austrian government, ironically enough as a member of the guild of goldsmiths, to buy a glass and brass pendulum clock.

In the fall he decided to come to Minneapolis, for what he called the last round of interviews for his memoirs. It was during the "ten days of atonement" preceeding Yom Kippur that Berk called to arrange his visit. He was very gay when he arrived and seemed deceptively robust. There were no wasted words, no introduction. He began speaking, as he lowered himself, a bit askew, so as to settle on his solid hip into a chair.

"These are all my notes from the Lincoln Center Dance Collection. I'm giving you the bibliography on Jewish dance to complete." He opened the package and I saw countless xeroxed pages systematically divided into different groupings of Jewish dancers, folk dance,... the headings caught my eye as I thumbed through the stack of pages. In his clear, bold script it said DANCE: A bibliography of sources relating to Jewish dance and dancers. Works on the Old Testament, films and books. Available at the Dance Library of Performing Arts, by Fred Berk.

As he went over the pages in the hotel lobby where we met, he looked pained. "What's wrong?" I asked.

"No, I can't give it to you yet, it is still too unfinished." He put the pages back into the package and tied it up with string again.

Was this why he had come?

I sat bewildered, in silence.

He looked straight ahead at a dark column in the hotel lobby where we sat. The package rested askew on his knees, his hands folded over his work. Tears began streaming down his face, but he never changed the tone of his voice, he never faltered in what he said. His bald head shone in the harsh light of the hotel lobby and I looked down at the grotesque shoe building up his shorter leg. It was always so well polished. He must have polished it out of spite, I thought.

Tears rolled down his cheeks and dropped onto the package.

"I'm not an authority — for that I'd have to pretend that I knew all kinds of

dates. I'm a researcher, a collector, an organizer, a folk dance teacher. I hate pretense and I hate incompetence. Artistry isn't any of that. An artist is a hard worker, same as a factory worker, but in a creative way.

"I'm not on a higher plane than anyone else. I acquired something that isn't in the books by working hard, by noticing that special 'It.'

"At night, I lie down — sleeping is out of the question — and I think the whole couch is going to fall into a sea of nothingness. I never thought there was a God, but maybe I remember 'It' — something universal, something that drives me to continue my work.

"I think 'It' makes us go forward, to grow, to learn and to continue with our projects. If someone else finishes my project, it's only one of many, but for me it's the most important. I know how it should go."

He took up his package and put it under his arm.

In February I traveled to New York and we met for dinner at his favorite Chinese restaurant. After the meal Fred took out two packages from inside his coat neatly folded beside him. One was small and flat in yellow paper, neatly taped at each end. It simply said "For Shai'le."

"This is for Shai's Bar Mitzvah."

He was handing me a present for my son, who would be thirteen in nine years!

Then he handed me another, fatter package. "For Mrs. Ingber," said the card in his big, black handwriting. I laughed — not Judy? Mrs. Ingber?

He watched me as I opened the box. Inside, nestled in tissue paper, was a pair of grey-green mother-of-pearl opera glasses.

"These were my mother's, for the Vienna Opera."

There seemed no more to say.

We walked out of the restaurant and he insisted on taking the bus. He held onto his cane, and then lifted it like in an old vaudeville routine as the bus came. We both laughed as he boarded it, stepping carefully up the big steps. The door closed behind him, and his back was to me, when I realized I hadn't said goodbye.

Two days later, before leaving from the airport, I tried to telephone, but there was no answer. After returning to Minneapolis, we received a phone call from a friend of Fred's. He had died. It was February 27, 1980.

Judaism requires that the bereaved family say *kaddish*, the prayer for the dead. It is first said at the gravesite and then once a day for a month and finally on the yearly anniversary of the death. *Kaddish* is not a private prayer; it can be recited only in a *minyan* or congregation of at least 10 adults gathered together for prayer. One may say it anywhere, but there has to be a group of 10 adults present.

Fred has no gravesite and no family. But he was used to a *minyan* — not the minimum of 10 adults needed for congregational prayer, but in a broader sense — a number of people. His *minyans* are his lifework, whenever they dance, it is as if a secret *kaddish* is being said. Fred instructed his friends to carry out a cremation and scatter his ashes at sea.

He counted on all kinds of people to find a way to communal identification and expression. He was talented and unusual in his ability to orchestrate the feelings in a group through dance. In many different settings — at rallies and festivals, with professional dancers or with youths and amateurs — he could draw out the qualities of joy and excitement.

He channeled his work for the community and with the community at synagogues, Jewish centers, universities, colleges and summer camps, through established organizations. But beyond his knowledge of how to work within the systems of Jewish

organizations and hierarchies was his power to touch individuals. Even Orthodox Jews joined with atheists and liberal Jews to dance under Fred's direction. He knew how to emphasize everyone's humanity and the desire to express it in dance. In the midst of a group, individuals felt Berk was speaking to each one individually. This capacity brought out the best in his dancers.

Yet, apart from his work, he was a private person. Although he exuded humor, he rarely offered personal reflections of his own experiences. Most of the things he did remained a mystery to those who worked with him, to those he taught, and to those he befriended. But his privacy in no way narrowed his circle of friends.

He had to choose between life and despair many times. And he chose life in the midst of the worst drama of our civilization. He could argue his case many times over — with hostile border guards, callous doctors, greedy agents, indifferent government officials, on any number of occasions, when his survival was threatened. And he was victorious in a battle with years of crippling physical ailments, becoming a master teacher of movement in spite of physical handicaps.

He continued his search while on a trip, with friends and with strangers, always examining, thinking, mulling over things in his mind. The challenge that dominated his life and gave it a unique meaning was: what is Jewish life?, what makes it survive?, who are the Jewish dancers, what is their work and what is its meaning?

Perhaps the answer to all these questions would be the life of Fritz Berger, now known as Fred Berk, who danced his way through life, battle after battle, in a series of victory dances.

FOOTNOTES:

1. Schorske, Carl E., *Fin-de-Siècle Vienna,* Alfred A. Knopf, New York, 1980, p. 31.
2. *Ibid.,* p. 31 and 45.
3. *Ibid.,* p. 37.
4. An undated program of the "Tanzabend der Tanzgruppe Gertrud Kraus" shows that Kraus and Cilli Wang continued to work together. Fritz himself performed on a program with Cilli Wang at the Margaretener Volksbildungshaus in Vienna with other Kraus dancers including Helli Broida, Nelly Frank, Trude Goodwyn, Mizzi Holger, Margit Knöpfler, Stella Mann, Carola Mare, Bertl Reidinger, Bertie Spielmann. Fritz's name was listed as Fritzi Vorberger.
   The dances included a "Farandole" to Bizet's music; a suite called "Kampf," "Guillotine," "Abgrund," and "Finale," concluding with "Hopak; Trojka; Wodka." Wang's dance was titled "Felix Salten: Die Musikanten."
5. March, 1973.
6. Manor, Giora, *The Life and Dance of Gertrud Kraus,* Hakibbutz Hameuchad Publishing House, Tel Aviv, 1978, p. 12-21.
7. *Ibid.* p. 19.
8. *Ibid.,* p. 13.
9. Butler, Aria, "Dance: Chassidic Chai," unpublished Master Thesis at the University of California at Los Angeles Dance Department, 1977, p. 16 and p. 36.
10. *Ibid.,* p. 11.
11. Koegler, Horst, "In the Shadow of the Swastika," *Dance Pespectives* Vol. 57, Spring, 1974.
12. Angela Sartorio, the director of the Balletto della Città di Firenze was the daughter of an Italian sculptor and a German Jewess. Angela had toured with Jooss' first world tour, performing in the "Green Table." Today she lives in Santa Barbara, California.
13. Lisa Czobel created the role of the young girl in Jooss' "Green Table" in the premiere performance in 1932. She toured with Jooss and also performed in the company of Vera Skoronel. She lives in Hamburg where she still teaches. (Information from Claudia V. Kauffman.)
14. Goth also worked as Sartorio's assistant and teacher. Later she fled to Cuba and eventually to New York where she established herself as a dance critic and also initiated the dance series called "The Choreographers' Workshop." See *Dance Magazine,* Oct. 1951, p. 12.
15. Naima Prevots in her paper delivered at the Congress on Research in Dance

Conference with the National Dance Guild on June 21, 1981 at University of California at Los Angeles spoke about the cabaret tradition in Europe where people "came to an environment of political commentary and song." Zurich pre-World War II offered a refuge for artists and politicians and Berk briefly benefited from the artistic underground of the cafes in 1938.

16. *Encylopedia Judaica,* The Macmillan Co., Keter Publishing, Jerusalem, 1972, Vol. 12, p. 719.
17. Dürer survived the war and later became a director of movies in Austria and Germany. Information from interviews with Fred Berk.
18. Morse, Arthur D., *While 6 Million Died, A Chronicle of American Apathy,* Random House, 1967, p. 270.
19. *Ibid.,* p. 85
20. Leland Windreich, "The Career of Alexandra Denisova, Vancouver, de Basil and Cuba, " *Dance Chronicle,* 1979, Vol. 3:1.
21. Calendar of Pro-Arte Performances. Courtesy of the collection of Celida Parera Villalon. Ted Shawn and his dancers performed on Jan. 4 and 6, 1937; Nimura and Kay on March 22 and 24, 1937.
22. Information from interviews in August, 1978 and July, 1980, Los Angeles, California with Claudia V. Kauffman.
23. The program was printed in Pro-Arte Musical de Habana's official magazine of September 1, 1939. It listed "Danza de saltos y cabriolas," a dance of war to Schumann; "Lucha de los elementos" and a dance of romance to Chopin; a dream of love to Liszt; "Danza Campesino" to Graupner; Landlers and waltzes to Strauss; a march; and Russian and Croatian dances. From the collection of Celida Parera Villalon.
24. Woon, Basil, *When It's Cocktail Time in Havana,* Horace Liveright, New York, 1928, p. 27 and p. 98.
25. From the collection of Claudia V. Kauffman.
26. Celida Parera Villalon, a balletomane at that time, remembers that Riabouchinska and Lichine did not stay all the time, nor did de Basil and his wife Olga Morosova or Grigorieff. But the rest of the company went through very hard times. "A group of my friends and I used to bring them food and invite them to our houses to eat so they would not starve." In the fall, they reassembled in New York for a short Canadian tour and resumed their south American junket at the end of 1941.
27. Information courtesy of Leland Windreich.
28. Information and probable diagnosis courtesy of Dr. Bert S. Horwitz.
29. Wilson, John S., "How a Famous Dance Troupe Came Through the Long War, *Ballet Review* p. 29, p. 30.
30. Glazer, Nathan, *American Judaism,* Second Edition, University of Chicago Press, 1972, p. 85.
31. *Ibid,* p. 91.
32. Blau, Joseph L., *Judaism in America,* University of Chicago Press, 1976, p. 63.
33. Glazer, Nathan, *American Judaism,* p. 91
34. These institutions, fundamentally shaped by Fred Berk, became in time, institutions for Israeli folk dance and Jewish dance. At this early stage, however, the dancers were working intuitively.
35. Rabbi Davis later became the director of the Jewish Theological Seminary and eventually moved to Israel where he currently directs the Institute of Contemporary Jewry at the Hebrew University in Jerusalem.

36. The *Reconstructionist Magazine,* Vol., IX, 6, Ap. 30, 1943, p. 18.
37. Some of the ideas developed by programming of the committee included Jewish Music Month and Jewish Book Month reported in *The Reconstructionist Magazine,* New York, Vol. XI:7, May 18, 1945, p. 7. These programs are now commonplace and make up the programming in Jewish Community Centers and Jewish institutions throughout the United States.
38. Hering, Doris, *Twenty-Five Years of American Dance,* Orthwine Publishers 1951, p. 104.
39. *Ibid.,* p. 99
40. Rosen, Lillie F., "The What of the Y," *Eddy,* Spring, 1975, p. 23.
41. *Dance Magazine,* February, 1954, p. 29.
42. Terry, Walter, *I Was There,* Marcel Dekker, 1978, p. 139.
43. Rosen, Lillie F. "The What of the Y", *Eddy,* Sp. 1975, p.22.
44. File on Zemach from the Dance Collection of the Performing Arts Research Center, the New York Public Library at Lincoln Center, New York City.
45. Archives of the 92nd St. Y. Letter from Dr. William Kolodney to Fritz Berger, Nov. 4, 1942.
46. Shreiber, Ben Zion, "The Brandeis Camp Institute, An American Jewish Educational Institution," *Reconstructionist Magazine,* Vol. XV:7, May 13, 1949.
47. *Ibid.*
48. Herman Popkin wrote in letters of April 29, 1978 and October 21, 1981 to the author about the beginnings of Camp Blue Star in Hendersonville, North Carolina based on his own camping experience at Brandeis Camp. In 1950 he hired Katya Delakova and Fred Berk to join his Blue Star staff. Berk continued on as head folk dance teacher until 1979. Also, see Herman Popkin's "Tribute to Fred Berk," published in *Viltis Magzine,* Sept.-Nov., 1980.
49. Kummel became an avid student of Berk and Delakova's and on their recommendation he went to Israel to work with their former teacher Gertrud Kraus. He later danced with Balanchine's New York City Ballet and in the mid-70's directed the Dance Notation Bureau in New York City.
50. Today Shulamit Bat-Ari Kivel, co-director of the Jewish Dance Division at the 92nd St. Y, is an accomplished Israeli folk dance teacher. "I've never really been able to disassociate myself from them or those years," she said in an interview in New York in 1978.
51. Many of the original Jewish Dance Guild group have remained in dance throughout the years, including Paula Levine, today Director of Dance at Hollins College; Irving Burton of the Paperbag Players, a renowned theatre group for children and Herb Kummel (see note 49). "They taught you how to teach, not just to amass new material," said Kummel. "Also, they had an ability to define dance, to clearly dissect the movements and to invest it with that certain joy of dance at all times."
52. These program combinations of Jewish legends, folk, holiday themes and modern history were being developed by the dancers at a time when there was hardly even a concept of Israeli folk dance or modern Jewish art in America.
53. "Hagadah, A Story of Spring," was performed at the 92nd St. Y on March 15 and 16, 1947. From the archives of the 92nd St. Y.
54. Delakova and Berk also took this dance on their cross country tours as evidenced in an undated Ohio State University program.
55. Stodelle, Ernestine, *The Story of Louis Horst and the American Dance;* The

First Frontier, Connecticut, 1964, p. 4.
56. Komarack, Edward, ed., *Arts in Society,* University of Wisconsin, 1976, p. 327.
57. From an unpublished interview with Ruth Grauert, Nov. 29, 1978 at the University of Wisconsin, in the collection of Nancy Hauser.
58. Barzel, Ann, *Dance Magazine* review, undated.
59. The Joint Distribution Committee has been the organization responsible for care and resettlement for Jewish refugees from anywhere in the world, receiving funds from Jewish communities worldwide. Today it still operates and helps, for example, refugees from the USSR.
60. The Delakova-Berk tour to Israel in 1949 was organized by the Kibbutz Hameuchad. They traveled to the following kibbutzim: Alonim, Gvat, Ein Gev, Kfar Szold, Chulata, Menara, Kvutzat HaZofim, Revivim, and also a tour to Eilat.
61. Berk, Fred and Delakova, Katya, "We Dance for the Jewish Soldiers in Eilat," *The Reconstructionist Magazine,* December 16, 1949.
62. Hering, Doris, *Twenty-Five Years of American Dance,* 1951, p. 181.
63. Letter from Claudia V. Kauffman to author, November 4, 1982.
64. Conversation with Dr. Judith Kaplan Eisenstein in May of 1981 in Minneapolis, Minnesota on the occasion of the celebration of her father, Mordecai Kaplan's 100th birthday.
65. October 21, 1981 letter from Herman Popkin to author.
66. Later programs that Berk started included the Israeli Folk Dance Workshop at Blue Star in 1961 which continued every summer although Berk was absent in 1958, 1959 and 1960. In the Folk Dance Camp he was able to concentrate on teaching folk dance and teaching teachers as well as conducting cultural programs in the evenings.
67. Banes, Sally, *Terpsichore in Sneakers,* Houghton Mifflin, 1980, p. 5.
68. November 17, 1980 lecture at Walker Art Center by Marcia Siegel.
69. *Dance Magazine,* "The 92nd St. Y and its new Policy," January 1954, p. 4.
70. In the second season of the "Stage for Dancers" on March 19, 1952 Glen Tetley presented "Lyric Dance." "Twilight Caller," "The Canary," and also Tetley danced in John Butler's "In the Pew."
71. Dzhermolinska, Helen, *Dance Magazine,* October, 1951, p. 13.
72. There were 10 cooperative programs between Nikolais and Berk produced at Henry St. Nikolais taught the Stage for Dancers' troupe his choreography of some of his dances, so the programs sometimes featured his company in "Extrados," and sometimes the Stage for Dancers' troupe, a most unusual example of cooperation.
73. *Dance Observer,* June-July, 1951, p. 91 signed J.S.
74. *Dance Observer,* January, 1953, p. 13, signed L.G.
75. *Ibid.*
76. Now housed in the Dance Collection of the Performing Arts Research Center, The New York Public Library at Lincoln Center.
77. Berk, Fred, The Story of Israeli Folk Dance in Israel and in America," *Israel Dance Annual,* 1976, p. 12.
78. From a taped interview aired on WEVD Radio, New York City, Feb. 6, 1976 during the centennial of the 92nd St. Y. Omus Hirshbein interviewed Fred Berk on the rise and spread of Israeli folk dance in the U.S. Tape in Archives of the 92nd St. Y , courtesy of Steven W. Siegel, Archivist.
79. Bulletin of the 92nd St. Y.

80. Berk's original dance "Holiday in Israel" for the Merry-Go-Rounders appeared in a special notated publication in 1977 thanks to Lucy Venable's notation and organization skills. The Dance Notation Bureau Press published the dance along with the accompanying musical score, an explanation of the original lighting plot, costume instructions and the script of the narration used during the performance. Lucy Veneble wrote to the author, "I had good notes on 'Holiday in Israel' from the original production and I always had hoped to do something with them. Around 1973, I had a graduate-associate in the Ohio Dance Department, Cathy Simmons, who was interested in interviewing Berk and Gary Harris, the lighting designer. I tried out a version of the score with the repertory class and later another was mounted at Brooklyn College. Berk agreed to come to polish the rehearsals and make corrections in the text that I had developed.

   The Dance Notation Bureau gave it a notation checking and published the score, the first one that they published which can be freely performed without payment of royalties to the choreographer. This is due to Berk's generosity and his desire to help spread the use of notation in the dance world."

   Letter to Doris Humphrey from Fred Berk, Jan. 13, 1955 on file at the Dance Collection of the Performing Arts Research Center, New York Public Library at Lincoln Center. "After all the time, energy and advice you have given the Merry-Go-Rounders, for which we have never been in a position to remunerate you except with our deepest thanks, we hope that the situation now has changed.

   Please accept, then, this first bit of long overdue royalty which we expect to establish as regular procedure hereafter. Perhaps this symbolizes our coming of age as a professional company! To us, it denotes an infinitesimal (sic) return on a great debt which we cannot ever forget.

   Sincerely,
   Fred
   P.S. Enclosed is a check for two performances in December on the 18 and 27 for $8.00."

81. When the new state of Israel was settled by people from all over the world, they brought with them their various folk dance and music customs. However, as the state emerged as a country, impulses for new folk expressions evolved as a result of the lack of organic material matched by a strong nationalistic desire for self-expression. Hence individuals such as Gurit Kadman were instrumental in creating new folk dance festivals and institutions based on Jewish cultural heritage as well as the new dynamics of the young nation. See Ingber, Judith Brin, "Shorashim: Roots of Israeli Folk Dance," *Dance Perspectives* Vol. 59, Autumn, 1974.

82. Belijus, F., ed., *Viltis Magazine,* undated article signed by Gertrud Kraus, most likely ghost written by Berk.

83. Interview with Rivka Sturman by Joyce Dorfman Mollov on May 25, 1982 in Tel Aviv, Israel.

84. Berk, Fred, ed., *Hora* Magazine, Vol. XI:2, 1979.

85. A gala reception in Berk's honor, one of the very few in his eventful life, to mark the publication of "Holiday in Israel" was held at the Capezio Foundation with hosts Ben and Estelle Sommers on June 1, 1978. The Dance Library of Israel and the Dance Notation Bureau feted Berk and his Labanotation work.

Israeli Folk Dance Party — Musical arrangements Shai Burstyn, Tikva No. 145

Panorama — Musical arrangements: Ami Gilad, Tikva No. 140

Potpourri — Musical arrangements by Ami Gilad, Tikva No. 117

Rikudey-Am — (Dances for Children, Popular Dances). Music arranged by Ami Gilad, Tikva No. 138

Souvenir — Music arrangement: Shai Burstyn, Tikva No. 148

The Jewish Dance, New York: American Zionist Youth Foundation, 1960.

>Includes articles by Benjamin Zemach, Dvora Lapson, Ann Halprin, Sara Levi-Tanai, Fred Berk.

— and Reimer, Susan, ed. *Machol Ha'am: Dance of the Jewish People,* New York: American Zionist Youth Foundation, 1978.

One Hundred Israeli Folk Dances, Edited by Barbara Taylor and Susie Hofstatter. New York: Zionist Youth Foundation, Israel Folk Dance Department, 1977.

The New Israel Folk Dances. Youth Dept. of the American Zionist Council, New York, 1962.

"Staging Folk Dance", *Dance Magazine,* May 1952.

— and Venable, Lucy. *Ten Folk Dances in Labanotation,* New York: Dance Notation Bureau, 1959.

ed. *Ten Years, 1968-1978,* The Hora Anniversary Issue, New York: American Zionist Youth Foundation, 1978.

Phonograph Recordings, with dance explanations and selections by Fred Berk.

Jewish Folk Dances — Music arranged by Roger Starer, LP from 1945 or 1947 (includes New Hora, Debka, Ari Ara and Circle dance from Sarid)

Six Dances — produced by Michael Herman's "Folk Dance House"

Hora — on Elektra label, music by Dov Selzer and Geula Gil, 1952: (Horas to listen to and to dance to), Elektra No. 186

Chassidic Dances — Musical arrangement Ami Gilad, Shai Burstyn, Yossi Shlomer, Tikva No. 147

Dance Along with Sabras — Tikva No. 69, arrangements by Ami Gilad

Dances for Children — Music arranged and directed by Shai Burstyn. Tikva No. 106

Debka — Musica arrangements by Ami Gilad, Tikva No. 100

Israel Folk Dance Festival — Arrangements by Ami Gilad and Geula Zohar, Tikva No. 80

LIST OF WORKS BY FRED BERK

Books and Articles

Berk, Fred, "A Dissenting Point of View about Folk Dance", *Dance Magazine,* Dec., 1957

The Chasidic Dance, New York: American Zionist Youth Foundation and Union of American Hebrew Congregations, 1975.

>Includes articles by Haim Leaf, Lois Bar Yaacov, Marsha Seid, Jill Gellerman, Zvi Friedhaber, Lillian Shapero.

— and Lucy Venable, *Dances from Israel in Labanotation,* a correspondence course for folk dancers. New York: Dance Notation Bureau, 1967.

— and Katya Delakova, *Dances of Palestine,* Drawings by Myril Adler. New York: Hilllel Resources, B'nai Brith Publishers, 1947.

>Eleven dances created in America and "Mayim Mayim" from Israel, "Tcherkessia" from Europe.

Guide for the Israeli Folk Dance Teacher, New York: American Zionist Youth Foundation, 1978.

ed. *Ha-Rikud, The Jewish Dance,* New York: American Zionist Youth Foundation, Union of American Hebrew Congregations, 1972.

>Includes articles by Benjamin Zemach, Sara Levi-Tanai, Dvora Lapson, Gurit Kadman, Fred Berk, 25 dances and guide.

Holiday in Israel. Music arranged by Beatrice Rainer, New York: The Dance Notation Bureau Press, 1978.

>Includes Labanotation score of dance, music and extensive explanation.

ed. *Hora,* a publication of the Israel Folk Dance Institute, American Zionist Youth Foundation from 1968-1980.

Jewish Folk Dance Book, New York: National Jewish Welfare Board, 1948.

>Includes explanation of Harmonica, Hora, Double Tcherkessia, Debka, Rikud Hazugot, Sher, Patch Dance, Shir-shir, Ari-Ara.

86. Loaned to the author by Anne Wilson Wangh.
87. From the files of the American Zionist Youth Foundation, an undated *New York Herald Tribune* clipping.
88. Berk, Fred, ed., *Hora* Magazine, Vol. IX;1, 1971.
89. Berk, Fred, ed., *Hora* Magazine, Vol. VIII:1,Issue ¡22, p. 2.
90. Berk, Fred, ed., *Hora* Magazine, Vol. VII:2, Winter, 1975.
91. Berk, Fred, ed., *Hora* Magazine, Vol. VI:6, Fall, 1973.
92. Letter to Ernestine Weiss and Helen Garbutt, given to the author by them September 28, 1979.

All quotations from Fred Berk are the result of extensive taped interviews conducted with him by the author April 3-8, 1978 in New York City; April 21-26, 1979 Minneapolis; December 15-20, 1979 in New York City; July 20-25, 1979 in Tel Aviv; September, 1979 in Minneapolis; Feb. 22, 1980 in New York City.

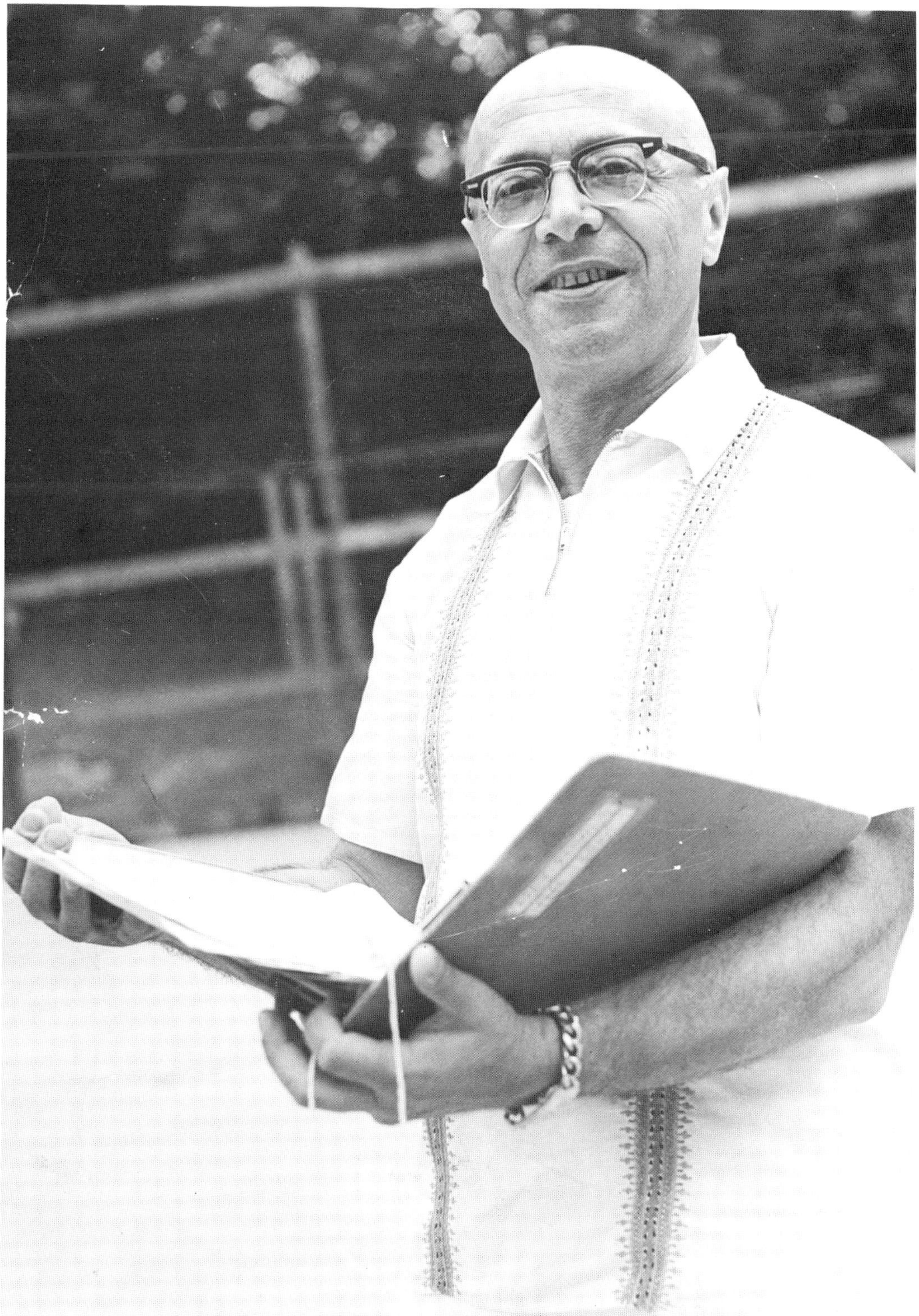

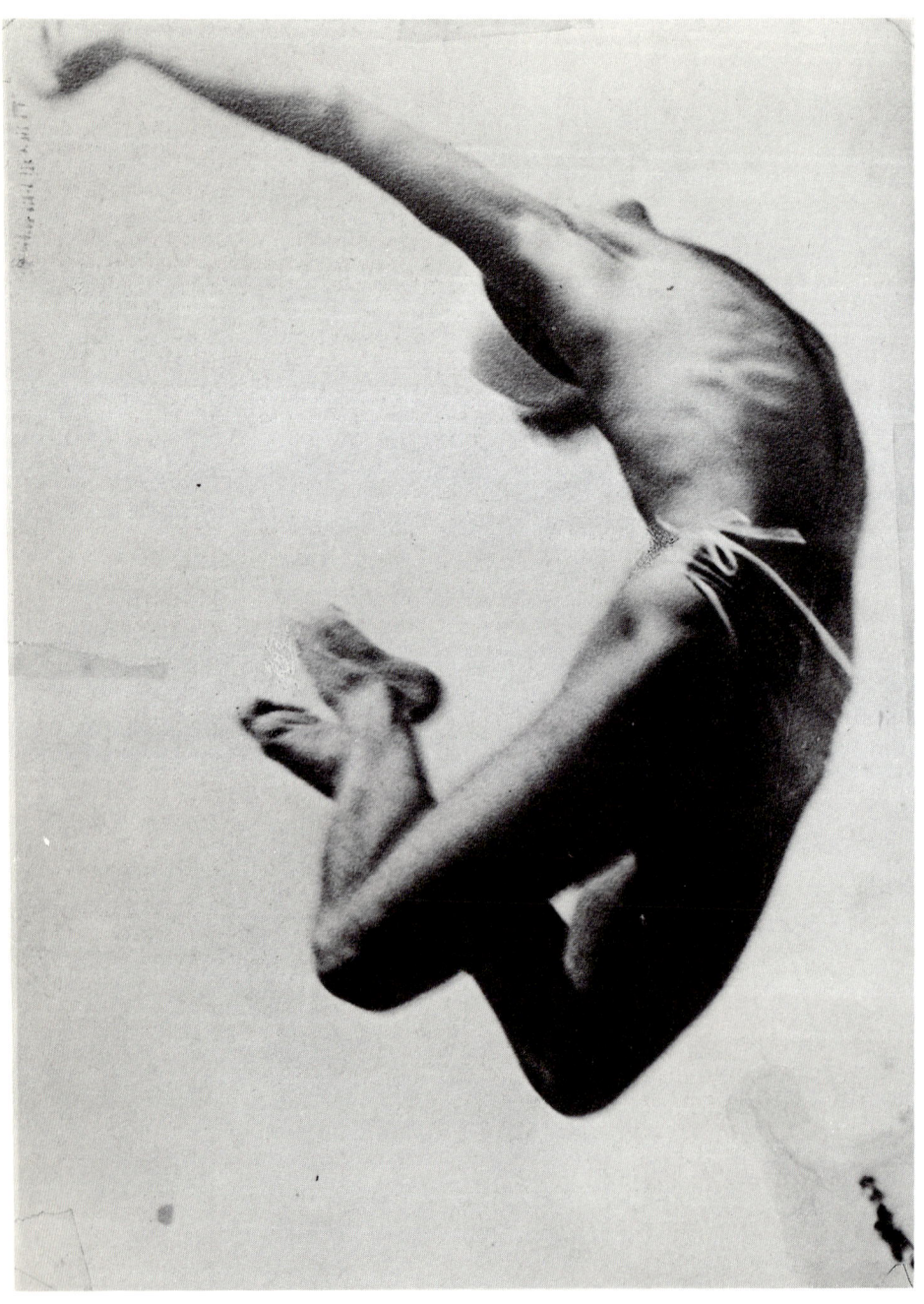

Vienna, 1931					רינה, 1931

פריץ ברג במחול הסולו שלו **העריץ**,
שזיכה אותו בפרס בתחרות בתחרות. וינה 1934

Fritz Berger in his solo
The Tyrant, Vienna 1934

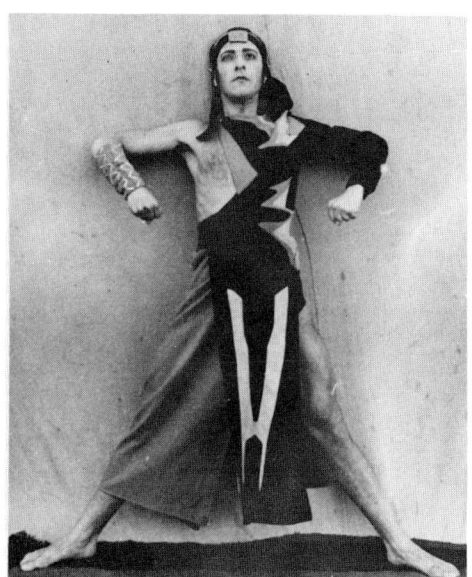

בית ההורים
והמחלבה בוינה

The Bergers'
home and dairy
in Vienna

גלויה לאבא
מטיולם של
פריץ ואחותו
ארנסטינה, 1916?

Fritz and his
sister Ernestine
on a postcard
sent home from
a trip, 1916?

עם ההורים
במרכבה, פריץ
ליד העגלון,
1918?

With his
parents, Fritz
sitting next to
the driver,
1918?

פריץ במחול רוסי
בלהקתה של גרטרוד קראוס,
וינה 1931?

Fritz in costume
in a Russian dance
in Gertrud Kraus' company,
Vienna, 1931?

פריץ באחד מתפקידיו
באופרה הממלכתית,
וינה 1934

Fritz Berger
in one of his parts
at the Vienna Staatsoper
in 1934

בהופעה עם
קלאודיה ואל,
קובה 1940

צלם:
לוטה גראהן

During
a performance
with
Claudia Vall,
Cuba, 1940

Photo:
Lotte Grahn

עם קלאודיה,
במחול־עם רוסי,
הבנה, קובה 1940

Claudia Vall
and Fritz
in a Russian
folkdance,
Havana, Cuba,
1940

In the U.S., 1949
Photo: Walter Strate

ארה"ב, 1949
צלם: ואלטר סטרייט

Finale of the 25th Israeli Folk Dance Festival, Lincoln Center, N.Y., 1976. Photo: Yitzhak Baer

The "Merry-Go-Rounders" in Austrian Wedding, 1954
Photo: Matthew Wisocki

חתונה באוסטריה, להקת ה"Merry-Go-Rounders", 1954. צלם: מתיו ויסוצקי

תמונת הסיום של פסטיבל המחול הישראלי העממי ה-25, לינקולן סנטר, ניו-יורק, 1976. צלם: יצחק ב

בכרמים, להקת "הבראיקה", 1964
צלם: ביל קארטר

In the Vineyards, "Hebraica", 1964
Photo: Bill Carter

Fred and Katya in their Jewish dance The Mehutonim
Photo: Walter E. Owen

פרד וקטיה במחול המחותנים
צלם: ואלטר א. אורן

Bride and Groom, 1944
Photo: Jan Kriegsman

חתן וכלה, 1944
צלם: יאן קריגסמאן

Hanya Holm, Katya Delakova and Fred Berk
in Holm's Trio,
Colorado, 1947

Photo: Knudson Bowers

פרד ברק, קטיה דלקובה והניה הולם
ב**טריו**, כוריאוגראפיה: הניה הולם,
קולורדו, קיץ שנת 1947

צלם: קנודסון בוארס

Fred and Katya, 1944
Photo: Gerda Peterich

פרד וקטיה בשנת 1944
צלם: גרדה פטריץ׳

Mary Hinkson and Katya Delakova
in Fred Berk's Timely Ballads,
"Stage for Dancers", 1950-51
Photo: Fred Fehl

מרי הינקסון (משמאל) וקטיה
בבאלאדות עדכאניות,
"בימת הרקדנים" ניו-יורק, 52-1951
צלם: פרד פהל

Glen Tetley, Alwin Nikolais and Hanya Holm
at Colorado Springs, 1947
Photo: Gerda Peterich

בקולורדו, קיץ 1947, עם גלן טטלי,
אלווין ניקולאיס והניה הולם
צלם: גרדה פטרייך

פרד וקטיה עם לואי הורסט,
ניו־יורק, 1948

Fred and Katya with Louis Horst,
1948

Fred Berk and Katya Delakova
with Alwin Nikolais and Hanya Holm
at Colorado Springs, 1947

אלווין ניקולאיס, הניה הולם
עם קטיה ופרד,
קולורדו, 1947

Shavuot pageant staged by Fred Berk at Camp Blue Star in the early 50's

"Blue Star" חג השבועות במחנה הנוער בבימויו של פרד ברק, ראשית שנות ה־50

פרד בשעת חזרה במחנה הנוער

Fred during a rehearsal at Camp Blue Star

1955 pageant
at Camp Blue Star
Hendersonville, N.C.

חגיגה במחנה הנוער "Blue Star"
בהנדרסונוויל, קארוליינה הצפונית,
שפרד ביים בשנת 1955

Fred and Katya at kibbutz Sassa,
during their Israel tour in 1949

בקיבוץ סאסא
בסיור ההופעות של פרד וקטיה בשנת 1949

פרד עם רבקה שטורמן
בתל-אביב

Fred with
Rivka Sturman
in Tel-Aviv

Fred and Katya during their visit in Israel　　　　　פרד וקטיה בביקור בארץ

פרד ושרה לוי־תנאי
בסטודיו של **ענבל**

Fred with
Sara Levi-Tanai
at the Inbal studio
in Tel-Aviv

The finale of Fred Berk's
Holiday in Israel

סיום מחול **ההורה** במחרוזת
חופשה בישראל

The "Merry-Go-Rounders" in Dundai
Photo: Matthew Wisocki

מחול ה**דונדאי** מאותה המחרוזת, 1953
צלם: מתיו ויסוצקי

מעשה בחמור מאת אלווין ניקולאיס, 1950; גלן טטלי בתפקיד החמור. צלם: פרד פהל

Alwin Nikolais' Fable of the Donkey, 1950; with Glen Tetley as the donkey and Anita Lynn, Harry Burstein and others. Courtesy of the Nikolais-Louis Foundation.
Photo: Fred Fehl

"Hebraica" dancers in Market Scene
(from the collection of B. Liebhaber)

להקת ״הבראיקה״ בתמונת השוק
(מאוספו של ברנרד ליבהאבר)

Three Old Mexicans from one of Fred Berk's international folk dance programs at the "Y" in New York in the late 50's

שלישית הזקנים המקסיקנים, שיצר פרד עבור תוכניותיו ב״Y״, ניו-יורק, סוף שנות ה-50

Jan Goldin
in Fred Berk's Bride of the Sabbath,
March 1957 at the "Y" and the Cooper Union in New York

ז'אן גולדין
במחול של פרד **שבת המלכה**,
ניו-יורק, מרס 1957

Finale of one of the Israeli Folk Dance Festivals at the Felt Forum, N.Y.
Photo. Itzhak Berez

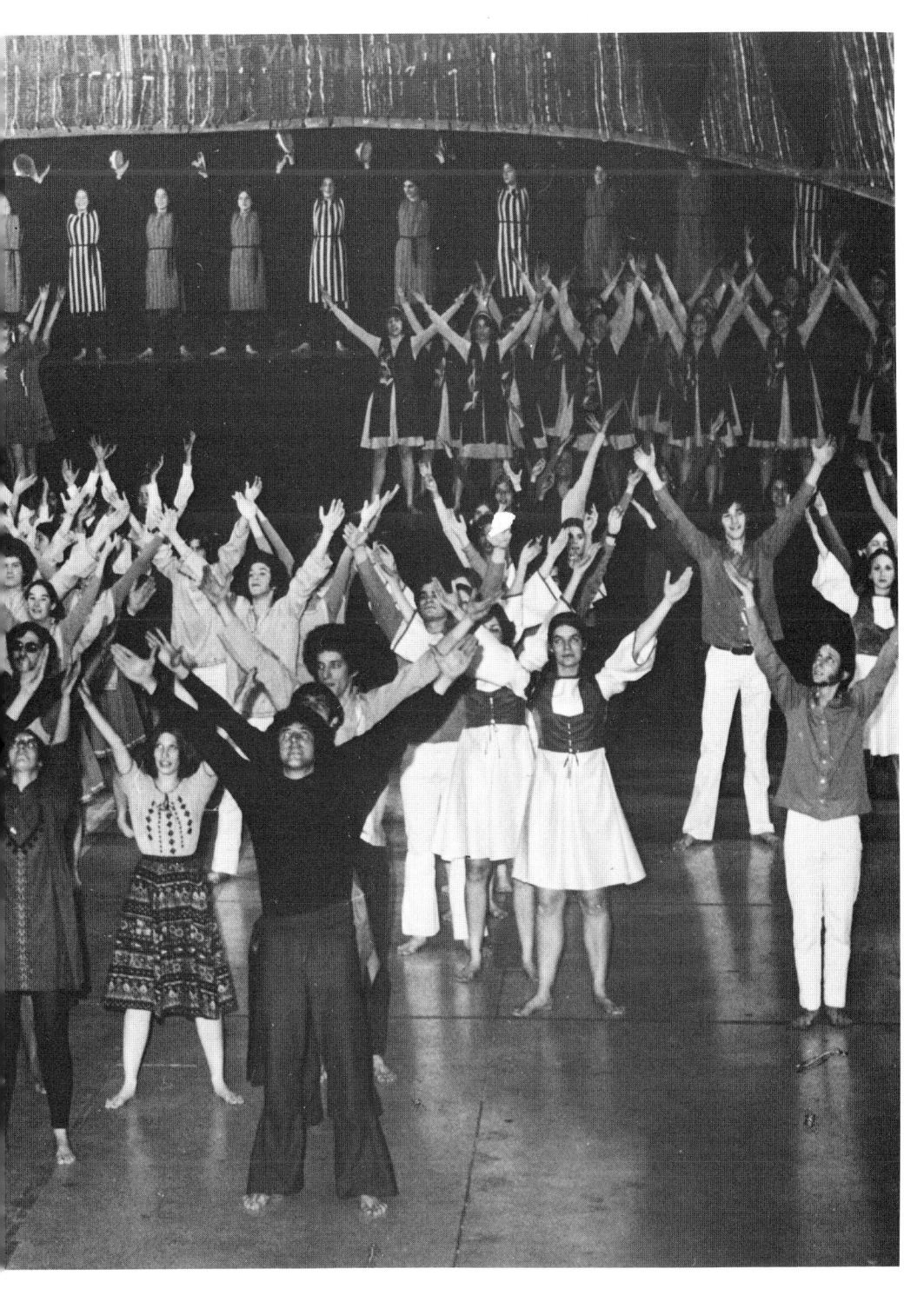

סיום חגיגי של פסטיבל המחול בפלט־פורום בניו־יורק

צלם: יצחק ברז

פרד וקטיה בתוכניתם
פנה דרך לעתיד
בכורה: 23.1.1944

Fred Berk and Katya Delakova
in their program
Make Way for Tomorrow,
1944

פרד וקטיה
בקולו יוגוסלבי
במחרוזת סביב העולם בשיר ובמחול,
ארה״ב, 1942–1952

Fred Berk and Katya Delakova
in their Around the World
in Song and Dance,
1942–1952

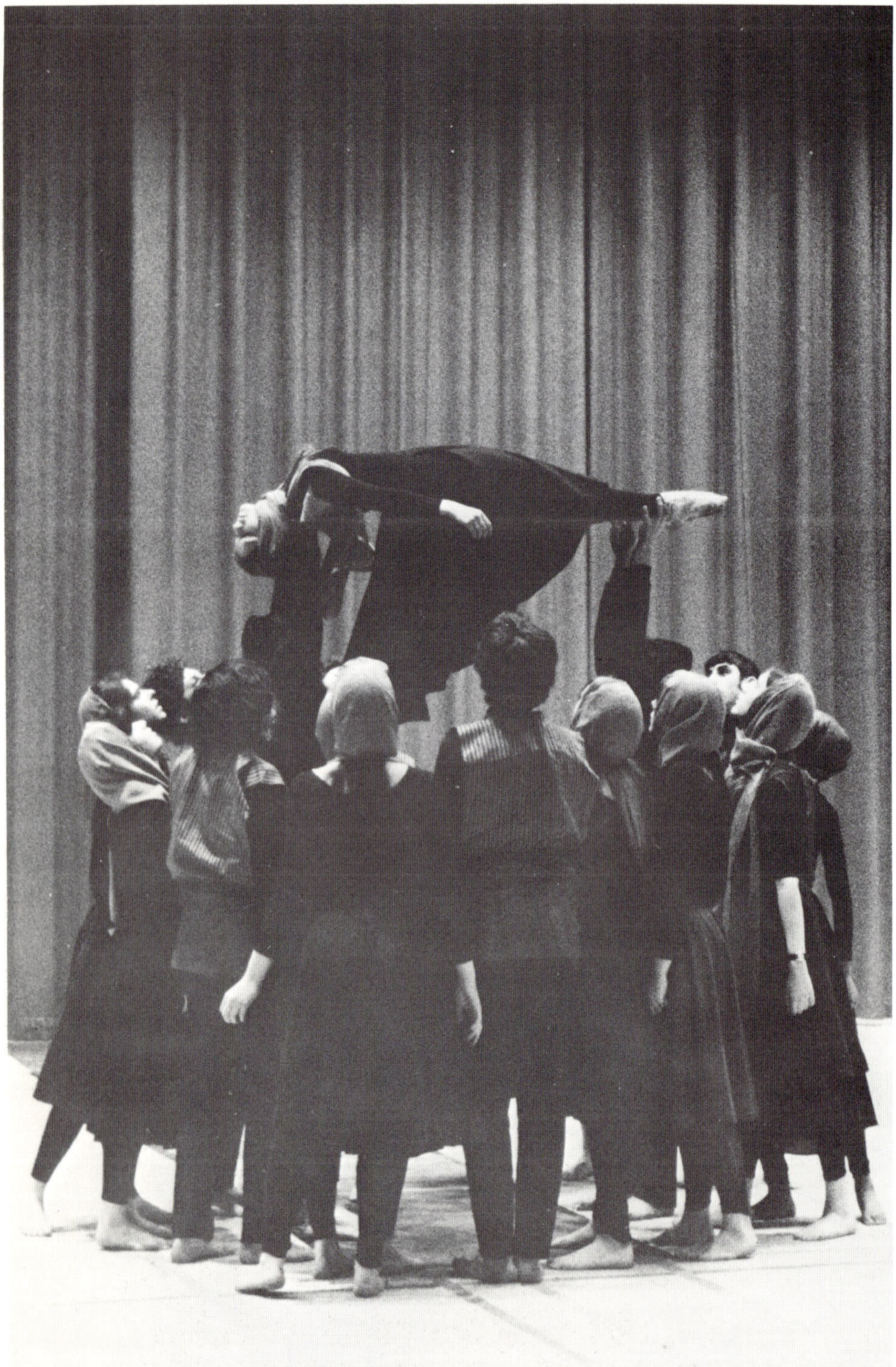

Fred Berk rehearses the "Hebraica" dancers in his Shepherd Dance at the "Y", 1967

Fred Berk's Ghetto Dance
Photo: Louis Peres

פרד בשעת חזרה עם להקת "הבראיקה" על מחול הרועים ב"Y", 1967

מחול הגטו מאת פרד ברק
צלם: לואי פרז

"Hebraica" dancers
in Chanuka by Fred Berk (rehearsal) 1960

"Hebraica"
in In Passing By by Fred Berk, 1960
Photo: Fred Fehl

רקדני "הבראיקה"
בשעת חזרה על **חנוכה**, 1960

להקת "הבראיקה"
ב**עוברים ושבים** מאת פרד ברק, 1960
צלם: פרד פהל

Fred Berk's Timely Ballads with dancers
Miriam Cole, Doris Rudko, Mary Hinkson
and Katya Delakova, 1950
Photo: Fred Fehl

"Hebraica" dancers
in Fred Berk's Celebration
Photo: Bill Carter

מתוך באלאדות עדכאניות מאת פרד ברק,
עם הרקדנים מרים קול, דוריס רודקו,
מרי הינקסון וקטיה דלקובה, 1950
צלם: פרד פהל

להקת "הבראיקה"
במחול חגיגה מאת פרד ברק
צלם: ביל קארטר

Fred with Shay Ingber in Tel Aviv. 1976

Fred Berk during a creative dance class at the 92nd St. Y, 1962

פרד עם שי אינגבר בתל-אביב, 1976

פרד בשעת שיעור של מחול יצירתי ב״Y״ בניו-יורק, 1962

למנצח על המחולות

חייו של פרד ברק,
מורה-למחול יהודי בימינו

מאת יהודיתברין-אינגבר

עברית: רון בן-ישראל

© יהודית ברין־אינגבר
1985

בהוצאת הספריה למחול בישראל, תל־אביב, רח׳ ביאליק 26

נדפס בדפוס אלף אלף בע״מ, רמת־גן, טל׳ 724931
סדר עברי: עט ואות, תל־אביב, טל׳ 459019
סדר אנגלי: תירוש, תל־אביב, טל׳ 444959

ISBN 965-309-000-3

התוכן:

הקדמה מאת אננה סוקולוב 5
תודות 6
פרק ראשון: פרד כפי שהיה 7
פרק שני: וינה 12
פרק שלישי: שוויצריה 26
פרק רביעי: אנגליה 29
פרק חמישי: קובה 31
פרק שישי: אמריקה 37
פרק שביעי: אופטימיות 40
פרק שמיני: בניה מחדש 43
פרק תשיעי: ריקוד אמריקני ב"Y" 46
פרק עשירי: ה"רקונסטרוקציוניזם" והמחול 49
פרק אחד-עשר: האגודה למחול יהודי 51
פרק שנים-עשר: מחוץ למסגרת היהודית 54
פרק שלושה-עשר: אירופה 56
פרק ארבעה-עשר: ישראל 58
פרק חמישה-עשר: במה לרקדנים 61
פרק שישה-עשר: עוד התחלה 65
פרק שבעה-עשר: לא במלים בלבד 68
פרק שמונה-עשר: ישראל ו"הבראיקה" 71
פרק תשעה-עשר: האסון 74
פרק עשרים: כתב תנועה 77
פרק עשרים ואחד: פסטיבלי המחול הישראלי 80
פרק עשרים ושניים: ישראל של ברק 82

מוקדש לבני, שי ונח, ולקלאודיה

הקדמה
מאת אננה סוקולוב

אני זוכרת את פגישותי עם פרד ברק בניו-יורק ובישראל. הוא היה אחד האמנים הראשונים שהכרתי, שהתענינו בצורה רצינית במחול-העם הישראלי. מסירותו לא תשכח. פרד ביקש תמיד להתחקות אחרי השורשים ולא הסתפק בהכרות שטחית, "תיירית" עם מחול-העם. וזה הביא אותו להתעמקות בשורשים ובמשמעותם של מחולות היהודים בעולם כולו. הוא לא היה רק מודע לחשיבות שימורם, אלא השקיע גם מרץ רב בהפצתם.

פרד היה פעיל מאוד בישראל בתחום מחול-העם. הוא נהג לנסוע לכל מקום בו הופיעו להקות בריקודי-עם ולבקר בכל מקום בו אפשר היה לחזות בביצוע מחולות העדות השונות. כך למד מחולות שבאו מכל ארצות תבל, מכל המקומות בהם חיו יהודים. הוא היה גם בקשרים אמיצים עם חלוצי המחול בישראל: גרטרוד קראוס, שרה לוי-תנאי וגורית קדמן – אם למנות רק אחדים מאלה.

הוא היה פעיל מאוד בהפצת המחול הישראלי בארה"ב. היה זה הוא שהביא את מחול-העם הישראלי לניו-יורק, שעה שאיש לא הכיר עדיין ריקודים אלה שם. נתמזל מזלנו, שיש בידנו ספר חשוב זה, המספר את סיפור חייו של פרד. הוא ידבר לא רק אל הרקדנים עצמם, אלא לכל האנשים, ממש כשם שפרד היה מסוגל לעשות זאת, בהזכירו לנו את המקורות האוניברסאליים שלנו. באוספו מחולות מהעולם כולו, הוא העלה בנו את שמחת-החיים – השפה המשותפת לכל בני-האדם המתענינים באמנות ובתרבות. משהתבררה לו חשיבותן של מסורות עממיות, הוא הקדיש את חייו למציאתן, שימורן, הוראתם וביצועם של מחולות אלה.

הערה: רשימת מראי-המקומות מופיעה בסוף החלק האנגלי של הספר.

תודות

ללא עזרתה המתמשכת והלבבית של דר' ריב-אללן פרל פולדש ספר זה לא היה נכתב. וברצוני להודות גם לדר' דאון ליל הורוביץ, שעזרה לי בניו-יורק, ולגיורא מנור, שעודד אותי במשך שמונה השנים, בהן אספתי את החומר וכתבתי ספר זה; לבעלי, יורם, שתמך בי ולבני, שי ונוח, על סבלנותם, שעה שהייתי הולכת לספריה "לעבוד על סיפורו של הדוד פרד".

בין האחרים, שעזרו לי בעבודתי, בעיצה ואינפורמציה, רות ברין, סלמה-ג'ין כהן, רות גודמן, אילה גורן, טוני הלשטיין, רות לרט, ברנרד ליבהאבר, גרטרוד ליפינקוט, סילביה רוזן, סטיבן ו. סיגל, סלידה וילאלון, לילנד וינדרייך וסיביל צימרמן.

סיפור חייו של פרד ברק לא יכול היה להכתב ללא הראיונות שהעניקו לי והמסמכים שהעמידו לרשותי באדיבותם דב אלטון, ויטס בליאיוס, בוני בירד, ברוס בלוך, ירדנה כהן, ראלף דייויס, קטיה דלקובה, אלזה דובלון, ג'ף דונקאן, יעקב עדן, יהודית אייזנשטיין, הווארד אפשטיין, לורי פרידמן-מאיירס, הלן גארבוט, רות גודמן, ראט ואיילה גורן, גארי האריס, דוריס הרינג, שלום ודבורה חרמון, קלאודיה ואל-קאופמן, סטפי קיי, שולה בת-ארי קיבל, הרב קימל, שרה לוי-תנאי, פאולה לווין, סופי מסלאו, סימה מיטמאן, ג'ויס דורפמאן-מולוב, מרדית מונק, אסתר נלסון, אלווין ניקולאיס, ג'נבייב אוסוואלד, הרמן פופקין, בסי שנברג, פאול ספונג, קארולין שטראוס, ימי סטרום, רבקה שטורמן, ליביה דראפקין-ואנאוור, לוסי ונאבל, אן וילסון-ואנג וארנסטינה וייס.

וברצוני להודות גם לעורכים של כתבי-עת, בהם התפרסמו קטעים מהספר תוך כדי חיבורו: דיאנה וודרוף, עורכת ה"Dance Research Journal" (חוברת אביב 1981); אדם לאהם, עורך כתב-העת "Arabesqué" (גליון ספטמבר 1983); גיורא מנור, עורך "מחול בישראל" (1983); ג'ורג' דוריס, עורך ה"Dance Chronicle" (גליון קיץ 1984).

רוב התצלומים שבספר הועמדו לרשותי על-ידי פרד ברק וקטיה דלקובה. אחרים באו מאוספיהם של ברנרד ליבהאבר וליביה דראפקין-ואנאוור. ניתנה לי, כמו כן, רשותם האדיבה של המשרד לכתב-תנועה בניו-יורק, שפירסם בשנת 1977 את "חגיגה בישראל" מאת פרד ברק, שרשמה לוסי ונאבל; ויליאם קומר, עורך ה"Dance Magazine" וסטיבן ו. סיגל, הארכיונאי של ה-"92nd St. Y."‎, להשתמש בחומר שברשותם.

פרק ראשון:
פרד כפי שהיה

לראשונה פגשתי בפרד ברק בשנה האחרונה, בה למדתי במכללת "שרה לורנס". זה היה באביב שנת 1967, כשבוע לפני סיום הלימודים. הייתי אחד משלושת הסטודנטים, שנשלחו להביא אותו ממאנהטן, כדי שיתן שיעור במחלקה למחול של המכללה. בסי שנברג, ראש החוג למחול, נהגה להזמין מורים-אורחים לימי ו'. פרד היה המרצה-האורח האחרון לשנה זו. הכרתי את שמו מאותה מודעה צנועה, ממוסגרת, שהיתה מופיעה בקביעות ב"דנס מאגאזין": "פרד ברק, מנהל המחלקה למחול יהודי ב'מועדון YM-YWHA' שברחוב מס' 92, ניו-יורק". הדבר תמיד עורר את סקרנותי, אבל שעה שנסעתי להביא אותו, לא הייתי בטוחה כלל, אם זה המורה-האורח שהייתי מבקשת לי לשיעור האחרון שלי במכללה. כרוב הסטודנטים במכללה, קיוויתי להתחיל בקאריירה בתחום המחול אחרי שאקבל את התואר האקדמאי ולא רציתי להקדיש את השיעור המסיים את חוק לימודי למשהו כמו ריקודי-עם ולוותר על עוד שיעור בטכניקה.

ברק התגורר אז בדירה בסמוך למועדון ה"Y" שברחוב ה-92. עדינה מרגוליס (מועמדת לתואר מוסמך בחוג למחול, שהיתה בשעתה אסיסטנטית של פרד ב"Y") נכנסה לבית, לקרוא לו. משחזרה עימו ועם האקורדיוניסט המלווה שלו, נדהמתי. פרד ברק אמנם נראה רזה ומוצק כרקדן, אבל ראשו היה קרח לחלוטין, הוא נראה קשיש למדי ורגלו האחת היתה נעולה בנעל אורתופדית כבדה. הוא צלע לעבר המכונית הממתינה, נשען על מקל הליכה עבה. גם המורה שלנו בסי שנברג צלעה בלכתה, אבל איש מאיתנו לא ייחס לכך חשיבות. היא היתה בנעוריה אחת מהמרקדניות האגדיות בלהקתה הראשונה של מרתה גראהאם, וידעה להפליא לאמן את גופותינו, ואת מוחינו הרגילה לחשוב בצורה מעמיקה על מחול ויצירה.

ברק והמלווה שלו נכנסו למכונית וישבו לידי במושב האחורי. ללא כל הקדמה של נימוסין פרד התכופף לעברי ושאל: "שמעת חדשות ברדיו היום?" ממש כמו בסי שנברג הוא דיבר אנגלית במבטא גרמני ניכר. לרגע התבלבלתי עד שתפסתי, שכוונתו היתה אם שמעתי חדשות מישראל. המלך חוסיין איים במלחמה, הנשיא נאסר חסם את מיצרי טיראן, צבאות מצריים ניצבו מול גבולות ישראל. שוחחנו על ישראל והמשבר הפוקד אותה במשך רוב הנסיעה בת ה-25 דקות מניו-יורק למכללת "שרה לורנס" שבעיר ברונקסוויל.

הדיבורים על מלחמה נגדו את אווירת השלווה של הקאמפוס, שכל גינותיו פרחו לתפארה באור השמש האביבי. הובלנו את מר ברק אל הסטודיו שבבניין המודרניסטי של החוג למחול, שתכנן האדריכל קורבוסייה. לאולפנה היתה צורה בלתי רגילה של משולש, שצלעו הרחבה ביותר מכוסה במראות ואילו ממול תלויים היו מסכים שחורים, שניתן היה לפורסם כדי ליצור מעין בימה למופעים. רצפת העץ הקפיצית הבריקה.

בסי חיכתה לפרד בסטודיו, ואנחנו מיהרנו לחדר-ההלבשה, להחליף את בגדי הרחוב שלנו לבגדי-ריקוד, לקראת השיעור במחול-עם ישראלי, שעמד להתקיים. הייתי בטוחה, שמה שנלמד יהיו אותן הורות, שהיו מוכרות לי מחגיגות בר-מצווה משפחתיות.

פרד ברק נכנס לאולפנה באיטיות, יורד בזהירות במדרגות. נראה היה שההשתחווה קלות, כשהרוצג לפני הכיתה. הוא ישב לו על אחד מכסאות הבאר הגבוהים, והאקורדיוניסט המלווה ניצב לידו. הוא הסביר בקצרה את היסודות והמרכיבים של המחולות שעמד ללמד,

את צורותיהם ואת מקצביהם. עד מהרה סובבנו במעגלים, קפצנו ורקענו ברגלינו עד שהיינו ממש שיכורים משמחת-החיים, שהוא החדיר בנו. הלכנו בעיקבות הוראותיו כאילו היינו רגילים לריקוד ריקודי-עם מאז ומתמיד, ואהבנו אותם יותר מכל, כאילו מעולם לא איבדנו את תחושת השייכות, שנוצרה במשך דורות של מחול עדתי. למרות השוני ברקע האישי של כל אחד מאיתנו, חשנו קשר חזק בינינו, כפי שמעולם לא הרגשנו בשעת שיעור של טכניקה.

הוא לימד בפשטות, אבל היתה זו פשטותו של רב-אמן אמיתי. ללא מלים מיותרות, ללא תנועות בלתי שייכות, ללא ״מילוי-זמן״. חשתי ששיעור זה שינה אותי לחלוטין. המחול כאילו פתח אותי, הגביר את קשרי עם חברי לכיתה בצורה חדשה, היה בו משמחת החברותא. זה קשר אותי לעמי החי בישראל, שהיה אז נתון בסכנה, באופן שמעולם לא חשתי בו קודם לכן.

בשבוע שאחרי סיום הלימודים פרצה מלחמה במזרח התיכון, מלחמת ששת הימים. ואני נתקבלתי למשרתי הראשונה בניו-יורק: התמניתי לעוזרת לעורכת ה״דנס מאגאזין״, כתב-העת החשוב ביותר בתחום המחול באמריקה, לידיה ג׳ואל (Lydia Joel).

במשרדי מערכת ה״דנס מאגאזין״, שהיו באותם ימים ברחוב ה-47, סמוך לברודווי, היה עלי לקרוא אינסוף רשימות ומאמרים על ענייני מחול, לפגוש אינספור רקדנים ולעבור תוך התפעלות על ערימות ענקיות של תצלומי-מחול. לאט לאט סיגלתי לעצמי השקפה רחבה יותר על מה כולל המושג מחול – כל דבר שאחד הכוריאוגראפים או חבורת רקדנים כינו ריקוד או מחול היה לנושא לגיטימי עבור דפי הירחון שלנו, ממש כמו היצירות הקלאסיות של הבאלט. מחול-העם קיבל עבורי משמעות נוספת, משבחרה לידיה בתצלום של רקדנים מיוגוסלאביה, המבצעים את מחול ה״קולו״, לשער הגליון הראשון שיצא לאור משהתחלתי לעבוד במערכת.

להפתעתי, יום אחד טילפן אלי פרד ברק. האם נוכל להיפגש, כדי לשוחח? מאוחר יותר נוכחתי, שאחת מהתכונות האופייניות שלו היתה להזמין אנשים לפגישה אישית, כדי לברר נושא כלשהו, שהעסיק אותו. מעולם לא נהג לסדר עניינים בשיחה טלפונית או בעזרת מכתב. הוא הגיע למערכת בשעת הפסקת הצהריים ויחד הלכנו למסעדה שקטה ואפלולית בשדרה השמינית. אני הייתי נבוכה מעט, כשהיה עלינו לעבור דרך איזור חנויות הפורנו שבאותה סביבה. פרד לא שם לב לכך, כי כבר היה שקוע בהסברת נושא פגישתנו. הוא הביא עימו כתב-יד של מאמר על מחולות-עם מנקודת ראות פעילות הנופש. הוא רצה לדעת, אם אסכים לשכתב את הרשימה שלו, והאם אני סבורה שה״דנס מאגאזין״ ירצה להדפיסו?

מאמרים פרי עטו הופיעו לא אחת ב״דנס מאגאזין״. עיינתי במאמר, שהיה מודפס בקפידה במכונת כתיבה. סגנונו היה מסורבל, וחסרו בו לגמרי השטף והקלות, שציינו את השיעורים שלו.

הוא שאל אותי, האם אני רוקדת? התעמקתי בתפריט, כדי להסתיר את מבוכתי, כשהסברתי לו שאין לי די כסף כדי לשלם עבור שיעורים. על מנת לשנות את הנושא, סיפרתי לו על מופעי-מחול, שהלכתי לראות כחלק מעבודתי במערכת. כמעט כל ערב הלכתי למופע ובסופי-שבוע אפילו פעמיים ביום, לצפות בלהקות אורחות, מופעי עליות-גג של יוצרים חדשנים, הופעות מחול מודרני בכנסיית ג׳אדסון שבגריניץ׳ וילידג׳ או לחזות ברקדנים נעולים נעלי-ספורט בתיאטרון היהודי הישן בחלקה המזרחי של מנהטן. בדרכנו חזרה אל המערכת שאל אותי פרד, האם לא ארצה לבוא ולהשתתף בשיעורי יום ד׳ שלו, הפתוחים למי שמעוניינים לריקוד ריקודי-עם, מתחילים ותיקים כאחד. ״זה לא רחוק מהדירה שלך. ותוכלי לקבל מילגת-לימודים,״ הוא אמר בפשטות. הוא חש עד כמה הייתי זקוקה לרקוד בפועל ממש וידע את מצוקתי הכספית. קיבלתי את הצעתו בשמחה.

ביום ד׳ הבא הלכתי אל ה״92nd St. Y״, אותו מוסד יהודי מפורסם, שבין כתליו זכה חלק נכבד מהמחול המודרני האמריקני להיות מוצג לפני הקהל. ה״Y״ היתה מעין מלת-קסם בעולם המחול של ניו-יורק. בדרכי לסטודיו שבקומה העליונה הצצתי לאולם, בו רק לפני שבועות מעטים התקבצנו כל המי ומי של עולם המחול לחזות במופע ראשון של להקתו של לואי פלקו (Louis Falco). קירות האולם היו מצופים בעץ בגוון כהה וסביב האולם, סמוך לתקרתו, היו חקוקים שמותיהם של הרמב״ם, מוצרט ומשה רבנו באותיות

8

זהב, כאילו להאציל מזוהר העבר על המופעים.

בקומה העליונה, בסטודיו בו נהג פרד ללמד, הסתובבו כמאה אנשים. נמצאו שם אנשים מכל הגילים והצורות, נועלים של נעליים מסנדל ועד לנעלי־באלט, לבושים במיגוון תלבושות שכללו בגדי־ריקוד, מכנסי התעמלות וסתם מכנסיים. ישוב על כיסא גבוה חיכה פרד, ליד שולחן ארוך ועליו מיקרופון, פטיפון וערימה שלמה של תקליטים. פרד הציע להתחיל במשהו, שהכל מכירים. הוא חילק את הכיתה לשני חצאים, שיצרו מעגלים, אחזו זה ביד זה והחלו לנוע בתצורות שהלכו ונעשו מורכבות יותר ויותר, לפי הוראותיו המדוייקות, הקצרות של ברק. התפעלתי מפשטותן ובהירותן של הוראותיו, ומהנכונות וההנאה של התלמידים, שהיו מוכנים בחפץ־לב לבצע כל מה שדרש.

בשיעורים הבאים דיבר פרד על מורים ורקדנים שהכיר. הוא הזכיר את גרטרוד קראוס, המורה הראשונה שלו בוינה, מולדתו, שעלתה אחר־כך לארץ. בשיעור אחר הדגימה הדסה בדוך את המחול התימני, שעד אז לא הכרתי כלל. הוקסמתי מהגלישה העדינה של "הדסה" התימנית. הופתעתי מצירופי המקבצים והצעדים שהדסה הציגה לפנינו. המשכתי להשתתף בשיעורים אלה במשך השנתיים, בהן עבדתי בניו־יורק.

משהחל סמסטר החורף, ביקשני פרד לבוא לחזרות של להקתו, "הבראיקה", שהתקיימו כרגיל בלילות יום ג'. עדינה מרגוליס יצרה אז עבור הלהקה מחול חדש משלה, "עלי באר". היה ברור שזו להקה של "חובבים" ושלא אקבל כל שכר עבור עבודתי, אבל זה לא היה בעל חשיבות עבורי. תחילה לא מצא חן בעיני הדבר, כשפרד השתמש במלה "חובבים", כי שייכתי כינוי זה למשהו נחות, המוריד את המחול לדרגת תחביב. אבל בחזרות נוכחתי עד מהרה, שההתלהבות והרצינות, ועצם איכות המחול לא נפלו מאלה שהכרתי בלהקות המקצועניות. רק הסיבות, שהניעו את הרקדנים להשתתף, והתוצאות היו שונות: הפרט המשתתף מצא את ביטויו האישי בתוך הקבוצה, וזה היה משהו ייחודי.

חלק מהמשתתפים היו מתלמידיו הקבועים של החוג, שנפגש בערבי יום ד'. רובם היו תלמידי בתי־ספר תיכוניים, שהתבגרו ממש תוך שיעורי הריקוד שבהדרכת פרד ברק, שעה שאחרים היו תלמידי הקורסים למחול מודרני שהתקיימו ב"Y". הכל התנהל בצורה מסודרת ומעשית. החזרות החלו בזמן ונסתיימו בדיוק לפי לוח־הזמנים. זמן לא בוזבז. פרד היה תמיד מוכן היטב לקראת החזרה, ומילא כל פגישה בשלל מיומנות מקצועית, יסודות כוריאוגראפיים והבטים טכניים־תנועתיים, ומעל לכל באנושיות חמה - כל המרכיבים ההכרחיים להתפתחותו של רקדן.

בשעת החזרות על הבימה לקראת המופעים היה פרד יושב במרכז האולם, אוזניות לראשו, ומדבר בצורה שקטה ולאקונית, מקצועית, עם מעצב־התאורה השמנמן של תיאטרון ה"Y", גארי האריס, דרך המיקרופון. נראה היה שהם מבינים היטב זה את זה. לא היו שום "סצינות" נרגשות משקרב ערב המופע. פרד היה שקט, מרוכז ודרש מאיתנו את מלוא הביטוי הבימתי. "חזרת־התלבושות היא עבורכם, לא למען התלבושות," נהג לומר.

הצטערתי לעזוב את ניו־יורק ואת ה"Y", אבל הייתי מאושרת להנשא לבעלי ולעלות לארץ בשנת 1972. ידעתי, שפרד נהג להביא בכל קיץ קבוצה של נוער אמריקני לישראל, כדי ללמוד מחולות־עם ועדות. הוא הזמין אותי לבוא להשתתף בשיעורים עם יוצרי מחולות־עם ישראליים כגון מושיקו, יעקב לוי ורבקה שטורמן שאירגן ובשנה הבאה הזמין אותי לתת מספר שיעורים לקבוצת הנוער שהביא איתו לישראל. הוא היה תמיד מעשי מאוד. הוא שילם לי ביד רחבה (בקנה־מידה ישראלי) ושילם תמיד מיד, עם גמר השיעור, כפי שהיה נהוג פעם בתיאטרון, כשהשחקנים היו מקבלים את שכרם עם תום המופע.

יום אחד בשנת 1974 הזמין אותי פרד ל"אייס־קפה" באחד מבתי־הקפה שבטיילת, מול חוף הים. הוא סיפר לי, שהחליט לצאת לגמלאות ולהתיישב בתל־אביב. לשם כך קנה לעצמו דירה סמוך לירקון, רחובות מעטים בלבד מהדירה בה התגוררתי עם בעלי, יורם.

משנעשינו שכנים, השתנו היחסים בינינו. התראינו לעיתים קרובות ולא רק בשעת שיעורי־מחול. יורם לקח אותו לחלונו, כדי לסדר את רישוי המכונית שפרד קנה לעצמו. עזרנו לו לסבל את החבילות עם ספריו ותקליטיו האהובים, שהחלו להגיע בדואר לתל־אביב. בטלפון היה מבקש לדבר עם "בעל־הבית", כשהיה זקוק ליורם, שיבוא לדירתו עם

המקדחה החשמלית. יורם ופרד נהגו להתבדח ביידיש, והוא אהב לבשל ולהזמין אותנו לסעודה: תבשילי בשר נהדרים, מרק עוף וסאלאט ריחני.

במיוחד אהב את חוף הים של קיסריה. בימי הקיץ נהג לבלות בשפת הים שם ומשתתקיימו באמפיתיאטרון הרומאי העתיק מופעי הפסטיבאל הישראלי, היה מבקר בהם לעיתים קרובות.

נהגנו לערוך פיקניקים על חולות קיסריה. פעם, בדרכנו חזרה לעיר, טעה יורם בדרך ואיכשהו הגענו לאיזור בלתי מוכר לנו של וילות.

"איפה אנחנו?" שאלתי.
"אין יענעוולט!" צחק פרד.
"מה זה 'יענעוולט'?"
"שום־מקום, ביידיש!" ענה פרד.

בערבי שבת נהגנו להתאסף בשעות אחרי הצהריים אצל גורית קדמן, לקפה ועוגות. גורית, מחלוצות מחול־העם הישראלי, עלתה לארץ עם בעלה, המומחה למטבעות ועם שולמית, והתישבה בתל־אביב עוד בשנת 1920. פרד הכיר אותה ואת משפחתה בביקורו הראשון בארץ, בשנת 1949. אני הכרתי את בית קדמן בשנת 1972.

גינת ביתם של הקדמנים היתה המקום בו חגגנו מאורעות רבים. את בואו של פרד להתישב בארץ; את סיום מלחמת יום־כיפור בשנת 1973; את הולדת בני הבכור, שי.

באחד מימי מלחמת יום־כיפור הקודרים ליוויתי את פרד לדירתו שלחופי הירקון. במשך שבועות שלמים כמעט ולא הגיע דואר מחוץ־לארץ. ברחובות נראו רק גברים מעטים, כאלה שהיו צעירים מדי או זקנים מדי מכדי להתגייס. רק מעטים מאזרחי החוץ נותרו בארץ בימי המלחמה. פרד היה נרגש מכך, שכוריאוגראפית יהודיה, אורחת מארה"ב, שבאה לעבוד עם להקת בת־שבע, עזבה מבלי לסיים את חזרותיה, עם פרוץ המלחמה. פרד סבר, שהמורל של הלהקה נפגע מעזיבתה של האמנית האורחת.

"יש חשיבות לשייכות," אמר פרד. לגבי פרד להקת מחול היתה בבחינת יחידה חברתית, ממש כמו העם היהודי כולו.

בביתה של גורית חגגנו את הולדת בני הבכור. היא מזגה לכולנו ליקר שזיפים לכבוד המאורע, והתברר שה־25 בינואר הוא גם יום הולדתו של פרד. מהרגע הראשון נוצרו יחסים מיוחדים בין פרד ושי שלי. אי אפשר היה כלל לשער, שלפרד מעולם לא היו ילדים משלו. הוא היה מסוגל להרגיע את התינוק ואהב לשעשע אותו ולהאכיל אותו בכפית.

מקץ חמש שנים, שעה שהחלטנו, בעלי ואני, לשוב לאמריקה, פרד לא שאל שאלות מטרידות. הוא אמר בפשטות: "נחוץ שיהיה באמתחתך רפרטואר של מחולות ישראליים, שתוכלי ללמד באמריקה." הוא טיפס מדי בוקר לדירתנו שבקומה הרביעית, עד שלימד אותי עשרה ריקודים, ועזר לי לרשום כל אחד מהם בפנקסי. ללמוד מחול כדי ללמדו הוא דבר שונה מאוד מלללמוד את המחול כדי לבצעו. היתה לו שיטת־רישום משלו. בראש העמוד היה כותב באותיות גדולות את שם המחול, את צורתו ציין באות מסויימת, אחר־כך בא רישום הקצבים ולפעמים היה רושם גם את המנגינה, את הליווי המוסיקלי וכמו כן מי האיש שיצר את המחול ובאילו נסיבות נוצר. הוא שבחר בריקודים למעני וכל אחד מהם היה אחד המחולות ה"קלאסיים" מאוצר מחול־העם הישראלי.

בני שי היה יושב לו מתחת לשולחן, כשפרד לימד אותי, ומלווה את התנועה בהמהום או שירה בקולו הנאה. לפעמים היה מושיב את התינוק על ברכיו, ובעדינות מקיש את המקצבים, כשהוא אוחז בעדינות באצבעותיו הזעירות.

כשהוא לימדני את "דודי לי" של רבקה שטורמן - המחול האהוב על פרד יותר מכל - הוא קם, ומבלי להשען על מקל ההליכה שלו, אחז בידי והחל לרקוד איתי. רקדנו יחד וזה היה מהנה ביותר. שלא כפי שהיה כשהיינו הולכים יחד ברחוב, הוא לא צלע. רקדתי עם פרטנר מנוסה ורקדן מקצועי.

לפעמים היינו נפגשים בגן הציבורי שלחופי הירקון, מול דירתו. הוא היה מקבל קטעי־עיתונות על מופעי־מחול של בני־יורק ותמיד התחלק בהם איתי. הוא הראה לי את "הורה", כתב־העת המוקדש לכל הבטי המחול הישראלי, שהיה מפרסם בני־יורק שלוש פעמים בשנה. "האנגלית שלי נשמעת כל כך גרמנית!" היה מתלונן. היה עלי לתקן

לפעמים מאמרים שכתב. הוא סיפר לי על ספרו החדש, שעסק בחיבורו: "מחול־העם היהודי" (Machol Ha Am: Dance of the Jewish People), שיצא לאור בשנת 1978. יכולתי לעקוב אחרי עבודתו. התיק עם התצלומים שאסף הלך ותפח. התרגשתי, כשהראה לי תצלום מהופעותיו של ברוך אגדתי בראשית שנות ה־20. והוא שכנע את שרה לוי־תנאי וגורית קדמן להשאיל לו צילומים מאוספיהן הפרטיים.

במשך הקיץ חלתה המורה הראשונה שלו, גרטרוד קראוס, שבזכותה זכה להתוודע אל חוויות הבימה 45 שנים קודם לכן בוינה. כל יום נהג לנסוע לבית־החולים בו היתה גרטרוד מאושפזת. לעיתים קרובות הצטרפתי אליו עם בני ש. הוא היה מבלה עם הילד בגינת בית־החולים ואחר־כך מתחלף איתי ועולה לבקר את גרטרוד. הוא היה מביא לה את השבועון הגרמני המצולם "שטרן" וטבלאות שוקולד מריר, שאהבה. הוא היה מסור לה מאוד.

יום אחד, בגינה שמול ביתו, אמר לי: "קשה לי להרדם ואני מרגיש חלש. אחד מתלמידי בעבר הוא רופא בבית־החולים רמב"ם בחיפה, והוא סידר לי שם בדיקה יסודית." ידעתי מתי תתקיים הבדיקה, אם כי לא הזכיר זאת עוד. הייתי מודאגת, כשביום הבדיקה לא התקשר אחרי שחזר מחיפה. לבסוף ענה לטלפון. "אינני יכול לדבר עכשיו," אמר ופרץ בבכי. הוא אילץ את עצמו להרגע ואז אמר, שהרופאים מצאו שיש לו סרטן שאינו ניתן לריפוי.

פרד החליט לשוב לניו־יורק. הוא בא להפרד מאיתנו וישב, שלא כדרכו, מאובן בראש השולחן. "ג'ודי," שאל, "האם היית מוכנה לכתוב את תולדות חיי? הרי גם את עומדת לשוב לאמריקה, והיינו יכולים לשוחח בטלפון, ותוכלי לבוא לבקר בניו־יורק או שאני אגיע למיניאפוליס. היית יכולה לשוחח עם תלמידי לשעבר ועם עמיתי. והרי את כבר מכירה את כל ידידי בישראל. היית רוצה לעשות זאת?"

לפתע התברר לי, שלמעשה איני יודעת על אודותיו דבר. היכן משפחתו? האם נספתה כולה בשואה? מתי הגיע לניו־יורק? האם הופיע באמריקה, כשם שעשה בוינה? זה משונה, שידעתי כה מעט על אדם כל כך קרוב אלי.

"אראה לך את כל התוכניות, הספרים, המכתבים שלי. כי אני מחשיב את עצמי לאסוף חומר על מחול יהודי יותר מכל דבר אחר."

וכך החלה החקירה שלי על חייו וסיפור "למנצח על המחולות", סיפור חייו של אמן מחול יהודי, קרם עור וגידים.

פרק שני:
וינה

בוינה של שנת 1911, יעקב והנרייטה (בלאו) ברגר גרו ברחוב יארטן (Jartenstrasse) מספר 14, ברובע השני המשתרע בין נהר הדנובה לתעלה, שהיה מרכז מסחרי ראשי וכן הרובע היהודי. יעקב ברגר המשיך להפעיל את המחלבה הקטנה שהוריו יסדו ממש בלב העיר. הוא היה אדם שאפתן, חם־מזג ואף אלים לעיתים. הוא התהדר בלבושו והיה גאה במיוחד, כשנולד ילדו השני, בן זכר. פרידריך ברגר נולד ב־25 בינואר, 1911.

במשך שנות מלחמת העולם הראשונה, כשרוב העיר רעבה ללחם, איכרים נהגו להביא למשפחת ברגר לחם, ביצים וירקות תמורת הזבל מהדיר והרפת ששימש לזיבול שדותיהם. החנות הקטנה שהיתה צמודה למחלבה שרתה את השכונה, ותלמידים חילקו את החלב מוקדם בבוקר. מספר פועלים עזרו בטיפול בשלושים הפרות שברפת ובחמישים ושניים הסוסים שבאורווה.

"אני זוכר שהעיזים, היונים והחתולים שלנו היו מתאספים מתחת לעץ הענק שבחצר. אהבתי להאכיל את החתולים. בערבים הייתי יוצא, מגלגל מיכל חלב ריק והרעש היה מקפיץ חמישה או שישה חתולים מגג האסם. העיזים היו זוכות לתשומת לב מיוחדת ממני. עז אחת אהבתי במיוחד. היה זה יום נורא, כשהצצתי מהמרפסת וראיתי כיצד שוחטים אותה.

"המקום המיוחד שלי לחלום בו בהקיץ היה מרתף ביתנו. הייתי יורד לשם לאור נר ומשחק לבדי מאחורי החביות והשקתות העצומות ששימשו לכביסה. הכביסה היתה אירוע חשוב, שנמשך שלושה ימים, שעה שנשאבו מים מהמשאבה שבחצר והורתחו בשקתות העניקות שבמרתף. כשהכל כובס ונרחץ, נתלו הכבסים לייבוש בעליית הגג. חוץ מהמרתף, אהבתי לשחק בין הבגדים שם. מעבר לחוטי הכביסה אוחסנו בחביות גדולות כל הכלים המיוחדים לפסח. גם חביות אלו שימשו כאביזרים נפלאים לסיפורי."

פריץ היה בן חמש כשפרנץ יוזף, קיסר האימפריה ההפסבורגית, נפטר. ממרפסת כל הבתים נתלו דגלי־אבל שחורים. סיום מלחמת העולם הראשונה בישר שינוי מהותי של מפת אירופה, ושושלת ההפסבורגים, אשר שלטה במשך 700 שנה, נכחדה אפילו מאוסטריה לאחר שהאימפריה התפוררה.

השינוי היחיד שהבחין בו פריץ היה, שמשפחתו שיכנה דיירים בביתם, משפחת פליטים שדיברו יידיש בלבד. "היה להם ילד קטן, בן גילי. למרות שלא יכולנו לשוחח, שיחקנו יחד באורוות ובאסם. לבושו היה שונה משלי, ויום אחד הוא הביע משאלה להיות דומה לי יותר, ללא הפיאות המסורתיות שלו. ובכן, נטלתי מספריים מהבית וגזזתי אחת מפיאותיו. הוא נבהל ורץ אל אמו. זו היתה הפעם היחידה בחיי, שהמכות שספגתי מאבי היו מוצדקות.

"זאת היתה המשפחה הראשונה שהכרתי שהיגרה לאמריקה. הם יצאו רק עם מעט המטלטלים שעל גבם. אני זוכר שחשבתי, כמה ענייה ועצובה נראתה האם. לא ידעתי אז כמה בת־מזל היתה לעזוב בזמן ההוא. מי יכול היה לחלום אז על מה שעתיד לקרות לכולנו."

במשפחת ברגר דיברו גרמנית בלבד. למרות פרוותיהם והאסם שבחצר, הם היו תושביה של עיר קוסמופוליטית. כמו שאר שכניהם היהודיים, הם זילזלו בזרים שמחוץ

12

לוינה, ואף ביהודים שמחוץ לעיר. יהודים דוברי־יידיש החלו זורמים בהמוניהם לוינה עם תום מלחמת העולם הראשונה, בהמלטם לא רק מתוצאותיה המרות של המלחמה אלא גם מהפוגרומים ברוסיה.

"כשהייתי בן 13 בערך, ידיד מבית־הספר לקח אותי לפגישה של קבוצת צעירים ציוניים בתנועת־הנוער BLAU-WEISS ("כחול־לבן"). הוקסמתי מעקרונות השיתוף שהיו נהוגים בין הצעירים. כשיצאנו לטיול של יום ראשון, כל אחד מאיתנו הביא איתו צידה. אחדים בינינו היו עניים מאוד ובאו לטיול כמעט ללא כל מזון. ערמנו את כל האוכל לתל גדול והתחלקנו שווה בשווה. להתחלק כך נראה בעיני נהדר! הייתי מאושר, וזו היתה החוויה הראשונה, שסיפרתי לאמי, משחזרתי הביתה. היא, לעומת זאת, נתקפה בהלה. מה אם אכלתי במקרה טריפה?! לעולם לא הורשיתי עוד להשתתף בפעולות."

בית ברגר היה אדיש לתסיסה הציונית שהורגשה אז בחוגים היהודיים של וינה. הרצל וחלומותיו על חברה יהודית חופשית בארץ־ישראל לא דיברו אליהם. כל אותם ערכים שייעשו כה חשובים ובעלי משמעות לפריץ מאוחר יותר – התייחסות רגישה לילדים, ציונות ואמנות – היו חסרי ערך בעיני הברגרים.

"אבי נהג ללכת לבית־כנסת אורתודוקסי ("שיל" בניב המקומי). כבן מסור ישבתי לצידו מדי שבת במשך התפילות, שנמשכו כמעט יום תמים. אמא, לעומתי, גדלה בבית־כנסת רפורמי־קונסרבטיבי. גם כאשה נשואה המשיכה להתפלל שם. לא שהיתה בלתי תלויה באבי, אך בזכות הוריה המיוחסים הוא הסכים שתמשיך להתפלל שם. רק לעיתים הורשיתי לאסוף אותה ואת אחותה משם.

"הדרת המקום הדהימה אותי. הנשים ישבו בעזרת־הנשים המוגבהת, ללא מסכים המפרידים את הנשים מהגברים, כמנהג בית־הכנסת של אבי. הרב, רבה הראשי של וינה, היה גבר גבה־קומה ואישיות כריזמטית. אני זוכר את המקהלה המזמרת, המלווה את החזן. רזה היה מאוד שונה מהתוהו ובוהו של קולות הגברים הרעשניים, המתפללים כל אחד בפני עצמו, שבבית־הכנסת של אבי."

אביו של פריץ התמיד בניהול עסקיו בצורה כושלת. היו לו תחביבים ראוותניים. הוא החזיק בסוסים יקרים והתלבש בטרזנות. כדי לשמור על תדמית המשפחה ולמרות מחאות האם, הוא הכריח את ילדיו לרכוב עימו במרכבתו המפוארת, הרתומה לסוס אציל.

"הוא אכל כל כך הרבה, שלא יכול להתכופף ולשרוך את נעליו. אחותי ואני הצטרכנו לבצע משימה זו עבורו. שלוש או ארבע פעמים ביום היה שולח אותי למסבאה, כדי להביא לו בירה מהחבית.

"לעיתים קרובות יותר ויותר באו הנשים אל ביתנו, ואני איבדתי את כל הדרת הכבוד כלפי אבי. במשך ימים שלמים היה מסתגר בחדרו ולא מדבר אפילו עם אמי. משהתחלנו לאבד את כל כספנו, נאלצתי לעזור. אחותי החלה לעבוד בגיל 15. לא היה מספיק כסף בבית אפילו עבור שמלותיה. אני מניח שזה היה בשנת 1924.

"משפחתי היתה מאוד גאה, בהתקרב מועד בר־המצווה שלי. היא ציפתה ממני לגדולות. תהליך לימוד השפה העברית ושינון הדרשה שהיה עלי לשאת היה היה מעינויי הגדול עבורי. הייתי מפוחד לגמרי ממשהיגע תורי לעמוד על הבמה בפני כל הציבור כדי לקרוא מהתורה. היה עלי להתחיל בדקלום נאום שלמדתי. כשהגעתי למלה 'סבתי', במטרה לכבדה, הפסקתי והתיישבתי לפתע. פשוט, שכחתי את כל שהיה עלי לומר, ונמלטתי אל ספסל משפחתי. התחלתי להתייפח. אנשים חשבו, שבבכיתי כי סבתי היתה אז חולה במצב אנוש.

"בהדרגה איבדנו את כל רכושנו, מלבד כמה סוסים. אחותי, הבכירה ממני בארבע שנים, נאלצה לצאת לעבוד בבית־חרושת כדי לעזור בכיסוי הוצאות מחייתנו. הנושים לקחו מאיתנו את ביתנו ואת המחלבה." אמו של פריץ שמרה את הבית נקי תמיד, ונהגה לנעול את חדר־המגורים הראשי כדי לשמרו מסודר בתכלית השלמות, עבור אורחים. בשמלותיה הארוכות והמסוגננות, תמיד נראתה כלילדי מושלמת. שלא כמו נשים אורתודוקסיות אחרות, לא נהגה לחבוש פיאה נוכרית, אלא סידרה את שערה הארוך לפי האופנה הוינאית.

"אבי פתח עסק של העברת מטלטלין עם מעט הסוסים שנותרו לנו. בקיץ נהגנו להסיע אנשים אל בתי־הקיץ שלהם, או אל המגורים השכורים בסמוך למעיינות המרפא. היתה לנו עגלה גדולה רתומה לסוסים. ובסתיו היינו מחזירים את הנופשים לבתיהם. זה היה בשבילי תענוג גדול, כל אותן נסיעות הלוך ושוב. בכל מסע בן יום שכזה ישבתי על

13

יד הרכב. לפעמים הוא היה נרדם ומרשה לי להחזיק במושכות בדרכנו הביתה. הסוסים אמנם היו מוצאים את דרכם בעצמם, אך לי היתה ההרגשה שאני עושה דבר מאוד חשוב.

"מסעות תמיד קסמו לי. בראותי רכבות חולפות, הייתי ממציא עבורן יעדים מסתוריים ביותר. הדבר האהוב עלי ביותר היה מסעות עם דודתי, אחותה חשוכת הילדים של אימי, שהיה לה בית נפלא באתר המעיינות באדן (Baden). הייתי מבלה את הקיץ שם.

"החיים עם דודתי היו כה שונים. היא היתה מקשיבה לי, בספרי לה סיפורים או בהראותי לה את אוסף הבולים שלי, וייחד טיילנו כל ערב. היא היתה האדם היחיד הקרוב לי, האדם הקרוב אלי ביותר. כמה חמה ומבינה היתה.

"בעיר הנופש היה תיאטרון קייצי, שהעלה את כל האופרטות המפורסמות והמחזות הקלים. כמלווה הקטן של דודתי ראיתי את כולם, ועולם חדש נפתח בפני, עולם המרתק אותי עד היום ממש כמו אז. בחוזרי לויינה, חיפשתי דרכים כדי שאוכל להמשיך וללכת לתיאטרון.

"לפעמים היינו הולכים במאורגן מטעם בית-הספר לאופרה או לתיאטרון, ואני הייתי אז ברקיע השביעי. כמובן שרציתי לראות מקרוב את השחקנים והשחקניות, שהפיחו חיים במחזות, והתחלתי לצפות להם בפתח כניסת האמנים. כך התוודעתי אל קבוצת אנשים צעירים שתמיד חיכתה שם.

"היה זה חוג קטן של חברים ללא כל קשר אל משפחתי, השכונה שלי, בית-ספרי או העובדה, שאני יהודי. בקבוצה קטנה זו, שציפתה לבוא האמנים, דיברנו באותה שפה. חלקנו בינינו משהו עמוק ויפה - התקשורת שבאמנויות. כתוצאה מכך קשרינו האישיים היו גם הם מיוחדים.

"מאחר שכולם ליקטו חתימות, גם אני הפכתי לאספן אוטוגראפים. ראיתי כיצד המעריצים מחכים ליד כניסת-האמנים עם אלבום החתימות, תוכניות ופרחים, וכך גם אני התחלתי להביא זרים כדי להעניק אותם לאמנים הנערצים. אני מניח שהגזמתי ברגשותי העזים, אך התיאטרון הביא אותי אל הדבר הטוב ביותר שידעתי אז - אפילו לקבוצת חברים ואחר-כך למועדון, שבו ניסיתי לראשונה את כוחי במשחק.

"הייתי חלק ממועדון מעריציה של השחקנית אלזה וולגמות (Else Wohlgemuth). היא היתה מושא תאוותי במשך כשנתיים. אני זוכר שניצלנו כל הזדמנות להעריצה ויום ההולדת של 'האלוהית' היה תאריך מיוחד עבורנו. ברשותי היו שישים צילומים שלה, כל אחד ואחד חתום על ידה. בחייה הפרטיים היא היתה נשואה לרוזן והתגוררה בצידו השני של הפארק, הסמוך לתיאטרון. פעם אחת הצלחתי לפתוח למענה את דלת מרכבתה, ואחר-כך רצתי דרך הפארק והגעתי לפניה לפתח ביתה. כך הצלחתי לפתוח את דלת מרכבתה בפעם השנייה, והייתי מאושר בתכלית.

"כל זה נראה כעולם דימיוני, עולם התיאטרון, ואפילו לא חלמתי, שאוכל פעם בעצמי להיות חלק ממנו.

"הלימודים בבית-הספר נעשו לי קשים ביותר. אף אחד לא הקשיב אלי, שם או בבית. הפסקתי לנסות אפילו להכין את שיעורי-הבית וויתרתי על הכל - חוץ מהרגעים הגנובים על-יד דלת הבמה של התיאטרון. קיבלתי ציונים איומים, אך לא מצאתי כל דרך לשפר את הישגי בלימודים. לא יכולתי ללמוד דבר מספרים. בסוף סולקתי מבית-הספר.

"אבי היה צורח עלי ולבסוף מכה אותי. אני זוכר כיצד צרח: 'יותר לא תוכל לבזבז את זמנך בבית! אתה בן ארבע-עשרה וחצי, והגיע הזמן שתתחיל לעבוד. אני אמצא לך עבודה אצל פרוון או כשוליה של צורף, באיזה מקום שלא תצטרך לעבוד בשבתות.' משלא הייתי מגיב, הוא היה נוטל חזון ומכה אותי עד שהמקל היה נשבר."

באביב, כשפרח הלילך, ב-16 באפריל 1926, החל פריץ בחניכותו אצל צורף-הזהב הוכבאום. "חובותי כללו את ניקוי הסדנה, רחיצת החלונות, הכנת חומרי-הגלם הנחוצים והסקת האש בתנור עב-הכרס במשך החורף. כשאלה היה עלי לעבוד בפרך כעבדו הנרצע של הצורף, זכיתי לשבת ליד שולחן העבודה על ספסל נמוך, והייתי מתיך, משייף ומבריק את המתכות לפני מגע ידו של האמן."

בשנתו הראשונה של פריץ כשוליה, שמונים וחמישה פועלים נורו למוות בהפגנת רחוב בויינה. שביתה כללית שפרצה בעיר נשברה רק בעזרת כוחות הצבא.

במשך חמש שנים תמימות היה פריץ מטפס את חמש הקומות המובילות לסדנה

14

מספר פעמים ביום. הצורף דיבר אליו רק לעיתים נדירות, ורק כשהיה זקוק למשהו. פריץ השתעמם מאוד ושנא את העבודה. מאחר שלא הראה בה כל עניין, מעולם לא זכה לעבוד עם המתכות היקרות, למרות שהיה עליו ללמוד את המקצוע. במשך כל השנים של חניכותו יצר פריץ רק טבעת אחת (וגם זאת בעזרת הצורף), כדי שיוכל לעמוד בבחינת-הגמר.

"הייתי מתחיל לעבוד בשבע בבוקר. מאחר שמעבידי היה קמצן גדול, הוא היה קוצב לי מכסה שבועית של עצי-ההסקה. לא היה איכפת לו אם הכמות תספיק לכל השבוע. הוא רק דרש שהמקום יהיה מחומם בהגיעו לעבודה בשמונה. הדרך היחידה להמלט משם היתה למלא שליחויות. משום שמעולם לא ניתנו לי דמי-נסיעה בחשמלית, היה עלי ללכת מלקוח ללקוח ברגל. הצורף לא ידע כלל כמה זמן דרוש לכך, ואני שילבתי את השליחויות עם טיולים לכניסות-האמנים באיזור התיאטראות."

פריץ הצעיר היה צועד לאורך ה-Ring, הרחוב הראשי המקיף ומפריד את העיר הפנימית, העתיקה, מהאיזורים החיצוניים של וינה. שדרה זו נבנתה במקום שהיתה בעבר חומת העיר העתיקה, והשדרה היתה מוקפת בבניינים ציבוריים ובתים פרטיים מפוארים.(1) ה-Ring נעשה למוקד הסמלי של התרבות הליברלית השלטת – היו בה בתי-ספר לחינוך העילית, בניני הממשלה, המוזיאונים והתיאטראות שנועדו להביא את התרבות הנשגבה לכל.(2)

לאחר שהיה פריץ עובר על פני הארמון הקיסרי, האופרה וה-Burgtheater, היה מגיע לבנין פשוט יותר, המכיל שלושה אולמות קונצרטים. כאן ניגנו התזמורות הגדולות ולעיתים הופיעו שם גם סולני המחול הדגולים. אלבום-החתימות של פריץ היה תמיד איתו, גם כשהיה סוחב על שכמו שקי פחם ועץ להסקה, או את עיתון הבוקר.

גזירי-העיתונים ותמונות השחקנים והשחקניות שבאלבום הודבקו בקפידה לדפיו. כך שפריץ יוכל לזהות את הדמויות המפורסמות, אם יתמזל מזלו וייתקל בהם ברחוב. "פעם אחת ראיתי את אנה פאבלובה עוברת במרכבת סוסים. היא היתה כה זעירה וחיוורת, והופתעתי למראה פניה העצובים. המרכבה עצרה והיא ירדה כדי להתבונן בחלון-הראווה של חנות עתיקות. מיהרתי אליה וכך השגתי את חתימתה.

"בטיול בר-מזל אחר ראיתי את הרקדנית אידה רובינשטיין, שהופיעה בוינה למחול מאת מוריס ראוול, עוזבת את בית-האופרה לאחר חזרה, בליווית המלחין. כמובן שהשגתי את חתימות שניהם."

לעיתים היה פריץ מתגנב לחזרות. "אני זוכר שראיתי את האליל שלי, אלזה וולגמות, אולי חמישים פעם על במת הבורגתיאטר ב"מרי, מלכת הסקוטים" מאת פרידריך שילר. תמיד אפשר היה לגלות מתי מתנהלות החזרות ומי ישתתף בהן. הייתי הולך רק לחזרות שלה. הקבוצה שלנו, בפתח כניסת-האמנים, נהגה להחליף מידע ולרגל על האמנים. כל פרט קטן בחייהם היה בעל חשיבות לגבינו. לפעמים היינו אפילו משחדים את הנהגים שלהם בברנדי, יין או סיגריות, שיספרו לנו היכן היו השחקניות האהובות עלינו ועם מי סעדו."

הבורגתיאטר, שהיה כה אהוב על פריץ, היה מקום מיוחד במינו. אכסדרת-הכניסה ושני גרמי-המדרגות שבה היו מפוארים. האחד נועד במקור לשרת את אנשי החצר ההפס-בורגית והשני יועד ליתר הקהל. המדרגות עוצבו בשיש עם עיטורי עץ, ובנרשות הבדולח מעל נגהו אור-יקרות על פסליהם של שחקנים מפורסמים. המדרגות המפוארות הובילו לאולם מתקל עם מרפסת, שעליה טיילו הצופים במשך ההפסקות בבגדיהם ההדורים. ציוריו של Gustav Klimt(3) קישטו את התיקרות והקירות. מי יכל לחלום אז, שהצעיר המתגנב ומחכה על-יד דלת הבמה, יופיע כאן בערב הבכורה שלו?

ככל שפריץ המשיך לעבוד רכון על שולחן עבודתו של הצורף, כן נעשה עגול-כתפיים יותר ויותר. יציבתו הדאיגה את אמו והרופא, שאליו היא שלחה אותו, המליץ על התעמלות או שיעורי ריתמיקה כתרופה.

"אחותי, שבדרך כלל לא היה לה הרבה מה לומר לי, שמעה על בית-ספר לריתמיקה, המנוהל על-ידי רקדנית בשם גרטרוד קראוס. בטיולי בעיר התחלתי להבחין בשמה של קראוס על לוחות המודעות." סקרנותו של פריץ התעוררה והוא הלך לצפות בהופעה של קראוס (יחד עם הפנטומימאית Cilly Wang(4)) באחד הפארקים בעיר.

"מחולות הסולו, בעלי האיכות יוצאת הדופן, הרשימו אותי מאוד. במשך ההפסקה

15

נכנסתי אל מאחורי הקלעים, כפי שהייתי רגיל, כדי לספוג את האווירה ואולי אף לראות את קראוס מקרוב. במקומה פגשתי את אמה, שחקרה אותי לרצוני. מבלי לחשוב הרבה השבתי, שאני רוצה ללמוד עם קראוס. האם נתנה לי את כתובת הסטודיו והורתה לי לבוא ביום שבת הקרוב, אחר הצהריים.

"למרות שמירת-השבת הקפדנית במשפחתי (אסור היה לטייל או לבצע כל פעילות חרף מתפילה עד צאת השבת), הלכתי לשם בשבת שלאחר ההופעה. ראיתי את קראוס לבושה באיזו גלימה מזרחית עומדת בראש מעלה המדרגות הלוליינית, שהוביל לסטודיו. היא נראתה כרוח שהועלתה באוב. מאובן מפחד, עמדתי שם בשתיקה והבטתי למעלה. בדרך כלל הייתי כבד לשון, אבל אז הרגשתי גרוע מתמיד. למרות זאת הזמינה אותי גרטרוד להשתתף בשיעוריה.

"הלכתי לרקוד שם מדי שבת אחר הצהריים. פעם אחת, אולי אחרי חצי שנה של שיעורים, אמרה גרטרוד לפתע: 'תלמידים, הסתכלו אחורה. התבוננו בפריץ ובצעו את התרגיל בדיוק כמוהו, כי הוא עושה זאת בדיוק כפי שהתכוונתי!' זו היתה הפעם הראשונה בחיי, שזכיתי לשבח כלשהו! היא לא ידעה כלל מה זה עשה לי. דבריה היו העידוד הגדול ביותר שקיבלתי עד אז. למעשה, כפי שלמדתי אחר-כך כמורה, לעולם אינך יודע כיצד ישפיעו דבריך על התלמידים. גרטרוד הצליחה לגעת בנפשי!"

בשיחות עם ברק במשך שלוש שנות חייו האחרונות הוא חזר פעמים רבות על תיאור שיעוריו הראשונים עם קראוס. "אני חושב, שמה שהרשים אותי בשיעוריה היתה דווקא המוסיקה. לא נחשפתי הרבה למוסיקה עד אז. אני זוכר שבגיל חמש בערך אמי לקחה אותי ל'כרמן' ב'אופרה העממית', והסבירה לי שמישהו ייהרג במערכה האחרונה. הייתי דרוך כל הזמן למותו הצפוי, ולכן לא זכרתי כלום מהמוסיקה. בבית בוודאי שלא שמעתי מוסיקה. גרטרוד נהגה להדגים את התנועות לפני התלמידים ואז היתה חופזת אל הפסנתר ומלווה בעצמה את כל התרגילים והאימפרוביזציות. במשך שלוש או ארבע השעות של השיעור היא סיפקה את כל הליווי, והתאימה את היצירות המוסיקליות לרעיונות התנועה. היא היתה בתחילה פסנתרנית ולפני שנעשתה לרקדנית הופיעה כפסנתרנית-סולנית ברסיטלים. היצירות שבחרה לנגן וחוש הקצב שלה חשפו בי משהו בזמן שרקדתי. המוסיקה הקלאסית נגעה ללבי, ונפשי נסקה אל על עם הצלילים.

"המחול המודרני היה אז חדש בתכלית ומהפכני בגישתו, בפילוסופיה ובטכניקה שלו. גישתה של קראוס היתה שונה מזו שהיתה נהוגה אז בבתי-הספר של הרקדניות הוינאיות האחרות, שניסו לעשות מתלמידיהן העתקים מדוייקים של סגנונן המסויים. גרטרוד עודדה אותנו ליצור בעצמנו מחולות, ולהיות רגישים לצורה בד בבד עם השאיפה לחשוף את רגשותינו. המגמה היתה להביע את עצמך, והריקוד יתבע את כל כולך."

תלמידים אחרים של קראוס תיארו לא אחת את דרכה המיוחדת לעודד ביטוי כוריאוגראפי אישי. מיה סלאבנסקה (Mia Slavenska), שהיתה אחר-כך בלארינה מפורסמת, ציינה בראיון איתה ב"Dance Magazine" (5) שהיתה גם תלמידתן של מורות לבאלט בפאריס, כגון אגורובה (Egorova), פראוברז'ינסקה (Preobrajenska) וקשסינסקאיה (Kschessinskaya) וגרטרוד קראוס בינהן: "אצל קראוס גיליתי אפשרויות בלתי נידלות להבעה וחופש יצירה במחול... היא עודדה את ניסיונותי הראשונים בכוריאוגראפיה." בזמן ההוא רקדו רוב הרקדניות הוינאיות בסגנונן הלירי של האחיות Wiesenthal או באורח הקומי הגרוטסקי של Cilly Wang או Gertrud Bodenwieser. קראוס הציעה משהו שונה לגמרי.

פריץ ניסה להגדיר ייחוד זה. "התרגשתי משילוב המרכיבים הרגשיים והפיסיים בתנועת הגוף שלי. ההתגברות על כוח הכובד והתנועה בחלל היו חוויה מרטיטה, מין פרץ רגשות דרך כל ישותי. רקדנו מיגוון של רעיונות ונושאים, לפעמים על הלילה ובדידותו הלוחשת, לעיתים על נושא תנ"כי או חברתי, נגד המלחמה והרודנות. גרטרוד במיוחד, אך גם כולנו, ראינו בעצמנו אמנים אוניברסאליים, השייכים לעולם כולו והיוצרים למענו. כתלמידים היינו מודעים יותר למורשת האוסטרית של שירים וריקודים עממיים מאשר לרקע הדתי שלנו.

"כמובן, שמעתי אז על הנצחונות שנחלה קראוס בקונגרס המחול הבין-לאומי במינכן בשנה הקודמת (1930)." **פריץ החל ללמוד עם קראוס שנה אחרי-כן, בהיותו בן 20 והיא בת 28.**

16

היא היתה בוגרת האקדמיה הממלכתית הוינאית לאמנויות, במגמה לפסנתר. כדי להרוויח למחייתה, קיבלה על עצמה ללוות בפסנתר את שיעורי המחול המודרני של בודנויזר, שהיתה ראש המחלקה. בודנויזר נהגה לבקש את תלמידיה להראות מדי פעם עבודות, שהכינו בבית, לכיתה. יום אחד הדהימה הפסנתרנית-המלווה, גרטרוד קראוס, את כולם, כשקמה מהפסנתר וביצעה מחול, שחיברה, למרות שמעולם לא למדה מחול ולא היתה תלמידת הכיתה. בשליש הבא נרשמה כסטודנטית אצל בודנויזר.

בצעירותה היתה אתלטית מצטיינת ואף זכתה במספר מדליות, והיא שמרה על כושרה הגופני. אבל לאחר חילוקי דעות עם בודנויזר עזבה גרטרוד את הלימודים והחלה בכוריאוגרפיה עצמאית. בשנת 1926 היא הופיעה בקונצרט הסולו הראשון שלה בוינה, וב-1930 לקחה עימה קבוצת רקדנים לקונגרס הבין-לאומי לריקוד. מנהליהן של להקות באלט וכוריאוגרפים מודרניים מכל רחבי אירופה באו למינכן למשך שבעה ימים, כדי לראות ולהיראות.(6) גם טד שאון (Ted Shawn) מארצות-הברית בא להופיע בקונגרס. יצירתה של מרי ויגמן (Mary Wigman) ''TOTENMAL'' (''גלעד''), היתה אמורה להיות האירוע המרכזי בקונגרס, אך לבסוף הוצגה רק כ''יצירה בתהליך-עבודה''. גרטרוד קראוס זכתה לשבחי הביקורת על יצירתה הקבוצתית ''שירי הגטו''. המבקר Fred Hildebrandt מברלין כתב על ''שירי הגטו'': ''ליבי נמלא חגיגיות, כה יפה היה חלום העצב והבטחון בבורא שלהן.''(7) הריקוד לא התבסס רק על דימיון אישי; היסודות המסורתיים של המחול החסידי הוסיפו לו עומק ומימד אובייקטיבי.

מבקר אחר תיאר את הקונגרס במלים: ''האירוע השאפתני ביותר ואחד הגדולים בתולדות הבאלט והמחול המודרני. בהשתתפות יותר מ-1,400 רקדנים, כולל Rudolf von Laban מגרמניה, גרטרוד קראוס מוינה, Gret Palucca מדרזדן ווארלי קרטינה מבית-ספרו של Dalcroze.''(8)

כשפריץ הצטרף לבית-ספרה של קראוס, הוא ידע שזכתה לשבחים על ''שירי הגטו'' שלה, אך הוא לא התייחס כלל לנושא היהודי של היצירה. לימודיו עם הכוריאוגרפית הנודעת היו מלאי-השראה עבורו, והוא היה מאושר לראות כל כך הרבה ריקוד. אולי יום אחד גם הוא יוכל להופיע על הבמה.

פריץ לא ידע אז שמה שקסם לו בריקוד, היסודות הגופניים והרגשיים כאחד של התנועה, היו בעצם תמצית הריקוד החסידי. זו היתה הגישה היהודית לביטוי במחול, שמאוחר יותר היתה למרכיב מרכזי כל כך בקריירה שלו. פעם אחת, בחוללו תחת כיפת השמים בהופעה יחד עם קראוס, ''משהו קרא לי, שאז עדיין לא יכולתי להסבירו לעצמי. כשרקדתי בחוץ, וראיתי את הכוכבים והשמים, את העצים והצללים, חשתי את שלוות הלילה, והייתי כאילו בעולם שונה. הייתי מאוחד עם היקום, וזו היתה הרגשה מאוד דתית, מרוממת. הרגשתי, שזו בהכרח תמצית המחול.''

הריקוד סיפק לאדם צעיר זה, שמעולם לא היה מסוגל להביע את עצמו, פורקן נלהב ליצרים ודרך נהדרת ליישם את כשרונותיו החבויים. היתה זו הפתעה עבורו לגלות, שהריקוד עזר לו למקד את רגשותיו הדתיים. הוא היה ''חסיד'' מבלי לדעת זאת - החסיד, שאינו זקוק לתיווך מלומד כלשהו בקשריו עם אלוהיו ועם הבריות, החסיד הרוקד באקסטזה, והמצרף בכל מעשיו את הגשמי אל הרוחני.

רבי זלמן, מגדולי החסידות, אמר, שניצוצות האלוהים נפלטים מהקדוש ברוך הוא והאדם הופכם לרוחניים באמצעות התפילה והמחול. ריקוד הוא אחד מהתהליכים המאפשרים הפשטת הגשמיות וגילוי הרוחניות.(9)

''קראוס עודדה אותנו ליצור מחולות חדשים ולהביאם לסטודיו. אני זוכר שאת סוויטת המחולות הראשונה שלי יצרתי עבורי ושתי נשים צעירות. המחול הראשון נקרא 'מרסייז' ('La Marseillaise'), השני היה ריקוד רוסי, שהסתמך על העניין הכללי במהפיכה הסוביטית שרווח אז, והשלישי היה מחול על 'קאפיטליסט'. אני גילמתי את הדמות הראשית של 'המנצל' המעביד את פועליו ונאבק בהם. כמובן שהעובדים ניצחו לבסוף ואני הובסתי, בהתאם לתקינות הדור ההוא.

''החלטנו, ששני הפועלים ילבשו בגד אדום ואני אהיה שחור. מאחר שלא היה לנו כסף, לא היה לי מושג כיצד להשיג את התלבושת. שאלתי בעצתה של אמי. היא כבר ידעה, שאני רוקד ברצינות, אך אסרה עלי לספר על כך לאבי. 'האם אין לנו דגל שחור בעליית-

הגג?' שאלה. כשהקיסר פרנץ יוזף מת ב־1916, כל בית נדרש לתלות דגל שחור מחלונו. ובכן, מצאתי בעליית־הגג את הדגל, מגולגל ועטוף היטב, שהיה מונח שם במשך חמש־ עשרה שנה ללא שימוש. לקחתיו לתופרת שגרה בשכנותנו. מאחר שהייתי כה רזה, היא הצליחה לתפור לי ממנו זוג מכנסיים, אבנט וחולצה רוסית רחבה. בזמן ההופעה, כשרכנתי לרגע, התפרצעו המכנסיים ונקרעו לחלוטין. לא התפר פקע, אלא הבד היְשן עצמו פשוט התפורר, וזה היה סופו של 'ריקוד הקאפיטליסט' שלי.״

אחת מהרקדניות שהשתתפו ביצירה היתה בחורה יוגוסלבית נאה ותמירה, בעלת עיניים רושפות וצחוק תמידי ושמה קלאודיה (Claudia Vall). הוריה רצו שתלמד מוסיקה ובאלט, והיא היתה מוכנים לשלם היטב עבור שיעוריה. האומנת של ימי־ילדותה המשיכה ללוותה אל השיעורים. אביה, שהיה בעל בית־חרושת לבני־בנין בזאגרב, סיפק לבתו הצעירה את המובחר ביותר. כבר בגיל 16 היא היתה למוסיקאית ורקדנית מעולה. הוריה רצו שתסיים בית־ספר לבנות־טובים לאחר לימודיה בתיכון, ולכן שלחו אותה, בלווית האומנת, לוינה.

״למרות שנשארתי בבית־הספר שהורי בחרו עבורי, הלכתי למבחנים והתקבלתי ללימודים באקדמיה לאמניות הבמה (האקדמיה שפריץ למד בה בשנת 1933). בבקרים למדתי מוסיקה ומחול ואחרי הצהריים משחק, אנטומיה וציור. תחילה אפשר היה לראותי כבתם הצייתנית של הורי: ילדה קטנה וממושמעת, לבושת מדים שחורים וסינר לבן, אך באווירת התחרות החיונית שבבית־הספר לאמנות השתניתי מאוד. נבחנתי והתקבלתי להפקתו של מקס ריינהרד (Max Reinhardt) 'הנס'. תארו לכם את הניגוד שבין הנערה המגיעה, מלווה על־ידי אומנת, עד לדלת־הבמה, ומיד לאחר מכן הייתי מופיעה על הבמה כזונה שיכורה בבימויו של ריינהרד!״

בתקופה זו צפתה קלאודיה בהופעת מחול של גרטרוד קראוס. היא כה התרשמה מסגנונה האקספרסיבי של קראוס, עד שהחליטה ללמוד אצלה מחול מודרני. במשך שלוש שנים שהותה בוינה למדה והופיעה עם קראוס. היא התוודעה אל פריץ ברגר, אלזה שרף, קטיה דלקובה (Delakova) ורקדנים אחרים בבית־ספרה ובלהקתה של קראוס. הקבוצה העריצה את קראוס, שאספה אותם סביבה, ונוצרו קשרים חברתיים הדוקים בין הרקדנים לבין עצמם.

החברויות בקבוצה היו עזות ועמוקות, מאחר שהם בילו שעות ארוכות בלימוד וחזרות עם קראוס. ״היו אלה שעות של קסם. באווירה זו שכחת את עצמך לגמרי, ועבדת רק למען מה שקראוס רצתה.״ הרקדנים אף עבדו יחד על יצירותיהם העצמאיות, והופיעו בעבודות חבריהם. אלו היו הכרזות עזות על אמנויותיהם הפוליטיות, הרוחניות והרגשיות, שבוטאו דרך הריקוד.

פריץ ביקש מקלאודיה לרקוד במחול שיצר ״על מצבם של העובדים המנוצלים על־ ידי המעבידים תאווי־הבצע״. השקפת עולמו היתה כה שונה משלה! היא נדהמה מצעיר רזה וביישן זה וגילתה שהוא כשוליה עבד אצל צורף ורקד בסתר, למרות שהוריו לא עודדו את שאיפותיו. היא חשבה על האהבה והעידוד המתמיד שקיבלה על מנת שתלמד את האמנויות. חברותם התבססה בזמן החזרות. זה הזמן שבו רקדנים באמת תלויים האחד בשני, בהכנותיהם לקראת החשיפה לביקורת התמידית של הכוריאוגראף והקהל. ועזרה הדדית זו, שביסוד כל עבודה קבוצתית, היא שתציל מאוחר יותר את חייהם של קלאודיה ופריץ.

כדי לגרות את היצירתיות של קבוצתה, הביאה אליהם קראוס אמנים ורקדנים שונים. היא הזמינה, כנראה בשנת 1932, את עזרו של פון לאבאן, Fritz Klingenbeck להרצות בפניהם על כתב־תנועה. לאבאן כבר ביסס אז שיטה שלמה של ניתוח תנועה, שמאוחר יותר תשפיע באופן מפתיע על הקריירה של ברק. אך במפגש ראשון זה פריץ רק למד כמה מההנחות הבסיסיות של ה־"Labanotation".

קראוס עצמה עבדה לעיתים עם לאבאן. תיאור עבודתה עימו נמצא בביוגרפיה שלה, שנכתבה על־ידי גיורא מנור ב־1978 ״חיי הריקוד של גרטרוד קראוס״.[10]

אוסטריה של שנות ה־20 סבלה ממאבקים אלימים בין האירגונים החצי־צבאיים של מפלגות הימין והשמאל. הלאומנים דרשו שאוסטריה תסתפח לגרמניה. מפלגות הפועלים הרבו לעסוק לא רק בפוליטיקה ומאבק אלים, אלא הקדישו משאבים רבים לבניית שיכונים, ניהול בתי־ספר ומוסדות תרבות. מדי שנה היתה נערכת תהלוכה ענקית,

מלווה מופעים תנועתיים, ב"יום האיגודים המקצועיים". להקות מחול רבות, ביניהן זו של קראוס, נטלו חלק. על חגיגות עממיות אלה ניצח לאבאן, שיצר את הכוריאוגרפיה ההמונית, וגרטרוד קראוס שימשה לא אחת כאחד מעוזריו במבצע הענק.

הכוריאוגרפים התמחו בהנחיית המונים על הבמה. אופרות כ"אאידה" הועלו מדי שנה תחת כיפת השמיים, כמשיכה לתיירים, וכן חזיונות המבוססים על ההיסטוריה האוסטרית, שהוצגו בחזית בנין העיריה.

"אני זוכר שגרטרוד הכינה את הכוריאוגרפיה ל'ואלס הדנובה הכחולה'. המוטיב שלה נלקח מהמיקול הגדול, שיוצר הנהר בזורמו בוינה. לרשותה עמדו, אולי, מאה וחמישים בנות, שצעדו לאיצטדיון וכולן ביצעו את אותו הצעד כשהן מחזיקות צעיף משי כחול וארוך שריחף מעליהן והתבדר ברוח. האנשים בקהל צעקו וצרחו, כה יפה היה החזיון.

"מפלגות פוליטיות מתחרות סיבצדו חזיונות ותהלוכות באיזורים שונים של העיר, ואנו ביצענו את מקהלות־התנועה שלנו למען כל מפלגה ששכרה אותנו, בעצם. אני זוכר שגרטרוד הכינה ריקוד רוסי של חג הפסחא עבור הקומוניסטים, ו־Mia Slovenska, Manon ואני השתתפנו בביצועו. חזיון אחד שאני זוכר נעשה לזכר החיילים שנפלו במלחמת העולם הראשונה. גרטרוד הכינה את הכוריאוגרפיה על גבי חמש במות בגבהים שונים ואנו התחלנו אותה בזחילה ממישור למישור, כשמסכות גז על פנינו. הייתי כה קצר־רואי, שלא יכולתי לראות מתי הגיע תורי לנוע, ואני זוכר שהרקדנית שמאחורי נאלצה לדחוף אותי מעלה".

שנה מאושרת של חייו החלה כשפריץ פוטר על־ידי הצורף. "השלמתי ארבע שנות חניכות איתו, ושנה אחת עבדתי בתשלום מלא. משפוטרתי, יכולתי להצטרף לשיעורים המקצועיים של קראוס, בבקרים. גם בזמן חניכותי הצלחתי למצוא דרכים־לראות הופעות תיאטרון ולשמוע מוסיקה. הייתי מחכה בתור במשך שלוש או ארבע שעות לפני פתיחת הקופה, וכך הייתי משיג כרטיס עמידה, זה היה כל מה שיכולתי להרשות לעצמי. כל העומדים בתור כבר הכירו זה את זה והתענוג הגדול היה לדון במוזמן לנו בקונצרט או לרכל על השחקנים בתיאטרון.

"למזלי הצלחתי להצטרף ל־claque ב'אופרה העממית', ז. א. נעשיתי 'מוחא־כפיים מקצועי'. אם כי לא קיבלנו שכר עבור עמלנו – התשואות – לפחות לא נאלצנו להמתין עוד לכרטיסים, והוכנסנו לתיאטרון בחינם. היינו נעמדים בנקודה אסטרטגית בפאתי האולם ומחכים להוראות ראש ה־claque. ברוב התיאטרונים הראשיים העסיקו אז מומחה שכזה, והכוכב הראשי היה משלם לו, כדי שינהיג את מחיאות־הכפיים עם כניסותיו ויציאותיו מהבמה, ובזמן שהיה משתחווה. בקבלנו את האות, היינו מתחילים לשאוג 'בראוו!' ולמחוא כפיים בהתלהבות. היינו אפילו זורקים פרחים לבימה. למרות שכל הקהל ידע על ה־claque ביחוד באופרה, זה היה מוסד מקובל, שהיה חלק מהאווירה והערצת הכוכבים".

השנה שבה השלים פריץ את חניכותו, 1931, היתה גם השנה שבה נכנס לחיים שמאחורי הקלעים. במקום הצפיה על־יד כניסת האמנים, או בתפקיד של מוחא כפיים, החל להשתתף בעצמו בהפקות.

"הנסיון הראשון שלי היה כניצב, במשך חודשים, כקולי בחזיון גדול על סין, 'Brulle, China!' ('זעקי, סין!'), ובהחזרה הכללית קיבלתי צבע איפור צהוב וכובע של קולי סיני. לאחר ההופעה התבוננתי היטב כיצד כולם מורידים את האיפור וניסיתי לעשות כמוהם. לא יכולתי להבין, מדוע זכיתי למבטים מוזרים ברחוב, בדרכי הביתה. רק בבית גיליתי, שפני היו עדיין משוחים בפסי צבע צהוב. לא ידעתי שיש להוריד את האיפור בעזרת שומן.

"לאחר זאת השתתפתי ברוויו 'Quer durch Wien' ('חתך דרך וינה'), ורקדתי בתפקיד כדורגלן. שמעתי אז שהכוכבת ההוליוודית Anna May Wong באה לככב ברוויו באותו התיאטרון. היו בהפקה זו תפקידים לשישה גברים, היודעים לשיר ולרקוד. אני הייתי היחיד שנבחר להשתתף מצוות ההפקה הקודמת, למרות שמעולם לא למדתי זימרה! היה עלינו לזמר ולרקוד את ריקודי התקופה עם וונג. היתה זו שנתי המאושרת ביותר. הייתי על הבמה וחשתי שדבר לא יכול לעצור אותי עוד!"

סימני אנטישמיות התרבו בכל יום. יהודי וינה הרגישו כמי שאינם מקובלים במישורים רבים. זו היתה עובדת יסוד מוכרת בחיי הוינאים, והיהודים תמיד הסתדרו

עימה. מי שם אז לב לכרוז, כדוגמת זה שהופץ על־ידי מפלגת הפועלים הנאצית כבר ב־1928? האופרה הממלכתית הכריזה על בכורת 'Johnny spielt auf', יצירתו של המלחין ממוצא יהודי Ernst Krenek. האופרה תיארה את חייו של מוסיקאי כושי, נגן ג'ז בארצות־הברית. הכרוז הנאצי הכריז ש"הנושא הרקוב הזה על יהודים וכושים משפיל את בית־האופרה הממלכתית והמפואר שלנו. כל האנטישמים מוזמנים למצעד מחאה ב־13 בינואר, 1928. ליהודים ההשתתפות אסורה!"

פריץ הוזמן להצטרף ללהקתה של קראוס ב־1931. "איזו חוויה! השנתיים שעבדתי עם גרטרוד פתחו אותי. היא העניקה לי בטחון, כיוון חדש ואת תחילת זהותי האמיתית. אף אחד מהרקדנים היהודיים שבינינו לא היה מודע לרקע שלו. כולנו ראינו עצמנו כחלק מחיי העיר, וחשבנו שכך צריך להיות. למרות זאת, גרטרוד ניסתה לעורר אותנו להתמודד עם נושאים השאובים ממסורתנו."

סיור מופעי־הסולו הראשון של קראוס לחיפה, ירושלים, תל־אביב וקהיר באפריל 1931 היה "מאוד מרשים עבורנו," נזכר פריץ. "היא הוקסמה על־ידי הקבצים והמראות של אותם מקומות אקזוטיים, ודרכה הם השפיעו על כולנו. היא הכינה את המחול שלה 'הנער התימני' לארבע נשים ולי, בתפקיד הנער. תלבושתי הוכנה מבדים ויריעות שהביאה מהשוק בירושלים. ריקוד זה הציג בפני לראשונה את הנושא של יהודי המזרח, על תנועותיהם המתפתלות, בעדינות. כמובן שהחומר סונן דרך תפיסתה הכוריאוגרפית של גרטרוד. מאוחר יותר אף רקדתי בשחזור מחרוזת 'ריקודי הגטו' שלה.

"גרטרוד יצרה את 'חתונה חסידית' עבור עצמה בתפקיד הכלה ואני הייתי החתן. היה זה לא רק תפקיד ראשי אלא גם חוויה נפשית עמוקה בשבילי, הטעם הראשון של מסורת יהודית, שבאמת דיברה אלי. כמו כן אני זוכר את 'ריקוד מרים', בו הופעתי כאחד מארבעת הצעירים הלבושים כעבדים. המחול אורגן על הבמה ועליה משטחים בגבהים שונים, כשגרטרוד רוקדת על בימה נישאת במרכז וממנה יורדות מדרגות אל מזבח. במחול הנצחון הצטרפנו אליה, כשאנו אוחזים במיני מגינים עגולים בידינו וגרטרוד מנגנת בטמבור. כל זה יצר תמונה מהממת.

"המחול שלה 'הכותל המערבי' היה הנסיון המרגש ביותר של חיי המחול שלי דאז. במשך החזרות עבדנו על סדין, שהיה תלוי לרוחב הסטודיו, שסימל את הכותל העתיק שבירושלים. בהתיחסה לשמו המקובל, 'כותל הדמעות', היא עיצבה את ראשינו וידינו במצבים מסויימים כאילו ניסינו להציץ מעבר לו ופיסלה את גופותינו לפי דימויים של חסידים מתפללים. היתה לי הרגשה, שהיא מסתתת אותנו מאבן, הטמונה עמוק בליבה."

בהקדמה לספרה "המחול החסידי" כתב פריץ: "ריקוד זה עורר בי רגשות רדומים של זהות יהודית שלא שיערתי, שהם קיימים אצלי... רק כשהגעתי לארצות־הברית בזמן השואה, בשנת 1941, התגבשו רגשות קהים אלו למסירות גדלה והולכת למחול היהודי."

בזמן שפריץ היה חבר בלהקתה של קראוס היא הכינה כוריאוגרפיות לתיאטרון יידי מולינה, ה"וילנער טרופע", שהופיע בוינה באותו זמן. "היא שיתפה אותי בעבודת הקבוצה והופעתי איתם מספר פעמים. הקבוצה התנהלה על בסיס שיתופי, ולבי הלך שבי אחריהם. היו לכך מספר סיבות, אך אולי העיקרית היתה, שזה היה מגעי הקרוב הראשון עם סביבה יהודית מזרח אירופית. בכל הקשר אחר, מחוץ למסגרת התיאטרון, ודאי הייתי מגיב ככל יהודי וינאי אחר - בבוז וקרוב לוודאי בזלזול.

"גרטרוד יצרה במסגרת זו מחול עברי, עבור גבר נוסף ועוד ארבע נשים. אהבתי להגיע בערב לתיאטרון ולהתאפר לקראת ההופעה. התלהבתי, למרות ששאר חברי הקבוצה היו ענייני מרודים וסגנונם כה טראגי, מלא פתוס והגזמה.

"את שפת היידיש כבר שמעתי קודם, אך לא הבנתי הרבה. התידדתי מאוד עם אחת השחקניות, אשר סיפרה לי לראשונה על הפוגרומים ברוסיה. סיפורים אלה היו מנסיונה האישי. היא סיפרה לי כיצד רכבו הקוזקים הרוסיים אל כפרה ושחטו ללא רחם את היהודים בו. מפיה שמעתי על הקשיים העצומים העומדים בפני הפליט בהתחלת חייו החדשים במקום אחר. מעולם לא חלמתי, שגם אני אתנסה במצבים כאלה. נהגתי לשבת עם השחקנית בחדר ההלבשה שלה, שקוע בדבריה ממש עד תחילת ההופעה.

"איני זוכר עוד מה היו המחזות ואילו ריקודים רקדתי שם, אך האווירה היתה רבת משמעות עבורי. התיאטרון בו הופענו היה בחלק היהודי של העיר, בסמוך לגן שעשועים.

20

שכרי הדל הספיק רק עבור נקניקיה, שהייתי קונה בפארק לאחר ההופעה, אך לא יכולתי להיות מאושר יותר."

הריקוד גרם לפריץ להעריך את עצמו והביא לו חברים וקהל, שהיה מעוניין לשמוע את דיעותיו ולראותו רוקד. הוא הפיק בעזרתו של רקדן אחר של קראוס, אוטו ורברג, מספר קונצרטים. הקונצרט הראשון נערך באולם "אורניה" (Urania), ב-8 בנובמבר 1932, ואיתם הופיעה הרקדנית גרטה בק, בליווי כינור וחליל. בדרך כלל הם היו שוכרים אולם קטן, לעיתים בית-מרזח עם במה קטנה בפאתיו, משהו כמו אוף-אוף ברודווי. כמו כן היו שלוש ה"מכללות העממיות" של המפלגה הסוציאליסטית, שם החברים התאספו להרצאות ותוכניות אמנותיות. אחת היתה בלב העיר והשתיים האחרות בפרבריה. עבור שכירת האולם נדרש פריץ לשלם תשלום סמלי בלבד, ואם כי היה עליו לארגן מחדש כמה מהריקודים בהעדר מסך בקדמת הבמה, לא היה עליו לדאוג לפרסומת או למכירת הכרטיסים. המחשבה על התיאטרונים הגדולים היתה רחוקה ממנו. אפילו רקדנים נודעים יכלו לשכרם רק להופעות-מנחה, מאחר שכולם העלו את הצגותיהם בערבים.

לבסוף הבחין אביו של פריץ בפעילותו. "במשך כל שנות לימודי ובשנתיים בהן הופיעתי עם גרטרוד, חששתי שאבי יגלה זאת. לבסוף אזרתי אומץ וסיפרתי לו, שברצוני להשתתף בחוג להיסטוריה של המחול והמוסיקה מדי שבת באקדמיה הממלכתית. לאחר ששמע כי עלי לנסוע לשם בחשמלית ולהפר את מנוחת השבת, הוא צעק: 'ובכן, רק שלא תרד מהחשמלית ברחוב שלנו, ושלא יראו אותך השכנים.'"

בהזדמנות אחרת שמע ברגר האב מחבר בבית-הכנסת שלו, ששמו של בנו מופיע על לוחות המודעות. "הוא חזר הביתה ודרש לדעת אם רקדתי בפומבי.

"'כן,' השבתי.

"'האם אתה מרוויח מזה כסף?' שאל אבי.

"'כן,' אמרתי בעצבנות.

"'אם כך, מבחינתי זה בסדר.'"

לאור הצלחותיו בשטח הריקוד אזר פריץ אומץ ופתח סטודיו משלו, ברובע השישי. אנשים צעירים רבים באו לשיעורי הכושר והתרגילים וכן לשיעורי הריקוד שלו. בת זוגו לריקוד, קלאודיה קאופמן-וואל, אף זוכרת שלימד סטפס. פריץ אירגן את הסטודיו בצורה כה מוצלחת, שיכול היה לעזור להוריו ככל שהעסק שלהם התדרדר.

ביומו העמוס היה פריץ נחפז מהסטודיו לאולם הקונצרטים ומשם לפגישות עם חבריו, כשההסדר הדהוי של בירת ההפסבורגים לשעבר משמש לו רקע מתאים לפעילותו. אנשים ביקשו את חברתו. הוא היה רזה ויפה-תואר, בעל חוש הומור, דמות שונה מאוד מאותו ילד בודד, מכונס בעצמו ובלתי-מובן של משפחת ברגר.

פריץ וחבריו לא הקדישו הרבה תשומת לב לשינוי שחל במצבם של האמנים בגרמניה. גישת הנאצים ליצירה האמנותית החלה לתת אותותיה המפחידים. הפילהרמונית של ברלין ניגנה ב-1934 סויטה מהאופרה החדשה של פול הינדמות, "מאטיס הצייר", למרות שהנאצים יצאו כנגדו בעיתונות וקראו לו "אמן מנוון". השפעתם גרמה לפיטוריו של המנצח לאחר הבכורה. שר-התעמולה גבלס התקיף כל מי שסטה מהקו התרבותי הרשמי של המפלגה הנאצית כ"רקוב, סוטה והרסני". (11)

הוכרז על תחרות בינלאומית למחול, שתתקיים בוינה ביוני שנת 1934. עיתון צרפתי שדיווח על התחרות היוינאית ("Archives International de la Danse Revue") טען כי "מטרת התחרות היא לגלות כשרונות חדשים". היתה חלוקה לעבודות סולו וליצירות לקבוצה; לכל מתחרה הוקצו חמש-עשרה דקות להופעה. הזוכה בכל יום המשיך עד ליום החמישי, בו נבחרו המשתתפים להופעת-הגמר החגיגית. ראש העיר של וינה היה אמור להעניק מדליית זהב, מדליית כסף וחמש מדליות ארד לזוכים.

על-פי מאמרו של דר' וולפגנג בורן בכתב-העת הצרפתי מה-15 ביולי, 1934, חבר השופטים הבינלאומי כלל אורחים מאמריקה, פולין, הונגריה ויפן. בתחילה, פריץ אף לא חשב על סיכוי להכנס לתחרות. תסביך הנחיתות של ילדותו גבר עליו. אך חבריו ושותפיו למחול דחקו בו. לבסוף גבר בו הרצון לזכות בהופעה במסגרת כזו, אשר בה, כך ידע, יכל אף לזכות באחד משלושת הפרסים בני 1,000 שילינג, אשר נתרמו על-ידי משרד החינוך האוסטרי. כמו כן הוצעו פרס לסולנים על-ידי הרקדנית המהוללת גרטה ויזנטאל ומדליות-

זכרון חגיגיות מטעם הארכיון הבינלאומי למחול והעיר וינה.
הוא בחר להציג שלושה ריקודים, שיצר בזמן חניכותו עם גרטרוד קראוס. "מחול־שיר ארגנטיני" היה ריקוד קליל, מלא שמחה ובו נפילות מהממות לאחור וסיבובים מסחררים. "כורל" למוסיקה של צזיר פרנק היה תולדת הרושם המיסטי שעשה על פריץ הפולחן הקתולי בקתדרלה, ו"הרודן" היתה הצהרתו האישית נגד היטלר, למרות שניסה לתת לדמות הרודן משמעות אוניברסלית על־ידי שימוש בדמות פרעה המצרי.
ביום החמישי של התחרות פריץ היה עדיין בפנים. יום זה החל עבורו בחלחלה, והמתח הרב של התחרות עירער את שלוות רוחו, איים להרוס את נוכחותו הבימתית. אבל בסופו של היום, שמו של פריץ ברגר הופיע בין הזוכים בתחרות, הרקדן הויניאי היחיד (שאר שבעת הזוכים במדליות היו מצ'כוסלובקיה, פולין, שבדיה ולטביה), שעלה לגמר וזכה במדלית ארד. מבקרי העיתונות הללו את הזוכים.
פריץ ממש נסק לתוך עולם המחול הויניאי המוכר. אחת מהסולניות המפורסמות והאהובות של האופרה הויניאית, הדי פונדמאייר, באה אל מאחורי הקלעים לאחר ההופעה של פריץ. והוא, שהכיר אותה מהאופרה וזכר אותה בייחוד בתפקיד אשת פוטיפר ב"אגדת יוסף", היה המום, כשביקשה אותו להפגש עמה בביתה. מה היא רצתה ממנו? בפגישה הסבירה הרקדנית, שברצונה להרחיב את רפרטואר הופעות הסולו שלה. היא כבר למדה צעדי מחולות עממיים אוסטריים ממומחה לפולקלור באוניברסיטה, ועתה חפצה בצעדים אף מארצות אחרות. למרות שהרקע שלה היה זה של להקת הבאלט האופרה הויניאית, היא היתה צמאה להרחיב את אופקיה. האם יוכל פריץ ללמדה את ה"הורה" עבור מופע־יחיד, שרצתה להכין, בשם "הנערה מפלשתינה"? הוא לימד אותה בשמחה את ההורה והיא לימדה אותו, בתמורה, את מחול ה־Landler, מחול מרחף לזוג, בקצב הולס. בעתיד, יתברר, שמחול זה יהיה שימושי ביותר עבור פריץ ובמסעותיו בארצות שונות הוא יציג את הלנדלר לעומת ההורה, ביטוי לשני הפנים של זהותו.
פונדמאייר פרשה חסותה על פריץ; היא השיגה עבורו תפקידים במספר סרטים, כולל הגרסא המצולמת לאופרה "הנסיך איגור". אך עתה כבר החלה ההשפעה הנאצית לחלחל בחיים הויניאים ולהשפיע על עבודתו. "היה עלינו להצהיר בכל חוזה על היותנו יהודים. לעיתים נמנעה מאיתנו האפשרות להשתתף בסרטים חדשים ובפעמים אחרות הוחרמו בגרמניה סרטים בהשתתפות רקדנים או שחקנים יהודים."
ה"בורג־תיאטר" המכובד נזקק לעיתים לרקדנים ופנטומימאים לתפקידים מיוחדים. הסידור היה, שהאופרה סיפקה אמנים אלו עבור המחזות. רקדני האופרה השתייכו למוסד ממלכתי זה מילדותם, שם קיבלו את חינוכם, ובעוברם את הבחינות היו נכנסים ללהקה כרקדנים ורקדניות צעירים מן המניין. האופרה והבורג־תיאטר דאגו לאמניהם לכל ימי חייהם. בין אמני במה קבועים אלה לא היה יהודי אחד.
בהמלצתה של פונדמאייר התקבל פריץ לבורג־תיאטר כרקדן מחליף וכפנטומימאי. "זה היה כמו חלום. אם כי כבר מזמן הפסקתי לחכות ליד דלת הבמה עם צילומים וחתימות, אך התיאטרון המכובד הזה נשאר עדיין מעין מקום מקודש עבורי. בהכנסי דרך כניסת האמנים לראשונה, ובדרכי לחדר ההלבשה שלי, ראיתי את כל השמות המפורסמים על הדלתות ונזכרתי בחלומותי ובשאיפותי של תחילת דרכי. הייתי בטוח שהגעתי לגן־עדן.
"השמועה על כך שאופיע בבורג־תיאטר נפוצה, ומשפחתי, שכני וחברי הקודמים החלו להקדיש לי תשומת לב. הרגשתי שאני בדרכי להצלחה, ובעיני האנשים בשכונתי הייתי למישהו!"
פריץ הוזמן ב־1936 על־ידי אחד האמרגנים להכין ולהופיע ברקודים אוסטריים בנשף שעמד להתקיים בשגרירות האוסטרית בהאג. תוכננה חגיגה בהשתתפות מיטב אמני הזמר והמחול בחלק האמנותי. חלק מהתשלום עבור הולס והלנדלרים המסורתיים, שפריץ הכין לעצמו בלוויית שתי רקדניות, היה כרטיס־הטיס. "איזו התרגשות! לא יכולתי להחליט מה היה יותר מרגש, ההזמנה להופיע בשגרירות האוסטרית בהולנד או הסיכוי הראשון שלי לטוס במטוס. לא העזתי לספר על כך מראש להורי, אך שלחתי להם מברק מאמסטרדם! היינו אמורים לטוס חזרה לאחר הערב הנפלא והמסיבה המפוארת בשגרירות. אך מזג האוויר היה כה גרוע, שקרקיעננו למשך שבע שעות, וכשהשמראונו לבסוף, נאלצנו לנחות כבר בדרזדן שבגרמניה. שם עמדה בפנינו האפשרות לחכות עד למחרת ולנסות

לטוס שוב, או לחצות את גרמניה ברכבת עד לוינה עוד בו בלילה. בחרתי ברכבת. מעמדו של היטלר היה כבר מבוסס ולא היה לי כל רצון להשאר בגרמניה, ולו יום נוסף אחד.

"הזדעזעתי עמוקות בדרך משדה התעופה לתחנת הרכבת. דרך החלון, ואף באוטובוס עצמו, נתלו שלטים האוסרים את הכניסה על היהודים. זה היה בלתי יאומן ואני הרגשתי בחילה עד עומק נשמתי. כמובן שקראתי על האיסורים בעיתונות ואף הרגשתי את האנטישמיות על בשרי, אך איך שהוא תמיד הסתדרנו. וינה, אחרי הכל, היתה ביתנו. הורגלתי לשמוע הערות מהסוג שבעלה של הדי פונדמאייר היה מעיר: 'כמובן שאנו יודעים שהנך יהודי, אך אשתי כה אוהבת את עבודתך.' רק אחוז מסויים של יהודים הורשה ללמוד באוניברסיטאות או לעבוד במקצועות מסויימים. משרות ממשלתיות כמעט שלא ניתנו להשגה ליהודים. אך עדיין לא הייתי מוכן למה שראיתי במו עיני בגרמניה.

"כשהגעתי הביתה, סיפרתי למשפחתי על כך, אך הם הקלו ראש בדיווחי ואמרו, שדבר לא יקרה לנו בוינה."

חברתו קלאודיה כתבה לו מאיטליה. הוא ידע שהיא עזבה את גרטרוד קראוס כדי ללמוד עם ורה סקורונל בברלין, אך הוטרדה מהאווירה שם וחזרה לזאגרב. שם כה חסרה לה חברת אמני־במה אחרים, עד שנסעה לזלצבורג ושם פגשה באנג'לה סארטוריו(13) ובליזה סובל(14), אשר רקדו בעבר עם קורט יוס. הרקדניות שכנעו את קלאודיה לבוא לאיטליה ולרקוד עימן באופן מקצועי.

בחורף של שנת 1937 קלאודיה והלהקה האיטלקית הופיעו בוינה. לאחר הקונצרט, שהתקיים באולם הקונצרטים הגדול, החברים נפגשו שוב, ופריץ הוצג בפני אנג'לה סארטוריו.

"הייתי כה מאושרת, ויכולתי לראות שגם הוא היה מאושר. הוא כה השתנה, עכשיו, שכבר היה מעצב ריקודים, מלמד ומופיע כמקצוען מן השורה. הוא צחק בנימה אירונית בהזכירו את הורי, שעתה תמך בהם באמצעות רווחיו מהריקוד."

קלאודיה התגוררה בחדר זעיר בפנסיון קטן בפירנצה. "כל שאני זוכרת משם הוא, שהיה מקום עבור נעלי הסטפס שלי, נעלי הבאלט, האקורדיון והגראמופון. הדיירים השלווים האחרים חשבו, שאולי אני אמנית־קרקס! אני זוכרת, שבערב החופשי שלי נהגתי להוציא את הגראמופון למרפסת ולהתאמן. לעיתים הייתי מדמה לעצמי, שאני ג'ינג'ר רוג'רס, ואז הייתי צוחקת ונזכרת בפריץ, הנמצא בסטודיו שלו בוינה. זה היה תענוג ללמוד אצלנו ריקודי סטפס בסגננונו של פרד אסטר." סרטו של פרד אסטר עם ג'ינג'ר רוג'רס, "Swing Time", יצא לאקרנים ב־1936 והכל צפו בו וב־"Flying Down to Rio". כל צעד מהסרט "Top Hat" שוגן בקפדנות. בחלולה על המרפסת כאילו היתה לבושה בשמלה ארוכה והדורה, היתה קלאודיה מדמה לעצמה סציניות שונות מאותם סרטים. דייר אחד בפנסיון נהנה כה מההחזרות שלה על המרפסת, והחל לעזור לקלאודיה במתיחת קפיץ הגראמופון, כדי שלא תיאלץ להפסיק לרקוד כל כמה דקות. בהדרגה החלו הרקדנית הזעירה והגבר המבוגר גבה הקומה לקשור שיחה בין הריקודים. הוא סיפר לה, שמוצאו מצפון גרמניה, שלמד רפואה באיטליה, ועתה עבד כרופא בבית־חולים בפירנצה.

לאחר זמן מה, הזמינה לארוחה ש"היתה מעננת במיוחד, כי אכלתי בימים ההם בעיקר רימונים. אמנם אהבתי רימונים, אך גם לא יכולתי להרשות לעצמי לקנות הרבה מזונות אחרים. הייתי אוכלת ארוחת־בוקר גדולה ומשלימה אותה בפירות לארוחת־הערב."

כשפשפה פצעה את ברכה בשעת חזרה ונאלצה להפסיק את החזרות על המרפסת, החליט הרופא לטפל בה בעצמו. בפנסיון, בעזרת מכונה רפואית חדשה שהביא מבית־החולים. "המכונה נגהה באור מיוחד והוא הראה לי כיצד לכוונה, כדי שתרפא את ברכי."

להקת המחול הזדקקה לרקדן־גבר, וקלאודיה כתבה והציעה לפריץ להצטרף אליהם לסיור באיטליה, צרפת ושווייצריה. האם ירצה פריץ לבוא לפירנצה? זו לא היתה ההזמנה הראשונה שקיבל לרקוד באיטליה. הוא הופיע שם לראשונה בהזמנתה של טרודי גות(14), גם היא תלמידה לשעבר של גרטרוד קראוס, אשר חזרה למולדתה איטליה בשנות השלושים המוקדמות, כדי לייסד שם להקת מחול מודרנית. היא פעלה לעיתים גם כאמרגנית עבור אמני במה אחרים, ובהיותה בת למשפחה עשירה מאוד, יכלה לטפל באמנים בינלאומיים מהשורה הראשונה.

פריץ קיבל את ההצעה לרקוד בקבוצתה של טרודי גות משום שרצה לראות את

23

איטליה יותר מאשר להופיע עימה. הוא חשב את יצירותיה ליבשות וחסרות דימיון, אך הצד החיובי בכך היה, שהיא הרשתה לו לכלול את מחולות-הסולו שלו בתוכנית. במהרה הוא גילה, שהקהל האיטלקי מגיב היטב לחוש ההומור שבריקודיו ונהנה להופיע בפניהם.
הוא אף אהב לטייל ביחידות ברחובותיהן של הערים האיטלקיות בהן הופיע. הבניינים בגוני החומר הזכירו לו את כל התפארות לאופרות האיטלקיות אשר ראה כילד, באותם רגעים גנובים בחזרות האופרה הוינאית. עתה היתה זו מציאות, רחובות איטלקיים רוחשי חיים. הוא אהב לסעוד בבתי-הקפה תחת כיפת השמיים, לטייל לאיטו ליד החנויות הקטנות, ונהנה להתבונן בדרך בה ברכו הגברים האחד את השני ברחוב, בחיבוקים עזים ובטפיחות שכם מלאות חיבה. הוא התענג למראה שמלותיהן הסרוגות של הנשים האיטלקיות, אשר נעו ורצעדו בצורה כה מצודדת. האוירה הים-תיכונית היתה כה מנוגדת לזו של וינה! מבחינת מזגו הרגיש שם ממש בבית.
הוא שמח לקבל את ההזמנה מלהקת ה־"Balletto" ונמשך לרקוד שוב עם קלאודיה. היא היתה כה מאושרת ותוסטת בטיולים הראשון ברחובותיה של פירנצה, חיבקה את פריץ וקראה: "או, פריץ, עליך להכיר את הגבר שאני עומדת להנשא לו!" פריץ הוצג בפני גיאורג קאופמן הגבוה וההדור תמיד, שהיה היפוכו הגמור. בעוד שפריץ אהב לשוחח, לבלות בחברה ולעבוד בקבוצה, היה קאופמן שתקן והעדיף להקדיש את עצמו לקריאת ספרים והאזנה למוסיקה מובחרת בחדרו שבפנסיון. אך למרות הניגוד, נקשרו הגברים מיד זה לזה ונהנו לשוחח. שניהם העריצו את קלאודיה.
פריץ נשאר לרקוד בפירנצה רק לזמן קצר. הסיור בארצות אירופה האחרות נדחה והיה עליו לחזור לוינה.
הוא המשיך לעבוד למרות האבטלה הגוברת והאנטישמיות. היו לו תלמידים נאמנים רבים בסטודיו שלו, והוא רקד הרבה במיגוון תוכניות ומחזות מוסיקליים בפרברי וינה. לעיתים קרובות היו המחולות שלו בעלי אופי עממי וכללו את הטנגו, הלנדלר, הולס הוינאי, הפולקה והמזורקה. אלה היו רק מרכיב אחד מהרפרטואר המודרני המוכר שלו, וזוהו בקלות על-ידי הקהל, שאהב אותם. זאת בניגוד לעבודתם של הרקדנים המודרניים באמריקה, שהתגאו במקוריות החומר התנועתי שלהם ונושאי המחולות. עבודתה של מרתה גרהם "Primitive Mysteries", או "New Dance" של דוריס האמפרי למשל, היו בלתי תלויות בחומר תנועתי עממי אמריקני כלשהו ויציגו תופעה חדשה בתכלית במחול התיאטרלי.
ב־1937 הוזמן פריץ על-ידי מנהל התוכניות של ארגון העובדים הסוציאליסטי ללמד כיתה בני-נוער, וזה היה ניסיונו הראשון בעבודה עם קבוצת-גיל כזאת. הם היו מגיעים פעמיים בשבוע מכל קצות העיר, כדי ללמוד איתו מחול, וכן על מנת להכין הפקה קטנה, שתכלול ריקודים אוסטריים עממיים. בכל קבוצה היו לפריץ יותר מחמישים תלמידים, ושמונת הזוגות שבחר להפקה נעשו למעריציו הנאמנים. הוא הכין את "Annen-Polka", למוסיקת של יוהן שטראוס, שהקהל דרש תמיד לראותו שלוש פעמים ברציפות, כהדרן. הוא הבין, שריקוד זה שימש מענג כפורקן לצעירים ולכן ההיבט הטכני של הביצוע היה חשוב פחות בעניו מרגשות החדווה והשיתוף שבריקוד. גם בהדגישו כוונה זו, הוא עדיין הצליח להשיג תוצאות נאות, ושיטת עבודה זו עם רקדנים בלתי מקצועיים הוכיחה את עצמה שוב לאחר שנים רבות, בעבודתו באמריקה.
היטלר פלש לאוסטריה ב־11 במרץ, 1938. "אני זוכר שהייתי בצהריים בחנות המכולת ושם שמעתי את החדשות. רצתי הביתה לבשר להורי שסופם של היהודים הגיע. הם אמרו: 'אל תשטתה! הכל חיים עם זה בגרמניה מאז 1933. זה לא יהיה נורא כל כך.' כמה אומללה היתה טעותם! אנשים התאבדו מרוב פחד ואחרים מצאו דרכים להבריח את עצמם מעבר לגבולות. בימים הראשונים של ה'אנשלוס' איש לא שיער עד כמה הצליחו הנאצים לשתק את היהודים באימתם.
"בעל-הבית של הסטודיו שלי אמר שלא אוכל ללמד שם עוד, אלא רק לערוך חזרות לבדי. בשביל מה אתאמן? תמהתי. אף אחד לא יזמין אותי להופיע! אפילו הפסנתרן, שניגן עבורי במשך שנים, בסטודיו ובהופעות, ונראה כחבר קרוב ביותר, הודיע לי, שלא יעז עוד לנגן עבור יהודי. מישהו היה עלול לדווח עליו... התלמידים היהודיים הספורים שלי הפסיקו לבוא, כי חששו לצאת לרחוב, והנוצרים לא היו מוכנים ללמוד עוד אצל יהודי.

כל החזים להופעותי בוטלו. ההבנה הפתאומית, ששותקנו בחיינו המקצועיים והפרטיים היתה מפחידה. נותרת לבדך, ללא חברים, שרוי בפחד מתמיד שמישהו עלול להסגירך. תוכניותי ללמוד בקיץ עם המורה הרוסית המפורסמת לבאלט, אולגה פראוברינסקיה, בפריס, נגוזו כחלום. הפסטיבלים האיטלקיים בוטלו. חששנו לחיינו. יכולת לחוש בסכנה בכל בנין, בכל משרד ובכל רחוב. בבנין שבו גרנו התגוררה גם משפחה נוצרית ולה שבעה ילדים, ששלושה מבניה היו חברים במחתרת הנאצית. מיד לאחר פלישת היטלר הם החלו לרגל אחר אחותי, שנטתה להשמיע את דיעותיה בגלוי. היא נישאה ועזבה את הבית, ופתחה מפעל משלה לייצור כפפות. מאוחר יותר היא נאסרה ונשלחה למחנה ריכוז.

"באותו שבוע של פלישת היטלר התקשר אלי מנהל קבוצת הצעירים של ארגון העובדים הסוציאליסטים ואמר שהיותי יהודי אינה משנה דבר, כי 'חברינו הצעירים אוהבים אותך ואנו רוצים שתמשיך.' אך אני השבתי, שאני חושש לנוע ברחובות. המנהל שלח חמישה או שישה נערים ללוותני אל שיעורי הריקוד, והם הקיפוני ברחוב ובחשמלית כחומה.

"קבוצת הצעירים היתה מתאספת בחדר האחורי של בית-בירה באחד מפרברי העיר, ואני הייתי נכנס לשם בדלת האחורית. פתאום הבנתי עד כמה היה המצב בעייתי לגבי הקבוצה. 'מלווי' נאלצו לשוב איתי אל העיר בלילה ואז היה עליהם לנסוע לבתיהם בחשמלית במשך שעה ארוכה. בפעם השניה שלימדתי שם נכנס אחד מבעלי המקום לחדר והתלחש עם הצעירים. ראיתי את פניהם המודאגות והודעתי למנהל, שלא אוכל להמשיך עוד. כולם היו מסתבכים בגללי.

"לפתע פתאום קיבלתי מברק, ובו הצעה להופיע בשווייץ. הובטח לי, שאוכל לקבל רשיון-עבודה חוקי שם למשך תשעה חודשים. לא שאלתי שאלות, לא בדבר שכרי או עם מי אהיה אמור לרקוד והיכן. קיבלתי את ההצעה מיד! עזבתי את וינה עם מזודה אחת מלאה בתלבושות ותווים. הורי עדיין התעקשו להתלות באמונה המיושנת, שהכל יהיה בסדר ושנפגש בקרוב בזמנים טובים יותר."

פרק שלישי:
שוויצריה

הקבוצה הקטנה שאליה הצטרף פריץ הופיעה בתוכניות של סטירה פוליטית במרתפי בתי-קפה.(15) ה־"Kleinkunstbühne" או "הבימה הזעירה", היתה צורה נפוצה של תיאטרון, שהתפתחה בין שתי מלחמות העולם. קבוצה כזו היתה מורכבת, בדרך כלל, מארבעה או חמישה משתתפים ופסנתרן מלווה, שכתבו בדרך כלל בעצמם את הסקצ'ים והבדיחות בסגנונם של ברט ברכט וקורט וייל, ואף רקדו עיבודים בימתיים של מחולות-עם להנאת הקהל. פריץ החל לעבוד עם קבוצה שכזאת בציריך, וסייר עימם בערים דוברות הגרמנית שבשוויצריה.

"כולנו היינו פליטים יהודיים: הזמרת היפהפיה, הפסנתרן, המנחה אשר הינחה את הערב וסיפר בדיחות בארבע שפות, שחקן נוסף ואני ובת-זוגי למחול. לאחר ההופעה היינו מתחלקים ברווחים, המטבעות שנזרקו אל כובעו של המנחה.

"לאחר שלושה חודשים של עבודה עימם, מצאה הזמרת פטרון עשיר, שרצה שתשכב ברווחי בין-לאומי. אני הכנתי את הכוריאוגרפיה לכוכבת ולשש רקדניות, וסיירתי עם ההופעה המוצלחת, שכללה אף לוליינים ערביים ונערת-גומי לוליינית צרפתיה."

פריץ התידד עם אשה צעירה זו, אשר היתה מגיחה, להפתעת הקהל, מתוך קופסא זעירה, שהיתה מונחת על שולחן במרכז הבמה. למרות העובדה שפריץ לא דיבר צרפתית והיא לא ידעה גרמנית, הם בילו את כל זמנם יחד. אם היה משהו חשוב לומר, היה פריץ מזעיק את המנחה כדי שיתרגם. הלהקה סיירה יחד במשך חודשים והופיעה בתיאטרונים הגדולים של שווייץ. השכר היה טוב ופריץ היה מאושר מאוד.

לפתע הוא קיבל מכתב מהמשטרה - אשרת העבודה החוקית שלו בוטלה. נאמר לו, שעליו לעזוב מיד. נוסף לכך הבהיר המכתב את החוק החדש הקובע שעל כל האזרחים האוסטריים להפקיד את דרכוניהם בשגרירות הגרמנית.

"בבואי לשגרירות הגרמנית, ראיתי את תמונתו הגדולה של הפיהרר, וכל הצדעות ה'הייל היטלר!' שנשמעו במסדרונות היו מחזה מעורר אימה. חששתי שלא אקבל דרכון גרמני תמורת הדרכון הישן שלי, ושלא אוכל לחזור הביתה, לוינה. אבל נתנו לי דרכון חדש, ועל העמוד הראשון שלו הוטבעה באדום בולט האות "J", משמע: יהודי. בין כך וכך לא היה לדרכון זה תוקף רב ביותר, מאחר שליהודים לא הוענקו ממילא אשרות-כניסה לרוב המדינות. לא יכולתי לקבל את חסותה של אף שגרירות."

כששמעה נערת הגומי הצרפתית על תלאותיו של פריץ, כעסה מאוד. "אתה תבוא עימי לפריס!" הכריזה.

"ואיך אגיע לשם?"

"הצרפתים עדיין מאמינים במהפיכה, באחוות אחים, בשיוויון ובחופש. רק היטלר משוגע!"

הרקדנית הזעירה לקחה עם פריץ המוחה לשגרירות הצרפתית בציריך. לבקשת הפקיד הציג בפניו פריץ את דרכונו הגרמני החדש, הדרכון הנאצי של הרייך השלישי, אשר הוצא ב-12 בדצמבר 1938. "איננו יכולים להתיר לך כניסה לצרפת," אמר הפקיד בקרירות, "אתה עלול להישאר בארצנו."

"על מה אתה מדבר," צווחה הרקדנית הקטנה. "אתה מייצג את ארצי, את צרפת,

26

ראנו מייצגים את החופש. אינך יכול להתנהג בצורה כזאת." היא צעקה בקול כה רם עד שהמשטרה נאלצה לפנותם מהבנין.

הזועע והכעס של הרקדנית הצרפתיה הקטנה נגעו לליבו של פריץ. הם היו כאבן קטנה הנזרקת בידי ילד כנגד בית-אבן ענק, אך מעשה חסר-תועלת זה נגע לו עמוקות והוכיח לו, שיש עוד אנשים המסוגלים להתנהג באנושיות.

לא היה עוד דבר שיכול היה לעשות. מכל מקום, הלהקה התפזרה כשהכוכבת היפהפיה הצליחה לקבל אשרת-כניסה לרפובליקה הדומיניקנית. היא אמרה לפריץ שאין לה מושג היכן מצויה אותה רפובליקה, אך היא תיסע לשם בכל מקרה. אנשים היו עוזבים, אם רק היה להם להיכן.

הוא ארז את התלבושות ואת תווי הנגינה במזוודתו, נפרד מחבריו והלך לתחנת הרכבת. התחנה היתה מוצפת אנשים, אשר התנקזו מכל הכיוונים. פריץ לא מיהר והתנהל לאיטו בהמון, מפלס דרכו בין החבילות, המזוודות והילדים הקטנים.

"פריצל!" שמע קול מוכר קורא. הוא הסתובב וראה את קלאודיה ואל בלווית בעלה ג'ורג' ממהרים לעברו. הם הגיעו ברכבת מפירנצה ועתה היה עליהם להגיע לנמל, שם המתינה להם אוניה.

"לאן מועדות פניכם?" עקב השאון הרב נאלץ פריץ לחזור על השאלה הבלתי נמנעת מספר פעמים.

"אנו מפליגים להאבאנה."

שנה לאחר שהותו של פריץ בפירנצה הצטרף מוסוליני, אבי הפשיזם, לעמיתו היטלר וסיווג את היהודים כבלתי טהורים גזעית והאשימם במפלותיו באתיופיה ביולי שנת 1938. הוא הנהיג תקנות גזעניות באיטליה, בהן נאסר על יהודים לעסוק ברפואה.(16) לא היתה כל דרך פתוחה בפני קאופמן, בעלה הרופא של קלאודיה, אלא להגר שוב. הזוג החליט לעזוב את איטליה, והם נישאו בצריך והחלו בחיפושים אחר מדינה שתתיר להם להכנס לגבולותיה.

"התחלנו לחזור על פתחי הנציגויות הזרות בצריך. היה לי הדרכון היוגוסלבי שלי, אך הדרכון הגרמני של ג'ורג' הקשה על העניינים. מה שנראה בתחילה כמשחק והרפתקאה, הפך למשימה בלתי אפשרית. ואז גילינו, שקובה תתיר לנו להכנס בשעריה! חזרנו לבית המלון שלנו כדי לארוז, ושם חיכה לי מברק מטרודי גות. היא עזבה את איטליה והגיעה בינתיים לקובה, והציעה לי לבוא להאבאנה, כי יש לה שם עבורי עבודה כרקדנית."

קלאודיה מצאה פיסת נייר בארנקה, שירבטה במהירות את כתובתה בהאבאנה ונתנה אותה בידו של פריץ. לא היה להם פנאי לברר כיצד הצליחו להשיג את אשרות הכניסה. הוא התבונן שוב ושוב במלים "האבאנה, קובה", ושם את פיסת הנייר בכיסו.

פריץ המשיך לפלס את דרכו לרכבת. הקיטור שריחף על פסי הרכבת הענקית אווירה שלא מהעולם הזה לפרידתו משוויצריה. הוא מעולם לא שם לב לערפל זה, מעשה ידי אדם. גלי העשן מול פני האנשים, הכל נראה מכני ולא טבעי - אפילו העננים לא היו במקומם הנכון.

להפתעתו, בשובו לביתו הוא מצא מכתב מהאמרגן(17) שהשיג עבורו את העבודה בשוויצריה. הוא כתב לו מאמסטרדם: "ברצוני להוציא את אחותי מוינה. אם תארגן להקה של חמישה רקדנים ותכלול בה את אחותי, אשיג לכם חוזה להופעות במועדוני-לילה ובבתי-קולנוע בהולנד למשך שלושה חודשים."

פריץ קפץ על המציאה והחל לרקום תוכניות. האמרגן דירר סידר ניירות חוקיים עבור החמישה. ללא בעיות שכר פריץ ארבעה רקדנים, ותוכנן, שיורדים מהרכבת בהולנד תיפול האחות, כאילו במקרה, ותנקע את רגלה, כך שלא תיאלץ להופיע. פריץ הכין את הכוריאוגרפיה לשלושה רקדנים ולעצמו. החזרות התנהלו בוינה, והקבוצה יצאה לדרך כמתוכנן.

הכל נראה לו כהרפתקא אחת גדולה. הוא לא האמין, שמשהו יקרה לו באמת. מי יכול היה להאמין ש"הפתרון הסופי" יחול על כל משפחתו, על שכונת מגוריו ועל הקהילה בה חי?

ביום השלישי לשהותו החוקית בהולנד בוטל תוקף האשרה שלו. אף ההולנדים היו

חשדנים לגבי מבקרים יהודיים מהרייך השלישי. הותר לו אך לסיים את שבוע ההופעות במועדון־הלילה. למרות זאת היה עליו לקנות בשארית כספו המועט את כרטיסי הרכבת לרקדני הקבוצה כדי שיוכלו לחזור לבתיהם שבבלגיה, שווייצריה ואוסטריה.

"גרתי תחילה בחדר בפנסיון מהודר. מדי לילה עברתי לחדר זול יותר, עד שהגעתי לעליית־הגג הבלתי מוסקת וזה היה בחודש ינואר הקר. כספי אזל. בראשי לא ידעתי מה לעשות." ממדי התפשטות הנאציזם נעשו ברורים יותר ויותר. מחוסר יכולת לעבוד בוינה, ועתה אף בשווייצריה והולנד, הוא החליט לעזוב את אירופה לגמרי. הוא כתב לרקדנית לשעבר מקבוצתה של גרטרוד, אשר השתקעה בלונדון ושאל אם יוכל לבקרה. היא כתבה לו בתשובה, שאם אכן יצליח להגיע לשם, המשפחה תדאג למזונו והוא תמיד יוכל לישון על הרצפה.

פריץ ניגש לקונסוליה הבריטית במטרה לברר מה נדרש כדי להשיג אשרה עבור קבוצת רקדנים. היה עליו להשיג חוזים ממשיים להופעות באנגליה וכן בהולנד, וכרטיסי הלוך וחזור מאמסטרדם ללונדון. בלי כל אלו לא תינתן אשרה זמנית לבריטניה. למרות שהדבר נראה כבלתי אפשרי, החל פריץ בנסיון להגשימו.

הוא מכר את שעונו של סבו, החפץ בר־הערך היחיד שהיה ברשותו, ובכסף זה רכש כרטיס הלוך־חזור ללונדון. דרך חבר, אף הוא סוכן־אמנים, השיג חוזים מזוייפים להופעות אשר כביכול הבטיחו לו עבודה בהולנד למשך חודשיים.

הבעיה שנותרה עדיין היתה, כיצד להשיג אשרת כניסה שתאפשר לו לשוב מאנגליה להולנד לאחר שכבר גורש ממנה בפתאומיות. הוא החליט לגשת למשטרת הזרים באמסטרדם ושם הוא הסביר את תוכניתו בפשטות וביושר ככל האפשר. "אינכם רוצים בי בהולנד, ואף אני לא רוצה להשאר. יש לי סיכוי להשאר באנגליה, אך אני זקוק לאישור כניסה חוזר. אם תעניק לי אותו, אני מבטיח לא להשתמש בו לעולם."

הפקיד ההולנדי הביט הישר בעיניו. "כבר נמאסו עלי כל הסיפורים והדראמות. אף אחד לא מגיע אלי עם סיפור אמיתי. מאחר שאתה הראשון האומר אמת, אתן לך את אשרת־הכניסה החוזרת, אך אני מטביע צלב קטן בפינת דרכונך. זהו הצופן שלנו והוא מבטל את תוקף האשרה. אם תחזור להולנד, תשלח אותך משטרת־הגבולות ישירות לגרמניה."

למחרת חזר פריץ לצירות הבריטית, כשבידיו אשרת הכניסה בחזרה להולנד, חוזים מזוייפים וכרטיס הלוך־חזור. הוא קיבל אשרת־תייר בת עשרה ימים לאנגליה.

החותמת האחרונה בדרכונו הגרמני בעל סימן ה־"J" היתה "בתוקף לכניסה אחת, בתנאי שנושא התעודה לא ישאר בממלכה המאוחדת לאחר השבוע השלישי של פברואר 1939, ולא יעבוד בשכר או שלא בשכר." הוא עזב את האג ב־23 בינואר והגיע ללונדון ב־25 בינואר 1939 - יום הולדתו.

פרק רביעי:
אנגליה

פריץ ניגש לארגון היהודי הלונדוני שנקרא "בית־זוברון", כי חשב שהם יוכלו לעזור לו במציאת עבודה ומקום מגורים. נאמר לו שם, שאין זה כך, מאחר שברשותו רק אשרת־תייר לעשרה ימים.

אולם הפקיד בארגון היהודי שלח בשם פריץ בקשות לארוח הפליט היהודי. כמו כן הוא היפנה אותו לעורך־דין, אשר היה מוכן לטפל בהארכת אשרת השהיה שלו באנגליה ללא תשלום.

בזמן שחיכה לתשובה לבקשת ההארכה, ניסה פריץ למצוא עבודה בלונדון. הוא פגש רקדנים שונים, אך כולם היו מובטלים ולא יכלו לעזור לו.

כשחזר ל"בית־זוברון", נאמר לו, שאם כי היתה תשובה אחת לבקשתו, כדאי לחכות לתשובה נוספת. האשה שענתה לבקשה נראתה בעצמה במצב קשה ולפקיד לא נראה, שהיא תהיה לעזר רב.

אך בפני פריץ הנואש לא נפתחו אפשרויות אחרות והוא החליט לנסוע למרות הכל לעיירה רותרפילד במחוז סאסקס ולבקר את אליזבת גראהם, האשה שענתה לפניית הארגון היהודי. להפתעתו הוא מצא מונית, שהמתינה לו בתחנת הרכבת, והסיעה אותו אל ביתה המקסים של העלמה גראהם. אם כי היא חייתה בצמצום, היא החזיקה משרתת, גנן ונהג. פריץ התארח בביתה במשך ארבעה חודשים, שבהם הוכיחה גראהם, שהיא נותנת חסות מיוחדת ונדיבה. היא סיפקה לו שיעורי אנגלית, דאגה להשיג לו עבודה כמורה פרטי למחול ואף לקחה על עצמה להביא את הוריו של פריץ מויינה ודאגה להם למחסה בלונדון במשך שנות המלחמה. אליזבת גראהם היתה אחת בימי מלחמת העולם הראשונה, ולאחר שראתה במו עיניה את אכזריות הגרמנים, נשבעה לעזור לפליטים, שיצליחו להמלט מהם.

מיד בהגיעו לביתה הוגש התה בכלי־כסף בוהקים, בליווית צלחות עמוסות עוגיות וכלים מלאים ריבה ושמנת. לאחר שהחליפו מספר מלות נימוס, הם אכלו בשקט, מאחר שלא דיברו בשפה משותפת. מחדרו של פריץ בקומה השניה נשקף הגן המטופח ומעבר לו נוף השדות והגבעות.

בתשע בערב הוא נקרא שנית לחדר הטרקלין ושם הוגש קפה, שעה שגברת גראהם האזינה לחדשות ברדיו. הוא חש תסכול כי לא יכול היה להבין את החדשות בגלל שליטתו המועטת בשפה האנגלית, אך לאחר מספר שבועות כבר היה מסוגל לשוחח מעט עם המארחת שלו, בהעזרו בתנועות ידיו ובפנטומימה.

היא היתה נדיבה אך גם החמירה עם פריץ. היא האמינה בחשיבות העבודה ובחנה את אופיו של פריץ על־ידי מטלות קטנות שהעסיקו אותו תדיר. הוא קיצץ ענפי עצים בגן, תיקן את הגדר ואף עזר להזיז רהיטים בבית.

פעם בשבוע הוא היה מוצא שתי לירות אנגליות מתחת למפיתו בארוחת הבוקר, הקצבה נאה ביותר. היא סרבה במבוכה לקבל את תודותיו והיתה שולחת אותו לבקר את חבריו בלונדון ומציעה לו לבקר בסרטים או להפגש עם עורך־הדין שלו בקשר לאשרת־השהיה שלו. במשך החודשים שחלפו תפס פריץ באיזו התחשבות והקרבה עצמית היא טיפלה בו.

איש מהשנים לא הכביד על השני בשאלות. הם חשו בצורך בפרטיות וכבוד הדדי.

29

מיס גראהם היתה חכמה ורגישה. כששמעה, שפריץ הוא רקדן, היא היתה שולחת אותו מדי יום להתאמן בגן.

האימונים היומיים, תחת השמיים האפורים והערפילים, היו לתוספת מבורכת בסדר יומו. הוא התרגל למזג האוויר הקודר, כשם שלמד להתעלם ממוסיקה מלווה מיגעת בשיעורי-מחול. למרות התנאים הקשים הוא לא ויתר על השיעור היומי שלו.

הריקוד הוא שאיפשר לו להכיר אנשים חדשים, לשפר את האנגלית שבפיו ואף להשתכר כסף, שהיה נחוץ לו ביותר. היתה זו שוב מיס גראהם, שארגנה עבורו פגישה עם שכנה צעירה ועשירה. לאחר ראיון מוצלח בחווילתה, הוא הוזמן ללמד את ילדיה ריקוד. אך כאשר האשה סיפרה לו שהיא אוהבת לרקוד במסיבות ולצערה בעלה לא שותף לאהבה זו, הרגיש פריץ, שהוא פוסע על קרקע לא בטוחה.

"האם תתלווה אלי ואל חברי ביום שבת הבא בערב כבן-זוגי למחול? נשלם לך עבור שירותיך."

אם כי פריץ השיב בחיוב, הוא חש כג'יגולו ושנא בקרבו את הרעיון כולו. הוא התלווה פעמים רבות אל האשה לאחוזות שונות בסביבה. יחסיהם היו תמיד מהוגנים, אך הוא תיעב את הרעיון שאמנות הריקוד היקרה לו, והוא עצמו, ינוצלו בצורה כזו.

מאוחר יותר, בזמן חג הפסח, הזמינה אותו האשה לביתה לאחר שבילו את הערב יחדיו. היא שילחה את המשרתים מהספרייה, סגרה את הדלת והציעה לו ברנדי.

"אני מתחננת בפניך לא לספר זאת לאיש. לא לבעלי, לא לילדי ולא לגברת גראהם. אני הייתי מעוניינת בך, בעזרה לך, כדי שתוכל למצוא מקום טוב יותר לחיות בו. איש אינו יודע כאן שגם אני יהודיה." והיא נתנה לו כסף כדי שיפתח בחיים חדשים.

ברור שהיא חיבבה מאוד את פריץ. הוא היה בעל נימוסים נאים ואדיב, למרות מיגבלות השפה. החייט של מיס גראהם תפר עבורו חליפת טוויד אנגלית, שהדגישה את גיזרת הרקדן החטובה שלו. מפניו הנעימות, פני הנער והמבוגר גם יחד, נשקפו עיניו הכהות, מישירות המבט, אך הרגישות. המרכיב הסותר היחיד בהופעתו המושכת היה ראשו המקריח. היה קשה לנחש מהו גילו האמיתי.

פעם אחת הלכו פריץ והאשה לסרט אמריקני. "ישבתי במשך כל הסרט ולא הבנתי מלה. כל כך צחקנו, כשחברי האנגלים התוודו, שגם הם לא יכלו להבין את המבטא האמריקני שבפי השחקנים."

בסוף אפריל, בזמן ארוחת הבוקר, בישרה לו גברת גראהם, שהשיגה עבורו מקום על סיפונה של "אורביטה" המפליגה לקובה. היא נאלצה לרכוש עבורו כרטיס הלוך וחזור, אך היא לא יחסה חשיבות לכסף שבוזבז בשל כך. העיקר שיעבור בשלום לארץ, בה יוכל לפתוח בחיים חדשים. היה עליו לגשת מיד לחייט ולהזמין חליפה חדשה לנסיעה. והיא סרבה לשמוע תודות על כל מה שעשתה.

פרק חמישי:
קובה

פריץ הגיע לקובה כנראה ב־12 במאי, 1939, באוניה האחרונה מאירופה שנוסעיה הורשו לרדת לחוף. האוניה "סנט לואיס", אשר הגיעה לקובה שלושה ימים אחר־כך, נאלצה לחזור להמבורג בגרמניה, כשעל סיפונה 907 פליטים יהודיים, אשר מצאו את מותם מאוחר יותר בשואה באירופה.(18) קובה סבלה משפל כלכלי שנגרם עקב נפילת מחיר קני־הסוכר, תעשיית־היצוא היחידה באי. האבאנה היתה מוצפת בכוח עבודה זול מהאיטי השכנה, שם התנאים היו קשים עוד יותר. שפע של מהגרים הגיע מאירופה. האווירה היתה כבדה ביותר.

למרות שהאיגודים היהודיים באמריקה וחמש קבוצות של יהודי קובה פתחו משרדים בהאבאנה לעזרת הפליטים, הממשלה תמכה בצעדים אנטישמיים במדיניות הפנים שלה.

הנמל נסגר לאחר בואה של האוניה "אורביטה".(19) למעשה, העיתונות הכריזה עליו מכבר כסגור, מפחד הצוללות הנאציות.

לגבי האירופאים, האיים הקאריביים יצגו תמיד רומנטיקה, מסתורין וחום תמידי. עתה הם הפכו למקום מקלטם של רבים, אשר חיכו לאשרת־הכניסה הנכספת לארץ החיים החדשים, ארצות־הברית. למרות החלטתם הנחרצת של הנאצים למחות את היהודים מהעולם, מספר ארצות נתנו להם מחסה, ועד בואו של פריץ לקובה, אף היא היתה אחת מהמדינות אלו.

על סיפון ה"אורביטה" נהנה פריץ מההרגשה הנדירה של פנאי מתמשך, שמעניק השייט באוניה. הוא היה קם בשעה 6 מידי בוקר, ומתאמן ומתרגל במחול הסטפס. ביום השלישי להפלגה נתבקש פריץ לתת שיעורי־מחול לנוסע ספרדי אחד, שלחם במלחמת־האזרחים לצד הרפובליקנים ואיבד בה את זרועו. פריץ הבהיר לו בשפת סימנים, שיתן לו שיעורים תמורת לימוד השפה הספרדית. בסופה של ההפלגה בת השבועיים ידע פריץ את המלים הנחוצות למקצוע הריקוד, כגון ימין, derecho, שמאל, iizquierdo, ואף מלים וביטויים שימושיים בספרדית, והחייל לשעבר יכול היה לבצע צעדי־מחול פשוטים אחדים.

פריץ היה מהרהר לעיתים קרובות בידידתו קלאודיה ומדמיין אותה עומדת על הרציף בהאבאנה ומנפנפת לו לשלום.

בעומדו על הרציף בהאבאנה, הזיע פריץ תחת השמש הטרופית בתוך "החליפה האנגלית הקלה" שלו. הוא לא יכל לראות בשום מקום את קלאודיה וג'ורג'. לאחר שחיכה מעט, סחב את מטענו דרך רחוב מתעקל עד שהגיע לשדרת דקלים וקקטוסים רחבה, צמחים פלאיים בעיניו האירופיות. הוא הראה את כתובתם של הקאופמנים לעוברים ושבים ולנוסעי האוטובוס, וכך הגיע לבסוף לדירתם. הם היו מאוד מופתעים לראותו, מאחר שקראו בעיתונים שהנמל נסגר. מרוב שאלות ותשובות נרגשות היה קשה לברר, מה עלה בגורל חבריהם השונים.

קלאודיה הסבירה, שהאבאנה היא מרכז מחול פעיל. ארגון ה"Sociedad Pro-Arte Musical", שנוסד בידי פטרונים עשירים ב־1918, במטרה להעשיר את חיי התרבות בעיר, דאג להביא להקות וארגן קונצרטים.(20) ב־1937 לקח הארגון תחת חסותו את הופעותיהם של Ted Shown, Yeichi Nimura, Lisan Kay(21) ובשנת 1938 הציג ה"Ballet Caravan"

31

האמריקני תוכנית מהממת. מאוחר יותר באותה שנה הופיעו התלמידים המתקדמים של בית-הספר לבאלט ה"פרו-ארטה" בתוכנית משלהם. בשנים 1931-1938 נוהל בית-הספר בידי ניקולאי יבורסקי, לשעבר חבר להקת אופרה בפריס. בין תלמידיו היו Alicia Martinez המוכשרת, בעלה לעתיד Fernando Alonso ואחיו אלברטו. שני הבחורים הצעירים היו בניה של נשיאת ה"פרו-ארטה", Laura Rayneri de Alonso. בסוף שנות ה-30 עזבו שלושת הרקדנים המאומנים היטב את קובה. אלברטו הופיע עם הבאלט הרוסי של דה באזיל, שעה שאליסיה ופרננדו רקדו בברודווי ועם ה"באלט תיאטר" בניו-יורק.

בנין ה"פרו-ארטה" נבנה ב-1928 באתר שבין האבאנה הישנה למיראמר, רצועת חוף שבה גרו עשירים קובנים, שחפצו להיות קרובים למועדונים המשובחים של העיר ואף סמוכים לחוף. הבנין הכיל ספריה, אולם קונצרטים קטן עם פסנתר משובח, סטודיו למחול, משרדים ותיאטרון ובו 2,500 מושבים.

נזכרת קלאודיה:(22) "הגעתי לקובה באופן חוקי, כחברה בלהקת הריקוד החדשה Mozart Opera Troupe. טרודי גות השיגה עבורי את המשרה, אך למעשה להקת האופרה התפזרה מיד לאחר בואי. הרקדנים החליטו להופיע יחד עם אחת מזמרות הסופרן של הקבוצה, והופענו במועדוני-הלילה הפרטיים של האבאנה." היא למדה ספרדית ואנגלית, שהיו לשונותיה החמישית והששית, משאר הרקדנים. "לא סבלנו מהשינוי וההסתגלות לחיים החדשים, מאחר שנעשינו לחלק ממושבת האמנים שבהאבאנה."

פריץ רצה מאוד להתחיל בחזרות עם קלאודיה. בלי ספק יוכלו להכין תוכנית יחדיו, אך היכן יערכו את החזרות? הוא הביא עימו תלבושות ותווים. מתי יוכלו להתחיל בעבודה? קלאודיה צחקה. עליו להרגע. הדברים מתנהלים אחרת בהאבאנה, ואין מה למהר. אנשים מקדישים זמן להנאות החיים, ועליו ללמוד להסתגל לקצב האיטי.

היא וג'ורג' חזרו עם פריץ לאזור הנמל, שם היו להם חברים שידעו על דירה בת שני חדרים פנויה. היא נמצאה בבנין סמוך לנמל, באזור שירד מגדולתו ובו גרו בזול זונות, סרסורים ופליטים.

כדי שיוכלו להשתכר, החלו קלאודיה ופריץ בחזרות. הוא פירסם על קיומם של שיעורי התעמלות ומחול לנשים. הפליטים החלו לבוא לשיעורים, מאחר שלא היה להם דבר לעשותו מלבד לצפות לאשרות כניסה לאמריקה. התועלת המובטחת שבתרגילים ובאמנות שבשיעוריו של פריץ עזרה לשבור את המתח הבלתי נסבל שבציפיה לחדשות בדבר קרובי משפחה באירופה ובדאגה לעתיד.

פריץ אהב את האקלים הטרופי, את דרך החיים הנינוחה ואת חוסר הרשמיות של האבאנה. "הכל היה עדיין כה תמים. הקובאנים שפגשתי היו שואלים אותי מדוע עזבתי את אירופה. כשעניתי, שנאלצתי לעזוב בגלל יהדותי, הם היו שואלים - מה זה יהודי?" הוא השתעשע ברעיון להשאר בקובה, למרות שמצא את החום מתיש. "כל כך חם!", "!Hace calor", היה אחד הביטויים הראשונים שלמד בקובה. קלאודיה נזכרת, שבאחת החזרות הוא זרק את כובע הקוקים עשוי הפרווה שחבש באחד הריקודים וזעם "חם מדי לרקוד!"

הצוות ואל את ברגר היה מבוקש כבר בהתחלה. תוך חודש מבואו של פריץ, ארגן עבורם אמרגן ידיד הופעות בתיאטרון ה"פרו-ארטה", למרות שהיה זה סוף העונה. ב-19 ביוני 1939(23) הם הציגו את תוכנית הדואטים שלהם למוסיקה של שופן וליסט, שכללה גם ריקודים עממיים מרוסיה, קרואטיה ואוסטריה.

הריקודים שיקפו את סגנון המחול הוינאי המודרני שעליו חונכו - אהבה ואחוות-עמים הוצגו על-ידי ריקודים בעלי קצבים ונושאים תנועתיים שהושפעו ממחולות עממיים מסורתיים, וריקודים שנושאיהם ביקורת חברתית הצטרפו למחולות של אווירה. "מחול קפיצות וניתורים" למוסיקה של שומן היה מחאה כנגד מלחמות. "מאבק הניגודים" למוסיקה של שופן היה מחול על הרפתקאת אהבים. לקטעים שונים של שופן (שנוגנו בפסנתר על-ידי תיאה גלוסמן) רקד הזוג את "רומנסה של אהבה", ו"המהפכן" תיאר את הבריקדות בזמן המהפיכה של 1848. ריקוד שקיבל את השראתו מתמונה של ברויגל, "מחול כפרי", בוצע למוסיקה של גראופנר.

בחלקה השני של התוכנית הופיע הצמד במחולות עממיים מרוסיה, פולין וקרואטיה, כשבאחרון הם לבושים בתלבושות מקוריות שהביאה קלאודיה מיוגוסלביה,

32

מולדתה. התוכנית הסתיימה בשני ריקודים אוסטריים, החביבים על הקהל, ה"לנדלר" למוסיקה של שוברט וואלס ויגאי למוסיקה של י. שטראוס.

"לא הייתי רגיל לקהל כה עירני בהבעת רגשותיו ולצעקות והקריאות, שבהן קיבלו אותנו," נזכר פריץ. "אך כבר היכרתי את מנהגי החבורה המתאספת בפתח כניסת האמנים מהזמנים בהם הייתי "מוחא-כפיים מקצועני" בוינה. אך עתה הפכתי ממעריץ נלהב לכוכב עצמו!" האמרגן שלח את צמד הרקדנים, כשהם לבושים בחלוקים ועל פניהם עדיין האיפור, מנהג שלא יתואר בוינה, כדי שיעניקו את חתימותיהם לקהל המעריצים ליד פתח התיאטרון. "התקבלנו בתשואות והמון המעריצים התחנן לחתימותינו. אחר זאת נסוגנו בדרמטיות חגיגית."

בעתון בשפה האנגלית, ה"Havana Post", הופיעה ביקורת אוהדת. Clotilde Pujo, בעלת הטור הפופולרי "פינת המוסיקה", ציינה לשבח את "הביצוע ואת איפיון הדמויות." היא התפעלה מעבודת הצוות הטובה, מהתלהבות הרקדנים, מהידע שלהם ומהתלבושות הציוריות.

לאחר מספר חודשים הוצע לפריץ ללמד בבית-ספר למוסיקה. בעזרת שאלות רבות לתלמידים הצליח פריץ ללמד מחול בספרדית בסיסית. הוא וקלאודיה היו לחלק של קהילת האמנים בהאבאנה. "עבדנו במועדוני-הלילה בכל העיר," סיפרה קלאודיה. "זו היתה תקופה נהדרת. לא היינו כמו שאר הפליטים, שחשבו רק על החיים החדשים העתידיים באמריקה."

העונה הבוערת בהאבאנה החלה בדצמבר. למרות המלחמה באירופה, נפתחו מירוצי-הסוסים והקאזינו פתח את שעריו; תיירים מצפונה ודרומה של אמריקה הציפו את העיר מדצמבר ועד לסגירת הקאזינו במרס.

קלאודיה ופריץ הוסיפו ארבעה ריקודים חדשים לרפרטואר שלהם: פרודיה על מחולות פסטורליים למוסיקה של Grainger, ריקוד סקוטי, ריקוד ספרדי למוסיקה של אלבניז וריקוד הונגרי למוסיקה של דבוז'ק. עם אלה הם הופיעו בתיאטרון "Lyceum" ב-6 בדצמבר, 1939.

הם הופיעו במועדוני-הלילה המפוארים, שהיוו שרשרת של בניינים הדורים לאורך הטיילת בחוף. רוב חיי החברה של העיר החל לאחר שקיעת השמש, כשהחום פג במקצת. את ימי הקיץ בילו האנשים על שפת הים; בחורף טיילו ברחובות וישבו במרתפי-היין ובבתי-הקפה.(24)

המלונות החביבים על התיירים העשירים היו ה"נסיונל", ה"פרסידנטה" וה"סוויליה", כשה"נסיונל" בראש הרשימה. לקלאודיה כרזה באנגלית המודיעה על הופעתם של "קלאודיה ופרדריק" באכסדרת מלון "נסיונל". תוכניתם כללה ריקודים מארצות שונות ובינהים המזורקה הפולנית, הטרפאק הרוסי, ריקודי ארצות מולדתם, קרואטיה ואוסטריה, וכן ריקודי המחאה שלהם נגד המלחמה.(25)

הצמד אף השתתף בנשף ראש-השנה האזרחית שנערך במלון. ידיעה ב"Havana Post" מתארת את ההכנות לחגיגה: "אולם הנשפים הראשי של מלון 'נסיונל' יקושט בהתאם בצבעי כסף וכחול עליזים לכבוד מסיבת ראש-השנה, שתיערך ביום ראשון בערב. ארוחה מיוחדת תוכננה ושני רקדנים מוכשרים בצורה יוצאת מן הכלל, קלאודיה ופרדריק, יופיעו בביצועים בימתיים של מחולות עממיים מארצות שונות." קלאודיה נזכרת שזרם החשמל נפסק באמצע המופע החגיגי ושני הרקדנים נותרו לפתע על הבמה החשוכה לחלוטין.

הם סיירו באי והופיעו בליוויית תזמורת או לעיתים עם פסנתרן בלבד. תוכניתם הורכבה ממחולות סולו ודואטים, המבוססים על נושאי תנועה עממיים שראו באירופה, אך פריץ גם רקד את מחולות הסולו הנודעים שלו, אשר היקנו לו את מדליית הארד בתחרות בוינה.

אך לא כל הסיורים בוינה היו מוצלחים. מספרת קלאודיה: "נשכרנו להופיע בסנטיאגו דה קובה, בצידו השני של האי. כשהגענו לשם, לא מצאנו את התזמורת שהובטחה לנו. הבמה היתה במצב נורא. איך שהוא הצלחנו להשיג חצוצרן וכנר, ששימש גם כסנדלר הכפר. בנקודה מסויימת במהלך ההופעה שאלתי לפתע את פריץ תוך כדי ריקוד: 'האם עלי לעקוב אחר החצוצרה או הכינור?' ושנינו פרצנו בצחוק כה עז, עד שלא יכולנו להמשיך עוד."

33

למרות הקשיים קובה המשיכה להאיר פנים לפריץ. הוא לא יכל לרוות את צמאונו לחיי הרחוב בה: רוכלי הדגים ומוכרי ספוגי-הים, העליצות, הריחות והתנועה. לגביו היה קצב פועם בכל. תמיד נשמעה נגינתם של תופי הבונגו. ה-Maracas והגיטרות, והמוני אדם היו רוקדים לעיתים קרובות ברחובות. ריקודי הרחוב הנפלאים ביותר התקיימו בפברואר, חודש ה-Mardi Gras. ביום שלפני צום הפסחא ואף במשך מספר ימים לאחריו, בעיקר ימי ראשון, יצאו לרחובות מצעדים של Comparsas ועניי האבאנה רקדו את הקונגה בבגדיהם הצבעוניים ותלבושותיהם המזהירות. מכוניות מקושטות ועמוסות לעייפה נעו באיטיות לאורך הרחובות. מוסיקה ושירה נשמעו מכל עבר.

"אנשים היו מתחילים לפתע לרקוד את הרומבה," נזכר פריץ. "מעולם לא נתקלתי באהבה כזו לתנועה. המקצבים הללו כישפו אותי בתכלית. לאחר החזיון היומי של הקרנבל החלטתי ללמוד מחול ספרדי, אך המורה שמצאתי לא יכל להסביר לי מה לעשות. אז פשוט חיקיתי את תנועותיו בהתלהבות."

באביב שנת 1941 ראה פריץ בפעם הראשונה את הבאלט הרוסי. להקת ה"Ballet Russe de Monte Carlo" בניהולו של הקולונל דה-באזיל, הגיעה להאבאנה. האמרגן סול יורוק אירגן את סיורה של להקה במרכז ודרום אמריקה. בשבוע האחרון להופעותיהם בקובה התנגדו הרקדנים לקבל את שכרם במטבע המקומי. מאחר שלא הגיעו להסכם עם ההנהלה פתחו הרקדנים בשביתה. כתגובה ביטל יורוק את שאר התאריכים להופעות, והלהקה נתקעה בחוסר כל בהאבאנה מאפריל ועד אוגוסט.(26)

פריץ הוקסם מרקדני הבאלט הרוסי. הוא שמח לפגוש רבים מהם על חוף הים, אשר הפך לאולם חזרות בלתי רשמי. רבים מרקדני הלהקה היו פליטים, ממש כפריץ עצמו, ומשפחותיהם נפוצו לכל עבר על פני העולם. רבים מהם החזיקו בדרכוני "חבר הלאומים", מה שכינה דרכוני-ננסן לאנשים חסרי נתינות, שסופקו לפליטים ולא הוכרו בכל מדינות העולם. כתוצאה מכך היו הרקדנים מוגבלים במסעותיהם. בשיחה איתם התברר, שרובם היו מודאגים מהמצב באירופה וחששו שארצות-הברית תסתבך במלחמה. אך מכל מקום עליצותם הנמרצת שבה אליהם, כשהחלו בתרגיליהם ובמפגני האקרובטיקה על החוף.

בערך בזמן זה פתח יאבורסקי, שעזב את בית-הספר לבאלט של ה-Pro-Arte ב-1938, סטודיו משלו וארגן להקה קטנה. הוא הזמין את פריץ להצטרף אליו כרקדן אופי, הצעה ששימחה אותו מאוד. רקדנית אירופית אחרת, נינה ורשינינה, שהוזמנה אף היא להצטרף, היתה בשעתה אמנית מועדפת על-ידי מיאסון ותלמידתו של לאבאן, ונתקעה בהאבאנה יחד עם יתר אמני הבאלט הרוסי.

פריץ היה מדוכא, כשחברתו ובת-זוגו למחול, קלאודיה, קיבלה אשרת-כניסה לארצות-הברית יחד עם בעלה. ג'ורג' לא רצה להשאר רק בחזקת "מר ואל". ככלות הכל, הוא היה רופא ורצה מאוד לעסוק במקצועו ולבנות חיים ממשיים חדשים לעצמו ואשתו. באמריקה היה לו סיכוי להשיג כל מה שחפץ ולבטח יהיו שם הזדמנויות לקלאודיה לרקוד. הקאופמנים החליטו לעזוב למען עתיד בטוח יותר והם הבטיחו להשיג לפריץ את "ההצהרה בשבועה", שהיתה נחוצה כדי שגם הוא יוכל לבוא בעקבותיהם.

למרות ההזדמנות להופיע לצידם של רקדנים טובים בלהקתו של יאבורסקי, שקל פריץ בזהירות את צעדיו. לפניו עמדה עונה מעניינת של מחול: להקתו של קורט יוס היתה אמורה להופיע בהאבאנה ומרתה גראהם היתה עתידה לבוא בחורף. כוכב הבאלט הרוסי דויד לישין עבד על מופע קברטי מהמם בשם "Congo Pantera" עבור מועדון-הלילה "טרופיקאנה".(27)

פריץ החליט לחתום על חוזה עם להקתו של יאבורסקי למשך שישה שבועות, ובזמן זה הוא קיווה לקבל את אשרת-הכניסה שלו. אז הוא יוכל להצטרף לקאופמנים באמריקה ולהבטיח את עתיד עבודתו. הוא דן במצב עם האמרגן שטיפל בו במשך 18 החודשים שחלפו מאז הגיע לקובה. הלה הציע לו, שישנה את שמו בעל הצלצול הגרמני. זה יכול היה לעזור בקבלת הויזה, כי שם כמו פרידריך ברגר עלול לעורר אסוציאציות עם הנאצים, שאמריקה היתה קרובה למלחמה איתם. פריץ חשב על שם פשוט יותר, פרד ברק, והשתמש בו לראשונה במסמכים הרשמיים, שהגיש לקונסוליה האמריקנית.

למרבה המזל הצליח ג'ורג' להשיג עבודה כרופא בקולורדו, וזה איפשר לו לכתוב משם לקונסול האמריקני בהאבאנה, לתמוך בבקשתו של פריץ ולהוכיח שיש משפחה

34

באמריקה שתדאג לו עד שימצא עבודה. כתוצאה מכך הוענקה לפריץ האשרה. נותר לו זמן אך להשלים את החוזה עם יאבורסקי בטרם יפקע תוקף האשרה.

בבוקר אביבי אחד הוא הלך לחזרה ואחר-כך לחוף הים. הוא חש בשמחה בשל הידיעה, שמשהו חדש ממתין לו בפתח ובקרוב יחליף את האקלים הטרופי באחר. אך למחרת התעורר, כשכאבים עזים ברגלו הימנית והוא רועד כולו. למרות זאת התלבש וידידה איך שהוא אל מחוץ לדירתו בדרכו לחזרה. בקושי הצליח להגיע לתחנת האוטובוס, אך לא היה מסוגל לעלות עליו מרוב הכאב שבטיפוס במדרגה. חרד כולו הצליח לחזור הביתה ולזחול למיטתו.

הוא קרא לאחד משכניו, שהיה רופא פליט מלטביה. האיש הזקן אילתר מיתקן למתיחה ולקיבוע הרגל, בעזרת קומקום-תה, שקשר לכף רגלו של פריץ. הוא הורה לפריץ הקודח להמשיך לשכב במטה במשך ימים רבים. פריץ לא יכול לעשות דבר. יום ולילה סבל מהתכווצויות שרירים עזות וכאב במפרק הירך.

לאחר שאיש לא ראה אותו או שמע ממנו במשך מספר ימים, באה לדירתו אחת מתלמידותיו לשעבר. היא הזדעזעה ממצבו והודיעה על כך ל"ג'וינט", ארגון העזרה לפליטים יהודים, אשר שלח רופא קובני ועובדת סוציאלית. בחושבו שפריץ אינו שומע ספרדית, מסר הרופא את תוצאות הבדיקה לעובדת הסוציאלית: "ארתריטיס חמור במותן כתוצאה מזיהום, שהרס את מפרק הירך."(28) הרופא סבר שאין הרבה סיכויים להחלמה.

"שליטתי בספרדית היתה טובה וללא כל בעיות הבנתי את חומרת מצבי. הייתי מפוחד מאוד, אך מה יכולתי לעשות? אושפזתי בבית-חולים שבו שררה צפיפות איומה, כשרק אחות אחת ואח השגיחו על כל המחלקה. חלקתי את החדר עם עוד שמונה חולים, כשרק אחד מאיתנו יכל לזוז - היה זה נער, אשר דידה על רגל אחת. הנער המסכן ביצע שליחויות עבורנו, מאחר שלא היה מי שיעזור לנו. המזון היה מועט ביותר ואף פעם לא היו די מים טריים בחדרים המצחינים. אי אפשר היה להשיג אז בקובה אנטיביוטיקה. בערבי שבת היה משרד ה'ג'וינט' שולח לי עוף לכבוד שבת ואני הייתי מחלק אותו לשמונה חלקים וחוגג עם האחרים."

חברים הביאו לפריץ לבית-החולים את ספריו הראשונים על מחול באנגלית. "אחד מהם היה על סרגי דיאגולב והאחר על אנגה פבלובה. את השבועות שנשארתי בבית-החולים בילתי בקריאת הספרים שוב ושוב, בעזרת מילון. לא רק למדתי את פרטי חייהם של שני האישים הללו, אלא גם שיפרתי את האנגלית שלי."

בשוכבו במיטתו, קרא פריץ את עתון המהגרים הגרמני האמריקני. מודעות רבות הכריזו על מוצרים למכירה על-ידי מהגרים חדשים. מודעה קטנה בדבר סטודיו למחול בניו-יורק משכה את תשומת לבו והוא קרא אותה בקפידה. המורה, קטיה דלקובה, היתה מוכרת לו מאירופה! היא שרדה! הוא כתב לה ובקש לדעת את קורותיה. אולי יוכלו להפגש, אם יגיע לארצות-הברית, אם יוכל לחזור לכושר ולהופיע שוב.

הם רקדו יחד, כל אחד ביצירות חברו, תחת חסותה של גרטרוד קראוס בוינה. דלקובה נישאה, ואחר-כך התגרשה, ביוגוסלביה. היא הזמינה אותו פעמיים לבוא ולרקוד עימה שם. הוא אהב מסעות והתרגש מאוד לקראת ביקור בארץ כה עשירה במחולות-עם. הם לא טיפחו יחסים חברותיים מיוחדים במשך הסיורים המפרכים המשותפים שלהם, אך היו לו זכרונות נפלאים מעבודתם המשותפת. הוא חיכה בצפיה דרוכה לתשובתה מאמריקה, ותהה מה עלה בגורלה.

דלקובה ענתה לו, אך לא סיפקה פרטים. מאוחר יותר שמע פריץ על אביה העיתונאי, אשר נשאר זמן רב מדי בוינה, בכסותו את המאורעות הפוליטיים. היא חזרה מיוגוסלביה לאוסטריה כדי לנסות לשכנע את הוריה להצטרף לדודה באמריקה. היא הגיעה מאוחר מדי - דוד אחד כבר היה במחנה הריכוז הנאצי בוכנוואלד. אביה נאסר, אך אחותה הצליחה לחמוק ולעבור ברגל את ההרים והגיעה לצרפת. בנס, עם שיחרורו הפתאומי של אביה ממחנה הריכוז, הגיעה עבורם אשרה נדירה ומיוחדת לאמריקה. דלקובה נשארה בוינה עם דרכונה היוגוסלבי, כדי לנסות ולשחרר את דודה ממחנה הריכוז, והיא המשיכה לבקר אותו עם חבילות מזון ובגדים, אך לאחר שנה היא נואשה והצטרפה לאחותה והוריה באמריקה.

החוויות שעברו ערערו אותה, והיא היתה שרויה במעין קפאון חושים. היא רצתה

35

להתעלם מרגשותיה, להתעלם מהעובדות ולשכוח את הזכרונות. היא החלה לעבוד בבית־חרושת לייצור בובות כפועלת. לאחר שעות על גבי שעות, בהן החזיקה בידיה אברים זעירים חסרי חיים, השתוקקה לנסיון יצירתי. היא הגיעה להכרה, שברצונה להעביר את רגשותיה כלפי העם היהודי לשפת המחול. היא פנתה ל"ועד אירגוני הצדקה היהודיים" ופגשה בז'נט וייסמן, אשר האמינה בעתיד עבודתה ונעשתה לסוכנת מייצגת האישית שלה. דלקובה נשלחה להופיע בפני קבוצות נשים יהודיות כגון אסיפות "הדסה" ומועדונים בניר־ג'רסי.

שם היא הופיעה במקרה בתוכנית משותפת עם בנימין צמח. אף הוא היה יוצרם של ריקודים על נושאים יהודיים ועבודתו נגעה לליבה. היא הצטרפה ללהקתו ונעשתה בת־זוגו למחול.

דלקובה כתבה בתשובה למכתבו של פריץ, שהיא עובדת עם צמח ושהם יחד מנסים לפתח מרכז תרבותי יהודי ועל פריץ לנסות לבוא!

"עזבתי את בית־החולים על קביים. שחיתי בים ופינקתי את עצמי בשכיבה על החול החם על שפת הים. התידדתי מאוד עם דויד לישין, מיכאל פאנאייב וטטיאנה ריאבוצ'ינסקה,(29) מרקדני הבאלט הרוסי, שהיו באים לעיתים קרובות לחוף. הם עודדו אותי בהתמדה ואמרו שאוכל לשוב לרקוד תוך מספר חודשים. הם צדקו, אך זה לקח שנה תמימה.

"בינתיים פג תוקף האשרה שלי לארה"ב, בזמן שהותי בבית־החולים, ולא היה לי מושג, כיצד אצליח לעבור את הבדיקות הגופניות בשגרירות. כדי להכנס לאמריקה היה עליך להיות בריא, ונכה לא הורשה להכנס. ובכן, לאחר שניכנסתי לבנין הנציגות, נטשתי את הקביים שלי ואיך שהוא, בהשעני על הקירות ובהאחזי ברהיטים בלא־איכפתיות מופגנת, הגעתי עד לפקיד, שכלל לא הבחין במצבי. קיבלתי אשרת כניסה חדשה." שלוש שנים לאחר שנמלט מוינה, היתה הדרך לארצות־הברית פתוחה לפניו.

פרק שישי:
אמריקה

את הלילה הראשון שלו בארצות־הברית, ביוני 1941, בילה פריץ במעון למהגרים חדשים, שנוהל על־ידי אירגון תמיכה יהודי, ברחוב לפייט. ניתן לו מקום ללינה שם, מאחר שלא היתה לו משפחה, שיוכל לפנות אליה. פעמים רבות מאז חזר פריץ אל הבניין, שהפך להיות ברבות הימים תיאטרון ה"אוף־ברודווי" המפורסם, ה־Public Theatre של Joseph Papp.

"הרושם שקיבלתי מאמריקה בערב ראשון זה היה מאוד מוזר. חשבתי תחילה מהאנגלית המוגבלת שבפי והנה בחלק המזרחי התחתון של ניו־יורק כולם דיברו יידיש – האנשים ברחוב, השוטרים והמלצרים."

הוא לא נשאר בניו־יורק, אלא נסע מיד ברכבת לקולורדו, לפגוש את חבריו, קלאודיה וג'ורג' קאופמן. הוא התרשם מדרכם הניחוחה של האמריקנים ומגישתם הישירה. בקרון־המסעדה ברכבת, כשהוגש לו כריך ענק שהזמין בעזרת תנועות ידיים, הוא ניסה לאוכלו בנימוס באמצעות סכין ומזלג. "עם החינוך שקיבלתי, מי יכול לאכול בידיים? אך כשהבחנתי שכך אוכלים כל האנשים האחרים, נטשתי את הסכו"ם והתחלתי ללעוס."

ברק עדיין סבל מהארתריטיס, וידידו ד"ר קאופמן נתן לו זריקות וטיפול במפרק הירך. הוא החל לרקוד בזהירות. לשמחתו לקחו אותו הקאופמנים למסיבת Square-dancing. "לא יכולתי להבין את הוראות הכרוז. חשבתי שקריאותיו נועדו ללמד אותנו את הצעדים. לכן, כשהמוסיקה חזרה על עצמה בשנית, ביצעתי את מה שראיתי קודם, ולא יכולתי להבין מה קורה! תמיד הגעתי למקום הלא נכון, והרסתי את צורת הריבוע. לא הבנתי, שהכרוז אילתר את קריאותיו."

מצב רגלו השתפר בהדרגה וקלאודיה והוא יכלו להתחיל להופיע שוב יחד. הם אף הוזמנו להופיע בארוחת צהריים באמצעות כרוז של "ריקוד הריבוע". הצמד פנה אז אל הכוריאוגרפית והמורה המפורסמת הניה הולם, שבאה לניו־יורק מגרמניה בשנות השלושים כדי לפתוח שם את הסטודיו הרשמי של מרי ויגמן, ומאוחר יותר נעשתה לעצמאית, ובקיץ שנת 1941 הגיעה לקולורדו, כדי לפתוח במכללה שם קורס־קיץ למחול (אשר התפתח למוסד שנתי בעל חשיבות רבה לעולם המחול). הולם היתה אדיבה ומתחשבת כלפי הצמד המרקד של ואל וברק, ויעצה להם בדבר עבודתם והיכן יוכלו להופיע.

במשך כל הסתיו ובתחילת החורף הם הופיעו במועדונים פרטיים ומלונות, כשם שעשו בקובה. לתקופת חג המולד הם נשכרו להופיע במועדון־לילה בדנבר. האולם היה מלא חיילים, ששרקו וצעקו ולפתע נראה לדר' קאופמן, שזו בהחלט אינה סביבה הולמת לאשתו להופיע בה.

"היה לנו סוכן, שדאג לארגן הופעות עבורנו. בדרך כלל הופיענו במקומות טובים, אך ככל שנמשכה המלחמה התקיימו פחות כנסים וההזמנות נתמעטו. הקש ששבר את גב הגמל, לגבי ג'ורג', היה ההופעות במועדון־הלילה בדנבר. בקרוב היה 'מר ואל', בעלה של הרקדנית, אך עתה הוא היה רופא הפותח בקריירה חדשה, ובבית־החולים הקתולי לא ראו בעין יפה את העובדה שאשתו רקדנית."

עד רגע זה הם תכננו לעקור יחד לקליפורניה. קלאודיה ביקרה בלוס־אנג'לס וידעה ששם מצויה רק להקת־מחול מודרנית אחת, להקתו של לסטר הורטון. סוכן שראה

37

צילומים שלה מהופעות באירופה וקובה אמר לה: "לא הייתי חוצה את הרחוב כדי לצפות במשהו מסוג זה." היא ידעה שהדרך היחידה, בה ברק והיא יוכלו לרקוד יחדיו היא במלונות ובמועדוני־לילה. כדי להמשיך כך, היה עליהם להשיג תלבושות חדשות ואת רשותו של ג'ורג'.

הם גרו יחדיו בבית קטן בקולורדו ספרינגס. כלומר, במשך ימות השבוע היה ג'ורג' לן בבית־החולים ולמד את שיטות הרפואה האמריקניות, והצטרף אליהם לסופי השבוע. "הסתדרנו יחד באופן יוצא מן הכלל. היינו חברים, וכולנו היינו פליטים. התחלקנו בכל, וזה היה נהדר בתחילה."

אך דוקא כשדר' קאופמן קיבל עבודה בלוס־אנג'לס, הוא החליט שאינו רוצה שפרד ישאר עימם. "זה היה נורא. לא ידעתי כיצד לספר על כך לפרד. אני הייתי זקוקה לו כל כך כשותף וכיועץ, ועתה היה עלי לבשר לו, שלא נוכל לעבוד יחד עוד. אך פרד היה אדם מעשי ביותר, ורגליו היו שתולות היטב בקרקע. הוא הבין את המצב. היה ברור, שההזדמניות במחול מודרני עבור פריץ היו בניו־יורק, ולא בלוס־אנג'לס. וכשעבר לעבוד בניו־יורק, עלה בידו להחזיר לנו את כל הכסף שלווה מאיתנו עד לפרוטה האחרונה."

ברק נסע למנהטן והקאופמנים ללוס־אנג'לס. קלאודיה ניסתה לארגן כיתה למחולות־אופי בסטודיו של לסטר הורטון. הוא עצמו התעניין בנושא, אך לא כך תלמידיו. בבתי־הספר למחול מודרני באירופה היה מקובל להעביר שיעורים במחול־אופי, אך לשיעוריה של קלאודיה לא הגיע אפילו תלמיד אחד. היא חזרה לבאלט כמורה וכתלמידה. ללא פרד לצידה, על גישתו החברית וניסיונו האמנותי, לא הוסיפה להופיע עוד כרקדנית.

"כמובן שקינאתי בקטיה (דלקובה) במשך זמן מה. לאחר שפרד עזב, היא נעשתה לבת־זוגו.

"הוא שלח לי מכתב מהרי הקטסקיל שם רקדו יחד. 'הירח זורח,' כתב, 'וזה הקיץ המאושר בחיי.' הוא היה מאוהב בקטיה וכתב לי מיד לאחר שהחליטו להנשא.

"למעשה, חברותנו העמיקה גם מבלי שנופיע יחד. סוף סוף הייתי חופשיה מביקורתו ומהציפיה לשבחיו ואישורו. משנה לשנה הרגשתי כיצד החופש בינינו גדל. עמוק בתוכו הוא לא היה מסוגל באמת להסכים ולקבל. רציתי להיות איתו בשל דברים אחרים."

פרד לווה כסף מחבריו ונסע באוטובוס במשך שלושה ימים וללילות לניו־יורק. רוחו היתה מרוממת, כשהגיע לעיר הגדולה; הוא קנה לעצמו חליפה לפי מיטב האופנה, מעיל משיער גמלים ומגבעת, זוג נעליים. זו היתה הפעם הראשונה, מאז שהותו באנגליה אצל גברת גראהם, שרכש לעצמו בגדים. הוא שכר חדר קטן והלך לחפש את ידידתו קטיה.

היא הזמינה אותו לבוא ולרקוד אצל בנימין צמח. ברק הצטרף לקבוצה כמעט מיד, ורקד כל בוקר בחזרות ובשיעורים יחד עם שש או שבעת האחרים. צמח עמד מהר על יכולת היצירה שלו וביקש ממנו להכין שני ריקודים חסידיים להופעה עתידה בסטודיו. ברק קרא לאחד "שבת" ולשני "תמונות מכפר חסידי".

"בשניהם לא הצטרכתי לזוז הרבה, מאחר שעדיין הייתי מטפל במותן הכואבת שלי." אך למרות זאת הוא היה מרשים ביותר והיה אפשר לראות בתנועתו את שרידיהם של הסיבובים והצעדים המחליקים על פני הקרקע, שכה איפיינו את סיגנון תנועתו. אף כשרונו לארגון קבוצות עזר לו בקונצרטים של צמח. בחודשים הבאים הוא הופיע עם הקבוצה ב"קרנגי־הול", בבית העיריה ובמוסד־לשעבר, שהיה ברבות הימים ל"City Center" ולמרכז המחול המודרני בניו־יורק.

דלקובה זוכרת שברק רקד את תפקיד הבל מול קין של צמח, והיא רקדה את אשתו של קין. הם אף רקדו יחד סוויטה חסידית. למרות העבודה על נושאים יהודיים הם מצאו את גישתו של צמח רחוקה ממה שבאמת עניין אותם. לבסוף החליט הזוג שברצונו לפתח רפרטואר משלו.

"חשבנו, כשהתחלנו לרקוד את הצ'רקסיה, ריקוד מזרח־אירופי בעל נושא פשוט של ארבעה צעדים קדימה ואחורה, שנוכל לעורר אנשים להתעניין בנושאים יהודיים. אך התעניינו גם בריקודים של עמים אחרים ורצינו ליצור תוכנית, שתבליט את כוחו של 'האדם הפשוט'." במהלך עבודתם נוכחו לדעת, שצעדי הצ'רקסיה אינם יהודיים במהותם, והם הזדקקו למשהו מסויים וייחודי יותר בחיפושים אחר הביטוי היהודי. מה ידבר אל

38

קהלם החדש ואל נשמתם שלהם? הם שאלו את עצמם.

כדי לכסות את הוצאות מחייתו קיבל ברק על עצמו להופיע במועדוני-לילה. השניים הכינו שני מחולות שזכו להצלחה רבה - טנגו על אודות בעל קנאי וה-"Femme fatale" שלו וריקוד אפאצ'י. "כמו כן ביצענו ריקודי-נשף אופנתיים עם קפיצות וסיבובים. השתמשנו בריקודים הסלוניים ובמחולות העממיים שידענו מאירופה בהזדמנויות רבות, כבסיס תנועתי לרעיונות המחול הרציניים יותר שלנו. זאת היתה רק ההתחלה, כי נאלצנו קודם כל להשיג כסף למחייה," סיפרה דלקובה.

ההופעות במועדוני-הלילה היו מבחן קשה עבור פרד. הוא הוטרד לא רק מהעובדה, שהופיעו כל לילה במקום אחר, אלא אף השתעמם כשהיה עליו להמתין לתורו לעלות לבימה בין המספרים השונים. הוא מאוד לא אהב את המנהג המקובל, שהרקדנים יורדים לקהל ורוקדים עם האורחים ריקודים סלוניים. אך כל זה הכניס את הכסף הנחוץ ביותר.

הזוג רקד בהפקות של התיאטרונים היהודיים בניו-יורק. זו היתה עבודה מאומצת עבור תשלום קטן, אך כך הם לפחות לא נאלצו לנסוע ולעבוד באווירת מועדוני-הלילה. הם עבדו ב"תיאטרון הלאומי" ויתר התיאטרונים היהודיים שבשדרה השניה.

"עבור סוף שבוע, שבו הופענו תשע פעמים, קיבלנו שמונים דולר. ביום שישי נתנו הופעה אחת, בשבת שלוש וביום ראשון חמש! תמיד היינו חלק מתוכנית בידור שכללה מערכונים, זמרים, סרט קולנוע וסיום חגיגי עם כל המשתתפים. מעולם לא עשינו חזרות על הפינאלה. כשעה לפני עליית המסך היה קורא לנו הבמאי ואומר לנו מה יהיה ומתי יגיע תורנו לעלות על הבמה. קהל המהגרים התמוגג תמיד, כי התוכנית הזכירה לו את ארץ המוצא, כי געגועיהם לעולם שחרב היו עזים ביותר.

"בדרך כלל היתה התוכנית חובבנית, אך לעיתים היינו פוגשים בכמה מהשחקנים האידיים הגדולים, והתנסינו בחוויות המקצוענות והמסורת של משפחות שחקנים אלו.

"במכתב למלאך המושיע שלי באנגליה, מיס גראהם, ניסיתי לתאר את כל הקורות אותי. תשובתה היתה, שאם לשפוט לפי כתיבתי, כבר שכחתי את כל האנגלית הטובה שלמדתי בבריטניה."

לקראת הקיץ הם החלו לחשוב על עזיבת העיר החמה והלחה. דלקובה הכירה מישהו באחד ממקומות הנופש היהודיים שבהרי הקטסקיל. הם קיבלו חדר וכלכלה עבור עשרה שבועות של הופעות והשתתפות בתוכניות לחגיגות ראש השנה וסוכות. רוב הלקוחות דיברו יידיש ורוסית בלבד. הם אהבו את תוכנית הבידור, שכללה זמר והצמד דלקובה / ברק בליווי מוסיקלי. בכל לילה מלילות השבוע הם הציגו סוג אחר של מחול, למשל, ריקודי-עם ביום שלישי, קונצרט מחול "רציני" ביום שישי ובידור מגוון בשבת.

זו היתה פעם נוספת שהזוג נאלץ להתפשר ולהציג את אמנות הריקוד כבידור למשפחות נופשים אמידות בערבי-הקיץ.

במשך כל הקיץ עבדו השניים קשה מאוד, וברק נוכח לדעת בין החזרות וההופעות, שהוא נמשך מאוד לדלקובה. הוא התאהב בה והיה נלהב ונרגש. הוא כתב לקלאודיה בקליפורניה: "אני רוצה לשאת את קטיה לאשה."

הזוג פגש במשך הקיץ הרבה משפחות עם ילדים, והם קיוו שיצליחו לשכנעם לבוא לשיעורי ריקוד. הם החלו לתור את העיר ניו-יורק ולחפש אחר דירה שתהיה מספיק גדולה עבור מגורים וסטודיו כאחד. במשך שנות המלחמה היה כמעט בלתי אפשרי למצוא מגורים, מאחר שהרבה פועלים באו לעיר ככוח-עבודה בייצור המלחמתי. אבל פועלים אלה לא נזקקו לדירות מפוארות וגדולות, וכך הצליחה אמה של דלקובה לשכור עבורם דירה גדולה בקומת הקרקע, בקרן הרחובות ריברסייד ורחוב 72. זו היתה דירת-חלומות המשקיפה על נהר ההדסון. הזוג הצעיר גר בה יחד עם הוריה של קטיה, ולפרד היתה לפתע משפחה חמימה, כפי שמעולם לא היתה לו. מאחר שהדירה היתה סמוכה לכנסיה, הרקדנים לא הפריעו לאיש, ולא היו שכנים שיתלוננו. היה שם שטח לסטודיו וחדרי הלבשה, חדר לאחסון התלבושות, שניים וחצי חדרי רחצה, חדר מגורים גדול, הפונה לנהר וחדרי שינה להוריה של קטיה ולזוג עצמו וכן מטבח נוח. הם קנו ארבעים כסאות מתקפלים, למקרה שיזמינו קהל להרצאות והופעות סטודיו. בעל-הבית אף הבטיח להם לוותר על שכר-הדירה למשך שלושה חודשים, אם יצבעו מחדש את הדירה על חשבונם. הם היו מוכנים לפתיחת בית-הספר למחול הראשון שלהם.

39

פרק שביעי:
אופטימיות

ברק עזב את אירופה ערב השואה. הוא הגיע לארצות-הברית מספר חודשים לפני שזו התערבה במלחמת העולם השנייה, ב-1941. אמריקה היתה בתקופה של שינויים, ולפרד ברק היתה יד בעיצוב השינויים שחלו בחיים התרבותיים של יהדות אמריקה. הרקדן המודרני הוינאי, השקט והבלתי ידוע, באופן יחסי, הפך לאיש יצירתי ובעל סמכות, אשר נתן כיוון לשינויי ביהדות האמריקני. ברק היה בין אלו שהגיעו מאירופה והדליקו ניצוץ באמריקה, למרות הבדלי השפה, השוני בקצב החיים והסביבה החברתית.

הוא שמר באמריקה על עמדתו ההומניטרית והבלתי פוליטית, אך נושאי ריקודיו ומבנה הקונצרט הראשון שלו בניו-יורק הראו, בעצם, את אמנותיו. יחד עם בת-זוגו למחול, קטיה דלקובה, הוא הופיע ב"פני דרך למחר" ב-23 בינואר 1944, ב-"Times Hall Theatre" שברחוב 44. בתאריך זה מלאו בדיוק ארבע שנים (פחות יומיים) מאז נמלט מאירופה הנאצית.

ברק ודלקובה שילבו נושאים אמריקניים עממיים, כגון החלוץ המתישב באיזורים הבלתי מיושבים לזימרתו של ג׳יימס פיליפס, בריקודים על חלוצים יהודיים העובדים את קרקע ארץ-ישראל. השילוב של מוסיקה אמריקנית עממית ויהודית ורעיון ההתישבות יצר אחדות רעיונית נפלאה ואווירה של אופטימיות. התוכנית אף כללה ריקודים עממיים מיוגוסלביה, אוסטריה, רוסיה ואמריקה.

המלים הפשוטות שבתוכניה הביעו את גישתם: "אנו מדברים על דברים קטנים בחיי היום-יום של האדם הפשוט ולא על צערם וכאבם של עמים, משום שפחד אינו יכול להיות מורגש אלא אם כן נחווה באופן מעשי. אין אנו רוצים ברחמים אלא בהבנה. אנו מדברים על ההומור, הגבורה והאהבה של עמים שונים - ונמשיך לדבר עד שהשונה והזר יעשו לאחיכם." במחולותיו עם דלקובה ביטא ברק חום רב, והאופטימיות שלו היתה משכנעת בתכלית.

שלא כרקדנים המודרניים האמריקניים, שהתענינו בראש וראשונה בטכניקה של תנועה, ברק ובת-זוגו הדגישו את אישיותם העצמאית ואת רגשותיהם, מלאי השמחה או הרצינים, הקופצניים או הנלהבים. נראה כאילו קומתו הממוצעת של ברק, כ-165 ס״מ, השתנתה בהתאמה לאיכויות השונות שדרשו התפקידים והסיפורים. הוא יכול היה להיראות גדול ומאיים או קל ושנון, בהתאם לתפקיד שגילם.

"הכל נבע מתוכנו, וזה היה כה חי," נזכרת דלקובה. אף אחד לא הורה לרקדנים מה להביע על הבמה. למזלם הטוב הם אומנו באסכולה האירופית של המחול האקספרסיבי. חינוך זה פתח לפניהם את הדרך ליצירת ריקודים משכנעים, אשר דיברו בשפה שלמרות זרותה היתה מובנת לקהל האמריקני שלהם.

מרשימה במיוחד היתה הדרך, שבה ביצע ברק תנועות החלקה, בסגנון הלירי של הלנדלר האוסטרי ומחולות הוואלס. הוא אהב סיבובים וקפיצותיו היו גבוהות ורבות עוצמה. אם כי לא היה בעל טכניקה מסחררת, הוא נראה גברי מאוד בתנועותיו וביצע סיבובים בקלות ובעונג. ברק דחה שיחות ודיונים על המלחמה, על אירופה ומשפחתו. מעולם לא היה גלוי בדבר חייו הפרטיים, ושמר על מעין ריחוק אישי. אך חוש ההומור שלו והעידוד שהעניק לאחרים עשו אותו מושך ואהוב על תלמידים ורקדנים.

40

השמירה על פרטיות גרמה לריחוק מסויים אפילו מהקרובים אליו ביותר. בתחילה הוא עצמו לא הבין את הצורך שלו בפרטיות. הוא האמין בדבריו של אביו, שטפשותו ויחסיו הבלתי מוצלחים עם אחרים מעידים על נחיתות. הוא נסוג עמוק יותר אל דמיונותיו, עד אשר הריקוד חילץ אותו והעניק לו יכולת התבטאות. "למרות שתמיד נשארתי כמעין אי, כדי שאוכל להמלט מניצול ומסחריות, ספגתי צעקות פעמים רבות. תמיד אמרתי לעצמי, שאם ברצוני במשהו שונה, אוכל לעשות דברים אחרים. הייתי נעשה איש עסקים, אם הייתי רוצה כסף; הייתי נואם, אם הייתי רוצה לדבר." והוא רצה לרקוד.

הריקוד היה עבורו מוצא ותענוג. פעם בזמן קונצרט בבית־העיריה של ניו־יורק, בו רקד בתפקיד נביא תנ"כי בליווית מקהלה תנועתית, התמקד עליו הזרקור והאיר אותו. לפתע חש בסערת רגשות, כאילו היה רוקד בשמש ויכול להמריא אל על. בהבזק מהיר הבין את הדימויי של אליהו הנביא הממריא במרכבת אש השמימה. כוחו כמבצע על הבמה וכמורה נבע מאמונתו הפנימית, לא מהסברים.

"ומה יכולנו לעשות בזכרונותינו מאירופה? לא עשינו דבר ולא יכולנו לדבר על אירופה. הרגשנו אשמים בכך ששרדנו, ולא יכולנו להבין את ההגיון שבקיומנו, אז רקדנו."

גם ניצולים אחרים במקומות שונים רקדו, תגובה שנראתה תחילה כבלתי הולמת. במרחק של אלפי קילומטרים מברג ודלקובה התרחשה חוויית־מחול חדשה בתכלית, אשר מאוחר יותר תיעשה לציר ולנקודה המרכזית בחייו המקצועיים של פרד. בזמן שהמלחמה המשיכה להשתולל באירופה ובמזרח הרחוק, המשיך הישוב היהודי הקטן בפלשתינה־א"י, שמנה לא יותר מ־600,000 איש, לבנות את חייו בכל המישורים, כולל התרבותי והאמנותי ואף את חיי הריקוד שלו.

גרטרוד קראוס, מורתו לשעבר של פרד ואמנים רבים אחרים מאירופה, התישבה בארץ־ישראל לפני המלחמה ולימדה, יצרה והופיעה. חברתה הקרובה, גרט קאופמן (גירות קצמן), מורה למחול שהיגרה לפלשתינה ב־1920, היתה אולי הראשונה שראתה את הצורך במחול עממי ישראלי.

בשנת 1944 האזינה גרטרוד לא פעם לתוכניתה של גרט קאופמן בדבר מחול ארץ־ישראלי חדש. חייב להיות משהו, שיבטא את רוחו של הישוב – הקהילה היהודיה החיה במולדת העתיקה. הריקוד היה נחוץ כעידוד לקיבוצים, כאמצעי־ביטוי לשמחת היהודים השבים לאדמתם וכגורם מלכד בין הקיבוצים, המושבים, הכפרים והערים הגדולות. היה צורך למצוא חוט מקשר, שדרכו יוכל הישוב להראות לעולם את אחדותו, והמחול בודאי יוכל לעשות זאת.

אולי הזמן המתאים ביותר להביע זאת הוא חג השבועות. קיבוץ דליה, השוכן בהרי אפרים, הזמין את קאופמן ליצור מחול על־פי "מגילת רות". היא רצתה לאסוף אף רקדנים אחרים, להזמינם להראות את המחולות שיצרו, לבקש מהם ללמד את מחולותיהם לרקדנים האחרים ולדבר על יצירת מחול עממי חדש.

לא כולם הסכימו איתה. ירדנה כהן מחיפה התנגדה לרעיון וטענה שאין דרך ליצור מחול עממי. היא עצמה יצרה ריקודים עבור קיבוצי הצפון כחלק מהגיגותיהם. "אך את משתמשת בסממנים עממיים במחולותיך, וכללת כלי נגינה נהדרים וסלי־נצרים צבעוניים והענקת לעבודתך אוירה עתיקת־יומין. היצירה מראה את החדש ואת הישן ולכן היא תשאר. את יוצרת את המחול החדש."

אך ירדנה טענה: "אך זה אינו מחול עממי." לבסוף היא התרככה והסכימה לבוא לדליה עם מלוויה המוסיקליים. קבוצתה רקדה את המחול הפשוט, שחיברה למנגינה יהודית ספרדית עתיקה. ירדנה קראה לו "מחול עובדיה", על שם המלווה שלה. שיער הנחושת שלה נצץ בשמש בחוללה ודרשה דיוק ביצוע מרקדניה. לימוד המחול המודרני באירופה עזר לה להבהיר את שרצתה, אך הסגנון לא היה מערבי. אכן היה זה משהו חדש, אך גם ישן ומזרח־תיכוני.

גרט הזמינה את שרה לוי־תנאי להביא לדליה קבוצת רקדנים מקיבוץ רמת־הכובש. שרה עבדה אז כגננת, אך בערה בה התשוקה להתאים מוסיקה ומחול לשיריו של ביאליק. מלותיו של ביאליק היו כה רבות השראה. ושמא תשתמש במלות "שיר השירים"? היא נזכרה באמה, השרה בתימנית וחולמה בהקיץ על אנשי המדבר החזקים, המחדשים את חייהם. הריקוד היה עבורה הכלי להביע רעיונות אלו.

גרט הצליחה לשכנע אף אותה לבוא לדליה. והיא אף שכנעה את רבקה שטורמן מקיבוץ עין-חרוד להצטרף. היא הביאה עימה קבוצת נוער, כדי שירקדו את המחול החדש שלה "הגורן".

לאה ברגשטיין יצרה מחול לחג העומר בקיבוץ רמת-יוחנן. אף היא הסכימה לבוא לדליה, להראות וללמד אותו. גרט שכנעה את הקיבוץ להכין אמפיתיאטרון, כך שהקהל יוכל לשבת ולחזות ברקדנים.

בעיה חמורה היה העוצר, שהיה אז בתוקף בפקודת השלטונות המנדטוריים. איש לא הורשה לנוע בכבישים משקיעת החמה ועד לבוקר. איך יגיעו הצופים הביתה אחרי המופע? גירות החליטה שפשוט אין ברירה, ועל הרקדנים לבלות את כל הלילה במחולות. התוכנית ערכה כ-12 שעות!

בדרך נס היה האירוע להצלחה מסחררת. הקהל נשאר כל הלילה. כנס דליה היה לכוח מניע בתנועת המחול העממי הישראלי החדש, ממש כשם שגירות רצתה ותכננה.

42

פרק שמיני:
בניה מחדש

בעזרת עינם החדה של מי שבאו מבחוץ, הצליחו קטיה דלקובה ופרד ברק למשוך קהל מגוון להופעותיהם. הם פיתחו דרך עבודה, שתאמה את כשרונותיהם והביאה להשגת מטרותיהם: בניה מחדש של החיים היהודיים בארה"ב בשנות ה-40. דרך עבודתם הם תרמו לתחייה התרבותית של יהדות אמריקה.

תכנון ההופעות מוכיח עד כמה מגוון היה הקהל שלהם. הם יכלו למשוך ולרתק את הקהל דובר היידיש, תלמידי אוניברסיטאות או קבוצות נשים ציוניות, והם הופיעו בתיאטראות, בעצרות וגם בהתרחשויות דתיות. קהל מגוון זה הגיב תמיד בהתרגשות לאותה בשורה: אחווה והזדהות עם היהודים העקורים, חוויה שהיתה רחוקה ביותר מההוויה האמריקנית. ריקודים אלה הציגו את קיומה של ישראל כיסוד חיוני ביהדות, ואת היהדות, באמצעות התנועה, כתרבות רבת פנים.

הם הופיעו בתיאטראות שונים, החל בקרנגי-הול עבור מועצת "הפועל המזרחי"; בבית-הספר למבוגרים ללימודי היהדות שב"YM–YWHA" של רחוב 92 בקונצרטים על נושאים יהודיים; בפסטיבל לאמנויות יהודיות שנערך במרכז היהודי בברוקלין ובתוכניות של ריקודים עממיים במוזיאון למדעי-הטבע במנהטן. הם הופיעו בתוכניות בסמינר התיאולוגי היהודי של אמריקה ובפני קבוצות צעירים מתנועות הנוער הציוניות. הם חזרו והופיעו מספר פעמים ב"חברה לקידום היהדות" מיסודו של הד"ר מרדכי קפלן.

באופן כללי, קהל זה היה חלק מהיהדות האמריקנית האמידה. יהודים רבים עזבו עד אז את משכנות-העוני הדתיים הצפופים ועברו לשכונות החדשות יותר ולפרברים. הסוציולוגים טוענים, שבמקומות אלה התפתחו הדפוסים של החיים היהודיים באמריקה. התוכניות שהציגו ברק ודלקובה נגעו ללבם של רבים מהצופים בקהל, אשר היו בנים למהגרים שנטשו את היהדות.(30)

הפופולריות של ברק ודלקובה גדלה יחד עם עליית תנועת המרכזים הקהילתיים היהודיים בשנות ה-40. בתחילה היה תפקיד תנועת ה-JCC לעזור למהגרים יהודים להתאקלם באמריקה וללמוד אנגלית, מנהגי היגיינה ולרכוש מקצוע. משהבינו הכל את הקורה לקהילות היהודיות באירופה, החלו המרכזים הקהילתיים להכין תוכניות כדי לחזק את הזהות היהודית באמריקה. הארגון למרכזים קהילתיים יהודיים ו"YM–YWHA" (ההתאחדות העברית לגברים צעירים ולנשים צעירות), הקימו משרד, שסיפק אמנים, מרצים ותוכניות אמנותיות למרכזים ברחבי אמריקה.

"ההתאחדות העברית" החלה כמעין מרכז חינוכי וחברתי עבור צעירים יהודים מגרמניה באמצע המאה ה-19, בבלטימור. משגברה ההגירה, היה קשה להבחין בין מטרות ה"התאחדות" לאלו של ה"Settlement Houses", אך כשהאוכלוסיה היהודית התבססה והתאזרחה, השתנו התוכניות ב"Y". כמו הנהגת ה-JCC, הבינו אנשי ה"התאחדות", שאפשר למקד את הפעילות סביב היהדות לאו דוקא בקשר לקיום מצוות דתיות. הם רצו למצוא את המכנה המשותף היהודי במיגוון הפעיליות – הדתיות, הפוליטיות, האינטלקטואליות, התרבותיות והפילנטרופיות. הם קיוו, שסוג חדש כזה של פעילות קהילתית המותאם לאמריקה יחליף את האורתודוקסיות האירופית הגוועת.(31)

מרדכי קפלן, פרופסור ורב בסמינר היהודי התיאולוגי (סמינר רבנים לתנועה

היהודית הקונסרבטיבית), ראה זאת כהזדמנות להחיות ולחזק את היהדות האמריקנית. בספרו "יהדות כתרבות" הוא טוען בעד ייסוד מחדש של קהילות יהודיות מרכזיות באמריקה, אך במימדים חדשים. אלה יכללו פיתוח האינדיבידואליות היוצרת של אמנים במטרה להעשיר את ההבעה הדתית היהודית. קפלן היה תעמלן נמרץ והשפעתו החזקה אצל הקונסרבטיבים והרפורמים גם יחד עוררה אף רבים שלא היו חברים בקבוצות אלו או בתנועתו של קפלן עצמו, ה"Reconstructionists".(32)

בשנות ה־20, ה־30 וה־40 לימד מרדכי קפלן בסמינר התיאולוגי היהודי. תלמידיו הוקסמו מהסינתזה של "התרבות היהודית" שיצר מהציונות, הדת, האמנויות ושטחים אחרים בעלי ענין ליהדות. השפעתו ניכרה במיוחד בתנועה הקונסרבטיבית.(33)

רעיונות אלה של קפלן תאמו את עבודתם של ברק ודלקובה. הם עבדו עם מוסדות שהושפעו מתנועתו, כגון המשרד להרצאות של המרכזים היהודיים. לקפלן היתה השפעה גם על תוכניות ה"Y" ברחוב 92 ועל מחנות־הקיץ היהודיים.(34) ג'נט וייסמן, מנהלת משרד ההרצאות, הכירה את דלקובה. מאחר שהיא חיפשה דרכים לגוון את התוכניות מעבר להרצאות המקובלות על היסטוריה וספרות, היא ביקשה מדלקובה והפרטנר החדש שלה, ברק, להבחן בפני נציגי המשרד. בדרך זו הם יוכלו לקבל את אישורו של המשרד ולהופיע בפני המרכזים הקהילתיים היהודיים בכל רחבי אמריקה.

וייסמן הזמינה את הזוג להופיע בפני קהל של עובדים סוציאליים בניו־ג'רסי. היא הצטרפה אל הרקדנים, כדי שתוכל לעמוד בעצמה על טיב ההופעה ולראות את תגובת הקהל. היא ראתה רפרטואר, שהחייה דמויות תנ"כיות, אגדות ותמונות מהחיים היהודיים באירופה המזרחית. כמו כן היו ריקודים על ציון, כגון "הורה" ו"חלוצים", שני ריקודים שנעשו לסמלם המסחרי של דלקובה וברק.

וייסמן החליטה לא רק לשכור את הרקדנים אלא אף לדאוג לקידומם ופרסומם. הזוג החל מיד במסע הופעות נרחב בחוף המזרחי. היא אף סידרה להם הופעות ב"בתי הלל" בקמפוסים של קולג'ים יהודיים רבים ותחת חסותה של מועצת הסעד היהודית הם נתנו כארבעים הופעות בשנה. ברק נזכר בהופעה ב־Madison Square Garden הענקי בניו־יורק, שבה התקבלו הרקדנים בצורה יוצאת מן הכלל: "למרות שריקוד ה'חלוצים' שלנו נרקד ללא מוסיקה, הקצבים של כל קטע נבעו מתנועות־עבודה שונות כגון סיקול הקרקע והנטיעה של אדמת ישראל. הטכנאים במדיסון סקוור גרדן התקינו מיקרופונים מתחת לריצפת העץ של הבמה, והקהל השתולל ממש, כשבסוף כל אחד מחמשת הקטעים טפפו רגלינו בקצב הולך וגובר."

הרקדנים הציעו את עצמם כמורים במרכזים הקהילתיים הרבים באיזור ניו־יורק, וכך נחשף הציבור להשפעתם.

אם היה צורך בחומר חינוכי כתוספת להופעה, היה הזוג כותב דפי מידע, שהודפסו על־ידי האמרגנים. בדרך זו יצאו לאור ספריהם הראשונים "The Dances of Palestine" (הריקודים בפלשתינה) ו־"Jewish Folk Dance Book" (ספר ריקודי עם יהודיים). בעידוד ה־JWB הפיקו דלקובה וברק את התקליטים הראשונים של מוסיקה למחולות־עם יהודיים. לפי הענין שגילה ה־JWB בדלקובה וברק, מומן הריקוד היהודי על־ידי ארגונים אחרים. ה"ועד לאמנויות יהודיות", בהשראתו של קפלן, תמך בקבוצת ריקוד, "ריקוד עמי", מאז 1936. מנהלת הקבוצה, Corinne Chochem, הפיקה קונצרטים, כתבה ספרוני־מחול לחגים היהודיים והופיעה בשידור טלויזיה ב־1942.

לאחר התחלה זו נעשתה "הועדה לאמנויות יהודיות" לרבת עוצמה בתחום האמנות היהודית, לא במעט בזכות תלמיד מוכשר בסמינר לרבנים Moshe Davis.(35) הוא ראה קשר בין האמנויות ליהדות ולצמיחה הספונטנית של תנועת הנוער היהודית, ליסוד מחנות־הקיץ ולמספרם הגדל של מורים והדיוטות המעוניינים בעברית. כל אלה היו סיבות מעודדות לפיתוח "הועדה לאמנויות יהודיות". מטרות הועדה היו לשרת דרך האמנויות יהודים שדיברו עברית, וכן את אלה שלא שלטו בשפה. על האמנויות להיות "כלים להבעת רגשות, אשר באמצעותם תובא היהדות לעם בבהירות, בהחלטיות ובצורה מאורגנת."(36)

אמנים מהשורה הראשונה, כלאונרד ברנשטיין למשל, היו מעורבים בפעילות ומטרות רבות הושגו. הועדה קיוותה, שאמנים ישתמשו ביצירתם בנושאים יהודיים ובשפה העברית. "בריקוד, וכן באמנויות הגראפיות והפלסטיות, הנושאים מבוססים על מקורות

עבריים." וזה הובן, באופן כללי, ככולל נושאים מהתנ"ך, מעולם האגדה היהודית והשפה העברית המתחדשת.(37)

לועדה עצמה היו מחלקות לתיאטרון, לארגון, לספרות יהודית ולקבוצות מוסיקליות. הועדה יזמה את הקמת בית־הספר לאמנויות עבריות בניו־יורק.

קטיה דלקובה ופרד ברק נעשרו לחלק מתוכניות אלה. בזמן עבודתם עם "הועדה לאמנויות יהודיות" הם אף עבדו ב"Y" של רחוב 92, שהתפרסם כבמה למחול המודרני האמריקני, מלבד היותו מקום לאמנות, ספרות ומחשבה יהודיים.

ברק ודלקובה נבחנו ב־1942, כדי שיוכלו להופיע על בימת ה"Y". המבחן עשוי היה לקבוע את השתייכותם לקבוצה עילית של רקדנים מקצוענים, שנבחרו להופיע בתוכנית מחול חדשה, ללא השתתפות בהוצאות ההפקה מצידם. כך הם יוצגו בפני קהל המחול הגדול של ניו־יורק על־ידי אחד מהמוסדות התרבותיים המכובדים ביותר של העיר.

ה"Y" של רחוב 92 נמצא בפינה הדרומית של שדרת לקסינגטון ורחוב 92. זהו בנין לבנים לא יומרני בן שלוש קומות, שחזותו מתמזגת עם המדרכה. ה"Y" נוסד ב־1874 על־ידי קבוצת אנשי עסקים יהודיים עשירים, שרצו לעזור למהגרים היהודיים החדשים ממזרח אירופה להתאזרח באמריקה.

פרק תשיעי:
ריקוד אמריקני ב"Y"

ב-1934, שעה שפריץ ניסה בהצלחה להשיג הכרה למחול שלו בוינה, נאבק המחול המודרני באמריקה על ההכרה בו.

ביוני 1934 נפתח קורס הקיץ למחול במכללת בנינגטון, שבמדינת ורמונט. את שיעורי הטכניקה הבסיסית לימדה מרתה היל וקורסים בני שבועיים הועברו על-ידי הניה הולם, דוריס האמפרי וצ'רלז ויידמן. שניים או שלושה קורסים בטכניקות שונות התנהלו בעת ובעונה אחת, ומטבע הדברים היו הרבה עימותים של דעות ותיאוריות.

שתי דמויות במחול האמריקני המודרני, האמפרי והולם, דיברו במיוחד אל פרד, שמצא את עצמו בעולם חדש. אישיות-מפתח אחרת בעתידו של פרד, הדר' וילאם קולודני, החל באותם ימים בתוכניות מחול ב"Y" של רחוב 92. החל ב-1934, השנה בה הצטרף קולודני לארגון כממונה על החינוך, חדלה בהדרגה הפעילות להיות מכוונת לעידוד תהליכי ההסתגלות החברתית של המהגרים היהודיים. במשך כמעט 40 שנות כהונתו, הוא יצר תוכניות שהשפיעו רבות בתחומים שונים, ונעשו לאבני-דרך בחיים התרבותיים והאמנותיים של העיר. תוכניות שעסקו בפיוט ושירה שאירגן תרמו להתפתחות הספרות האמריקנית, וערבי הריקוד היו למוקד התפתחות המחול המודרני בארצות-הברית.

חשיבותו של ה"Y" של רחוב 92 גדלה בזמן קולודני, ומאמציו התרכזו בעיקר ברקדנים וכוריאוגרפים צעירים. החל ב-1942 נערכו תקופתית מבחנים, שהזוכים בהם השתתפו בסדרות מופעים ורבים שהחלו את הקריירות שלהם על במת ה"Y", הפכו ברבות הימים לדמויות רבות השפעה בעולם המחול המודרני האמריקני, וביניהם אגנס דה-מיל, ואלרי בטיס, הלן טמיריס, פרל פריימוס ופול דרייפר. (38)

המחול המודרני הצליח בדרך כלשהי להתקיים בשנות המלחמה, וזאת באמצעות יוזמות של רקדנים בודדים ומעט תמיכה ממסדית, שניתנה בחודשי הקיץ. בנינגטון קולג' בורמונט סיפק במה, כוח-אדם, קהל ואוירה המעוררת ליצירה. אך ב-1941 עזבה הניה הולם את בנינגטון ויסדה מרכז למחול משל עצמה בקולורדו. אתר-קיץ חשוב אחר להופעות היה ב-Jacob's Pillow שנוסד על-ידי טד שון. מכל מקום, במשך עונת המחול הרגילה, כל אחד נאבק על קיומו. מרתה גרהם, למשל, קיבלה מימון בעיקר מגב' קולידז' (E. Sprogue Coolidge) ואפילו הצליחה להציג עונה בברודווי ב-1944, שבה הציגה את גולת הכותרת של מחולותיה על נושאים אמריקניים, "אביב בהרי האפלצ'ים". רבים מהכוריאוגרפים התענינו בנושאים אמריקניים.

דוריס האמפרי המשיכה ליצור את הכוריאוגרפיות שלה, אך כתמיד היתה מעונינת בפיתוח כוריאוגרפים אחרים. ב-1940 יצרה יחד עם הפרטנר שלה, צ'רלז ויידמן, אפשרות נוספת לדרך המקובלת של הופעות מחול מודרני, שהיתה מורכבת כרגיל מסיורי-הופעות, קונצרטים ולעיתים גיחות לכוריאוגרפיה בתיאטרוני ברודווי. הם פתחו את התיאטרון שברחוב 16, שהעניק להם אפשרויות רבות. המקום הכיל שורות אחדות של כסאות וכתפאורה שימשו מחיצות מתקפלות. בהופעותיהם מדי יום ראשון (לדברי אחד המבקרים), "בקעו מקליפתן כמה מהיצירות המעולות של המחול בן זמננו." (39)

עבור אמני-המחול שעבדו מחוץ למסגרת להקות בשנות הארבעים, נמצא פתרון חדש, שבמהרה אומץ על-ידי כל הרקדנים בסגנונות השונים - הופעות ב"Y" של רחוב 92.

46

ב-1942 כינס קולודני ועדה של מורים ודמויות מעולם המחול, שתפקידה היה לבחור את המשתתפים להופעות אלה. בזמן מסויים כללה הועדה את מרתה היל, בסי שנברג וג'רום רובינס.(40)

מאמר ב"דנס מגזין"(41) מתאר כיצד יצרו ההופעות ב-"Y" קריירות חדשות. "רק לפני שנה הגיעה ג'נט קולינס לניו-יורק, מבלי שאיש ידע על אודותיה דבר. לא יהיה זה בלתי מדויק לומר, שהיא נעשתה לכוכב בין לילה. מספר ימים בלבד חלפו, למעשה, לפני שהביקורות על הופעתה הרשמית הראשונה בניו-יורק התפרסמו בעיתוני יום ראשון. על סמך שני מחולות סולו בלבד בהופעה ב-'Y' היא כונתה 'התגלית החדשה, המוכשרת ביותר מזה עונות רבות', 'הרקדנית המרגשת ביותר מזה זמן רב...'"

ואלטר טרי, מבקר המחול של ה"הראלד טריביון", תיאר את השיטה, בה בחן קולודני את הרקדנים:

"כל הרקדנים נאבקים על קיומם. אפילו למפורסמים שבהם קשה למצוא סידורי-הופעות ורסיטלים בניו-יורק. הרקדנים הצעירים נמצאים בתחתית הערימה, כי מתי, היכן וכיצד יוכלו להציג את עבודותיהם בפני הקהל? ב-YMHA הבינו את מצבם החמור של צעירים אמריקנים אלו ומצאו דרך לעזור להם. במשך שש עונות הציג תיאטרון המחול של ה-YMHA סדרות של הופעות מחול מהדרגה הראשונה, באולם הנוח והמצוייד היטב של תיאטרון קאופמן ברחוב ה-92... בשנה זו, וילאם קולודני, מנהל הסדרות, וועדה מייעצת של מורים למחול בחנו ובחרו לבסוף ששה אמנים צעירים להופעות באולם קאופמן בחסות ה-'Y'. הרקדנים לא לקחו על עצמם כל סיכונים כספיים, אך קיבלו הזדמנות להופיע במסגרת מקצועית במרכז מחול מוכר ובפני קהל מבין; אולי עזרה זו למחול האמריקני היא בקנה מידה קטן, אך זו התחלה חשובה בכיוון טיפוח ועידוד האמנות המקומית. בודאי יתייחסו כל הרקדנים הצעירים ל-YMHA כאל מקור עידוד ואולי ימצא מר קולודני, שהעניין שהוא מגלה בדור הצעיר של הרקדנים האמריקנים ישמש כמנוף להתחלתה של קריירה אחת או יותר."(42)

השנים הוכיחו שטרי צדק. קריירות התחילו ב-"Y" ולעיתים אף המשיכו שם. גם מאלה שלא היו חלק מתהליך הברירה על-ידי הבחינות נדרש סכום נמוך במיוחד עבור שכירת התיאטרון. בשנת 1939 התעריף הגבוה ביותר עבור שכירת האולם היה 75 דולאר. סכום זה כיסה את הוצאות הדפסת הכרטיסים והתוכניה, את התשלום לצוות עובדי הבמה, לקופאים ולשאר ההוצאות הטכניות של ההופעה. התעריף הנמוך של ה-"Y" בהשוואה לתיאטרונים אחרים עשה אותו לאחד ממקומות המפגש הפעילים ביותר בעיר ניו-יורק. "אף אדם, לפניו או אחריו (מלבד הדר' קולודני), לא השתדל כל כך להשכיר את במת ה-"Y" במחירים מגוחכים לרסיטלים וסדנאות של חלוצים כמרתה גרהם, דוריס המפרי, פולין קונר ואחרים."(43)

קולודני גם דאג לכך, שמרכיב חינוכי חשוב יעמוד מאחורי ההופעה. הוא לא היה חסיד של השקפה או סגנון מסויימים בריקוד. הוא רצה באיכות ובכשרון גבוהים. הוא יצר מרכז מחול, שהיה לא רק מסביר פנים ומעשי, אלא גם קורא תגר. קולודני רצה לפתח קהל למחול כשם שפיתח רקדנים.

מרתה גרהם היתה המנהלת החינוכית הראשונה של המחלקה למחול ב-"Y". מספר שנים מאוחר יותר החליפה אותה דוריס האמפרי, ולאחריה באו הניה הולם, בוני בירד ואחרים. השיעורים למחול היו מרשימים ממש כמו במחלקות הריקוד של הקולג'ים המובחרים: הרצאות בהיסטוריה ובתיאוריה של המחול ושיעורים במיגוון סגנונות וטכניקות. במשך השנים כללו שיעורים אלו את שיטותיהם של דלקרוז, האמפרי-ויידמן, גרהם וכן אימפרוביזציה ובאלט.

ב-1944 החלה דוריס האמפרי ב"כיתות ליצירת מחול לכוריאוגראפים" ב-"Y", אשר יועדו לכוריאוגראפים ורקדנים מקצועניים ונעשו לבסיס ספרה ("אמנות עשיית המחולות", בתרגומו של דב הרפז ובהוצאת הספריה למחול בישראל, 1984). נוסף למחלקה מיוחדת לילדים, התקיימו שיעורים למורי-מחול, למקצוענים, למבוגרים ולסוגים רבים אחרים של תלמידים.

הרצאות מודגמות הוגשו על-ידי לואי הורסט ורקדני להקתה של מרתה גרהם (1.4.1939); יסודות המחול וחשיבות החלל בריקוד על-ידי הניה הולם ולהקתה (14.12.1941);

דיון והדגמה של מחול ככוח חברתי על-ידי ולטר טרי בעזרת הדגמות של רקדנים בעלי שם (בשנים 1951–1952); "מוסיקה בת זמננו למחול" על-ידי טד שון וג'סי מיקר; ג'רום רובינס ומורטון גולד; ולרי בטיס וברנרד סיגל (15.12.1947); סדנאות על "השימוש בשירה בריקוד" על-ידי ג'ן מלקולם ברינין (1948); וראיונות פומביים שנוהלו על-ידי ולטר טרי עם רקדנים בכירים, שדיברו על גישתיהם ליצירת מחול: ג'ורג' באלנצ'ין, ג'רום רובינס, דוריס האמפרי, הלן טמיריס ואגנס דה-מיל.

קולודני התעניין בפיתוח מחול יהודי בה במידה, שהיה מעוניין במחול כללי: כמפעל חינוכי, על-ידי הופעות ופיתוח קהל.

קולודני העלה עודד תוכניות של מחול יהודי מאז נכנס לתפקידו ב-"Y". ב-1937 הופיעו בנימין צמח וקבוצתו עם המקהלה של מקס הלפמן. צמח הופיע ברוסיה ויצר ריקודים על החסידים והחיים היהודיים במזרח אירופה. הוא עורר עניין באמריקה ואסף סביבו רקדנים אחרים.(44)

ריקוד גם הוצג בבית-הספר למבוגרים ללימודי היהדות שב-YMHA. ב-28 בפברואר 1942 הופיעה קורין חוכם (Chochem) ולהקת "ריקוד עמי".

באוקטובר 1942 הגישו פרד ברק וקטיה דלקובה בקשה למבחן לסדרות המחול של ה-"Y". הם כתבו בבקשתם, שערכו סיורי הופעות ברחבי יוגוסלביה, רומניה ואוסטריה ב-1936. לאחר שנפגשו שוב בניו-יורק הם הופיעו ברוצ'סטר ב"לילה בפלשטינה" (7.6.1942) ובפני הוועידה הציונית במלון "ניו-יורקר" ב-14 באוקטובר 1942. למעשה, פרד שהה אז בארצות-הברית רק שנה אחת. תשובת קולודני להצעתם היתה:

מר ברגר היקר!(45)

תודה לך עבור מילוי הטופס למבחנים להופעה בקונצרט של חמישה רקדנים בתיאטרון המחול של ה-YMHA ביום ראשון אחר-הצהריים, 14 בפברואר, ב-3.30.

קבעתי לך מבחן ביום ראשון, 13 בדצמבר, בשעה 11.50. לרשותך יעמדו 15 דקות, כולל החלפת תלבושות, שבהן עליך להציג שני ריקודים. עליך להיות מוכן להציג שניים נוספים, בהתאם לדרישה.

על הבמה יהיה תלוי מסך אחורי מקטיפה כחולה כהה, ושתי "רגליים" מקטיפה כחולה כהה יאפשרו שתי כניסות מכל צד. התאורה תהיה פשוטה וללא כל אפקטים מיוחדים. לרשותך יעמוד פסנתר-כנף קונצרטנטי "סטיינווי", ופונוגרף חשמלי בעל רמקול.

עליך לבצע את ריקודיך בתלבושת מלאה.

באם תתקבל, אנו מצפים שתבחן שנית עם הרפרטואר שלך ביום ראשון, 24 בינואר. מטרת מבחן שני זה תהיה לבחור את הקטעים מהרפרטואר שלך עבור התוכנית הסופית ב-14 בפברואר, אשר בה יוקצבו לך 15 דקות מההופעה.

שכר האמנים עבור הופעה של רבע שעה הוא 35 דולר.

קולודני הציג את ברק ודלקובה, ורבים אחרים, פעמים רבות.

פרק עשירי:
ה"רקונסטרוקציוניזם" והמחול

לאחר שהופיעו לראשונה ב"Y", לימדה דלקובה מחול יהודי במחנה קיץ יחיד במינו לצעירים יהודיים בשם Brandeis Camp. ברק עבד בקירבת מקום, באתר הנופש היהודי. הוא לימד קבוצות גדולות של נופשים שלא התענינו במיוחד במחול. למרות שזו היתה הזדמנות להתמחות בהוראת קבוצות גדולות, שבתחילה לא התענינו במחול עממי, הוא שאף ליותר. הוא מצא זאת בביקוריו אצל דלקובה. היא לימדה צעירים שהיו צמאים לביטוי עצמי ולמציאת משמעות ואלה הוצעו להם במחנה המיוחד.

מחנה ברנדייס נוסד על־ידי שלמה ברדין, מחנך חלוצי שפעל בפלשטינה ובאמריקה, אשר ערך ניסויים חינוכיים במסגרת מחנות הקיץ. הוא נשען על שני מקורות: הקבוצה החינוכית לפי הדגם הישראלי, שבה רעיונות שיתופיים ודגש על לימודים; ו"בית־הספר הגבוה העממי הדני", מוסד שאימן בהצלחה מבוגרים להיות להנהגה קהילתית תוך מספר חודשים.

ברדין היה מנהיג רב השראה, שחיפש דרכים חדשות להקניית תחושת היהדות לצעירים. רעיונותיו עלו בקנה אחד עם כוונותיהם של מספר ארגונים יהודיים כגון הסתדרות ציוני אמריקה, הדסה, בני־ברית, שסברו שההנהגה היהודית הצעירה לא עמדה על רמה נאותה. ללא מידע על יהדות והכשרה להנהגה נדונה תוכנית פעולתם להסתפק בפעילות שטחית.(46) צוותו המוכשר של ברדין כלל את מקס הלפמן המוסיקאי ואת משה דייויס, רב צעיר, את קטיה דלקובה ורבים אחרים.

הריקוד נעשה למסלול עיקרי לליבם של הצעירים במחנות. במידת מה יש לזקוף את ההצלחה לזכות סגנונה הדרמאטי של דלקובה. היא נעזרה בעבודתה מושכת הלב במוסיקאי החדשני מקס הלפמן. הם השתמשו בריקוד כדי להגביר את איכות החיים היהודיים שהורצגו במחנה ברנדייס כטקס ופולחן. "נתנו לאישיות המחנאים לצמוח בכל הכיוונים. רצינו לעזור, באופן מתמיד, לתלמידינו להגיע אל מעבר לטכניקת המחול," אמרה קטיה דלקובה בהזכרה בתקופה זו.

התיאורטיקנים כתבו: "הצעיר האמריקני הממוצע הוא רקדן נלהב. הריקוד הוא גרעין חייו החברתיים. לפיכך היה זה טבעי ביותר שהריקוד יהווה חלק כה חשוב בתוכנית מחנה הקיץ. אך כיצד יוכל הריקוד לקבל אופי יהודי מיוחד? היתה הרגשה, שכדאי להתנסות בריקודי־עם מהסוג הנפוץ בישראל... די בכך שהמחנאי יזכר בישראל, שם שלמד לזהות עם משהו חיובי ויצירתי באופיו. בהיסטוריה, בהישגים ובנצחונות של ישראל הוא ראה תשובה לשאלות, שכה הטרידו אותו. האם היו היהודים עם טפיל? בהתבוננו בישראל הגיע לתשובה שלילית. האם הם מוגי־לב? לא, הבט בישראל. האם היה בכוחם לשגשג? כמובן, ראה את ישראל... ריקודי־עם נעשו למשהו מקובל, וריקודי־חברה הפכו לאתגר, לאופיו המיוחד של המחנה... על־ידי קישור בין סמלים ומנהגים יהודיים ותרבות יהודית דינמית נוצרה ההזדמנות להעשיר את הצעיר היהודי במשמעויות חדשות."(47)

שנים אשר בילו בצעירותם במחנה, הרמן מ. פופקין והרברט קימל, סיפרו מאוחר יותר על משמעות הריקוד ב"ברנדייס" עבורם. פופקין אמר, ששיעוריו עם דלקובה היו ההתנסות הראשונה שלו עם ריקודי־עם יהודיים. הם, כמובן, לא נקראו "ישראליים" בטרם קום המדינה. דרך הריקוד השתנתה כל גישתו לציונות.(48)

קימל הוא דוגמה נוספת של צעיר, שמחול־העם נגע בנשמתו. הוא גדל בבית־כנסת בברוקלין, שם שימש ריצ'רד טאקר כחזן ומוס הארט ניהל פעילות תיאטרונית. למרות הביטוי היהודי התרבותי, מעולם לא חלם קימל על האפשרות לבטא את עצמו דרך נושאים יהודיים באמנות. ב"ברנדייס" הוא פגש את דלקובה וברק.

"ברק ביקר לעיתים קרובות במחנה 'ברנדייס', הכיר את המחנאים, רקד איתנו במפגשים הכלליים, העלה רעיונות והשתתף בחלק מהתוכניות הבלתי רשמיות," אמר קימל.(49)

קימל גילה, שקיימת דרך לשלב את אהבתו לישראל עם הריקוד. הוא הופתע לראות שאין צורך בבית־כנסת או באמצעים דתיים חיצוניים, כדי לבסס קשר זה.

משה דייוויס שוחח לעיתים קרובות, במשך קיץ, אחד עם דלקובה וברק. הוא החליט, שברצונו לערב אותם בפעילות הועדה לאמנויות יהודיות. כשחזרו כולם לניו־יורק, שיער דייוויס, שהרקדנים יזדקקו למקום בו יוכלו לערוך מפגשים בנושאי הריקוד היהודי. הוא נזכר, שאולם ההתעמלות בסמינר התיאולוגי היהודי פנוי לעיתים קרובות, וערך את הסידורים הנחוצים, כדי שדלקובה וברק ילמדו בו.

לאחר חזרות הבוקר שלהם בליוויית הפסנתרן בין תשע לאחת, ולאחר הכיתות לילדים אחר־הצהריים, הם לימדו בערבים ב־JTS. כשם שניבא דייוויס, השיעורים שהעבירו היו מרשימים. תלמידיהם היו מורים לחינוך יהודי, מורים בסמינר התיאולוגי, רקדנים המעונינים בנושאים יהודיים, סטודנטים ורבנים צעירים. לגבי כולם הריקוד נעשה בעל משמעות מיוחדת. "זה סחף אותנו - אותו צורך פנימי לביטוי יהודי. חשנו, שאנו מקימים אנדרטא חדשה, המושרשת עמוק מתוך השורשים של עמנו," אמרה דלקובה, בהזכרה בימי 1943.

דלקובה וברק החלו ללמד את הסטודנטים לרבנות, כיצד לחגוג את החגים וכיצד להכין טקסים בעזרת המחול. "כי ללא רבנים ופילוסופים אי־אפשר ליצור תנועה גדולה ולהגיע לחקר אמיתי בנושאים מהותיים," אמרה דלקובה.

הרקדנים מצאו בריקוד דרך לאחד את האובדן האישי שלהם, התוהו ובוהו שהתנסו בו באירופה, עם רעננותו של הנוער האמריקני והצורך העצמי שלהם בביטוי החוויה היהודית. מורי המחול מצאו עידוד בועדה לאמנויות יהודיות ובסמינר התיאולוגי היהודי.

הועדה הזורמה הזרימה כוחות חדשים לאפיק היצירה. נערכו פגישות רבות והתנהלו ויכוחים בין חברי הועדה. "נפגשנו במשך ערבים רצופים. שקלנו והתווכחנו על אמנותנו, בצורה כללית ואף במושגים של יחס אישי לאמנות. אחדים מאיתנו תהו בדבר ערכה הכלכלי של אמנות יהודית, והאם נוכל להפכה למקצוע? אחרים העלו את השאלה, האם אמנות עממית נופלת בחשיבותה מאמנות טהורה? אחדים מאיתנו היו קשורים לאמנות־העם, וכל זמר בלדות וזמר־עם נחשב בזמן ההוא לקומוניסט, והם השתמשו בשירי־העם שלהם לויכוחים פוליטיים במקום למטרות אמנותיות. אנחנו, מכל מקום, רצינו להשתמש באמנות העממית למטרה מתוחכמת יותר: לעצב מחדש עם שלם בדרך חדשה. לא מיהרנו לקבל ריקוד ומוסיקה עממיים בפני עצמם, אך יכולנו להעריך אותם כאמצעי לפיתוח חוש השיתוף והאחווה שהיקנו," אמרה יהודית קפלן־אייזנשטיין, אחת מראשי האגף למוסיקה בועדה לאמנויות יהודיות.

יהודית, בתו של מרדכי קפלן, ובעלה, אירה אייזנשטיין, רב צעיר בתנועה הרקונסטרוקטיבית, חברו עם הרקדנים דלקובה וברק, למרות הויכוחים ללא סוף שהתנהלו ביניהם. "כל תחיה של האמנות היהודית, אם ברצונך לכנותה בשם זה, החזיקה מעמד בזכות הדחף והאומץ," אמרה יהודית אייזנשטיין. דרכה התקשר ברק לרעיונותיו של קפלן. עבורו לא היתה זו אידיאולוגיה, או לימוד בספרים וחינוך בסמינר. הוא הבין את אשר קפלן לימד על אחדות היהדות דרך האמנות לא כעוד פעילות בועדות השונות.

הוא חש בחיוניות רעיונותיו של קפלן באמצעות העבודה המעשית עם אמנים והוגי־דעות מוכשרים אחרים. שיעור אחר שיעור שיכנע את ברק בצמאון הצעירים היהודיים לביטוי תרבותי. הוא החל לראות שיש מקום עבורו ושמחה לו תפקיד בעידוד הצעיר האמריקני היהודי להגשים את עצמו דרך הריקוד.

פרק אחד־עשר:
האגודה למחול יהודי

בזמן קצר יצרו קטיה ופרד שלוש קבוצות תלמידים נפרדות ב"חברה התיאולוגית היהודית". קבוצה למחולות-עם רגילים בהדרכתו של פרד; קבוצה ליצירת מחולות עבור טקסים וחגים כגון ל"ג בעומר או חג-הביכורים, בהדרכת קטיה דלקובה וקבוצה בהדרכת שניהם ובה רקדנים מנוסים, שהתענינו בשימוש בנושאים יהודיים בהופעות־מחול: "האגודה למחול יהודי" ("The Jewish Dance Guild"). הם חיפשו אחר חוויה אמנותית קבוצתית ייחודית יהודית עבור אנשים צעירים אלו. הם כתבו ופרסמו עלון על פעילותם ובילו יחדיו שעות לאין ספור, בחזרות, ביצירה, בהופעות ואפילו בעבודות משותפות, כדי להרוויח כסף. רק חמש שנים קודם לכן היה פרד צעיר נרדף, שמצא בריקוד אמצעי לקיום גשמי, שאיפשר לו לחצות גבולות ולהמלט מהנאצים. עתה, בארצו החדשה, הוא למד, שהריקוד הוא גם אמצעי להשרדות רגשית.

אחת מהתלמידות בשיעורי הערב בסמינר התיאולוגי היהודי היתה פליטה צעירה מבלגיה, שולמית בת־ארי קיבל, שלמדה ריקוד באירופה.(50) במשך המלחמה היא התחבאה במשך שנתיים בכפר בצרפת. "נשבעתי שאם אחיה, אמשיך לרקוד." היא הגיעה לבסוף לניו־יורק, החלה לעבוד ובכספה המועט שילמה עבור שיעורי באלט ומחול מודרני. "אך באמת רציתי לרקוד ולהביע את החוויה היהודית שלי." היא חיפשה, עד שמצאה את השיעורים בסמינר.

"שיעוריהם של קטיה ופרד היו מאוד מספקים ורבי משמעות. לא הייתי יהודיה שומרת מצוות, ואף הם לא, אך חיפשנו יחד אחר תוכן יהודי וביטוי למה שעבר עלינו. יצרנו ריקודים, שהיו קשורים לנושאים יהודיים ומשמעותיים עבורנו.

"שילוב הכשרונות של קטיה ופרד היה יוצא מן הכלל. קטיה נהגה לומר, שגברים הם שלווים ופיוטיים יותר ואילו הנשים - ארציות. היא לימדה את ההיבטים המודרניים, האילתוריים והדרמאטיים של העבודה. מגעו של פרד היה קל יותר והוא התרכז בתנועות עממיות יותר מאשר במודרניות. היינו שמונה בקבוצה החצי־מקצועית. אז הקימו המנהלים את האגודה (גילדה) למחול יהודי, שכללה אותנו. פרד וקטיה חלמו, שכולנו נחיה יחדיו בבית גדול וישון וניצור ונעבוד שם.

"הם עודדו אותנו ליצור ריקודים משלנו, וכללו אותם בהופעות, עזרו לנו להשיג עבודה, כדי שנוכל להתקיים ולהמשיך לעבוד עם הקבוצה. במשך זמן רב רב עבדנו בסטודיו שלהם, ואחר־כך עברנו לחזרות יומיות ב'Y'. גישתם היתה כה כוללת ולרשותך עמד נסיון עצום. הם היו לדוגמה, כמורים וכבני-אדם.

"אישורו ועידודו של פרד היו חשובים לנו מאוד. הוא היה בעל יכולת שיפוט נהדרת, ויכל לראות כהרף עין מה היה הכיוון שלך, כרקדן. והוא הענייק בטחון לאנשים ביכולת הריקוד שלהם. גישתו החיובית לאנשים איפשרה לתלמידים לפתח רעיונות תנועתיים משלהם בשיעור.

"אבי, שהיה ציוני, מורה ודובר עברית, בא פעם אחת לצפות בהופעת ריקוד שלנו ב'חברה לקידום היהדות'. הוא הגיב במשפט אחד: 'אבל זה לא יהודי במיוחד.' על הבמה אלה בני־אדם.' יכול להיות, שעבור הצופים נראה היה, שאנו משתמשים בטכניקת המחול המודרני ורק הריקודים החסידיים הם בעלי אופי אתני. מאחר שהיה כה מעט ריקוד יהודי

51

באותו זמן, נאלצו פרד וקטיה להסתמך בעיקר על רעיונותיהם שלהם ולמצוא פתרונות אישיים לבעיות האמנותיות. הזהות היהודית שלהם נבעה מההומניזם שלהם."

דלקובה וברק יצרו סביבה תרבותית מיוחדת והפיחו רוח־חיים במושג ציונות דרך הריקוד שלהם. הם ראו בריקוד אמצעי רב־השראה, העוזר לצעירים למצוא את שורשיהם ואת זהותם האמיתית. "החומר התנועתי היה קל להבנה ורגיש את הצופים. למדנו כיצד להופיע בפני הקהל. חווית הריקוד היתה משולבת בישראל וביהדות. אפילו החגים קיבלו טעם מיוחד לאחר שעבדנו יחד. פרד וקטיה שפעו אידאלים של שיוויון, דמוקרטיה, נעורים ורוחניות. ניתנו לנו שורשים ומין ציונות לא־דתית, אך נובעת מהלב," אמר הרב קימל.(51)

הרקדנים עבדיו יחדיו מדי בוקר בחזרות - כולל שיעורי טכניקה ולימוד הדדי. "אני זוכרת, שכשקטיה נתנה את השיעור, היה פרד עושה אותו עימנו," נזכרת הרקדנית ג'ויס דורפמן־מולוב. "כבר ידענו אז, שהיו לו בעיות וכאבים במפרק הירך והתפעלנו לראות, כיצד התאים את התרגילים וביצע אותם בעזרת חלקים שונים של גופו, אם הטרידו אותו הכאבים. החמיאה לנו העובדה, שאחד המנהלים 'למד' איתנו.

"ידענו שהם נאלצו להופיע במועדוני־לילה ולצאת לסיורי הופעות כדי להתפרנס ושלעיתים הוכרחו להתפשר ולהוריד את רמת ההופעות," מספרת ג'ויס מולוב. "בוקר אחד נגנבו $20, שהשאירה קטיה בחדר־ההלבשה, שנועדו לקניית נעליים חדשות. היא הרגישה רע מאוד עקב כך ופרד ניחם אותה ואמר - 'אז נרקוד עוד ערב אחד ושוב יהיה לך הכסף לזה'."

ברק ודלקובה פיתחו תוכניות על שלושה מישורים שונים עבור העדה לאמניות יהודיות. הם החלו ליצור כוריאוגראפיות עבור הקבוצה המקצועית; הם נטלו את האגדה היהודית מימי הביניים על "הגולם", דמות החימר שיצר המהר"ל מפראג, על מנת לעזור לעמו המדוכא. במצוות הרבי ביצע הגולם מעשים טובים, אך כשקם הגולם על יוצרו, החזירו הרבי לעפר, שממנו נוצר. בריקוד שיקפו ברק ודלקובה את שעבר עליהם באירופה על־ידי שינוי סוף האגדה המקורי, כפי שנכתב בתוכניה: "התוצאה הסופית אינה ניתנת לחיזוי, כי מי יוכל לשער את התוצאות לאחר שהתעוררו כוחות השחור." הם הופיעו בריקוד זה פעמים רבות.

ההופעה מרגשת עבור הקבוצה התקיימה בבוסטון, בסתיו שנת 1946, בנוכחותו של מי שהיה ראש ממשלת ישראל, דוד בן־גוריון. "הכנו תוכנית יחד עם מקהלתו של מקס הלפמן בנושא חג־הביכורים. בין קטעי הקבוצה והמקהלה שולבו מחולות של קטיה ופרד, כולל מחול 'החלוצים' המרשים. ביצענו את 'הגולם', וכן את 'שיר קם לתחייה' ואת 'הורה'," נזכרת מולוב.

"מהבמה ראיתי את דוד בן־גוריון יושב בשורה הראשונה. בנאומו, לאחר ההופעה, הוא דיבר על הרקדנים הצעירים והבעת פניהם, כשהניחו את הביכורים על ריצפת הבמה. הוא דיבר על התרגשותו הרבה מכך. נקל לתאר את השפעתה של הכרה זו בנו. אני הגעתי רק זמן קצר לפני כן מוויניפג, קנדה, כדי ללמוד מחול יהודי - הרקע שלי היה אורח חיים של 'עיירה יהודית' יחד עם ציונות. זה היה מדהים עבורי להיות באותו אולם יחד עם בן־גוריון, שהיה שם מלא קסם באותם ימים טרופים שלפני יסוד מדינת ישראל."

במשך 1946 התבקש ברק על־ידי הסמינר התיאולוגי היהודי להכין תוכנית טלוויזיה מקורית לכבוד ט"ו בשבט. דלקובה וברק הסכימו להופיע בשני ריקודיהם המפורסמים, "הורה" ו"חלוצים", אשר התאימו לנושא החג. התוכנית שודרה, כפי שהיה נהוג אז, בשידור חי. מנחה התוכנית היה רב צעיר ובלתי מנוסה, שלפתע סיים את דבריו 14 דקות לפני סוף התוכנית. "אלה היו הרגעים הגרועים ביותר של במה, שעברתי מעודי," נזכר ברק בצחוק. "נאלצנו לאלתר ולהמשיך לרקוד כדי למלא את הפער, וכל דקה נראתה לנו כשעה."

ב־1947 הצטרפו קטיה ופרד לצוות המורים של מחלקת הריקוד שב־"Y", שנוהלה אז בידי דוריס האמפרי. הם לימדו(51) ארבעה בקרים בשבוע, והדריכו קבוצה של מחול יהודי, קורס למדריכי מחול ואחד למחולות־עם יהודיים וישראליים. הם צרפו את ה"גילדה למחול יהודי" לתוכניותיהם ב־"Y", והלהקה הופיעה שם לראשונה בקונצרט חנוכה ב־9 בדצמבר 1947. הריקודים בתוכנית היו מסוגים שונים, ולא התייחסו לנושא חנוכה דווקא, וכללו את "שיר קם לתחייה"; ריקוד חדש, שהוצג כמערכון, את "הגולם"; "הורה"; "נטיעת עצים"

52

ו"גיבורים ללא שם".(52)

לקראת אביב שנת 1947 יצרו דלקובה וברק ריקוד חדש, "הגדה - סיפור אביבי".(53) הבשורה שבריקוד היתה, שהאביב הוא זמן שחרורם של העבדים וחסרי התקוה. ריקוד חדש אחר היה "אין צדק", שתאר מעשיה על אנשי חלם, אותה עיירה קטנה אי־שם בפולניה, שאחדים מכנים את תושביה טיפשים ואחרים "חכמי־חלם", כפי שנאמר בתכניה.

כל תוכניות המחול היהודי שהוצגו עד אז ב־"Y" כללו זכרונות מאירופה, ויהודי אירופה הוצגו, לעיתים, בנימה הומוריסטית. ברק ודלקובה יצרו ריקודים כאלה, אך גם טיפלו בנושאים חמורים אחרים: מחנות הריכוז ומשמעותם לגבי יהדות אמריקה. את ההשראה לריקוד "הקול הנצחי" קיבלו ממכתבו האחרון של חבר, שנשלח בספטמבר 1940 ובו נאמר: "דבר לא נותר. נמלטתי לעיר הבאה בתור".(54)

הופעה של "הגילדה למחול יהודי" בדצמבר 1947 כללה את "דמויות ממזרח אירופה - הרהורים" מאת פרד ברק. מחול זה בלט אפילו במסגרת המחול הכללי, שיוצריו לא התענינו ביותר בנושאים של חיפוש זהות וחידוש תרבויות. ב־Dance Observer של ינואר 1948 נכתב, ש"שמחת החיים היתה מרעננת ומעגנת בתוך עונת מחול, שהתעסקה בעיקר בפסיכואנליזה... הרקדנים הופיעו בצורה מכובדת והיו מרשימים באופן מיוחד... הם מילאו חובתם באופן מעורר הערצה, והופעתם מבטיחה, שיתפתחו לתוספת בעלת ערך לקבוצות המחול העממי שלנו. המנהלים והרקדנים כאחד ראויים לשבח על הטעם הטוב, שגילו בהופעתם הראשונה."

ב־28 בינואר 1948 הופיעה "הגילדה למחול יהודי" בסדרת "אמנות יהודית בת־זמננו" בפטרסון, ניו־ג'רסי והם רקדו בפסטיבל האומות המאוחדות. ב־25 במאי אותה שנה הופיעו קטיה דלקובה, פרד ברק ו"הגילדה למחול יהודי" במרכז היהודי בברוקלין, במסגרת הפסטיבל לאמנויות יהודיות. נוסף לסויטת המחולות המקורית "שיר קם לתחיה", למוסיקה של המלחין מקס הלפמן, הם הופיעו בריקוד שיצר אחד מרקדני הקבוצה, "קולות צעירים קמים עולים", נחום בלקמן (שחר). הקבוצה ניסחה את ההסבר בתכניה כך: "'הגילדה למחול יהודי' היא קבוצה שיתופית של צעירים וצעירות אמריקניים, אשר חשו צורך להביע את מורשתם היהודית (תלבושות, טקסים וחגים של העם היהודי), באמצעות המחול - מחול עממי ומודרני־הבעתי גם יחד."

קבוצת המחול העממי נעשתה חשובה יותר ויותר לברק. "זה היה נסיוני העצמאי הראשון ביצירה." עד אז אשתו היתה בעלת הקול המכריע והוא לא בטח בעצמו ויצר במסגרת הגדרותיה ודרך הוראתה. בריקוד שיצר ברק באותו זמן הוכיח לעצמו, שהוא יוכל להצליח. "זה היה מחול בימתי ובתוך הקשר האמנות היהודית. "רציתי להעלות את הרוח של ישראל, את תחושת האחווה בין הרקדנים וכן משהו יהודי ייחודי. באותו זמן לא שלטתי מספיק בעברית, ועל־כן ביקשתי מאחד מתלמידי־הרבנות שרקדו איתי להכנס לבמה בריצה ולצעוק 'מים, מים!', עד שהפכנו את המלה למזמור קיצבי וכך הבענו את תחושת התחיה והחיים החדשים בישראל."

ב־1948 כבר ניכר, שפרד פיתח תבנית מושלמת להוראה, יצירה והופעות־מחול. בעלון הפעילויות החינוכיות ב־"Y" נאמר, ש"קבוצת המחול היהודי מנהלת חזרות בימי שלישי, רביעי, חמישי ושישי, במשך שעתיים בכל פעם." פרד נהג כלפי רקדניו באופן מקצועי ביותר, ואף עודדם ללמוד סגנונות אחרים של מחול.

פרק שנים-עשר:
מחוץ למסגרת היהודית

מאמצע שנות הארבעים ואילך היו דלקובה וברק מעורבים לא רק בחוגים התרבותיים היהודיים, אלא השתייכו גם לגרעין יוצרי המחול המודרני. הם התידדו עם לואי הורסט, מנהלם המוסיקלי של רות סנט-דניס ושל מרתה גראהם מ-1926 עד 1948. חברותם עם לואי הורסט החלה, כשקטיה השתתפה בשיעורים לכוריאוגרפיה עימו בסטודיו של ג'ין ארדמן. הורסט האמין, שכוריאוגרפיה היא מלאכה, הניתנת ללמידה, כשם שהיא אמנות, והיתה לו השפעה מכרעת על התפתחות המחול המודרני באמריקה. "השתתפתי בקבוצת ההרצאות המודגמות שלו במשך שלוש שנים. היו לו, להורסט, השקפות וגישות ברורות כבדולח והוא יכול להסביר כל תנועה, מבלי שהיה בעצמו רקדן," נזכרת דלקובה.

למעשה, היה הורסט רחוק מלהיות רקדן.(55) הוא היה גבר גבה-קומה ורחב גרם ומעולם לא רקד בעצמו, אלא היה יושב ליד הפסנתר ומציב משימות לתלמידיו. הביקורת שהעביר ממקומו ליד הפסנתר גרמה לעיתים לאלה שהאזינו לו להתקפל מבושה. לדברי ברק, הורסט היה בעל חוש הומור יבש ועוקצני כשדיבר עם חבריו, אך כלפי תלמידיו היה ממש אלים, מילולית. "אני זוכר שכששבתי פעם אחת בכיתתו, הוא ביקש מאחד התלמידים תשובה לשאלה. התלמיד היסס ולא ענה מיד, והורסט המוקנט דרש תשובה מידית. 'אני חושב' - אמר התלמיד בהיסוס, והורסט קטע אותו: 'בעזרת איזה אבר?'"

ברק לא הסכים תמיד עם הורסט, במיוחד עם דעתו, שעל התלמידים למצוא תמיד מוסיקה חדשה לליווי ריקודיהם. "אני חשבתי שהוא היה בעל השפעה רבה מדי בעולם המחול המודרני, והיה חד-צדדי: הוא התעסק רק בוריאציות על נושא. בנסיעותינו מחוץ לעיר הייתי מתווכח עם קטיה על מה שחשבתי שהיתה גישתו השכלתנית מדי לריקוד. טענתי, שתמיד יכולתי לזהות תלמיד שלו על הבמה - לעולם היתה בתחילה תצוגה של הרעיון ואחר-כך חזרה עליו בחלקי הגוף השונים, למשל ברגל, בזרוע או בראש. ואני לא רציתי להיות מתמטיקאי, כשם שנראה לי שדרש. אולי זה אחד הדברים שמשכו אותי למחולות-עם בארצות-הברית. אלה היו רגשיים, ויכולתי לראות את הצעירים רוקדים ונהנים מהם.

"אך תמיד נהננו לצאת ולסעוד עימו במסעדות," אמר ברק. הורסט למד מוסיקה בוינה, והשלושה חשו בקשר משותף.

בנסיעותיהם להופעות במכללות לאורכה ולרוחבה של ארה"ב, נתקלו ברק ודלקובה ברקדנים שעבדו מחוץ לעיר ניו-יורק. אחד מסיוריהם הראשונים היה לאוניברסיטת ויסקונסין במדיסון, סיור שאורגן על-ידי מרכז "בתי-הלל". שם הם פגשו את Margaret H'Doubler, מיסדת המחלקה האוניברסיטאית הראשונה למחול באוניברסיטת ויסקונסין (ב-1926). מרגרט ה'דובלר כתבה ש"על הצעירים להיות מוכנים לחיות חיים יצירתיים ופרודוקטיביים בחברה הרוצה בשינוי. השפה, התלבושות והמנהגים - יש ללמוד את הכל בדרכים שיביאו למודעות, התמחות, מקצועיות וייצרו ערכים, שיתרמו לחברה." יתכן שבעיני השנים, שעזבו חברה הרוסה, נראו רעיונותיה בלתי מציאותיים, אך הדרך בה לימדה היתה משכנעת ביותר. מלבד זאת, לדלקובה וברק היו רעיונות דומים. הם הסכימו איתה כשאמרה: "האמנות היא האמצעי היחידי, שבעזרתו יכול האדם להביע ערכים

ומשמעויות, אליהם הגיע בחייו היום-יומיים – ערכים שנוצרו כתוצרה ממגעו של האדם עם המציאות."(56)

דלקובה וברק אף פגשו באסיסטנטית של ה'דובלר, Louise Kloepper, שהיתה האמריקנית הראשונה שסיימה את בית-הספר של מרי ויגמן בגרמניה.(57)

הם נפגשו לארוחת צהריים. "בפעם הראשונה בחיי נפגשתי עם רמת מרץ כה גבוהה אצל אדם מבוגר. נראה לי, שככל שהאדם נשאר יצירתי, הוא שומר על נעוריו. הייתי פשוט הומם מהמרץ שלה. באופן בלתי מודע היא הציבה בפני אתגר, שנשאר עימי לתמיד," אמר פרד.

המבקרת אן ברזל משיקגו כתבה על הקונצרט באוניברסיטה של ויסקונסין: "תגובת הקהל באולם המלא היתה כה חזקה, עד שהצופים כמעט נעשו לחלק מההופעה... רקדנים טובים בעלי תנועות לירית מתנת-אלוה וגופות מאומנים היטב, אשר רקדו ברגש, בידע ובהומור." (58) אף ה'דובלר כתבה להם, כי "משום שחשנו באמת האמנותית בריקודכם, הצפיה בכם ובמחולותיכם העניקה לנו הרגשה חמה כלפיכם."

דלקובה וברק נשאו רשימת ב-1 באוקטובר 1946, בניו-ג'רזי, לפני סיור ההופעות שלהם לדרום. הם החלו את הסיור באטלנטה, וברק הזדעזע, כשראה לראשונה את המחלקות הנפרדות ללבנים ולשחורים ברכבות. הוא נחרד, כשראה שעל הכושים נאסר לשתות מברזי-שתיה של לבנים או להשתמש בחדרי השרותים. ההתפקחות היתה מרה והיה קשה לו להאמין, שהוא עדיין באמריקה.

דלקובה וברק הגיעו למכללת Black Mountain הקולג' לאמנויות היוצא-דופן שבקרולינה הצפונית. "המקום, על אווירתו השיתופית, נתן לנו את התחושה של קיבוץ. התקבלנו שם כאמנים, ולא דווקא כרקדנים יהודיים," נזכר ברק. "אני זוכר, הצייר בן-שאן שהיה שם באותו זמן, והראה לנו את ציוריו. מצב מפרק הירך שלי התדרדר והגביל את אפשרויות ההופעה שלי, ולכן בירכתי על ההגדרה של עצמי כאמן ולא רק רקדן." מודעה מאותו זמן מבשרת על "תוכנית מגוונת של מחול מודרני" של הזוג, כשמחירי הכרטיסים הם $3.00, $2.65 ו-$1.55.

במשך קיץ שנת 1947 חזר ברק לקורס-הקיץ של הניה הולם בקולורדו. הוא רקד עם הולם לראשונה בבואו לארצות-הברית ב-1941. הפעם הוא ודלקובה באו למרכז כדי להופיע. נקודת השקפתם האירופית המשותפת על מחול מודרני משכה אותם אל הולם. היא החלה לעבוד איתם ויצרה את "The Triad", שלישיה לעצמה, ברק ודלקובה. הריקוד תאר את התחבטויותיה של אשה בין אהובה לילדה. ברק גילם את האיש, הולם את האם ודלקובה את הבת.

ברק נזכר בקשיים "בספירת" התנועות. "הספירות נראו כה שרירותיות. אני זוכר שעמדתי בקלעים עם אלוין ניקולאיס, שהיה האסיסטנט של הולם באותו זמן. זה היה לפני אחת מהחזרות האחרונות ואני התלוננתי בפניו על קשיי בספירת הצעדים. הוא ענה בדרך המתלוצצת הרגילה שלו, 'מדוע לא תסכם את כל הספירות ואז תחלק אותן בארבע?'"

במשך קורס הקיץ התוודע ברק לגלן טטלי, שהיה ברבות הימים לכוריאוגראף מפורסם. "האוויר היתה מלאת מרץ. בשיעורים, במשך החזרות ואפילו בשיחות שניהלנו בזמן הארוחות ובהפסקות. אולי היה זה בגלל אוויר ההרים הדליל. בסיום כל הופעה הבנתי, מה משמעות הקיום בראש הרים. חשבתי שאמות מחוסר חמצן.

"אני זוכר, שבוקר אחד בנה של הולם, קטיה ואני טיפסנו במעלה ההרים. יצאנו לדרכנו מוקדם מאוד וכשקרבנו לפסגה, החלה לעלות השמש. הפרדה שרכבתי עליה האיטה את צעדיה והדביר נעתק מפי, כשראיתי את כל צבעי השחר משתקפים ברקיע. התרשמתי מהמאבק הפיסי שבטיפוס, וחשתי שהוא שיקף משהו ממאבקנו הסמלי לחיים. הטבע יכול להיות מהמם ורענן, ללא כיעור או סבל. לא היתה לי כל סיבה לבכות את חולשת מפרק הירך שלי. למרות המכשולים הרבים ידעתי, שעדיין אוכל לנצח. חשבתי לעצמי, החיים הם נצחון – מחול נצחון!"

פרק שלושה-עשר:
אירופה

בקיץ 1948, שלוש שנים לאחר סיום מלחמת העולם השניה, החליטו דלקובה וברק לצאת לסיור הופעות באירופה עם תוכניות המחול שלהם. הקהל שלהם לא היה באולמות התיאטרון של וינה או מינכן, אלא במחנות-העקורים באירופה - היו אלה המחכים עדיין להתחיל חיים חדשים, למציאת ארץ או בית לאחר הנסיונות המחרידים שעברו במלחמה ובמחנות-המוות. "שנינו רצינו לעשות משהו למען עמנו. הגענו למסקנות מסויימות בדבר מה עושה את החיים לערכיים, ורצינו לחלוק זאת עם אחרים. הרגשנו כה אשמים, ששרדנו מהשואה. איני בטוח כיצד הגענו לתוכנית הופעות בפני ניצולי מחנות-המוות. אך גילינו שארגון "Joint" (59) הקים מחלקת בידור, שמימנה הופעות במחנות העקורים. היה עלינו לשלם את הוצאות הנסיעה לאירופה ובחזרה, אך הג'וינט שילם את כל הוצאותינו למשך הזמן שסיפקנו בידור בעל תוכן יהודי.

"לאחר שאירגנו את הסיור במחנות באירופה, החלטתי לבלות שבוע אחד בלונדון, כדי שקטיה תוכל לפגוש בהורי ובמיס גראהם. רציתי להביא להם מזונות שלא טעמו זמן רב, בשל הצנע שהיה עדיין נהוג באנגליה, ושמרתי בקפדנות על חבילה עבורם בתאנו על סיפון ה'קווין אליזבת'. לאחר שחצינו את האוקינוס והגענו לביקורת המכס, הזדעזעתי, כשגיליתי שהחבילה המעדנים הנפלאים נעלמה. לעולם לא אדע כיצד גילה הגנב, שהיתה זו חבילת מזון.

"זו היתה חוויה נוגעת ללב לפגוש שוב בהורי לאחר תשע שנים קשות של פרידה. כשביקרנו את מיס גראהם, היא, כדרכה, סירבה לשמוע כל מלות תודה, שניסיתי להביע בפניה. אך הרי היא שלמעשה הצילה את חיי!

"מלונדון טסנו לפריז. לארוחת הבוקר הראשונה שלנו לאחר הטיסה, ניסיתי להזמין בצרפתית עילגת קפה בחלב וחמניות. לא יכולתי להבין את אשר ניסו להסביר לי: פשוט לא היה קפה, לחם או חלב. המזון ניתן בהקצבה. לאחר אמריקה והשפע שלה זה היה הזעזוע הראשון שנאלצנו להסתגל אליו."

ביומם הראשון של הרקדנים בפריז הם נלקחו על-ידי נציג מהמשרד הראשי של הג'וינט לבקר בבית יתומים. למרות שהילדים איבדו את משפחותיהם במלחמה, פרד מצא את המקום מקסים. הילדים למדו לקשט את חדריהם למרות שכמעט לא היו להם חומרי קישוט. הם הדביקו על הקירות תמונות שגזרו מעיתונים, כאילו ניסו בכך לעורר מחדש את הצדדים היצירתיים שאיבדו במהלך המלחמה.

"לאחר שהגענו למינכן קיבלנו משאית ונהג, והובטח לנו שבכל מחנה-עקורים נמצא פטיפון. וכך, עם התלבושות והתקליטים שלנו, יצאנו לדרך. במחנה הראשון שהגענו אליו לא מצאנו פטיפון - הוא נמכר! הייתי כה מיואש, כשישמעתי על הספסרים בתוך המחנות, אשר מכרו את אשר נועד לטובת הכלל.

"באופן כללי, הסיור היה חוויה מחרידה עבורי. אתה שואל את עצמך, מדוע נחסך ממך הנסיון הזה? הדרכון האמריקני שלי אך הדגיש את רגש האשמה שלי.

"במחנות ראינו רק את אלו, שניסו פשוט להעביר את הזמן. ראינו את החולים וחסרי הישע, אלה שלא ידעו לאן ללכת או כיצד להגיע לשם. השתמשתי ברשמים אלו בריקודי 'הציפיה הארוכה', שנרקד רק לליווי נקישות המטרונום."

במסגרת הסיור נסעו ברק ודלקובה מפריז לאיטליה, אחר-כך שהו שבוע בוינה וזלצבורג וחודש נוסף בגרמניה, לפני שחזרו לפריז.

בכפר הררי אוסטרי קטן הם הופיעו במחנה ילדים, שלמרבה האירוניה נקרא "בוכנוולד" על שם מחנה הריכוז. ברק ודלקובה הופיעו בפני הילדים בריקודים מהרפרטואר שלהם, וגם לימדו אותם ריקודי-עם. אחד מפקידי הג'וינט כתב על אחת מהופעותיהם באיטליה: "ההופעה נערכה בוילה יפה, והיתה מבוססת על נושא חג-הביכורים. קבוצה של 15 נערים ונערות אומנו במהירות אך ביעילות על-ידי ברק ודלקובה במיוחד לאירוע זה... הקהל, צעירים וזקנים גם יחד, זכה להתרוממות רוח באמצעות אמנות המחול והנושאים היהודיים המוכרים, שהיו כה קרובים ללבם וכה עשירים בזכרונות."

ברק שב לוינה, עיר הולדתו. "מאיטליה עלינו לרכבת לאוסטריה, בעוברנו תחילה דרך השטח שבידי האנגלים. הרכבת עצרה בגבול האיזור הרוסי, בשדה פתוח למרגלות ההר הנהדר Semmering. הרוסים ערכו חיפוש ברכבת ובדקו את ניירותי. כשראו שאנו אמריקנים הם פשוט אמרו "Raus" (החוצה). הם זרקו את מטעננו דרך החלון, ולאחר שירדנו, המשיכה הרכבת בדרכה. ישבנו על מזוודותינו בחמש בבוקר, מוקפים בערפל קר, ולא ידענו מה לעשות. לפתע, הופיעה משאית עם חיילים בריטיים. הם הסבירו לנו, שהרוסים נהגו לפעמים להוריד נוסעים אמריקנים מהרכבות, ללא שום סיבה. הבריטים לקחו אותנו למטה שלהם, ושם בילינו את היום. בחצות הלילה הם החביאו אותנו, מכוסים בשמיכות, במשאית שהבריחה אותנו לוינה."

ברק מצא את עיר עלומיו יפה עדיין. "אך לא רציתי לראות את אנשי העיר. לא יכולתי להפסיק להביט בפניהם, ולתהות במותו של מי היו אשמים. דודתי האהובה ואחותי נהרגו. חשבתי שהייתי מכניס לעיר ילדים בלבד. חזרתי לשכונת מגורי היהודית העתיקה, לרחובות שגדלתי בהם. הבתים נותרו במקומם הישן, אך כל האנשים שהכרתי נעלמו. איש לא נותר מלבד רפד זקן אחד ממשפחה שהכרתי. כשנכנסתי לחנותו שמכבר הימים, הוא החל להתייפח - הוא סיפר לי על מה שעלה בגורלם של אנשי השכונה, ושהוא הניח, שאף אני מתתי. לא היה לו לאן ללכת לאחר המלחמה, ולכן חזר לוינה.

"אפילו לפני המלחמה לא היו רגשותי הפרטיים כלפי היהדות חיוביים במיוחד. הרושם שלי מיהדותו של אבי היה שלילי, והתנסיתי באנטישמיות בוינה. חסרתי אפילו את מושגי היסוד של הציונות, שארץ חדשה תציע גישה שונה וחופשית בתכלית לחיים היהודיים.

"למרות כל זאת, נהניתי לראות שוב את וינה, כי אי-אפשר לעקור שורשים הטמונים בנשמת אדם, יהיה מה שיהיה.

"אך מה עושה את החיים לשווים? המשכתי לשאול את עצמי. ניסיתי לבסס אהבה כנה, משיכה ומסירות כלפי סוג חדש של יהדות, אך לעולם לא נפרדתי מרגשות האשמה שלי. במשך השנים, כשישראל התמודדה בעוד ועוד מלחמות, נשארתי והתבססתי באמריקה, ורגשות אלו נעשו לי ברורים וחדים יותר. אך ידעתי, שבדרך מסויימת הפכתי ל'מוסד ציוני' משל עצמי. בהדרגה השפעתי על צעירים כה רבים לבקר בישראל ואף להשתקע בה, ואני יודע שהובלתי צעירים רבים לחשוב על יהדותם בצורה שונה. אני בטוח, שכל זה הוא תוצאה של החינוך המוטעה והשלילי שקיבלתי. זה גרם לי לרצות בשינוי עבור הצעירים של ימינו. רגשות אלו באו לא מהרצאות, ספרים או לימוד, אלא מהחיים עצמם, מהביקורים במחנות-העקורים והמחשבות התמידיות על אלו שמתו והמזל שליווה אותי תמיד."

פרק ארבעה-עשר:
ישראל

שנה לאחר הסיור במחנות-העקורים באירופה, כשמדינת ישראל היתה בקושי בת שנה, החליטו ברק ודלקובה לבקר בארץ.

הם תכננו להופיע בפני תשעה קיבוצים, כמה מהם באיזורי-ספר ובנגב. הם גם ביקרו בערים ופגשו בחברים ועמיתים מאירופה, כמו גרטרוד קראוס ואלזה שארף, והכירו דמויות חדשות מעולם המחול המקומי. אחת ממכרותיהם החדשות היתה גורית קדמן, לשעבר גרט קאופמן. מספר חודשים לפני שבא הזוג לישראל, אירגנה גורית את הפסטיבל השני למחול-עם בקיבוץ דליה, ושם היא הציגה יוצרים מקוריים כשרה לוי-תנאי, רבקה שטורמן וירדנה כהן. היא הכירה בין ברק ודלקובה ואמנים אלו והציגה בפניהם את הצדדים החדשים של המחול הישראלי.

"זו היתה חוויה מרנינה לראות את המציאות הישראלית," אמר פרד. "זה היה נסיון חיובי ביותר - סמל לחיים החדשים עבור היהודים, וניגוד גמור למצב, שבו מצאנו את היהודים במחנות-העקורים שנה אחת קודם. דבר לא עמד בדרכו של יהודי במדינת ישראל - ירדנו מהמטוס והסבל היה יהודי, וכן נהג האוטובוס, השוטר, האיכר, בעלי-הבתים ואנשי המקצוע. זה היה מלהיב ביותר."

ברק ודלקובה גילו, שהקיבוץ הוא נסיון יחיד במינו. כל צמח שראו בקיבוץ טופל וטופח כילד, ברצון להפריח את השממה. בקיבוץ הראשון שבו ביקרו, קיבוץ רביבים, הבחין ברק, שכל שתיל קטן כוסה בנייר שהגן עליו בפני החול. דבר לא נלקח כמובן מאליו. הוא שמע על היל הראשון שנולד בקיבוץ, וחש בגאווה המשותפת כשסיפר לו אחד מחברי הקיבוץ, לא אבי הרך הנולד, "נולדה לנו הבת הראשונה."

הצמד היהודי המרקד התקבל על-ידי הקהל בקיבוץ בעניין ובפתיחות. ברק אף אהב קהל זה, משום שנשאר לאחר ההופעה לדבר על מה שראה, ואפילו הציע ביקורת על רעיונות ונושאי הריקוד, והוא מצא זאת כגורם מעורר ביותר עבור האמן. בקיבוץ אלונים שבצפון, ברק אמר שהילדים היו בכל מקום, במיוחד במשך החזרות. המלה העברית הראשונה ששמע מהם היתה "קרחת". הוא החל להקריח בצעירותו, ונהג לחבוש לחבוש מיגוון כובעים ופיאות על הבמה. במשך ההופעה הוא שמע את הילדים לוחשים "אך היכן הקרחת?"(60)

ברק ודלקובה היו האמנים האמריקניים הראשונים שהדרימו עד אילת. קצין בכיר שצפה בהופעתם בקיבוץ הזמינם להופיע במחנה צבאי שם. הם סיפרו על כך ברשימה שפרסמו. (61)

"עזבנו את באר-שבע, הנקודה האחרונה של התרבות והמים, במכונית צבאית עם נהג ושני חיילים חמושים. נאמר לנו, שלא נמצא במדבר פסנתר או זרם חשמלי. אז החלטנו להביא עימנו את משה, מוסיקאי צעיר ומוכשר מקיבוץ חולתה, שניגן בחליל. הוא התאים את מנגינותינו לחלילו... פה ושם ראינו עדר גמלים, חול וחול ולעיתים איילות בין הסלעים וציפורים מוזרות... הנסיעה מבאר-שבע נמשכה 12 שעות, ואז נפרש בפנינו מיצר עקבה, ים-סוף המטהר... חשנו בחום ובריצנות המדבר התנ"כי... אחר-הצהריים החלה 'ועדת התרבות' להכין את הבמה עבורנו. הם חיברו כ-12 שולחנות יחדיו... חיכינו עד תשע בלילה, ואז שני ג'יפים סיפקו לנו את תאורת הבמה מפנסיהם הקדמיים... היה כבר חשוך

מכדי להתאפר, ומשה לא יכל לקרוא את התווים. ביקשנו להביא שלוש מנרות נפט... הקהל מנה כ-400 עולים חדשים ממרוקו בעלי זקנים ארוכים. אנו חייבים להודות שהם הפחידו אותנו קמעה, בחוסר השקט שלהם. למען האמת, אף הם לא ידעו למה לצפות... צליל החליל בקע מתוך הלילה ככישוף; כל הפנים המזוקנים התרככו כקטיפה...

״התוכנית נמשכה כשעה. היא כללה שלושה מחולות על נושאים חסידיים, קצת הורה, מחול עבודה ושירה בציבור בהנחיית משה. כשהסתיימה התוכנית, ירדנו לים לשחות, ויכולנו לשמוע עד שעה מאוחרת בלילה את החיילים שרים באוהליהם. הם שרו נעימות חסידיות.״

ביקורו הראשון של ברק בישראל היה עשיר בחוויות. רשמיו המגוונים מהכפר ואנשי הארץ נתנו לו ולעבודתו השראה רבה. הוא השתמש בדימויי כפר דרוזי, שעברו בדרכם, במחול שיצר, ״לילה״. שלוות הלילה ודמות האשה הדרוזית היושבת עטופת שחורים למרגלות ההר לאור הירח. הקשר שלו לארץ לא ניתן להתרה, והוא שב לישראל ב-1955, 1959, 1968 ואחר כך מדי שנה. בכל ביקור למד את ריקודי-העם החדשים ביותר ולימד אותם באמריקה. עם כל מחול חדש גדלה מעורבותו בחיי הריקוד של הארץ.

למרות התרשמותו החיובית מישראל, כשחזר ברק לניו-יורק הוא היה שלם עם החלטתו לעבוד בגולה. הוא הרגיש, שברצונו ללמד וליצור עבור יהדות אמריקה. ניו-יורק היתה ביתו, והוא רצה להמשיך לחיות בבית חדש זה, אך נקודת מבטו של אשתו נעה בחריפות לכיוון ישראל. הם מילאו את התחייבויותיהם ללמד ולהופיע, והדימויים הציבוריים שלהם היה חזק. דוריס הרינג כתבה בספרה ״עשרים וחמש שנות מחול אמריקני״, ש״תוכניותיהם עתה הם שילוב מרתק של הישן והחדש.״(62) לואי הורסט, אף הוא מבקר חשוב, כתב ביקורת אוהדת על הצמד לאחר הופעה עם להקתם ב-YM—YWHA, ב-25 במרץ, 1950. הביקורת התפרסמה בעיתונו של הורסט, ה-״Dance Observer״. ״שני אמנים ידועים אלה רכשו מוניטין ראוי לקנאה לפירוש הכוריאוגרפי המצויין שלהם, המבוסס על פולקלור תנ״כי ויהודי. אך בהופעה זו התעורר עניין מיוחד עקב העובדה, שבפעם הראשונה הם הציגו עבודות, שהשקיפו תחום חדש, המחול המודרני האמריקני... ברק הצליח מאוד ככוריאוגראף ביצירתו 'Timely Ballads', שהיא שלושה קטעים סאטיריים על אמריקה העירונית, שנרקדו באופן מצויין ובחוש הומור עוקצני... בחלק הפולקלוריסטי של הערב היצירה הטובה ביותר היתה עבודתו של ברק 'הרהורי שבת'...״

למרות הצלחותיהם, חבריהם הבחינו במתחים שבין פרד וקטיה. קלאודיה קאופמן באה לביקור מקליפורניה והלכה עם דלקובה לבתי-ספר בסגנונות מחול שונים. ״הייתי נבהית, אם לא היו יחסיהם כה מתוחים.״(63)

אך מכל מקום, ברק ודלקובה המשיכו להופיע כצמד במנהטן, ב״קפה חביבי״, שהיה מועדון לילה חדש ברחוב ברודוויי פינת רחוב 46. קהל רב נהר למועדון, כדי לראות בדרנים ישראלים בעלי-שם. בשנה השניה נאלצה ההנהלה להזמין גם אמנים אמריקנים כדי למלא את התוכנית, ביניהם היו ברק ודלקובה.

״קיבלנו חוזה לחמישה שבועות עם אפשרות הארכה לחמישה שבועות נוספים. אני חושב שהיינו אמורים להופיע בשלוש הופעות בשבת,״ אמר ברק. ״רקדנו על רצפת בטון, וכשאני נזכר בכך, אני חושב שזה מאוד הזיק לרגלי, שכבר היתה במצב קשה. רציתי להפסיק להופיע לזמן מה בגלל רגלי הכואבת, ועלה במוחי רעיון. החלטנו ללמד ריקודי-עם בשבת אחר-הצהריים. זו היתה הצלחה גדולה וההנהלה החליטה להפריש לנו אחוז ממחירי הכרטיסים, מאחר שמשכנו משתתפים כה רבים. לימדנו את ההורה והצ׳רקסיה ואת המחולות שראינו בסיורינו בישראל. פרד וקטיה ביטלו חלק מפעילויותיהם המשותפות. הם לא הופעיו עוד ב״Y״.

הפגישות עם הועדה לאמנויות יהודיות נמשכו. ג׳ודית קפלן נזכרת בזמן ששני הזוגות היו קרובים. ״התווכחנו הרבה על האמנות, על חינוך יהודי ועל רעיונותינו השונים. רבנו על יחסנו לישראל.״(64) היינו בקבוצת חברים, שחשבה על עליה והשתקעות בישראל. היינו נפגשים באחד מבתי החברים ומשוחחים במשך שעות. איירא ואני חשנו, שהישראלים רוצים רק באמנים מפורסמים, שלא כמונו, למרות שאחדים מאיתנו היו מוסיקאים ורקדנים ידועים. ברק אמר, שישראל מעוניינת רק במישהו כמו מרתה גראהם ולא בו או בקטיה. חוץ מזה, נמאס לו לעבור מעיר לעיר, מארץ לארץ. הוא רצה לתקוע

59

שורשים. בנקודה זו היו חיכוחים עם קטיה, שרצתה לעלות לישראל. ברק חש שהאמנויות היהודיות לא קיבלו עידוד בישראל, ושהיתה אווירה יצירתית יותר בארצות-הברית," אמרה איזנשטיין. ערבים אלו היו נגמרים בשתיקות מכבידות.

אך למרות זאת נסעו יחד קטיה ופרד ב-1950 למחנה-קיץ גדול בצפון קרוליינה, שנקרא "Blue Star Camp". הארי, בן והרמן פופקין היו בעליו המשותפים של המחנה המעורב לצעירים וצעירות יהודיים. הרמן פגש בפרד וקטיה במחנה ברנדייס, ורצה שיביאו למחנה שבניהולו את נסיונם. למרות התנגדות אחיו והורי החניכים, שחשבו שהמחנה נועד לענפי ספורט וחיים נמרצים בחיק הטבע, יצר הצוות המרקד ברק ודלקובה תוכנית, שכללה להקה להופעות של ריקודי-עם ישראליים, שהופיעה בהזדמנויות שונות. (65) כל המחנאים השתתפו בפסטיבל במתכונת פסטיבל דליה. (66) ברק ודלקובה החדירו במחנאים את אהבת התרבות היהודית, ולא רק את הריקוד כפעילות לשעות הפנאי. המחנאים יכלו לראות את המשמעות וההתרגשות שבמחול היהודי בחגיגות חג-הביכורים, שבדרך כלל חל בזמן המחנה. את החג היו חוגגים במחול וטקסים, כשם שחגגו את השבת ואת ההבדלה שבין קודש לחול.

ברק ודלקובה התלהבו מחניכיהם החדשים ומהתוכנית החדשה. ברק פיתה את הנערים בני ה-14 לבוא לשיעורי הריקוד באמצעות מדריך שהנערים העריצו. המדריך היה בעל כתפיים עגולות וגב כפוף, ולכן החליט ברק לעזור לו ולקרוא לשיעורים שיעורי פיתוח הגוף. "השיעורים שהעברתי היו, גופנית, קשים במיוחד, ובהדרגה החדרתי בהם מקצבים ואיכויות שונות של תנועה, עד שהנערים חלו לרקוד. הם התלהבו מכך מאוד."

המתח בין קטיה ופרד גבר, וכשג'ודית קפלן איזנשטיין ובעלה ביקרו אותם בקיץ, הם כמעט שלא דיברו עוד אחד עם השני. בחזרו לניו-יורק העסיק ברק את עצמו בכל מיני פעילויות, כי לא רצה להודות בקרע הגדל בינו לבין אשתו.

60

פרק חמישה-עשר:
במה לרקדנים

כשפרד ברק לא היה בסיורים או בהופעות, נהג ללכת להופעות של אחרים, על-פי רוב ב"Y". לעיתים קרובות צפה בהופעות שאורגנו ונתמכו על-ידי בת-זוגו למחול בשנות ה-30, טרודי גות, אך הוא לא החשיב תקופה זו כיצירתית במיוחד במחול באמריקה.

על הרקדנים היה למצוא את דרכם בחזרה אל הריקוד לאחר מלחמת העולם השניה, והיתה פחות עבודה עבורם עם חלוצי המחול המודרני.(67) ב-1949 הפסיקה דוריס האמפרי להופיע. הניה הולם עבדה בעיקר בברודווי, שרבים החשיבו כמין בריחה; מרתה גראהם החלה את התקופה "היוונית" שלה. אף אחד מאלה לא היה בשיא כוחו היוצר. המתמרדים, כגון אליין ניקולאיס, מרס קנינגהם, אריק הוקינס, דונלד מק-קייל, ג'ופרי הולדר ופול טיילור הכריזו על נטישתם את כור מחצבתם, אך עבר זמן עד שהמרד שלהם בא לידי ביטוי ממשי בעבודתם. תחילת שנות ה-50 היתה מעין זמן מעבר, כשהמחול המודרני היה יצירתי פחות.(68)

לרקדנים המודרניים היו אך מעט הזדמנויות להופיע. זה היה מעגל סגור, משום שללא הופעות היה קשה מאוד לפתח את המקצוענות הדרושה. בשנות החמישים חל שינוי אפילו בבמה המכובדת למחול מודרני ב"Y". "במשך שנות השלושים ובמידה רבה גם הארבעים, היה ה"Y" נמל-הבית לרוב ההופעות של המחול המודרני. כל תוכנית חדשה גרמה לתגובה עזה, להתרגשות ומשכה קהל חדש, שראה את התנועה הקיצונית החדשנית בהתפתחותה. במשך שנות החמישים שככה עוצמה זאת."(69) ברק החל לתת את דעתו ברצינות על בעיה זו של חוסר מקום להופעות. היכן יוכלו רקדנים צעירים לקבל את ההזדמנות הראשונה? יתכן, שזיכרונותיו של ברק מימי רינה, בהם זכה במדליית הארד, עוררו את דמיונו. הוא נזכר במסגרת שאיפשרו לאמנים עצמאיים רבים להציג את עבודותיהם יחדיו, בתחרויות שתמכו ברקדנים צעירים ושמומנו על-ידי עיריית רינה. הוא הבין, שיש צורך לעשות משהו לעזרת הרקדנים הצעירים.

"הלכתי להופעה ב'Y' וברכתי את הרקדן לאחריה. 'על מה אתה מברך אותי?' הוא אמר. 'הרי אהיה חייב כסף במשך שלוש השנים הבאות...'"

רעיון עלה במוחו למשמע הדברים. הוא ינסה ליצור מקום עבור רקדנים וכוריאוגרפים צעירים, שם יוכלו להראות את עבודתם ללא צורך למצוא מימון לשכירת האולם והוצאות ההפקה. ברק ודלקובה הופיעו לעיתים קרובות בגן-הפסלים שבמוזיאון של ברוקלין, בתוכניות מחול אתני. למרות העובדה, שמבקרי-המחול של העיתונים הגדולים של ניו-יורק לא כיסו ארועי-מחול מחוץ למנהטן, ושהנסיעה למוזיאון ברכבת התחתית נמשכת כ-20 דקות, ברק היה משוכנע שזהו רעיון טוב.

פרד נפגש לארוחה עם מנהלת התוכניות של המוזיאון, חנה רוז. "לקיים שיעורי מחול מודרני לילדים כאן זה אינו מספיק. ברצוני להציע לך סידרה של הופעות מחול מודרני בגן-הפסלים. תוכלי לבנות קהל חדש, והאווירה הבלתי רשמית של המקום, הגג הפתוח והבמה הקטנה שבפינה לא יהוו איום על קהל, שאינו רגיל למחול ולכוריאוגרפים ולרקדנים הצעירים. נמאס לי מקהל המחול, שהוא כעין משפחה מתאספת - והרקדנים מופיעים רק בפני רקדנים אחרים."

חנה רוז העלתה את הנושא בפני חבר הנאמנים והנהלת המוזיאון, שקיבלו את

61

הרעיון. כבר בשנת 1937 התקיימו מופעי תיאטרון-מחול בגן-הפסלים. בין אלה שהציגו אז את עבודתם היו ג'יין דאדלי וסופי מאסלוב. ההנהלה תרמה 75$ לכיסוי ההוצאות עבור כל הופעה. ברק התמנה למנהל האמנותי ומפיק הסידרה. רוז הציגה בפני הקהל כל תוכנית ואף מצאה שם לסידרה, "במה לרקדנים".

במשך שלוש שנות קיומה נעשתה "הבמה לרקדנים" למכשיר חיוני לרקדנים רבים. במשך עונת 1950, הופיעו הרקדנים על הבמה הקטנה בחצר הפסלים. הבמה היתה ללא מסך וקלעים, וללא הקסם שבתאורת במה. הקהל של שבת-אחר-הצהריים, ברובו ילדים והוריהם, נעשה יותר ויותר מרותק ופחות ופחות רעשן במשך העונה הראשונה, שכללה תוכניות של לוקס הובינג, אלווין ניקולאיס ולהקת המחול שלו, דלקובה וברק ושמונה אמנים אחרים.

כל רקדן קיבל 20$ עבור השתתפות בת עשרים דקות בערך. ברק שילב בתוכנית אחת רקדנים ידועים ובלתי ידועים. "הרעיון שלי היה לגוון ולכלול ריקודים מופשטים וריאליסטיים באותה תוכנית, ורקדנים מאסכולות שונות. זה היה עסק מאד עדין, שהצריך גישה דיפלומטית! מעולם לא בחנתי את הרקדנים. הם ידעו, שהשכר הוא סמלי - אך הם שוחררו משכירת-אולם והפקת ערב שלם בעצמם. בדרך כלל אמרתי לכל רקדן, 'ראה, אתה תרום את חלקך ואחר-כך פשוט לך לדרכך,' ואיכשהו זה עבד."

ברק ביקש מז'ק האריס, שהיה רקדן בלהקתו של ויידמן, להיות מנהל ההצגה תמורת 15$. בעצמו ראה בעבודתו "מחווה של אהבה" ומעולם לא לקח משכורת לעצמו. "הדנס מאגאזין" כתב על תוכניותיו של ברק, שהן בעלות "רוח בריאה של הרפתקה ותגלית".(69) לשם עריכת תוכניותיו המצליחות וכדי למצוא רקדנים, שוטט ברק בין הסטודיות בניו-יורק. "הגעתי לכל מרתף או עליית-גג, שהיו בהם רקדנים. בסטודיו של הלן טמיריס ראיתי את דניאל נאגרין. הוא סיפר לי, שיש לו סולו, אז אמרתי: מצויין!"

הוא הכיר את גלן טטלי מקורס-הקיץ של הניה הולם, ושכנע אותו ליצור כוריאוגרפיה לאחד מריקודיו הראשונים.(70)

מסגרת אחרת ליצירה היו הכיתות בקומפוזיציה בבתי-ספר כגון ה-The New Dance Group, המחלקה החדשה למחול בבית-הספר לאמניות הבמה, המחלקה למחול בבית-הספר "ג'וליארד" ובשיעוריו של לואי הורסט. ברק פנה לכל המורים - להורסט, דוריס האמפרי, מרתה היל, חואנה דה לאבאן והניה הולם - וביקש הצעות. בתוכניתו נהג לערב באופן חופשי, ובהצלחה, רקדנים משיטות וסגנונות שונות - כתלמידיהם של גראהם, האמפרי והולם.

הוא ריכז את האמנים הבודדים, אשר כנראה לא היו מצליחים להפיק תוכנית שלמה משלהם ללא יוזמתו. אלווין ניקולאיס נזכר בתקופה: "היה פשוט הכרחי להמשיך, כדי שמשהו חדש יקרה בסופו של דבר. פרד יצר את התשתית להמשכיות זו.

"הענין שלי בריקוד היה רחב ונדיב מאד. הוא ידע, שאם ישמור על מבחר מגוון בכל תוכנית, תהיה לו תמיכה רחבה יותר. לצד חזונו האמנותי, הוא היה איש ארגון מצויין."

ברק וניקולאיס הסכימו ביניהם על תוכניות מקבילות בברוקלין ובסטודיו שברחוב הנרי, שנוהל על-ידי ניקולאיס. ביום שני, ה-16 באוקטובר 1950, הם ניהלו יחדיו תוכנית בתיאטרון הקטן ב-Henry St. Play House, שהיה לבסיס להקתו של ניקולאיס, שניהל את המקום מ-1949 ועד 1970. דונלד מק-קייל הציג את יצירותיו "אקסודוס" ו"שיר מתוק" ולוקס הובינג הופיע בארבע מיצירותיו שכללו את "צעיר צנוע ביותר". רינה גלוק הציגה שניים מריקודיה. אלה היו רק הראשונים שהיוצגו בתיאטרון של רחוב הנרי תחת השם "במה לרקדנים".

ברק וניקולאיס קראו לנסיונם "סידרה המוקדשת לצורה והתפתחות במחול בן-זמננו". ב-18 במרץ 1950 הציג ניקולאיס את "משל החמור" ההומוריסטי, ואת "Extrados", שנרקדו על-ידי להקתו שכללה את פיליס לאמהוט, מארי לואיס ואחרים. ב-19 באפריל כללה התוכנית עבודות של ג'ון ארדמן, ניקולאיס ודונלד מק-קייל. בסתיו שאחר-כך הציג התיאטרון של רחוב הנרי את הכוריאוגרפיות של ברק "Timely Ballads" ו"סוויטה אמריקנית", שנרקדו על-ידי דלקובה וברק ולהקה של רקדנים מסדרת "במה לרקדנים" (כולל ג'ק מור ומרים קול).

כשברק והיועצת שלו חנה רוז עבדו על הפרטים במשך העונה הראשונה, התברר להם, שהסדרות בברוקלין לא יוכלו להמשיך להתקיים במוזיאון מחוסר במה מתאימה. במורד הרחוב עמד בנייננו של בית־הספר התיכון לכלכלת הבית, שלרשותו עמדו אולם ובמה בעלת מימדים טובים, המצויידים במסכים, ציוד תאורה וחדרי הלבשה. הסידרה הועברה לבית־ספר זה.

בתחילת העונה השנייה הם זכו לכיסוי נרחב בעיתונות. כתבת ה״דנס מאגאזין״ תארה את העונה החדשה בכלל ואת ברק בפרט:(71) ״אם הבמה בניו־יורק יכולה להחשב ברצינות לגן־עדן לרקדנים, אפשר ללא חשש להשוות בין חמישה אנשים וקוף המחט, כפי שהעדן מתואר בקוראן: יוסף מאן, טרודי גות, פרד ברק, הייזל מולר ווילאם קולודני... הם נמצאים בדרגה העליונה ואת הסיבה לכך אפשר למצוא, אף בין השורות, של לוח־ההופעות שבגליון זה. ללא יוצא מן הכלל אף אחד מאלה אינו תלוי בארגון הופעות מחול למחייתו, כולם עסוקים בקריירות מקצועיות נרחבות, כשהזמן והמאמץ האישי המופרש מהן כדי לעודד הופעות מחול מוחזר להם בדרך כלל כרווח רוחני ולא עובר לסוחר. מדוע הם עושים זאת?

״הם יודעים את מצבם של הרקדנים, שאינם יכולים לעשות דבר ללא $5,000 עד $10,000 כדי לשכור אולם בברודווי ולשלם לחברי איגוד פועלי הבמה וחשמלאים, שלא יוכלו לזכות בתשומת לב המבקרים במופעים שמחוץ למנהטן, אך אין באפשרותם לשכור אולם בעיר.

״ברק הקים את ׳במה לרקדנים׳ ב־1950. הוא רקדן שמקבל יותר הצעות עבודה משהוא ובת־זוגו יכולים למחול, קטיה דלקובה, יכולים לקבל על עצמם. בעשר השנים שחי באמריקה, מר ברק, שנולד באוסטריה, ראה בלא מעט תדהמה ולבסוף ברוגז, את התופעה של רקדנים מוכשרים העובדים על יצירותיהם בסטודיו שנה לאחר שנה, שעה שהקהל הולך לסרטים או יושב בבית.

״נמאס לי לראות את הרקדנים יושבים בסטודיו, והחלטתי שיש לעשות משהו, כדי להעלותם אל הבמה. הניחו לאלה הרוצים ליגע את עצמם בחיפוש אחר במות ברודווי; אנחנו נשתמש בכל במה שנוכל להשיג, ואם הקהל אינו יכול לבוא אלינו, אנחנו נבוא אליו...׳״

העונה השנייה של הסידרה במוזיאון בברוקלין נפתחה עם הרצאה מודגמת של לואי הורסט. למרות חילוקי דעות (פילוסופיים) בין השניים, ידע ברק כמה חשוב, שהקהל ישמע את הורסט. ״אני רק אמרתי לו שעברו שנתיים, מאז שמע אותו הקהל הניו־יורקי. בינתיים קם קהל חדש לגמרי, ודור חדש של רקדנים שצריכים לשמוע אותו.״ בין הרקדנים שהדגימו עבור הורסט היו מאט טוקי ומרי הינקסון. תוכניות אחרות כללו את מופעיהם של רות קארייר, סטוארט הודס, גלן טטלי ואלוין ניקולאיס.(72)

ברק אירגן סיום בלתי מקובל לעונת ה״במה לרקדנים״ בהופעה חגיגית ב־12 במאי 1951 ב״Y״. בין הרקדנים שבחר היו מרים קול, קטיה דלקובה, מרי הינקסון, גלוריה ניומן וג׳ק מור בכוריאוגראפיות משל עצמם וכן פרד ברק ואלוין ניקולאיס. הביקורת ב״דנס אובזרבר״(73) קבעה, ״הפסטיבל של להקת ה׳במה לרקדנים׳ סיים את העונה בתוכנית הראויה לחגיגה.״

ההופעות בעונה השלישית בחסות ״הבמה לרקדנים״ נערכו במנהטן ב״תיאטרון רחוב הנרי״, ובאולמות אחרים. גם הסידרה בברוקלין נמשכה, ועתה הרקדנים והקהל חובבי המחול היו בהחלט מוכנים לנסוע עד לשם. ה״דנס אובזרבר״ כתב בביקורת על התוכנית של ה־20 בפברואר 1952, כי ״יצירתו של מר מק־קייל ('Saturday's Child') הצדיקה את הנסיעה לברוקלין; ואפילו אם היצירה הצביעה על כשרון עצום יותר מאשר על הישג מיידי, למרות הכל היא הרשימה ביותר.״(74)

במשך העונה השלישית הציגו פרל לאנג ודוריס הרינג הרצאת־הדגמה, שהיתה בתבנית חדשנית. לאנג רקדה את מחולות־היחיד שלה ״Moonsong״ ו־״Windsong״ ואז הרינג, מבקרת ה״דנס מאגאזין״, ניתחה את הכוריאוגראפיה. לסיום בוצעו שוב שני הריקודים. ״העובדה, שניתן היה להנות מהם אפילו יותר לאחר שעמדו במבחן הלידה מחדש (שלאחר הניתוח), היא עדות מספקת ליכולתה של גברת לאנג ככוריאוגראפית ורקדנית,״ סיכמה אחת הביקורות.(75)

ברק הביא הרצאת-הדגמה מוצלחת זו למנהטן. זה לא היה עניין פשוט של הבאת שתי המשתתפות לבמה שענתה על דרישותיהן.

"הצגנו את הרצאת-ההדגמה ב-Cooper Union, שבימתו רחבה ולא עמוקה. לא היה מספיק מקום עבור הקבוצה לשלב ידיים וליצור מעגל. היה צורך לביים מחדש כל ריקוד ולהתאימו לממדים המוזרים של החלל. בעומק הבמה ניצבו ארבעה עמודים, שמסכים ביניהם. על הרקדנים היה להסיטם, כדי לצאת או להכנס לבמה. במהלך החזרה לאנג התבלבלה בשל הצורך להסיט את המסכים. היא ביקשה שיסומרו לאחור. האחראי החל לצעוק, 'את משוגעת? זהו בניין היסטורי, ואסור לשנות אותו בכל דרך!'"

ברק התייגע במציאת פתרון, כשלאנג איימה לבטל את ההופעה. אם רק יכל למצוא שקי חול כדי לשמור את הוילונות פתוחים! זה היה כבר ב-6.30 בערב. לפתע הוא נעלם. מספר דקות אחר-כך הוא חזר עם 20 חבילות סוכר מהמכולת הסמוכה. אלה שימשו כמשקולות שהחזיקו את המסכים פתוחים וההופעה התקיימה כמתוכנן.

במשך העונה האחרונה של ה"במה לרקדנים" הציג ברק תלמידים של מחלקות למחול של "התיכון לאמנויות הבמה", של מכללת שרה לורנס ומסדנת ההפקות של אליוין ניקולאיס. עניינו של ברק ביצירת הזדמנויות להופעה עבור רקדנים צעירים היה ברור מאוד בבחירת המבצעים בעונה האחרונה של "בימת הרקדנים" שלו.

פרק שישה-עשר:
עוד התחלה

התצלומים שבאלבום מהסיור לדרום ולמערב בפברואר 1951, אינם מראים את המתח הגובר שבין קטיה ופרד. הם הסכימו לסיים את כל התחייבויותיהם המשותפות להופעות. אך הקשר הפרטי שביניהם נשבר וקטיה החליטה לעזוב את פרד למען חיים חדשים בישראל. ברק שכר לעצמו עלייה-גג, ללא מים חמים ועם מדרגות רבות, שנחוץ היה לטפס עליהן, אשר הכבידו ללא רחמים על מפרק הירך שלו.

כלפי תלמידיו הוא היה עדיין הדמות הדינמית והתוססת. ובאופן מפתיע, בתקופה מכאיבה זו של חייו האישיים, הוא יצר כמה ממפעליו הפוריים ביותר. הוא פגש בשמחה לוין מקיבוץ נגבה, שנשלח על-ידי הסוכנות היהודית לאמריקה לעבוד עם צעירים כשליח. "הוא הזמין אותי ובערך עוד חמישים אנשים צעירים לחוות-ההכשרה של תנועת 'השומר הצעיר' מחוץ לעיר, שם הכינו את עצמם חלוצים לקראת החיים בישראל. במשך היום התקיימו הרצאות ועבדו בשדות, אך בלילה התחלנו לרקוד והמשכנו כמעט כל הלילה. שמחה הרקיד אותם בצורה שמעולם לא ראיתי כמוה קודם לכן. רוב הריקודים שהכרנו באמריקה כמחולות-עם יהודיים חוברו לנעימות חסידיות. לא היו אז בנמצא תקליטים למחול-עם, והיה קשה להשיג אקורדיוניסט טוב. לכן היה הליווי המקובל שירה בזמן הריקוד. אחדים מ'הריקודים היהודיים האמריקניים', כפי שנקראו אז, כללו תנועות מריקודי ה'Swing' וה'Square Dance'. (77)

"שמחה, שנקרא ששקה בפי כל, יצר אווירה משלהבת ומדבקת, והכניס את הצעירים למה שנראה ממש כטראנס. הם פשוט לא יכלו להפסיק לרקוד. שם ראיתי איזו השפעה יש למחול-עם על צעירים, הרוצים להתנסות בחוויות חזקות ומשמעותיות - במלים אחרות, צעירים הרוצים למצוא את הביטוי לזהותם במחול. החלטתי לנסות להשתמש בריקודי-העם בדרך זו."

לוין היה גם המארגן של פסטיבל המחול הישראלי הראשון בניו-יורק, שכלל מספר קבוצות של צעירים יהודיים, שרקדו ריקודי-עם ישראליים שונים. "התחרות והפסטיבל הראשון למחול-עם ישראלי" הוקדש ליובל הקרן הקיימת והתקיים במכללת האנטר, ב-13 בינואר 1952. לוין נזקק לרקדנים נוספים לתוכנית וביקש מפרד וקטיה להשתתף. תשעה חודשים מאוחר יותר, ב-29 בנובמבר 1952, הם התגרשו רשמית במקסיקו.

"לוין ראה את מחול 'השחר' שלי, וביקש ממני, מאחר שלא היה רקדן בעצמו, ליעץ לו לגבי הפסטיבל של השנה הבאה. אמרתי לו מיד, שלא אהבתי את רעיון התחרות. נכון שקבוצה אחת תזכה ותהיה ברקיע השביעי עקב כך, אך כל האחרים ירגישו נורא, וזה לא נראה לי כדרך מתאימה לתוכנית לכבוד ישראל."

ברק שמע שארגון חדש, המחלקה לנוער של ההסתדרות הציונית, יקח על עצמו את ניהול הפסטיבל ואילו לוין יחזור לישראל. הם ראיינו את ברק כמועמד לתפקיד מנהל הפסטיבל. הוא אמר, שבמקום לגרום לתחרות בין הקבוצות, הוא ישבץ בתוכנית באופן כזה, שכל קבוצה תציג את זו הבאה אחריה, וכך תבנה התוכנית עד שתגיע לשיא גדול, שבו יהיו כל המשתתפים על הבמה. ברק היה כמובן בקי ברושם שעושות מסות רקדנים גדולות מהופעותיו באירופה. כל נסיונו הקודם במחול התנקז בזום הפסטיבלים, שהפכו למסורת שנתית בחיים היהודיים בחוף המזרחי. הוא קיבל את התפקיד.

65

התנגדותו של ברק לרעיון התחרות מתקשרת עם השקפתו ותפיסתו את ריקודי-העם כאמצעי תקשורת חברתי בין רקדנים. החום האנושי היה לא פחות חשוב עבורו מההצלחה. "ריקודי-עם משמעם עשיית דברים יחדיו, כמעט כמו השתייכות למשפחה מעורבת בכך חברותיות מסוימת," הוא נהג לומר, "ואני באמת רואה בפסטיבל מפעל חינוכי." בעצם ימי בדידותו הוא עבד על מציאת דרכים לעידוד הרגשת הצוותא.

אחד הרקדנים מהפסטיבל הראשון שעבדו עם ברק היה דב אלטון. הוא לימד את אלטון ואת בת-זוגו את ריקודה של שרה לוי-תנאי "אל גינת אגוז" בעל הקצבים התימניים המסובכים, ואת "היין והגת" של ירדנה כהן. ברק השאיל לצמד הצעיר תלבושות והציע להם עיצה ועידוד כיצד להשיג סיורי הופעות. הרקדנים הצטרפו לשיעוריו ב-"Y". בימי ראשון לימד ברק ריקודי חברה לתלמידי תיכון. קולדוני, מנהל ה-"Y", ביקש ממנו להחדיר "משהו מיוחד, משהו יהודי"(78) לשיעורים, אך הצעירים לא התעניינו במה שהיה לברק להציע. היה עליו למצוא הקשר שונה למחול הישראלי. הוא רצה באנרגיה ובהתרגשות שהיו לקבוצות שעבדו עם לוין.

קולדוני וברק דנו בבעיה ומצאו פתרון חדש: ברק הצטרף לצוות המורים של מחלקת המחול, ולימד שיעור בימי רביעי, שהיה שונה משאר כל כיתות המחול שב-"Y". על התלמידים היה להרשם לעונה שלמה. הם יכלו לשלם בכל פעם שבאו, וערבים אלו נקראו "שיעורים פתוחים" ושילבו נסיון לימודי בבידור.

דב אלטון ואחרים שעבדו עם ברק באו בהתלהבות. השיעורים של ערבי יום ד' היו פתוחים לכל הרמות, ממתחילים ועד למקצוענים. הם החלו ב-8.15 ונמשכו עד 11. חברי ה-"Y" שילמו $0.50 ואחרים $0.75. השיעורים נקראו "ריקודי-עם יהודיים; המשתתפים בימי רביעי ילמדו כמה מהריקודים המסורתיים, כמה מהערביים והתימניים, ריקודי-עם יהודיים, שנוצרו כאן והריקודים הישראליים החדשים ביותר. השיעורים ילוו באקורדיון ויילמדו השירים."(79)

ברק קבע תבנית לשיעורים הפתוחים שנעשתה לסימן ההיכר שלו בהוראת מחול-עם ישראלי: הוא התחיל בחימום, שהתבסס על מספר צעדים פשוטים, שהופיעו אחר-כך בריקודים שלימד. יסודות אלו כללו את צעד הצ'רקסיה, צעד הדבקה, צעד המים-מים והצעד התימני, שבוצעו ללא שינוי המיקום. אחר-כך החל ברק לשחק עם ההדגשים והדינמיקה של הצעדים. "אחרי הכל, אם הכל מבוצע בלגטו אפשר להרדם, ואם הכל הוא גדול ופורטה אפשר לקבל כאב ראש. אתה חייב לגוון." לאחר 15 דקות הוא היה עובר למחיאות-כפיים יחד עם צעדים שונים, והאתגר עבור כל הרקדנים היה לשמור על ההתאמה בין הקצבים השונים בתנועות. "אחרי זה ביצענו את הצעדים בכיוונים שונים, קדימה, הצידה ואחורה, כשמחיאות-הכפיים הקצביות נמשכות. אפשר היה להתחיל לראות את הפנים הזורחות, ואז ידעתי, זה נצחון הריקוד - כה רב היה היופי וכה נעימה ההצלחה שהשיגו הרקדנים.

"רציתי שאפילו המתחילים יבינו את יסודות מחול-העם וכיצד יכלו גורמים אלו לשמש חומר בידי יוצרים של פולקלור. לעולם לא הבטתי ברגלי הרקדנים, אלא תמיד בפניהם. כשראיתי אותם מחייכים, ידעתי שעברנו את השלב הראשון, ואם הם התעניינו ידעתי, שנוכל להמשיך בפיתוח משהו חדש.

"תרגילי החימום הם כמו נגינת סולמות," הוא נהג לומר, "אשר משרתים מטרות רבות. חשוב מאוד להתחמם ולהתכונן לקראת הריקוד."

"לעיתים השתמש בתרגילי מקצב משעשעים כבמשחק, או בצורת שאלה ותשובה. הוא תופף, ובדרך זו נעשה מעורב פיסית בתנועה, והתוף נתן אוירה ישראלית - והרקדנים הגיבו ונענו לקצבים שתופף. הוא לא רצה להשתמש בשמות ומונחים שהיו עלולים, לדעתו, להרתיע. הוא פישט את הדברים בהוראתו, ועשה אותם לנעימים וברורים, וזו תופעה נדירה ביותר," אמרה רות גולדמן, תלמידה לשעבר, שכיום היא מנהלת מחלקת המחול היהודי ב-"Y".

יותר ממאה אנשים נרשמו לשיעורים הפתוחים של ערבי יום ד'. ברק החליט להוסיף עוד שיעורים במשך השבוע, ברמות מתחילים ומתקדמים, ואף קורס למדריכים לריקודי-עם. כל מיגוון התוכניות העשיר שב-"Y" של מחול ישראלי ויהודי נקרא למחול-עם ישראלי בניהולו של פרד ברק.

קארולין שטראוס זוכרת את אוירת לימוד ריקודי-העם הישראליים בשנות החמישים המוקדמות בניו-יורק. היא היתה חברה ב"יהודה הצעיר", קבוצת צעירים יהודיים באיזור לונג איילנד. "היו לנו פגישות, ולרוב רקדנו בהן ריקודי-עם ישראליים. אני זוכרת במיוחד את 'מים מים', 'הנה מה טוב', 'בא דודי', 'דודי לי', 'אל גינת אגוז' וריקוד דבקה מפרך עם כריעות שנעשו במהירות גוברת.

"כשעברתי מהקבוצה שלי לקבוצה איזורית רחבה יותר, האנשים שפגשתי היו מעניינים יותר והריקודים מגוונים. אהבתי את האוירה הישראלית; כולנו רצינו ללמוד עברית ולעלות לישראל. למרות שבמשפחתי מעולם לא השגנו במצוות, הלכתי לבית-הכנסת וניסיתי לשמור על כשרות.

"הריקודים החדשים שלמדתי בפגישות האיזוריות היו מורכבים יותר, ושייכים יותר לישראל המודרנית והלוחמת. בין אלו היו 'שיר הפלמ"ח', 'רועה ורועה' ר'כן יאבדו', ריקודי-שורות וכן ריקודי-מעגל ומחולות בזוגות. כולנו נגנו בחלילית הישראלית ורקדנו בכל הזדמנות, ביחוד בסופי השבוע שבילינו בכפר ובמפגשים.

"באופן כללי, מדריך אחד לימד את המחול למתחילים. המדריכים היו כולם בישראל וחזרו לאמן צעירים יהודיים או שפשוט חיכו עד שיתבגרו ויוכלו לנסוע לשם. כולם רקדו ב"Y"; הדבקות היתה עזה, למרות שנשמעה ביקורת על כמה מקבוצות הצעירים הציוניים האחרים. התחרות היתה ממשית; התחרינו אחד בשני על גודל ההתלהבות."

היא השתתפה בפסטיבל המחול הישראלי שנוהל על-ידי ברק, והיא זוכרת שהתרשמה מאוד מריקודי הקבוצות האחרות. "למעשה, רקדני 'השומר הצעיר', שחשבנו שהיה קומוניסטי, כמעט קרעו את הבמה. בהשוואה אליהם נראו ריקודינו מאולפים, עדינים וחסרי דם. ואנו הרי נתנו את הכל בהופעה! כתוצאה מכך התנהלו דיונים ללא סוף בשאלה האם יש צורך להיות קיצוני מבחינה פוליטית, כדי להיות בעל רגשות אמיתיים. בקשר אלי, לא היה לי מושג מה זה בעצם קומוניזם. כל מה שידעתי הוא, שעלי להסתיר את רוב פעילותי ב'יהודה הצעיר' מאבי, שהיה משוכנע שהם ניסו עלי 'שטיפת מוח'. המשכתי בריקודי-העם, הלכתי בהתלהבות לשיעורים הפתוחים ב"Y", וכן לפגישות של מחול-עם בינלאומי בגרינויץ' וילג'. הריקודים הישראליים היו האהובים עלי ביותר – אף קבוצה מלבד קבוצות הצעירים היהודיים ב"Y" לא יכלה ליצור התלהבות כזאת."

לביצוע כל עבודה שהיא יש צורך בכלים. במחול, הכלים שייכים בראש וראשונה למורה. הם נחוצים, כדי למסור את האמנות לתלמיד. לאילו כלים זקוק המורה, כדי ללמד ריקודי-עם ישראליים? ברק הקדיש לשאלה זו מחשבה רבה, ובשנים 1952-1980 הוא מצא תשובות, שהיו רבות השראה ונבונות. הוא הבין את הצורך במוסיקה מתאימה ובדרכים להסביר את צעדי מחול-העם הישראלי. ללא אלה, לעולם לא יוכל מחול-העם הישראלי להתקיים מחוץ לישראל. אף על פי כן, גם מי שנמצא רחוק מישראל, שלא ראה אף פעם מחול-עם ישראלי ושאינו דובר עברית, יש באפשרותו ללמוד את הריקודים. באמצעות הקלטות, שהופקו על-ידי ברק ובפיקוחו, אפשר להשיג את המוסיקה הדרושה. תקליטיו היו ההקלטות המקצועניות הראשונות של מוסיקה ישראלית עממית, שנוגנה על-ידי מוסיקאים מצויינים, בצירוף הוראות של ברק, המתארות את המחולות.

הוא נהג להתחיל את השיעור הראשון בקורס המדריכים שלו בציטוט מהתנ"ך וביקש מתלמידיו לבטאו במחול. "דברים מופלאים קרו. קיבלתי צעירים מארגונים יהודיים שונים, כמו 'הבונים', 'השומר הצעיר', 'מסדה' ר'בני-עקיבא', והארגונים הללו הענקיו מילגות-לימוד עבור חניכיהם ב"Y". אלה מעולם לא חשבו קודם במושגים של מחול, אך הם העלו פתרונות מעניינים. נתתי להם לעבוד גם עם אביזרים. כדי שהאביזרים יעזרו להשיג תוצאות טובות, הייתי מסביר, לדוגמה, שבריקוד-רועים עם מקלות אסור שהדבר הראשון הוא שיקרה שהמקלות יונחו על הרצפה, ועליהם להוות חלק מהריקוד. בסוף סידרת השיעורים, לאחר הדגמה מסכמת, הענקתי לתלמידים תעודה."

פרק שבעה־עשר:
לא במלים בלבד

נוסף להוראה, לארגון הפסטיבל השנתי למחול והופעותיו שלו, התייצב ברק בפני סוג חדש של התחייבות ב־1 בפברואר 1953: בכורת להקתו החדשה, הנושאת את השם: "The Merry-Go-Rounders". זו אמורה היתה להיות להקת מחול מקצועית חדשנית, שדוריס האמפרי, מנהלת מחלקת המחול ב־"Y", בוני ברד ופרד ברק יסדו, שנועדה להופיע בפני קהל של ילדים. תוכניתם הראשונה כללה מחול משעשע, "משל החמור" של אלווין ניקולאיס, "Goops" היה ריקודו של אוה דסקה על אודות יצורים חצופים מסרטים מצוייירים פופולריים והמחול החדש של פרד ברק, "חופשה בישראל".

אך פרד, שסבל מכאב בירך, היה מיואש. הרקדנים לא הצליחו להביע את הקצבים המיוחדים של העדות השונות בישראל, ורגלו הכואבת מנעה ממנו להדגים את אשר רצה: כוח בקריעות הרגליים והתרוממות בקפיצות. איך יוכל להעביר להם את תפיסתו בהסברים בלבד? אפילו המוסיקה נשמעה חסרת חיים, מלבד כשישב על־יד הפסנתרנית, באה ריינר, ותופף את הקצב.

שעה שישב בתיאטרון החשוך לצידה של דוריס האמפרי, הוא ניסה להביע את צערו. "לו רק יכולתי להדגים להם!" אמר, ואז לפתע בגד בו קולו ודמעות ניקוו בעיניו.

האמפרי עצמה סבלה משיגרון, שגרם לסיום בלא עת של הקריירה שלה כרקדנית. "פרד," היא אמרה, "אתה תוכל ללמד אותם את מה שאתה רוצה, אתה תמצא את המלים. אם אתה יכול ליצור את הכוריאוגרפיה למחול־עם כזה, יש כיוון חדש לגמרי בחייך. אז שב עכשיו על־יד הפסנתר, שיר בקול והכה בתוף את מקצבך. שים את רגשותיך בקולך והעבר את התנועה לרקדנים בתיפופך!"

ברק צלע לכיוון הבמה. הוא השתתל לספסל הישן לצידה של הפסנתרנית והוא שר ותופף בידיו והצית את הרקדנים בהתלהבותו. רקיעותיהם התחזקו וקפיצותיהם נעשו גבוהות יותר וברורות. הרקדנים השתעשעו ונהנו מהריקוד בצוותא וקרנו התרגשות. הוא ידע אז, שיוכל להכינם בעוד מועד לבכורה.

הרקדנים אומרו במחול מודרני, ורבים מהם הגיעו הישר מהמחלקה למחול של ג'וליארד. זה היה בהחלט רעיון נסיוני: להקים להקה של רקדנים מאומנים, שיופיעו רק בפני ילדים. פרד ברק אהב את הרעיון. לו רק יכול היה להעמיד עם הלהקה את הכוריאוגרפיות שלו, הוא ראה אותה כאמצעי לעזור לרקדנים. שנות החמישים היו קשות עבור רקדנים צעירים, והם נזקקו לתמיכה מוסרית ומעשית לאמנותם. הלהקה סיפקה נסיון מקצועי, שדרכו יוכלו להביט על אמנותם מזוית חדשה. הם לא נדרשו לביצועים טכניים קשים, אולם היה עליהם להשיג מהירות, צבע, רגש, דגשים ותנועות עבור קהל מאוד ביקורתי.

מי עוד מסוגל להבחין כילדים? הם רגישים יותר לכנות ואמת ממבוגרים. ומדוע לא **ייחשפו בפני הילדים הרקדנים הטובים ביותר? ומחול באיכות הגבוהה ביותר?** לא רק האמפרי וברק האמינו בלב שלם במבצע, אלא גם אלווין ניקולאיס ומספר רקדנים בולטים **אחרים של התקופה.**

לוסי ונבל (Lucy Venable) (80) אחת מהרקדניות ב"חופשה בישראל" המקורית מספרת, ששיטות עבודתו של ברק היו קשות, כמשגיח נעים הליכות, אך תקיף בחזרות,

68

תמיד דייק וניצל את הזמן במלואו, כשהוא מגיע לחזרה עם תוכניות ברורות. רקדנים עבדו היטב למענו.

"פרד לא נהג לסייר עם הלהקה בהופעותיה מחוץ לעיר, אך אני זוכרת אותו יושב ליד המלווה בהופעות ב־'Y', כשהוא שר ואף מכה בתוף בקטע המסיים."

ג'ף דונקאן, הרקדן הראשון ממין זכר בלהקה, מעיד על עצמו, שהיה רקדן מודרני טיפוסי, עד שפגש בפרד ברק. "לא רציתי לבצע אלא מנעד צר של תנועות. חשבתי, שידעתי ממה בנוי המחול המודרני, ולא רציתי לבצע כל מחול עממי. הייתי חצוף, אך במשך החזרות התחלתי לאהוב מאוד את התנועות. ונעשיתי מעורב. ברק עודד אותי ולימד אותי סודות מקצועיים רבים. הוא אחד מאות האנשים העוזרים לאחרים להתפתח ותומכים בהם, תופעה לא רגילה בניו־יורק, בה תמיד נראה שכל אדם דואג רק לעצמו. הוא היה אחד מאותם מעטים, אשר באמת היה איכפת להם מאמנותם. הוא ודוריס האמפרי היו כאלה, ולכן הם היו הנהלה מאוד נעימה וחזקה. ברק היה גם מעורב בניהול האדמיניסטרטיבי של להקת המחול, למרות שבוני ברד טיפלה במאבקי היום־יום, בפרסומת, בסידור ההופעות ובתלבושות. ברק שכנע את ניקולאיס לתרום את 'משל החמור' לתוכנית הבכורה."

אכן, בהופעתה הראשונה של הלהקה ישבו הילדים כמכושפים. כתב־העת "Life" שלח צלם ופרסם תמונות המעידות על ההשפעות המצויינות שהיו ללהקה על הרקדנים והריקודים. הביקורות ב"דנס מאגאזין" וב"דנס אובזרבר" היו נלהבות במידה שווה.

ה"דנס אובזרבר" דיווח ש"הלהקה הרפרטוארית של המבוגרים הקסימה את הקהל שלהם באחר־צהריים של שיחה קלה, שירה וריקודים... הצעירים השתתפו בפעיליות... כך שבעיה ניצבה בפני המבוגרים שבקהל: במי להביט, ברקדנים או בקהל. הילדים דרשו לפתוח שוב את המסך במחיאות־כפיים ובשירה, ומאחוריו נגלתה הסחרחרת, שהיתה העמודה צבעונית של סרטים וסוסי־עץ, שעליהם סובבו הרקדנים. כשהובטח לילדים, שהסחרחרת תוביל אותם למקומות נהדרים, הם עברו בקלות להתרחשות ב'חמור', שנרקד על־ידי מארי לואיס... ה'חופשה בישראל' של פרד ברק היתה בחירה מוצלחת, כיצירה היחידה של תנועה טהורה בתוכנית. הילדים התרגשו במיוחד, כשעוממעמו האורות בסוף ה'הורה', ונראו רק פנסי־הכיס שבידי הרקדנים, שהאירו את הדמויות שרקדו אל תוך הלילה."

בשיחה עם גרי האריס, שתכנן את התאורה ל"חופשה בישראל", אפשר לקבל רושם ברור יותר של הפעלול הבימתי החזק שיצר ברק, והוא אחת הסיבות להצלחתו של ריקוד מושך כל כך. האריס שיתף פעולה עם ברק לעיתים קרובות ב"Y" ובהפקות הפסטיבל הרבות במדיסון גארדן, באולם קרנגי ובלינקולן סנטר.

"מה שפרד עשה למעשה בסיום 'חופשה בישראל', שעה שהרקדנים ביצעו את ההורה כאילו מסביב למדורה בוערת, הוא שימוש ברעיון מקובל באירופה: צלליות. אלו נעשו פופולריות בארצות־הברית רק לאחרונה. על־ידי זריקור לבן אחד אפשר לשטוף באור את כל הרקע. כשהרקדנים רוקדים לפני הפנס, מטילים גופותיהם צלליות עצומות, הרוקדות על המסך האחורי. בסוף ההורה חזרו הרקדנים לבמה באופן מאוד מכובד. וכשהקצב גבר, החלו הרקדנים לחגוג. ואז, משירד הלילה, הודלק הזריקור והטיל צללים ענקיים.

"כשהקהל אינו יכול להפריד בין הצד הטכני למחול עצמו, אתה יודע שמשהו עובד כהלכה בתיאטרון. שאלתי מספר אנשים שהשתענייננו במיוחד בצדדים הטכניים של התיאטרון לתגובתם, והם הופתעו: על איזה אפקט אתה מדבר? זאת אומרת, שסיום הריקוד עבד בצורה מושלמת, משום שהצלליות הענקיות המסתחררות נבעו מרוח המחול עצמו. בתוך קטע סיום זה, שנמשך רק מספר שניות, נדחס עולם שלם של החינוך האירופי שקיבל פרד, רגשותיו כלפי הרוחני, רצונו לעשות את הרקדנים גדולים מהחיים, אהבתו למשמעות היהודית בצוותא של ההורה. כל רגע אמנותי שעובד, באמת ניתן לבדיקה מכל הזוויות. רגע מסיים זה בהורה הוא רגע שיא כזה."

למרות הצלחתו כמורה וכיוצר, ברק עדיין ראה את עצמו כאמן מבצע. ואכן עד ה־23 בפברואר 1953 הוא לא נאלץ לשנות את דעתו זו. הוא הופיע באותו ערב במפגן חגיגי שנערך במוזיאון ברוקלין לכבוד ישראל. הכאב במפרק ירכו כשביצע שני מחולות סולו שלו היה כה עז, שהוא הבין, שעליו לוותר על הקריירה של אמן־במה.

בדרכו הביתה מהכינוס הרהר מה יעשה במקום הופעתיו. בזמן שהגיע לדירתו

69

ונשכב במיטתו הוא כבר ארגן את מחשבותיו. הוא ייצור יותר כוריאוגראפיות עבור אחרים, וינסה ליצור קבוצת מחול יהודי ב-"Y". הוא יתרכז בהוראה ובלהקתו.
ב-1954 כבר נערכו מופעי ה-"Merry-Go-Rounders" בפני קהלים של מאות ילדים. לתוכנית של ה-12 בדצמבר 1954 יצר ברק ריקוד חדש, "חתונה טירולית".
אך הוא רצה להשתמש יותר בנושאי מחול יהודיים. הוא הבחין, שבמעט השנים מאז נוסדה מדינת ישראל לא יצרו עוד הרקדנים המודרניים ריקודים בנושאים יהודיים, כפי שעשו בשנות הארבעים. תפקיד זה עבר לרקדנים ישראליים, במיוחד תיאטרון המחול "ענבל". ב-28 בפברואר 1954 הפיק ברק את התוכנית הראשונה שלו על נושאים יהודיים עם הרקדנים הישראליים, ששהו אז בניו-יורק, נעמי אלסקובסקי, רינה גלוק ודינה נבם-צלת, ולהקתו בריקוד "חופשה בישראל". הוא החליט להקים את "רקדני אריאל" וליצור עבורם עבודות. ה"ניו-יורק טיימס" ציין, שהוא אסף קבוצה טובה, שאחדים מחבריה רקדו עם מרתה גראהם. דן ואגונר, כוריאוגראף עצמאי בעל להקה משלו כיום, שהיה אז בלהקתה של גראהם, נזכר בדרך עבודתו של פרד. פרד עדיין התבייש באנגלית שבפיו והעדיף פגישות אישיות. "הוא בא עד לדירתי," מספר ואגונר, "כדי לבקש ממני להצטרף ללהקתו. רקדנים הצטרפו לפרד כי הוא ידע היטב על מה רצה לעבוד. מרתה לא עבדה אתנו ברציפות, והוא הציע נסיון מעניין."
מפרק הירך של פרד הציק לו מאוד והוא נסע לקליפורניה, כדי שידידו הרופא ג'ורג' קאופמן יוכל להמליץ על טיפול עבורו. חוץ מהמנוחה הנפשית בחברת ידידיו האהובים, הוא קיבל זריקות קורטיזון, שהקלו עליו. כשחזר לניו-יורק הוא עבר לגור עם ידיד ותיק שלו, כדי לחסוך בהוצאות ולהיות קרוב יותר ל-"Y".

70

פרק שמונה-עשר:
ישראל ו"הבראיקה"

ברק חש הרבה יותר טוב והחל בתכנון מסע נוסף לאירופה וישראל. הוא נסע בתחילה לבדו לדובר ולונדון, לבקר את הוריו, ולרוטרפילד אל גברת גראהם שלו. היא לא היתה מוכנה לשמוע על קבלת כסף ממנו, למרות שכספה התדלדל, והוא נהג לשלוח לה חבילות מזון גדושות מעדנים מדי שנה, בחג המולד. בישראל הוא התארח אצל גרטרוד קראוס.

דירת המרתף של גרטרוד היתה במרחק גוש בנינים אחד מרחוב דיזנגוף התל-אביבי, גדוש החנויות ובתי-הקפה. ברק נהג לשבת עם גרטרוד בבית-הקפה האהוב עליה, "קפה דיצה", והקשיב לאמנים מפורסמים ולצעירים שבאו לשולחנם לשוחח עם גרטרוד. ברק אף ביקר את ידידתו גורית קדמן.(81) גורית וגרטרוד היו כוחות שעוררו את התפתחות המחול בישראל, גרטרוד את הריקוד הבימתי וגורית את המחול האתני והעממי. בחברתן חש וספג פרד את ההתרגשות שבתרבות החדשה שהן עזרו לבנות.

גורית הציגה בפניו קבוצה חשובה של רקדני-עם, את ועדת מחול-העם של המרכז לתרבות של ההסתדרות, שהכינה שיטה להוראת ריקודי-עם ברחבי הארץ. הועדה אף יצרה וארגנה פסטיבלים ולהקות, וקיבלה תקציבים וכח-אדם לפעילותיה. ברק הלך לפגישה בבנין הועד הפועל בתל-אביב. שם הוא פגש את רבקה שטורמן, שלום חרמון ותרצה הודס; הם עשרו אותו לאיש הקשר הבלתי רשמי שלהם באמריקה. בגלל מעמדו ב"Y" הוא יכול היה להפיץ בניו-יורק וברחבי אמריקה מידע על מחול-העם הישראלי, וכן, באמצעות תפקידו כמנהל פסטיבל המחול הישראלי השנתי בניו-יורק והמקומות הרבים בארצות-הברית בהם לימד, להפיק תקליטים של מוסיקה למחול-העם הישראלי (מלווים בהוראות כתובות). במשך השנים עזר ברק לחברי הועדה, ורבים אחרים, בביקוריהם באמריקה, על-ידי הזמנתם ללמד בסדנאות המוקדשות למחול-העם הישראלי.

ירדנה כהן זוכרת, שבמשך טיול הקיץ שלו ב-1955 הוא סייר רבות בחיפוש אחר ריקודים. ברק מספר במאמרו בעתון Viltis, שעלה בידו להביא חזרה לאמריקה את ריקודי-העם החדשים ביותר ולכלול אותם ברפרטואר שלימד.(82) הוא בחר מספר ריקודים שהראו לו יוצרים ישראליים, למד אותם והביאם לתלמידיו ב"Y".

רבים מהריקודים החדשים שאסף נעשו ללהיטים בקרב הקהל הישראלי, וזהו המבחן האמיתי של מחול-עם טוב. רבקה שטורמן זוכרת, שלעיתים קרובות, כשהראיתה לו את ריקודיה החדשים, "הוא כבר ידע אותם. בוודאי שהייתי שמחה וגאה שהוא בחר ללמד את מחולותי בניו-יורק."(83) אחד מהריקודים הראשונים שבחר ברק היה "הרמוניקה" של שטורמן, ריקוד שנעשה לא רק פופולרי בישראל ובאמריקה, אלא גם הפך לאחד מריקודי העם הישראליים האהובים ביותר בחוגי המחול הבינלאומיים. "הרמוניקה" ו"דבקה רפיח" של ויקי כהן, אשר לימדו בשיעורים הפתוחים של יום רביעי ב"Y", היו לשניים ממחולות-העם הישראליים האהובים עליו ביותר.

"אספתי את ריקודי-העם שמצאו חן בעיני," הסביר ברק, "אלה שהיו בעלי איכות מיוחדת, וזרימה חלקה מקטע אחד לשני. תמיד ניסיתי להביא את היוצרים לסדנאותי בניו-יורק, אך אם לא יכולתי להביאם, למדתי את הריקוד בעצמי. לעיתים הייתי חוזר עם 15 ריקודים, ולפעמים רק עם שניים. כשראיתי ריקוד שאהבתי, הייתי תחילה רושם אותו

במלים ומתאר את כל חלקיו כמיטב יכולתי. בלילה הייתי מנסה לשחזרו על-פי הכתוב, ואחר-כך הייתי הולך לראותו שוב ומשווה אותו אל הכתוב. למדתי בעיני במקום ברגלי. כמו כן למדתי, שמוטב לכתוב פחות מלים." מאוחר יותר הוא למד ברצינות את כתב התנועה של לאבן, שעזר לו לתעד את הריקודים עבור עצמו ולדייק כשלימדם.

לאחר ששב מהמסע לישראל ב-1955, המשיך לחפש דרך לבטא את רעיונותיו. הוא דיבר עם דר׳ קולודני, וכתוצאה מהשיחה נוצרה להקת מחול חדשה ב"Y", "הבראיקה".

קולודני הקציב $2,000 להקמת הלהקה ומחסן לאכסון התופים, התקליטים ו"השמאטעס", כפי שנהג ברק לכנות את התלבושות. "מעולם לא היה לי שולחן," הוא נזכר, "רק המחסן שלי." ברק החליט על להקה בת שישה זוגות. הם יערכו חזרות פעם בשבוע במשך שעתיים, ויכינו סוויטות של ריקודים חדשים, המתארים חגים והווי ישראלי. עם פיתוח הלהקה החדשה, נכללו כל פעילויותיו של ברק ב"Y" ב"מחלקת המחול היהודי".

"הבראיקה" היתה לגולת הכותרת של תוכניות המחלקה למחול יהודי. הרקדנים היו התלמידים המצטיינים משיעוריו של ברק. "הם היו חובבים, והריקוד היה תחביבם. הם באו פעם בשבוע לחזרה של שלוש שעות. האמנתי, שהם זקוקים למוטיבאציה חזקה. מעולם לא היו לנו יותר מ-10 או 12 הופעות בשנה, ותמיד הדגשתי את חשיבות כל אחת מהן. אחרת היה הריקוד נעשה מין משרה או הרגל, ואז קיימת סכנה, שההתלהבות והניצוץ יאבדו." כל הופעותיהם של ששת הזוגות שב"הבראיקה" היו בפני אולמות מלאים.

במשך הסתיו עבד ברק עם כמה מהתלמידים האהובים עליו ביותר. הוא הביע את רעיונותיו בכוריאוגראפיה בצורת הסוויטה, ויצר סצינות רבות בעלות אופי פולקלוריסטי: "כפר-דייגים", "השוק", "על מוכר-הפירות ודמויות אחרות, "הכרם", "המדבר". בחנוכה היו הרקדנים מוכנים להופעתם הראשונה, שאליה הוזמנו משפחותיהם. אחדים מהמרקדנים היו מקורביו של ברק כגון דב אלטון.

אמר ברק: "תמיד דימיינתי לעצמי את מבנה הסוויטה, לפני שהתחלתי בחזרות. ידעתי אם היצירה תכלול מחול לגברים, מחול בזוגות, ריקוד לבנות או סיום. בדרך כלל הייתי בוחר אביזר תיאטרלי כלשהו, שחזר במשך הסוויטה בשימושים שונים, כגון רשת דייגים. הבחורים יצאו לבמה עם הרשת, בקטע אחר הבנות גלגלו אותה והיא נעשתה לחבל, שהבנים רקדו עימו דבקה. בסיום עם כל 12 הרקדנים, השתמשתי בוריאציות רבות של תנועות עם הרשת."

סוויטות אחרות, שהצליחו במיוחד, היו על נושא השוק, המדבר, וסוויטה על ההשפעות האתניות השונות על התרבות.

דמות מוכר-הפירות בסוויטת השוק בא מדימויי, שזכר ברק מביקורו הראשון בישראל. "ראיתי איש מעניין עם מגש מתכת שטוח שהוא נשא על ראשו, וכשהתרוקן החזיקו כמניפה. זה נראה לי תיאטרלי מאוד." הוא כמעט לא השתמש בשירה כמקור השראה, אך ב"קולות האדמה" עזרו לו שירים מאת ביאליק ליצור ארבעה ריקודים מרשימים: "זכרונות" (על אודות פליטים), "מדבר", "לילה" ו"תקוה".

"זה מאוד קשה לנו, בני-תמותה, ליצור משהו שיש בו משום שאר-רוח, אך זה מה שספרד דרש, אפילו בחזרות," אמר ג׳ין האריס, מתכנן התאורה, בשוחחו על עבודתו של ברק. "מוטלת עליך האחריות לתת לאנשים הרשאה, כשכולם מסתכלים," הוא נהג תמיד לומר. צד חשוב אחר של עבודתו היה ה'ניקיון'. אם רעיון היה לא ברור, במיוחד אם הרקדנים העלו רעיון, הוא היה מנסה לפשט אותו. דימיונו תמיד שאף להיות ברור מאוד."

ליביה דראבקין, שרקדה ב"הבראיקה" במשך חמש שנים, אמרה שברק "לימד אותנו להיות אחראים. דרכו הבנתי מה משמעות איכות התנועה, ומה הם דינמיקה והשלכה לקהל. גם הבנתי כמה חשוב לקהל להרגיש, שאתה נותן את עצמך להם. הוא קרא לפגישות שלנו בימי ג׳ 'חזרות', אך אנו קראנו להן מסיבות. אפשר היה לחוש במוטיבאציה של ברק, והתלהבותו היתה מדבקת. הוא גרם לנו לרצות לרקוד, וזה מה שליכד את הקבוצה. בדרך כלל התחלנו בחזרות באוקטובר, ולקראת חנוכה, בדצמבר, היינו כבר קבוצה מלוכדת. הוא היה אדם מאוד אוהב, אך גם במאי מחמיר, אחרת לא היה יכול לעולם לרכז להקה של 12 בני נוער."

האריס מציע הסבר אחר להתנהגותו של ברק עם הרקדנים הצעירים. "המקצוענות שלו והשליטה בחומר היקנו לו סמכות, מבלי שיהיה רודן. היה לו סגנון מעולה, והוא עודד

את בני הנוער למצוא ולפתח את סגנונם האישי."

ביום ההופעה התאספו הרקדנים והצוות הטכני בשמונה בבוקר. בתחילה הם ניהלו חזרה כללית של התוכנית עבור האריס, המנהל הטכני, כדי לקבוע את מערך התאורה. אחר־כך היתה חזרת תלבושות, הפסקה של 15 דקות, ואז שתי הופעות, ב־3.30 וב־5. ברק הדגיש, שההכנה מאחורי הקלעים חשובה בעיניו ממש כמו ההופעה על הבמה. על כולם היה לגהץ את תלבושותיהם בעצמם, ולעזור אחד לשני בחילופי התלבושות. אחדים מהרקודים דרשו משמעת חמורה מאחורי הקלעים. הריקודים על העדות השונות בישראל, למשל, דרשו התאמה מדוייקת, מאחר שבכל קטע החליפו שני זוגות תלבושות לקראת הקטע הבא. הסיום כלל רקדנים בתלבושות רוסיות, חסידיות, ערביות ותימניות.

רקדנים מקצועיים רבים קיבלו את נסיון הבמה הראשון שלהם עם ברק ב"הבראיקה". ברק עודד כל תלמיד, שהיה בעל סיכוי להיות רקדן מקצועני, להמשיך בלימודיו. קהילית המחול התייחסה ללהקה ברצינות, ומבקרי המחול כיסו את ההופעות. ביקורת ב"דנס ניוז" קובעת: "רקדני 'הבראיקה' הם צעירים ומושכים למראה. הכוריאוגראף והמנהל, פרד ברק, נמנע בתבונה מלדחוף את רקדניו הבלתי מקצועיים מעבר ליכולתם, אך השתמש בחיוניותם הצעירה ובמרץ הטמון ברוב הצעדים היסודיים של המחול הישראלי."

ברק היה עסוק מאוד במשך חורף שנת 1955. בעת ובעונה אחת הוא ניהל חזרות עם להקת "אריאל" לקראת מופע בפברואר, שנקרא "מארצות רבות", ותכנן את ההופעה של "הבראיקה" בפורים שחל במרס. הוא הוסיף ל"הבראיקה" ריקודים חדשים: "נרשא חסידי", "תמונות מהאחזות", "רשמים" נוסף ליצירה האהובה על הקהל תמיד, "חופשה בישראל". הוא שיכלל את מבנה ההופעות של "הבראיקה" עד שתבנית זו היתה למסורת: המנחה הציג בפני הילדים תנועות פשוטות, הקשורות לריקודים שבאו אחר־כך, וכולם רקדו במקומותיהם. המלווה המוסיקלי לימד את הקהל שירי חג. בזמן שהמנחה והמוסיקאי העסיקו את הקהל, החליפו הרקדנים את תלבושותיהם בין הקטעים השונים, כך שהתוכנית זרמה ללא הפסקה. למרות שהריקודים יועדו לילדים, גם ההורים נהנו מהתוכניות.

73

פרק תשעה־עשר:
האסון

כלפי חוץ נראה הכל נהדר. אך מצב מפרק הירך של פרד הלך והחמיר. הוא התחיל לנסוע לעבודתו ברכבת התחתית במקום באוטובוס, שמסלולו היה ישיר יותר. כך הוא לא נאלץ לטפס במעלה המדרגות התלולות לאוטובוס כשאנשים עומדים בתור מאחוריו, וברכבת התחתית איש לא שם לב לצליעתו או אם ישב או עמד.

נוסעי הרכבת התחתית היו אדישים איש לרעהו, לעומת נוסעי האוטובוס, שפרד חש את מבטיהם אחר כל צעד מסורבל שעשה. בזמנים אחרים עקבו אחריו עיניים בריכוז, כשרקד בתיאטראות וינה, בלגרד, ציריך, אמשטרדם או ניו־יורק. הוא אהב סוג זה של תשומת לב. כמו האהבה, היא דחפה אותו לעשות יותר, אפילו להשיג תוצאות טכניות שהיו בלתי אפשריות בסטודיו. אז התקבל כל צעד שלו על־ידי הקהל בתשומת לב ובהנאה. הוא נזכר, עד כמה יכול היה למשוך את לב קהלו בקלות ובאופן שלם.

בעמדו ברכבת התחתית, כשהוא אוחז במתלה, הוא תכנן בדמיונו את החזרה הקרובה. מחשבותיו נקטעו, כשהרכבת נעצרה פתאום. דקירת כאב במפרק הירך שלו התפשטה מעלה, לכיוון החזה ומטה לתוך הרגל. הוא הכריח את עצמו לצאת מהקרון ולטפס לרחוב. במעלה המדרגות הוא שלף מטפחת מקופלת מכיס מעילו, ומחה את הזיעה ממצחו וראשו המקריח. הוא עיוות את פניו: "אני מזיע שוב, מבלי שביצעתי אפילו משפט אחד של ריקוד!"

בפינת רחוב 86 ושדרת לקסינגטון הוא הביט בשעונו. עדיין נותר לו זמן לאכול משהו בקונדיטוריה הגרמנית שאהב. מחלון הראווה רמזו לו צעצועי עץ מגולפים ועליזים ובפנים עציצי צמחים ירוקים כהים. מבלי לחשוב הוא הזמין בגרמנית את מאפה "לינץ'" האהוב עליו, והמלצרית בסינר הלבן הזעיר קדה קמעט קדה בפניו ואמרה, "בבקשה, הר דוקטור," כשהגישה לו את העוגה.

הוא נטש את חלומותיו בהקיץ והתרומם בעזרת כוח הרצון, כאילו היה עליו לרקוד תפקיד חדש על הבמה. דוקטור! בגרמנית לכל אחד צריך שיהיה תואר! תלבושתו היתה מתאימה: חולצה מעומלנת ומגוהצת, מכנסיים כהים בעלי קפל חד, ותיק ניירות שמן. עם ראשו המקריח והמשקפיים הוא נראה מכובד ורציני. הבעת פניו הרצינית הרגילה חזרה אליו. "הר דוקטור", הוא הרהר. אביו היה נהנה לשמוע זאת!

בהתקרבו ל־"Y", החל להחליק את רגלו הימנית קדימה, כך שלא ניתן יהיה לראות אפילו צל של צליעה. בשמונה בדיוק הוא פתח את דלת הסטודיו הקטן. הוא התבונן בקבוצה ואמר בהדגשה, "רקדנים, הבה נתחילו!"

המרץ שלו לא אזל לעולם. הוא ניזון בחלקו מהתלהבות רקדניו. הוא התווה צעד אחר צעד, צורה אחר צורה עבור הרקדנים הנעים במעגל. הוא הדגים את אשר רצה מהם, כשהחזהו סובב לימין ממקד את תשומת הלב לא אל רגלו הרוקעת, אלא לעוז ולכוח של גופו. הרקדנים צפו בו בתענוג אמיתי.

בביימו כניסה חדשה עבור הרקדנים, הוא תכנן את ריצת הרקדנים למרכז הבמה ופגישתם שם עם בנות זוגם, כאדריכל וקוסם. הוא ידע את כל כיווני התנועה ויכול לסבבם ולשלבם ללא כל התנגשויות. בשעה 10 בדיוק הפסיק, דיבר על החזרה הבאה והודה להם. הוא שפע בטחון וכוח. כמובן, הם יהיו מוכנים להופעת־החורף שלהם. הוא חייך אל אחת

74

הרקדניות הצעירות החדשות בקבוצת החובבים. "אל דאגה," הוא אמר לה כעידוד.

אל דאגה, הוא שינן לעצמו בהמתינו בחדרי השירותים. כשהיה בטוח שכל הרקדנים עזבו, הוא החל לצלוע בכאב ובאיטיות לכיוון המדרגות. העייפות והכאב שהתעלם מקיומם בשעת החזרה התגברו עליו. קומתו שחה.

הוא ראה את דר' ויליאם קולודני, מנהל ה־"Y" ותומכו הנאמן שלו, עולה במדרגות. הוא התמתח ליציבתו הבוטחת הרגילה, וכפה על עצמו חיוך.

הוא שאל ממעלה המדרגות, "האם אתה בטוח שאין עוד תקציב לתלבושות?" והרים את ידו בשאלה, כשהוא מכופף את מרפקו ומטה את ראשו כרב חסידי, המתווכח עם אלוהים. שניהם צחקו. "אדבר על כך עם ההנהלה," ענה קולודני.

באותו לילה לא הצליח ברק להרדם או לנוח. הכאב הבוער במפרק הירך שלט בכל. הוא ניסה לשכב על הספה, לבצע תרגילי מתיחה ולסובב הרגל בתרגילים שקיבל מפיסיו־תרפיסטים במשך השנים, ניסה לקרוא, לקח משכך כאבים, אך הוא לא הצליח להקל את הרעידות והכאב. בקושי יכול היה לבצע את הצעדים הפשוטים והרגילים ביותר, ולא יכול לסבול ישיבה או שכיבה. איזה מצב נורא עבור מי שרגיל לשלוט בגופו שליטה פיסית מושלמת. ללא חופש תנועה הוא חש ככבר ללא כינורו. או, כך חשב, כמכונאי, שאיבד את כלי עבודתו. מה יכל לעשות?

בהכנעה הוא קיבל עליו את התשובה - לקרוא לרופא. הוא חשב על כל הרופאים שבדקו אותו בעבר, הראשון בהבאנה, ב־1941, אחר־כך בקולורדו, לוס אנג'לס וניו־יורק. הם הצליחו לעזור לו להמשיך. הוא לא ביקש עוד להופיע, אך הוא רצה למצוא דרך לביצוע התנועות הפשוטות ביותר. הוא מצא במגירת שולחנו את שמו של רופא וינאי שהומלץ בפניו. בבוקר צלצל לקבוע עימו פגישה.

ברק לא ביטל שיעורים וחזרות. הוא המשיך באמצעות כוח הרצון שלו, למרות שנשאלץ לבקש מתלמידיו המצטיינים להדגים עבורו בשיעורים. קבוצת "הבראיקה" המשיכה בחזרות בהתלהבות הרגילה. הקבוצה הרפרטוארית "אריאל", ושיעוריו ב־"Y", נמשכו כרגיל. הוא לא סיפר דבר לאיש.

הוא דייק כרגיל לפגישה עם המנתח האורטופדי. לאחר הבדיקה נאמר לו, שיש לקבוע את פרק הירך. "כך נוכל לחסל כל כאב," אמר הרופא בחיוך של שביעות רצון.

פשוט לקבוע את התנועה שבתוכי? חשב פרד לעצמו. הוא לא יכל להגיב, ולכן לא אמר דבר. בדיוק כמו בילדותו, הוא הניח להסברים הרפואיים לזרום. "אחשוב על כך ואתקשר שנית," אמר ללא רגש, כביכול, בפנים חתומות.

במקום זאת הוא ניסה רופא אחר. עוד חדר המתנה, בדיקה נוספת וצפיה. "להחליף את פרק הירך," היה גזר־הדין. "כמה פעמים בצעת את הניתוח הזה?" שאל ברק, כשהוא יודע היטב את הסיכונים הגדולים שבניתוח חדשני כזה. הוא זכר את קשיה של דוריס האמפרי, לאחר שעברה את הניתוח בעצמה. הוא נרעד בתוכו, וידע שלעולם לא יוכל להסכים לניתוח. "ובכן, אחשוב על כך ואתקשר אליך שנית," אמר לרופא.

במשך חופשת החורף של 1956 נסע לקליפורניה, כדי לראות את ג'ורג' וקלאודיה. הפעם לא מצא שם נחמה.

לבסוף, כשחזר לניו־יורק, מצא רופא צעיר שהציע פתרון חדש: פשוט לשייף את הקצה הקעור של עצם האגן ושבו נעה עצם הירך. בדרך זו לא יצטברו עוד סידן וזיזי עצם, שיגבילו את תנועת המפרק, הסביר הרופא. זה יהיה ניתוח נקי ופשוט לתיקון הגבלת התנועה. אומנם נכון שרגלו הימנית עלולה להתקצר בכ־20 מ"מ, אך את ההבדל בגובה ניתן יהיה להסתיר בעזרת עקב מיוחדת בנעלו. הרופא הצעיר היה בטוח בעצמו ובתוצאות הניתוח.

ברק הסכים, והם קבעו את הניתוח לתאריך האפשרי הקרוב ביותר. זאת היתה הפתעה עבור חבריו לעבודה ולתלמידיו. אף אחד לא חשד שיש לפרד בעיה חמורה מעין זו.

בשולחן־הניתוחים הוא החל לחשוב בגרמנית, כשביקש ממנו הרופא המרדים לספור עד עשר. כשהתעורר לאחר הניתוח, כאב עז אחז בו. הוא לא יכל להזיז אבר כלשהו. הרופא דיבר על גבס, אך עד החזה? הוא שקע בחזרה בשינת סמים טרופה.

גלי כאב בחילה תקפו אותו בגלל הכאב, והוא ראה את האחות רוכנת מעליו וטורחת מסביב למיטתו. כשהגיע הרופא, ריכז ברק את מבטו על פניו. למרות ששכב כשראשו נסמך

בכר, הוא הרגיש כאילו עמד דום, אך הרופא ניבט אליו מלמעלה. כל היסודות הקבועים – ימין ושמאל, למעלה ומטה, קדימה ואחורה – כל הכיוונים שהכיר היטב מהריקוד על הבמה ומהוראה התבלבלו עכשיו.

"שומה עלי לגלות לחולים שלי את האמת. עצמותיך היו מאוד שבירות. במשך הניתוח נסדקה עצם הירך שלך במקומות רבים. לא יכולנו לסיים את הניתוח. לא עלה בידינו לבנות מחדש את מפרק הירך, אך הסרנו את העצם הפגועה. העצם הימנית שלך קצרה עתה בכ־70 מ"מ מהשמאלית. כרגע נראה, שלא תוכל ללכת עוד לעולם."

פרד היה המום מכדי לומר דבר.

האחות ניסתה ליישר את הכר עבורו. הוא הביט בה. "כה חבל," אמרה.

לפתע הוא חש בכעס גובר על הכאב, כעס על טיפשותו וחוסר יכולתה לעזור. שאלוהים יחסוך ממנו את הרחמים. הוא בז לרחמים עצמיים ומאחרים. הוא הכיר את רגש הרחמים כשגדל בוינה. הוריו ושכונתו ריחמו על היהודים, שנמלטו מרוסיה ומהפוגרומים. אך הוא הבחין בדבר מוזר אחד לגבי הרחמים: הם פטרו מהצורך בהבנה. לא היה נחוץ לעשות דבר, מלבד לרחם. האם רחמים שינו דבר? האם עזרו למישהו להשיג עבודה? "חבל על הבחור המסכן," אמר פקיד ההגירה הבריטי, אך האם זה עזר לו להשאר באנגליה, כשהנאצים רדפו את היהודים? "חבל שלא יוכל ללכת," אמר הרופא הספרדי בקובה, אך האם זה עזר לו?

הוא בז לרחמים. הוא לא רצה בהם. הוא כבר ימצא דרך.

פרק עשרים:
כתב־תנועה

סיום פתאומי של קריירת ריקוד הוא משבר עמוק. זהו לא רק סיומה של תקופת עבודה, אלא כביכול סוף החיים עצמם, מאחר שהקיום האמיתי של הרקדן הוא על הבמה. כל המאמצים, התוכניות והמחשבות התמקדו בבמה.

כשרקדנים לא יכולים להופיע עוד, הם מתנתקים לפתע מההכרה בהישגיהם. הקהל מגיב כשהרקדן מציג משהו שנון, גדול, מענג או מצחיק. הרקדן ניזון מתגובת הקהל, ויחסיו עם הקהל עזים מעבר למקובל בין אנשים רגילים. כשהאמן מתרגל לתגובה חזקה כזו ממאות צופים מדי יום, במשך חודשים ושנים, סיום הקריירה שלו הוא כניתוק מתמצית הוויתו, ניתוק מעצמו.

לעיתים קרובות הרקדן הוא אחד מאלה הזוכרים באופן מושלם את ילדותם והתבגרותם, מאחר שהאימון שלו מקיף את כל תקופות החיים. פרד יכול לזכור את ההרגשה שבהופעות בפני קהלים בעלי מזג שונה. קפיצה על הבמה אינה רק תנועה אחת - היא הרבה סוגים של שמחה, שהרקדן זוכר.

כשברק ניתר וקפץ, אנשים הביטו בו. עבורו זה היה כמו חצי חיוך של הצלחה, כניצחון בחיים. הוא זכר את הזמנים כשניתר על במת האופרה בוינה, וכיצד קפץ הרחק מרדיפתו של היטלר. קפיצתו היתה של שמחה, משום שגם האחרים הצליחו להינצל, וישראל היתה עבורו מין קפיצת־ניצחון של עם. הוא קפץ משמחה כשהתאחד מחדש עם חבריו, והקפיצה היתה חגיגת־ניצחון על שהוא עדיין יכול לנתר, למרות פציעתו. הוא רקד ריקוד ניצחון.

אך עתה לא נותר דבר. לא עוד ריקוד, אפילו לא הליכה. חוסר תנועה. מוות. פרד לא רצה לאכול וסירב לראות איש; הוא הורה לאחיות לא להכניס אורחים לחדרו ולא להעביר שיחות טלפון. זיפי זקנו צמחו, וכשהאחיות נכנסו לחדרו הוא פנה לקיר.

פיסיותראפיסטית שנשלחה לעבוד איתו נכנסה לחדרו ושאלה, "האם אתה פרד ברק, הרקדן?" היא זיהתה אותו כעצמו, ולא כחולה חסר תנועה. הוא הסתובב והביט בה, והיא חייכה ואמרה, "גם אני רקדנית. בוא ונעבוד יחד ונגלה את האפשרויות." היא באה לעבוד איתו מדי יום, כשהיא מלאת עידוד. הוא אמר לעצמו, "יכולתי לאבד את עצמי לדעת או להמשיך. החלטתי להמשיך."

הוא קיבל מבקרים. אחת מהם היתה יוצרת מחולות־העם הישראליים האהובה עליו, רבקה שטורמן, שהיתה בביקור בניו־יורק. היא מיהרה לחדרו, כשבידה זר פרחים גדול. פרד סיפר לה, שאמנית מחול אחרת מישראל, רחל נדב, מחלימה מניתוח בקומה אחרת של בית־החולים. הוא התעקש, שרבקה תיקח את הזר לרחל. לבסוף חילקה רבקה את הזר לשניים.(83)

לאחר עשרה שבועות הוסר הגבס שכיסה את גופו. התראפיסטית עזרה לו לקום על רגליו. אפילו בלי מפרק ממשי, הוא יכול לדחוף את רגלו קדימה, ולבצע צעד. הוא עבד ועבד כדי שיוכל לעמוד על רגליו ולנוע.

כשברק היה עדיין בבית־החולים, בא לבקרו מנהל אירגון "בית־הלל" של בני־ברית ושאל, אם יוכל ברק לקבל על עצמו לביים חגיגה גדולה ב־Ebbets Field.

77

ברק נועץ ברקדני קבוצתו, והם עודדו אותו לקבל את ההצעה. ה"דנס מאגאזין" פירסם תצלום של רקדנים, הערוכים בחדרו שבבית-החולים עבור המופע "מוסיקה מתחת לכוכבים". ברק קבע שיא אולימפי: הוא ביים שלושה ריקודים עבור ששים רקדנים להופעה ב-19 ביוני 1957, מחדרו שבבית-החולים.

למרות שהרקדנים קיבלו כסף עבור ההופעה מקרן תרבות אמריקה ישראל, הם סרבו לקבלו. הם היפנו את הכסף לכיסוי הוצאותיו הרפואיות של פרד.

כשיצא מבית-החולים במאי, הוא היה חייב $2,000. אך הוא לא היה מוטרד מכך. זעזוע גדול בהרבה היה מראה הנעל בעלת הסוליה העצומה, שהיה עליו לנעול. באורח פלא ובעזרת כוח רצון הוא הצליח ללכת על שתי רגליו, בעזרת מקל בלבד.

ברק נסע לקליפורניה, ובזמן שנה שם, החל באיטיות לבצע תרגילים. הוא תהה כיצד יצליח ללמד, מבלי להדגים את התנועות לתלמידיו.

מאמרים צנועים מאת ברק התפרסמו לעיתים בעיתוני מחול קטנים. במאמר שכתב על המונחים של שיטת לאבאן עבור רקדני מחול-עם(84), הוא האיץ ברקדנים להרחיב את אופקיהם. הוא הסביר, ש"ריקודי-עם נלמדים בדרך כלל על-ידי חיקוי המורה הנמצא במרכז הסטודיו. מורה טוב יפרק את הריקוד לקטעים...״ אך יש תהליך טוב יותר, והוא טען בעדו על סמך נסיונו האישי.

"הייתי מעורב בהוראת מחול-עם במשך 35 השנים האחרונות. בשנת 1957 עברתי ניתוח, שהותיר אחת מרגלי קצרה מהשניה ומנע ממני להמשיך לרקוד. במשך תקופת ההחלמה נתקלתי בספר על כתב-התנועה והתחלתי להתעניין שוב בתיאוריה של לאבאן. עולם חדש נפתח בפני.

"למדתי בהדרגה להביע תנועות שראיתי במלים. יכולתי להמשיך ללמד בעזרת המונחים של לאבאן. ראיתי, שתלמידים הלומדים כך, רוקדים לא באופן מיכני, אלא לומדים להבין את כל יסודות הריקוד.

"עוד כשהייתי עטוף בגבס קראתי את ספרי לאבאן; לא היה לי מספיק ידע להבין את כל הכתוב, אך המונחים משכו אותי. נראה לי שזו היתה דרך ברורה ביותר לניתוח תנועה. החלטתי ללמוד יותר והתקשרתי עם לוסי ונאבל, שרקדה בלהקה שלי, והיא כותבת כתב-תנועה מיומנת.

"בשנה הראשונה שלאחר הניתוח לא יכולתי להדגים דבר בשיעורים, לא יכולתי לזוז בכלל. אך התלמידים באו ושילמו עבור השיעורים. בשביל מה? תמהתי. מעולם לא דיברתי הרבה על ריקוד, ולא נהגתי לנתח ולפרט במלים. הרקדן לעולם לא מנתח בפרוטרוט את מחשבותיו ורגשותיו על הבמה, הוא פשוט רוקד אותם. אך בהדרגה הבנתי, שברשותי משהו שאין לאחרים. אפילו מבלי שיכולתי לזוז בעצמי, יכולתי לעורר ולפתוח תלמידים כלפי רגשותיהם הרדומים. יכולתי לערב אותם במחול בדרך מעודדת, לאחר שהתאמנו שנים עם מורים שהכבירו עליהם איסורים.

"המונחים של לאבאן העניקו לי יכולת לנתח ולראות תנועה, מבלי לבצע אותה בעצמי. הוראותי נעשו מדוייקות יותר.

"רקדני פולקלור אינם מאומנים במובנה הרחב של המלה. כשהם מלמדים או מנסים לרשום את הריקודים, בדרך כלל התוצאה לא ברורה, מאחר שהם משתמשים במונחים ובסמלים האישיים שלהם.

"לאבאן גורם לך להיות מדוייק יותר לגבי תנועה, קצב, כיוון ומישורים. אי אפשר לטעות בשיטה ברורה זו."

לוסי ונאבל זוכרת, איך ברק החל לרשום את מחולות-העם שלימד בכתב-התנועה של לאבאן, והחל לאסוף מחולות מאחרים. "מתוך נסיון זה צמח הרעיון של ספר קטן לרקדנים, עם כתב-תנועה פשוט. כתבנו יחד את 'עשרה מחולות-עם בכתב-תנועה של לאבאן' והספר יצא לאור. מאז נדפסו עוד שתי מהדורות נוספות. הרווחנו בערך רק $50 למהדורה, אך לא עשינו זאת עבור כסף. רבים השתמשו בספר להוראה ורבים עוד יותר למדו ונהנו מהריקודים.

"מטרתו של ברק היתה לשמור על הוראות פשוטות, ולרשום בכתב-תנועה רק את הצעדים. כך נשאר הכתב פשוט לקריאה, ותנועות הידים תוארו במלים. למדתי ממנו הרבה כיצד לשמור את החומר הכתוב בצורתו הפשוטה והישירה.״ אמרה ונאבל.

"מאחר שהעבודה על הספר היתה מוצלחת, הציע פרד שנעבוד על 'ריקודים מישראל'. הספר יצא לאור על־ידי המכון לכתב־לאבאן, ואף הוא יצא בשתי מהדורות. בחירת הריקודים והכתיבה הבסיסית נעשו בידי פרד; תפקידי היה תמיד להשוות את כתב־התנועה עם התנועה עצמה והטקסט המלווה, ולהעתיק ולעמוד את הכתב." בפגישותיו של ברק עם ונאבל הוא העלה את הצורך בקורס בהתכתבות לכתב־תנועה עבור רקדני־מחול־עם. המכון ערך קורסים בהתכתבות עבור המעוניינים במחול מודרני או באלט, אך הדוגמאות בהם היו קשורות לטכניקה וסגנון יותר מהנחוץ למחול־עם. "הוא הכין שתי סדרות של שיעורים. הן עדיין מופצות על־ידי המכון."

המכון פירסם את יצירתו המפורסמת של ברק, "חופשה בישראל", בספר ב־1978.(85) מבצע זה לא היה ביוזמתו של ברק, אך הוא פיקח עליו.

רקדנים רבים שמעו לראשונה על כתב־התנועה בשיעורי מחול־העם של ברק. רשימות שכתבה אן וילסון־זאנג בסדנה למורים בסוף שנות החמישים מראות את סוג החומר שבו השתמש ברק. בשיעור הראשון הוא הסביר את חשיבות הבהירות. "היו ברורים בכל, אפילו באיפיון הריקוד, והסבירו כיצד הוא מתייחס לעם מסויים. אינכם צריכים להיות מוסיקאים או רקדנים מקצועיים בכדי להבין את לאבאן, השיטה היא כה הגיונית."

פרד מצא את הבטחון הדרוש להמשיך בעבודתו דרך כתב־התנועה של לאבאן. היה עליו להכניע פחדים רבים, כשאחד העיקריים בהם היתה הופעתו החיצונית. הוא חשב, שאין זה הולם מורה לריקוד להופיע לסטודיו כשהוא צולע ונשען על מקל. לבסוף הוא אימן את עצמו להכנס לשיעור ללא עזרה. הוא תמיד ישב על כיסא גבוה וניהל את השיעור רק באמצעות קולו והתלהבותו, כשהוא שולט לחלוטין במצב, באמצעות הבהירות שרכש בעזרת כתב־התנועה.

"פרד נהג תמיד לומר: 'אתם מלמדים אנשים, לא חומר. יש לקבל את התלהבות התלמידים ואת רצונם לרקוד, ולהסביר להם גם את הפשוט בפרטים. זוהי, אחרי הכל, מלאכת ההוראה': כיצד לא להתרגז וכיצד לא להשתעמם עם החומר'." נזכרת שולמית קיבל, גם היא מורה לריקודי־עם. "גם אם עליך ללמד את 'זמר עתיק' בפעם החמישת־אלפים, עבור התלמידים זו עדיין חוויה חדשה."

מלבד המחלקה למחול יהודי של ברק ב"Y", היה לו אפיק פעולה אחר להפצת מחול־עם ישראלי ברחבי אמריקה. היה זה מחנה הקיץ Blue Star שבלב ההרים בצפון קרולינה. ברק עבד שם במ_ _ 18 שנה. לפני הניתוח שלו ב־1956, הוא לימד שם ריקודי־עם ישראליים והעמיד הופעות בהן השתתפו 700 מחנאים, ושילב את המחול בפעילויות הרגילות של המחנה.

הוא הפסיק ללמד שם במשך מספר שנים, וחזר כדי לנהל תוכנית מיוחדת למדריכי מחול־עם ישראלי. ממש כמו בעבודתו ב"Y", הוא פיתח מבנה מסויים, שהשפיע על מורים ורקדנים מכל אמריקה. הוא ניהל שני קורסים שונים, בני שבוע כל אחד, עבור 150 משתתפים.

בדרך כלל חל חג השבועות במשך המחנה, וברק יצר אוירת חגיגה מיוחדת באמצעות הריקוד. גם קבלת השבת נערכה בבית־כנסת תחת כיפת השמיים, ולעיתים קרובות כלל גם טקס ההבדלה מחול. בריקודי־העם במחנה "הכוכב הכחול" הורגשה רוחניות שמעבר למכניות של השיעורים והפעילות.

במשך הקורס היה על המורים שלקחו חלק להתאמן בהוראת מחולות למחנאים. לאחר שיעורי־נסיון אלו היה פרד מעריך ומבקר את עבודת המדריך. הוא גם לימד שיעור שנקרא "יסודות הכוריאוגרפיה", מלבד שני שיעורים יומיים של ריקודי־העם הישראליים החדשים. כמו כן היו שיעוריו בחירה במחול מודרני, זימרה ונושאים אחרים. בערבים ארגן הרצאות על ישראל או על מחול בתנ״ך. בערב האחרון של השבוע התקיימו הדגמות פתוחות של מחול ישראלי בפני המחנות השכנות ויתר המחנאים.

במחנה "הכוכב הכחול" כיום ניצב בניין רחב, שבו מתקיימות הסדנאות לריקודי־העם. זהו "ביתן פרד ברק למחול", מבנה פתוח עם רצפת ריקוד עצומה. מנהל המחנה, הרמן פופקין, תאר את שנותיו של ברק במחנה: "הוא היה כרב חסידי עם מאמיניו. אנו מודעים לכך שהוא הביא ל'כוכב הכחול', במחנה ובסדנאות, את אהבת ישראל שלו להרבה אנשים, צעירים ומבוגרים, באמצעות הריקוד."

פרק עשרים ואחד:
פסטיבלי המחול הישראלי

בהערה צנועה, אופיינית לברק, הוא אמר פעם, ש"אני לא מומחה לשום דבר, אך יש לי רעיונות. היה זה רעיון שלי לפתוח את פסטיבל המחול הישראלי, והוא נעשה לחלק בלתי נפרד מחיי הקהילה היהודית בעיר ניו-יורק." ברק התמחה בהפקה, שלא כללה נאומים והכרזות. תוכנית הריקודים (שנרקדו על-ידי ארגוני צעירים שונים), נבנתה כך, שהמתח וההתרגשות גברו לקראת סיום ענק, עם כל המשתתפים על הבמה.

רקדנים מודרניים אמריקניים מעטים, אם בכלל, היו מסוגלים לנהל מספר רב כל כך של רקדנים בבת אחת, שלא לדבר על המבנה הכללי המרהיב של המופע. ברק הכיר היטב את ההשפעה והשימוש במסות של רקדנים מהופעותיו בעצרות פוליטיות ושל ארגונים יהודיים עם להקתה של גרטרוד קראוס בוינה. הוא יכל להשתמש בכל נסיונו הקודם במחול בביומו את ההפקות בפסטיבל בני-יורק.

פסטיבל המחול הישראלי השנתי התקיים תחילה במכללת הנטר. בשנת 1962 עבר לקרנגי-הול, ב-1970 ל-Felt Forum שב"מדיסון-גארדן" וארבע שנים אחר-כך לאולם הפילהרמוני בלינקולן סנטר.

"התרוממות-רוח הורגשה מהרגע בו החלו לזרום המשתתפים מכל הכיוונים במאותיהם, בתלבושות ססגוניות, שרים ומוחאים כף. הם היו צעירים, מלאי און ושמחה... אולי הרגע המרגש ביותר בא בסוף הערב, כשכל הרקדנים התאספו לשירת 'התקוה', ומרוב שמחה פרצו בריקוד ספונטאני." (87)

ברק היה מרוצה במיוחד מארבעת הפסטיבלים, שהתקיימו ב"פלט פורום", בשל במת-הזירה שלו והיותו מתאים לתנועת קבוצות ולפינלה הגדול. אך, למרבה הצער, דרישות האיגודים המקצועיים עשו את קיום הפסטיבל שם לבלתי אפשרי, והיה צורך למצוא מקום אחר.

"פעם אחת, בפלט פורום," נזכר ברק, "נקבעה הופעה מסחרית ליום שני לאחר הפסטיבל, ואי אפשר היה לחצות את אחורי-הבמה בגלל כל מיני במות קטנות שהושקמו. הייתי ברקיע השביעי: השתמשתי בכל הרמות השונות ובימיתי את הריקודים באיזורים השונים, כך שהם תרמו לדרמאטיות של ההפקה. שכרנו מלון סמוך לאולם עבור כל קבוצות הצעירים, ומאחר שהיו כה הרבה משתתפים, נאלצנו להתחיל בחזרות בחמש בבוקר כדי שנהיה מוכנים להופעת אחרי-הצהרים. לו נותר לי עוד שיער, בודאי הייתי מאבד אותו אז מרוב המתח. 14 קבוצות השתתפו, כשלכל אחת 20 דקות על הבמה, עם הפסקה בין שתי ההופעות. עבור בני הנוער זה היה כמו פיאסטה ענקית."

האסיסטנטית של ברק לפסטיבל היתה רות גודמן, שמאוחר יותר קיבלה על עצמה את ניהול רוב המבצעים שהוא עסק בהם.

"אמן הוא מישהו, הרואה תמיד דברים חדשים. פרד היה כזה, והתפעלותו והתלהבותו התפשטו אל הצעירים. זאת היתה אמנותו. במשך עשר השנים שהייתי מעורבת בפסטיבל, נשארה מתכונת המופע זהה, אך תמיד היו צעירים חדשים, הורים חדשים וקהל חדש, ולכן חשנו, שלא היה צורך לשנות את המבנה."

במשך השנים פיתח פרד גרעין של צוות מקצועי עבור הפסטיבל. גארי האריס היה טכנאי הקול והתאורה המיומן; האטי וינר היתה ממונה על התלבושות ומוסיקאי מקצועי

80

נשכר להכין את העיבודים ולנצח. המנצח הראשון היה אליקום שפירא, שנעשה עוזרו של ליאונרד ברנשטיין, ואחריו באו מספר מוסיקאים ישראליים מעולים כולל דב זלצר, גיל אלדמע, אמיתי נאמן ובמשך שבע שנים היה שי בורשטיין האחראי, (שאף הכין הקלטות מוסיקליות עם ברק).

בפגישה הראשונה של מדריכי קבוצות צעירים שנערכה בסתיו, ברק נהג לספר להם על הנושא שנבחר לפסטיבל. אלו היו בהכרח נושאים רחבים, כגון "ישראל", מאחר שהריקודים היו בדרך כלל מבוססים על נושאים כגון "השבת", "הקציר" או "שמחה". "שינינו את הנושא משנה לשנה."

מדריכי־המחול שבו לקבוצות שלהם באיזור ניו־יורק ובחרו את הרקדנים הטובים ביותר לפסטיבל, על אף שברק הדגיש את הצד החינוכי ולא התחרותי של הפסטיבל.

כל אחד מהם לימד וערך חזרות לריקוד אחד, ואת התוצאות היו מראים לברק, שהציע שיפורים לפני החזרה הכללית של כל הקבוצות.

לאחר שצפה בכל הריקודים שהכינו הקבוצות להופעה, עזר להם ברק לשכלל את הביצוע הבימתי. עד ל"חזרת המעברים" כבר הכין ברק את סדר הופעת הקבוצות בהתאם לנושא הכללי, תוך כדי שמירה על איזון טוב בין קבוצות חלשות לחזקות יותר. "כאן אפשר היה לראות באמת את אמנותו ומומחיותו פורחות," אמרה רות גודמן.

"הוא יצר את המעברים כך, שלעולם לא היתה נקודה מתה על הבמה. כשקבוצה אחת הופיעה למרגלותיה של הקבוצה המסיימת, הקבוצה הבאה כבר היתה מוכנה לתורה. זרימה חלקה זו נתנה להופעה מראה מהוקצע ונקי. במשך החזרות היו הרקדנים שלא השתתפו בריקוד מסויים יושבים בצידי הבמה ולומדים מחבריהם. כל אחד היה חלק מהפעולה הכללית כל הזמן, מה שהעניק אווירה ישראלית לאירוע כולו. בריקודים של כל הקבוצות יחד, היה אפקט מדהים לתנועה השונה של כל קבוצת רקדנים. מעברים של תנועה קשרו בין הריקוד האחרון לפינלה."

הסיום היה התגברות הדרגתית, כשלבסוף כל הרקדנים מניפים את ידיהם מעל לראשיהם בתנועת V. תמיד נוצרה אחר־כך, ללא תכנון, הורה סוחפת - אי אפשר היה אחרת. זו היתה תמצית הרוח, שברק בנה בקפדנות במשך החזרות, שנמשכו שנה תמימה.

ראיון שפורסם בשנת 1974 מדגים את מעורבותו הבלתי רגילה ואת חזונו של ברק, וכיצד פעלו אלו בפסטיבלים:

"היו לי חששות כבדים בדבר קיום הפסטיבל ב־1974, לאחר מלחמת יום־כיפור. הייתי בישראל במשך המלחמה, ורעיון של פסטיבל המחול באותו הזמן נראה לי בלתי מתאים לחלוטין לזמן. האבדות היו כה רבות והטרגדיה היתה נוראה. אך יום אחד נתקלתי בשורה משיר אידי של מ. ורשבסקי, שבתרגום חופשי אומרת: 'אם אני מוכה על־ידי כל העולם - דווקא אז אצא וארקוד!' ברוח דווקא זו של היהודים הרגשתי שעל הריקוד להמשיך, שהוא נחוץ, למרות הכל. עלינו, על היהודים, להמשיך! נושא הפסטיבל בניו־יורק ב־1974 היה החג היהודי, הגדיר בצורה השלמה ביותר את עבודתו של ברק בפסטיבל הישראלי: "אם אינך עובד עבור הדור הבא, אתה במבוי סתום. הרבה אנשים מקימים אנדרטאות לעצמם, אבל ברק בנה יד־זכרון לצעירים."

פרק עשרים ושניים:
ישראל של ברק

בשנת 1968 קיבל ברק את המשרה הרשמית הראשונה שלו במוסד לנוער של ההסתדרות הציונית של אמריקה (AZYF). לפני מינוי זה הוא עבד למען הארגון כעצמאי, והשתכר כמנהל פסטיבל מחול-העם הישראלי, שנערך מדי אביב לכבוד יום העצמאות של ישראל, וגם עבור עבודתו ב-"Y" קיבל תשלום עבור כל פרוייקט בנפרד. הוא העדיף לעבוד בצורה כזו, למרות שיכל להרוויח יותר אילו ניהל סטודיו פרטי למחול משלו. הוא תיעב את הדאגה לפרטים הטכניים של ניהול סטודיו, והעדיף לנצל את פגרת הקיץ למסעות. מבחינה עסקית היה ברק כאי בודד בפני עצמו, והוא העדיף לדבוק במפעלים המיוחדים שלו ולא להתערב בעסקים מסחריים.

ברק יזם את הוצאתם לאור של ספרים על מחול יהודי ב-AZYF. הוא ערך בעצמו חלק מהספרים ואחרים כתב בשיתוף עם מחברים נוספים. כמו כן, בחסות התוכנית למחול של ה-AZYF, הוא ארגן מדי שנה סיור לימודים של קבוצת רקדני-עם לישראל. המשתתפים לקחו חלק במשך שישה שבועות בתוכנית מרוכזת של מחול עם כוריאוגראפים ישראליים של מחול-עם, וכן בשיעורים לטכניקה ותיאוריה של הריקוד. הם צפו בהופעות של להקות-מחול ישראליות ואף הופיעו בעצמם. במסגרת הסיור המיוחד שתוכנן ביד אמן על-ידי פרד, הם טיילו בישראל ושהו בקיבוץ.

"הגעתי לישראל בדיוק ביום שבו חל פסטיבל מחול-העם בדליה, ב-1968", סיפר פרד. "מאחר שאחת ממטרות הסיור היתה לראות את הפסטיבל בפעם הראשונה, נסעתי ישר ממשדה-התעופה לאמפיתיאטרון בדליה. שהיתי שם במשך יומיים, וראיתי את ההופעות והריקודים הכלליים. זו היתה חוויה, שלא אשכח לעולם." זה היה הפסטיבל האחרון בדליה, בו נטלו חלק 3,000 רקדנים ו-60,000 צופים.

כל מבצעיו של ברק החלו, פשוט, מאהבתו השלמה וממסירותו למחול-העם הישראלי. הוא רצה שרבים אחרים באמריקה יבינו אהבה זו, ולכן הוא יסד כתב-עת המוקדש למחול הישראלי בשם "הורה". בגליון הראשון (סתיו 1968), הוא כתב שכתב-העת "יפיץ חדשות, שעניינן פעולות מחול ישראלי באמריקה ובישראל, ויסביר לחובבי המחול את ההיסטוריה וההתפתחות של המחול היהודי." מטרות אלו הושגו בלי ספק ב-35 הגליונות שערך ברק בין 1968 ועד למותו ב-1980. בכל גליון היו חדשות על פסטיבלים למחול-עם ישראלי. בשער גליון הסתיו של 1978 (11:1) הודפסה מחדש התוכניה של הפסטיבל הראשון. הוא רצה לדווח על כל פעילויות מחול-העם הישראלי בארצות-הברית, קנדה וארצות אחרות.

הוא פרסם מאמרים על יוצרי מחול-עם ישראלי, ראיונות והדפיס כתבות מעיתונים אחרים, שחשב שעשויות היו לעניין את קוראי "הורה". אפשר לעקוב במאמרים כאלה, החתומים על-ידו וללא ציון המחבר, אחר השינויים שחלו ביחסו ובדיעותיו למחול-העם הישראלי.

אחת מההתפתחויות החשובות ביותר שתועדו ב"הורה" היא השינוי של ברק ברגשותיו כלפי האותנטיות שבמחול-העם הישראלי, והשימוש בשורשים ובמחול עדתי מסורתי בהופעות בימתיות. יש שוני ברור בין מחול-עם ומחול אתני, שהתפתח במשך דורות לסגנון ייחודי. תופעת מחול-העם הישראלי היא מיוחדת במינה, היות והיא אינה

82

תוצאה של התפתחות היסטורית ארוכה, במשך דורות, בעזרת המורשת הלאומית. מחול־העם הישראלי נוצר על־ידי יוצרים בודדים. מחול זה התייחס כמובן לצדדים האתניים של החיים היהודיים ולידע העממי העתיק שבתנ"ך, כשהעם היה חופשי בארצו. אך ברק הדגיש שוב ושוב במאמריו ב"הורה", שמחול־העם הישראלי הוא תופעה כוריאוגראפית, שנוצרה, הופצה ונלמדה על־ידי גרעין של רקדנים ישראליים קנאים לענין.

לאחר שגלי ההגירה הגדולים מאסיה וצפון אפריקה הגיעו לישראל, לאחר הכרזת העצמאות, יוצרי מחול־העם פנו יותר ויותר אל המורשת האתנית, שהובאה על־ידי הישראליים החדשים. גורית קדמן היתה בין הראשונים שהכירו בחשיבות הבסיס האתני להמשך ההתפתחות של מחול־העם הישראלי, אשר הודות להיותו יוצא דופן מבחינה היסטורית, רכש לעצמו תחילה את מבנה־העל של ההווה ורק אחר־כך את תשתית היסודות האתניים.

ברק חשב בתחילה, שאותנטיות וסגנון אתני אינם ממטרות מחול־העם הישראלי. "ריקודי־עם הם פעילות מרגשת לשעות הפנאי," אמר. אך מה שמפריע לפעילות בריאה זו הוא, שמורים רבים למחול־עם מתעקשים להדגיש שהכל 'אותנטי'. כמובן שיש ללמד ריקוד מסויים בדרך שבוצע במקור, אך אין להכריח את המשתתפים לבצע תנועות מסוגננות מעבר ליכולתם..."(88)

ברק התעמק בגרעין הבעיה של האותנטיות, וראה בה את "הידע וההבנה של אנשים ועמים, של הדת, הפילוסופיה, המנהגים והתלבושות שלהם ־ בקיצור, כל אורח חייהם. רקדנים רבים ספגו את גוני התנועות ואיפיונן... רק משום שהקדישו שנים רבות לחקר וללימוד עם אחד, ובדרך כלל אף גרו בתוכו."

הוא מתאר את נסיונו, בשנות החמישים המוקדמות, שהביא אותו למסקנה, שרקדני־עם אינם יכולים לספוג סגנונות אתניים מיוחדים ושלרקוד־העם הישראלי אין צורך בלימוד השורשים האתניים של מחול־העם הישראלי.

"לפני זמן מה הכנתי קטע מחול יוגוסלבי, עבור הופעה במוזיאון למדעי־הטבע בניו־יורק. הקבוצה כללה תשעה רקדנים מקצועיים, ורקדן אחד יליד יוגוסלביה. רוב תגובות הקהל לאחר ההופעה היו על הרקדן היוגוסלבי ־ חינו, סיגנונו ותנועתו השונה מזו של יתר המבצעים. העובדה החשובה היא, שכולנו היינו רקדנים מקצועיים, מלבדו. למרות שהוא למד והתאמן במשך חודשים רבים על הפרטים הקטנים ביותר של המחול העממי של ארצו ־ ולמרות שאנחנו עבדנו קשה מאוד על המשימה ־ כל מה שהשגנו היה חיקוי מלאכותי של הריקוד האותנטי שלו. זה מראה שוב, שכמעט בלתי אפשרי לרכוש טעם אותנטי בריקוד רק על־ידי חיקוי הצעדים."

ברק הגדיר את מטרות מחול־העם לדעתו כך: אם מתירים לאנשים לנוע בחופשיות במסגרת הצעדים הנכונים, הם יחושו בחופש ובשמחה, שהם, אחרי הכל, מטרת כל מחול עממי. "...ככל שמרגישים המשתתפים חופשיים, כך הם יפיקו יותר שמחה רגשית מהמחול... הם ישכחו את המתח והלחצים של חיי היום־יום, וישתחררו לחלוטין. **וכך צריך להיות.**"

אך לאחר הפסטיבל ה־25 למחול־עם ישראלי, שנערך ב־1976 בניו־יורק, שב והרהר ברק בבעית העבודה על הופעה עם רקדני־עם חובבים.(89) הוא אימן, ביים, הורה ויצר ריקודים והופעות רבים מספור. למרות שהוא עדיין הדגיש את שחרור הרקדן, סבר ש"הרקדן החובב אינו מצוייד בטכניקה להופעתו, אך הוא מביא עימו התלהבות עצומה, החסרה לעיתים אצל אמן הבמה המקצועי."

ריקוד־העם הישראלי רכש קהל מעריצים רב בחוגי ריקודי־העם בקרב הצעירים היהודיים ובעולם כולו. "עבורי, המעורבות, המשמעת ומציאת הזהות העצמית אצל הצעירים הם הצדדים החשובים והמספקים ביותר של מחול־העם. הוא טען, שעל הרקדן ללמוד להקרין "את חופש הריקוד על הבמה," אך הצד החשוב של ההופעה הוא, "שהרקדנים מונעים על־ידי נושא הריקוד; מה שמהמם את הקהל הוא צעירותם ורוחם... כל רקדן מעורב שכלית וגופנית במחול־העם הישראלי, המדבר על העם היהודי, על ישראל, על התנ"ך, על הרדיפות וההשרדות, על הרגלים ומנהגים ועל תקוות ושלום."(90)

הוא נעשה מעורב יותר ויותר בחיפוש אחר מחול־העם היהודי האותנטי. הוא ערב את תלמידיו ־ בני הנוער שליוו אותו בטיולי־הקיץ שלו לישראל ־ בחיפושים אחר ריקוד

יהודי בקהילות היהודים מחוץ לישראל, לא רק במחול-העם הישראלי של המדינה המודרנית.

שלום חרמון, דמות מרכזית בתנועת מחול-העם בישראל, נזכר, שבפסטיבל דליה האחרון (ב-1968), "רגליו של ברק הטרידו אותו כל כך, שלא חשבתי שיוכל להסתדר עם כל המדרגות שבאמפיתיאטרון שנבנתה בצלע הגבעה, אך הוא טיפס את כולן, כל אחת מהן, ואמר, 'אתה רואה? בישראל אני חי רצעיר מחדש.' ואז אמרתי לו, שעליו לעבור הנה כדי שיחלים."

ברק המשיך להביא, מדי קיץ, קבוצות צעירים של ה-AZYF. מתוכנית זו צמח הרעיון לקורס למחול-עם ברמה אוניברסיטאית. "אירגנו קורס באוניברסיטה העברית בירושלים בשנים 1972, 1973 ו-1974, שבו לימד ברק 'יסודות של מחול-העם הישראלי', והקורס התקבל בהצלחה רבה," מוסיף חרמון.

ברק דיבר עם חרמון ועם חבריו האחרים על תשוקתו להתיישב לבסוף בישראל. הוא הסביר, שיוכל לעשות זאת, כאשר יפרוש ממשרתו ב"Y", ויהיה זכאי להמחאות הביטוח הלאומי, שיספיקו למחייתו. אך הוא חשש, שמא לא יהיה לו הרבה מה לעשות בישראל. "הצעתי לו, שיצור ארכיון למחול יהודי אתני במסגרת המחלקה ההסתדרותית למחול, והוא אהב את הרעיון," אמר חרמון.

במשך מספר שנים הוא החזיק בבית-קיץ מקסים בוודסטוק, במדינת ניו-יורק, ומכר אותו וקנה תמורתו דירה בתל-אביב ליד הירקון. כשפרש מעבודתו בניו-יורק נהג לבלות יותר ממחצית השנה בתל-אביב.

בזמן שהותו בארץ מדי שנה, הוא המשיך לחפש אחרי מחולות חדשים, כדי להביאם לניו-יורק.

"זה היה שונה מאוד מהריקודים שנוצרו על-ידי רקדנים ישראליים, שחיו באמריקה (כמושיקו, שלום בכר וכו'). ברק סבר, שעצם העובדה שהם ישראלים בעצמם, לא עושה את יצירותיהם למחולות-עם ישראליים. הוא אף עורר יוצרי מחול בישראל, במיוחד בעזרת הקלטות שהביא עימו, בעלות מיקצב טוב והוראות ברורות ומדוייקות שכתב לביצוע הריקודים השונים. לדעתי, אלו היו טובים יותר מאלה שהופקו בארץ. ברק תקף ישירות את הישראלים שהתיישבו באמריקה והמשיכו לקרוא לריקודים שיצרו שם 'ישראליים'. 'טוהר האופי הישראלי' היה בסכנה, והוא לא יכל לקבל את הריקודים שנוצרו בארצות-הברית," אמרה רבקה שטורמן, היוצרת הותיקה.

צד אחר שתיעב ב"תעשיית המחול הישראלי" באמריקה היה ההתמסחרות שלה. בשנת 1973 הוא כתב, ש"ספרים, תקליטים ומאמרים התפרסמו כדי למלא את הדרישה למחול-העם הישראלי, הפופולרי במידה עצומה באמריקה..." (91) הטרידה אותו מאוד העובדה, שיוצרי מחול-עם רבים כל כך הפיקו תקליטים שליווּ את הריקודים החדשים שיצרו באמריקה, והוא לא קיבל את דרישתם לזכויות יוצרים ותמלוגים.

בישראל החל ברק לבקר שוב בהופעות של מחול מודרני. מזה שנים שלא נכח בהופעות, והוא חשש, שלא יוכל להבין עוד מהו נושא ריקודיהם או מה רצו להגיד. הוא, שהיה פעם כה מעורב בחידושי המחול, חשב שהיצורות החדשות של האמנות פסחו עליו.

עלידא גרא, רקדנית אמריקנית שהיתה בלהקתו הרפרטואריתב בשנות החמישים ועלתה לישראל, לקחה אותו להופעה להקת המחול "בת-דור". הוא הופתע מאולם הכניסה, על מראותיו, וגרם המדרגות משני עבריו, והמזנון הקטן, שבו הוגשו קפה, עוגות וממתקים. אולם הכניסה משמש למעשה גם כסטודיו, והמראות המשמשות את התלמידים בשעת השיעורים משקפות את הקהל ההדור הבא להופעות. בת-שבע דה רוטשילד, מי שהיתה הפטרונית של מרתה גראהם ועתה של בת-דור, עמדה בשקט בקהל, לבושה במעיל פרווה קצר. פרד ירד במדרגות האולם בעזרת מקלו, והטמינו מתחת למושבו. הם צפו יחד בהופעה; קרוב לוודאי שראו אחת מעבודתיהם של רוברט כהן, פול סנסרדו או ביצירות שנוצרו ללהקה בידי לאר לובוביץ' או צ'רלס צ'רני.

"אך היכן האופי היהודי או הישראלי?" קבל פרד. בודאי שהרקדנים מאומנים היטב, אך חסר לו הביטוי של המקום והזמן הישראליים של שנות ה-70. הוא מצא, שביכולתו להתרשם, להעיר ולבקר.

רקדנית אחרת שהופיעה ב"חופשה בישראל" שלו רקדה עתה בלהקת "בת-שבע".

84

הוא הלך לראות את לורי פרידמן ביצירתה של מרתה גראהם "שעשועי מלאכים", ושוב שמח לראות רקדנים מאומנים היטב. אך היתה זאת להקת "ענבל", שהקסימה ומשכה אותו. רעיונות המחול של שרה לוי-תנאי ריגשו אותו, מאחר שנראה שריקודיה מלאים בדימויים מהתנ"ך, מחיי המדבר וישראל ואלה מתבטאים בתלבושות, בצליל ובאיכות התנועה התימנית-יהודית. הרקדנים עוררו בו את שאהב ביותר בתיאטרון – העולם חובק-כל של יצירה ייחודית. הוא ראה את "ענבל" בסיוריה הראשונים באמריקה בשנות ה-50 המאוחרות, והביא את שרה לוי-תנאי ורקדניה, כולל מרגלית עובד, ללמד ב-"Y".

גיורא מנור, מבקר המחול של "על המשמר" ומחבר הביוגראפיה של גרטרוד קראוס, הזמין את ברק לעיתים קרובות להתלוות אליו לתיאטרון. "אהבתי ללכת איתו לכל הופעה בגלל התלהבותו העצומה, בגלל ה'או!' שלו, שהשמיע בצורה כה יהודית, כשהוא שואף את האויר לריאותיו בהתפעלות. היה בו משהו תמים ותמיד היה יסוד של פליאה שהביא עימו לכל הופעה, למרות מקצועיותו. הוא היה אדם סגור למדי, אך היה נהדר לשוחח עימו. הוא היה קהל נהדר, משום שהגיב על כל מה שאמרת, למרות שבעצמו לא נטה להביע רעיונות מופשטים."

הוא נהג לפטור ריקוד גרוע וכוריאוגראפיה בלתי מספקת ב-"אני לא מבין את זה," אמירה שלעיתים קרובות היתה הסוואה לעייפות מהעדר תקשורת עם כוריאוגראפים או רקדנים.

תיאבונו להופעות גבר עם התגברות נדודי השינה שלו. היה לו רצון עז לעשות דברים. עיניו קיבלו מבע חודר, למרות שגילה סבלנות מפתיעה כלפי שיגרות יומיות כתרגילי רצפה, שחיה, עריכת קניות, עבודה בארכיון, כתיבה וביקור אצל חברים.

אך בקיץ 1977 חש ברע והתאוּנה בפני חבר, שלא נותר לו כוח להכנות עבור הפסטיבל הבא בניו-יורק או להמשיך הסדנאות השונות, שילמד בתל-אביב. הוא חשב לוותר על התחייבויות ההוראה שלו בניו-יורק. יותר מאשר רגלו, הציקה לו עייפות כללית איומה. לבסוף התייעץ עם רופא ששלח אותו להבדק אצל מומחה.

נאמר לו, שהוא סובל מגידול ממאיר, שאינו ניתן לניתוח. דרך הפעולה היחידה הפתוחה בפניו היא לחזור לרופאים, כשהכאבים יעשו לבלתי נסבלים. הוא המשיך לעבוד כבתוך הזיה. למרות עייפותו, אירגן את הפסטיבל בניו-יורק ואפילו נסע ללמד במחנה "הכוכב הכחול" ב-1978. לבסוף הוא ביקר את חבריו הקאופמנים, שדחקו בו להוועץ ברופא נוסף בקליפורניה. שם ניתנו לו טיפולי קרינה, טיפולים הורמונאליים וניתוחים, אשר הותירו אותו תשוש, אך נראה היה שנעצרה התפשטות הסרטן.

רופאו של ברק היה מעודד ביותר והציג בפניו גישה חיובית: "לא נחסל את הכל, אבל המשך בעבודה." כשבפניו מצב חסר תקווה, המסוגל להכריע אף את האדם הנחוש ביותר, דחפה אותו להמשיך רוחו, שאינה יודעת ליאות. באמצע מחלתו הוא החל במבצע חדש. הרקדן שהפך למורה, לכוריאוגראף ומפיק הביט באוסף העצום שברשותו של מאמרים, ספרים, תמונות ומזכרות, שנערמו במשך השנים. אפילו אוסף הספריה הציבורית לאמנויות הבמה שבלינקולן סנטר, ניו-יורק, לא יכול היה להציע ביבליוגראפיה מיוחדת לעבודות על מחול יהודי. הוא החליט לתקן חסרון זה בעצמו.

הוא נפגש עם ג'נביב אוסוואלד, מנהלת אוסף המחול של הספריה והמוזיאון לאמנויות הבמה בלינקולן סנטר. היא הכירה וכיבדה את עבודתו, ושמחה להצעתו. אמרה אוסוואלד, "לברק יש הבנה עמוקה של כל סוגי המחול, והבנה מיוחדת במינה של המחול היהודי והישראלי. זו הבנה בהירה מאוד. יכולת הארגון שלו מצויינת, ומסיבה זו הצעתי לו שיתחיל בחיבור מפתח של כל המובאות על מחול יהודי בביליוגראפית המחול שלנו, בת 10 הכרכים."

לא היתה זו משימה קלה, לקרוא כל פריט בכרכים השמנים, לרשום הערות ואחר-כך לקטלגן. כשהיה בניו-יורק עבד על המחקר לעיתים קרובות בספריה. ניתן לו שם מדף מיוחד עבור הכרטיסיות המצטברות. היה קשה להחליט, מה ייכנס למפתח ולקבוע את תחומי הרשימה. אמרה אוסוואלד, לאחר אחד מדיוניהם הרבים: "ההשפעה היהודית במחול-העם, בריקוד הרנסנס, ובשימוש בחומר הדרמאטי האופייני לחיים היהודיים הם עשירים וחיוניים בהיסטוריה הכללית של הריקוד. אך השאלה היא אם לכלול בביליוגרפיה את כל השמות היהודיים במחול. מה ידריך את ברק בבחירתו? כמובן שהחלטנו לכלול את

כל המחול העממי והחברתי בישראל ואת כל הרקדנים הבולטים, שהיו ישראליים ואת כל אלה על נושאים יהודיים - החיים, התפיסה היהודית, התנ"ך - ללא הבדל מי יצר אותם. באופן בסיסי, החלטנו, שנמשיך לחקור את בעיית ההגדרה: מהו מחול יהודי."

למטרה זו כתב ברק לאחדים מהכוריאוגראפים היהודיים המפורסמים בני זמננו. למרות הניתוח והכימותראפיה, המשיך ברק במסעותיו, בכתיבתו, ואף בתוכנית מיוחדת למחול יהודי ב-"Y". עלון מ-1977 מודיע ש"לאחר חמישה חודשים בישראל, ילמד ברק ריקודים חדשים של שטורמן." הוא ביקר שוב בישראל ב-1978, ובאביב נסע לרומניה ולרוסיה לפני שחזר לטיפולים נוספים בבית-חולים באמריקה, ביוני.

בשנה שלאחריה, 1979, הוא הרצה ב-"Y" על מחול-עם ישראלי בליוויית סרטים ונשא הרצאה נוספת על מחול בישראל יחד עם אנה סוקולוב. הוא שמח במיוחד לפגישה מחודשת עם הרקדנים משנות "השיעורים הפתוחים של יום רביעי". הוא לימד ריקודים יחד עם רות גודמן ודני עוזיאל, בבחרו את הריקודים, שנוצרו בשנותיה הראשונות של המדינה.

כשהוא מתלוצץ על מצבו הגופני, הוא כתב לחבריו ש"הטיפולים הרפואיים הם נהדרים. אני חושב שבעוד מספר חודשים אוכל לחזור על הקטע הגדול שלי 'מות הברבור'." (92)

הוא שמח במיוחד לתוכניות להקים "במה לרקדנים" במוזיאון תל-אביב, ביוזמת הספריה למחול בישראל. את הרעיון לעודד כוריאוגראפים צעירים במתכונת שפיתח ברק בניו-יורק בשנות ה-50 הציעה למוזיאון ימי סטרום, שרקדה עם ברק בניו-יורק ועתה יושבת בישראל. העיתונות הישראלית הגיבה בחיוב ל"מוצא החדש לכשרון". דורה סודין כתבה ב-Jerusalem Post: "שלושים ושלושה רקדנים ואחד-עשר כוריאוגראפים השתתפו ב'במת הרקדן' הראשונה באולם רקאנטי, במוזיאון תל-אביב, שהתבססה על המבנה שהגה פרד ברק בניו-יורק... התוכנית הראשונה, של שבעה מחולות סולו וארבע עבודות קבוצתיות, נבחרה מתוך 30 הצעות שהוגשו. כדאי היה בהחלט לראות את העבודות שנבחרו - והיה קהל עברון: האולם היה מלא."

תיאבון הנסיעות של פרד הביא אותו לגרמניה ואוסטריה, ובחזרה לישראל בסוף האביב ובקיץ. הוא לא התחרט על שעזב את וינה. הוא השתמש בכסף המועט שקיבל מקופת תגמולים של ממשלת אוסטריה, למרבה האירוניה כמי שהיה בעבר חבר ב"גילדת צורפי הזהב", וקנה לעצמו שעון מטוטלת מזכוכית וארד.

בסתיו החליט לבוא למיניאפוליס עבור, מה שקרא, הסיבוב האחרון של ראיונות לקראת כתיבת זכרונותיו. היה זה במשך עשרת ימי תשובה שלפני יום כיפור, כשהתקשר לקבוע את ביקורו. הוא היה מאוד עליז כשהגיע, ונראה חסון באופן מפתיע. הוא לא בזבז מלים על הקדמות. הוא החל לדבר כשהוא מתיישב, מעט באלכסון בגלל ירכו.

"הנה כל הרשימות שלי מאוסף המחול בלינקולן סנטר. אני נותן לך את הביבליוגרפיה על מחול יהודי, כדי שתשלימי אותה." הוא פתח את החבילה וראיתי דפים מצולמים רבים מספור, מחולקים בשיטתיות לקבוצות שונות של רקדנים יהודיים, מחול-עם... הכותרות צדו את עיני כשעילעלתי בערימת הניירות. בכתב-יד הברור והבוטה שלו הוא כתב, "הריקוד: ביבליוגרפיה של מקורות המתייחסים למחול ורקדנים יהודיים. עבודות על התנ"ך, סרטים וספרים, שבאוסף המחול של הספריה לאמניות הבמה, מאת פרד ברק".

כשהוא עבר על הדפים, הוא נראה מוטרד. "מה לא בסדר?" שאלתי.

"לא, אינני יכול לתת לך זאת עדיין, זה עדיין לא כל כך גמור." והוא הכניס את הדפים בחזרה לתיק וקשרם שוב בחוט.

האם הוא בשביל זה בא עד למיניאפוליס?

ישבתי כועסת ושותקת.

הוא הביט הישר בעמוד הכהה שבאולם הכניסה של המלון בו ישבנו. החבילה נחה באלכסון על ברכיו, כשידיו מקופלות על עבודתו. דמעות חלו זולגות מעיניו. אך הוא לא שינה את נעימת קולו, הוא לא היסס בדבריו. ראשו הקרח הבהיק באור החזק שבאולם, ואני התבוננתי מטה, בנעל הגמלונית שלרגלו הקצרה יותר. הנעל היתה תמיד מצוחצחת להפליא. חשבתי שהוא ציחצח אותה במין הפגנתיות. הדמעות התגלגלו במורד לחייו

ונטפר על החבילה.

"אני אינני בר־סמכא. כדי להיות מומחה היה עלי להעמיד פנים, שאני יודע כל מיני תאריכים. אני חוקר, אספן, מארגן ומורה לריקודי־עם. אני שונא העמדת־פנים וחוסר יעילות. אין להן דבר עם אמנות. האמן הוא איש עמל, כמו פועל בית־חרושת, אך בדרך יצירתית.

"אני לא נמצא על מישור גבוה יותר מכל אחד אחר. אני רכשתי משהו שאינו נמצא בספרים על־ידי עבודה קשה, על־ידי חיפוש ה'זה' המיוחד.

"בלילה, בשכבי במיטה - אין בכלל מה לחשוב על שינה - אני חושב שהספה כולה תיפול לתוך ים גדול של כלום. מעולם לא חשבתי שקיים אלוהים, אך אולי אני זוכר את 'זה' - משהו כלל עולמי, משהו הדוחף אותי להמשיך בעבודתי.

"אני חושב ש'זה' גורם לנו להתקדם, לגדול וללמוד ולהמשיך במפעלינו. אם מישהו אחר יסיים את עבודתי, היא תהיה אחת מרבות, אך עבורי היא החשובה ביותר, כי אני יודע כיצד היא צריכה להיות."

הוא נטל את החבילה ושמה תחת זרועו.

בפברואר הגעתי לניו־יורק ונפגשנו לארוחת־ערב במסעדה הסינית החביבה עליו. לאחר הארוחה הוציא פרד שתי חבילות קטנות ארוזות היטב מתוך כיס מעילו. האחת היתה קטנה ושטוחה, בנייר צהוב, חתומה בקפידה משני הצדדים. עליה היה כתוב בפשטות "לשי'לה".

"זה בשביל הבר־מצוה של שי."

הוא נתן לי מתנה לבני, שיהיה בר־מצוה בעוד תשע שנים...

ואז הוא הגיש לי חבילה שניה, שמנה יותר. "לגברת איינגבר", היה כתוב עליה באותיות גדולות ושחורות. צחקתי. לא ג'ודי? גברת איינגבר?

הוא צפה בי, כשפתחתי את החבילה. בפנים נחה על מצע רך משקפת אופרה מצופה בצדפות אפורות־ירוקות.

"היא היתה של אימי, בשביל האופרה הוויאנאית."

לא נותר דבר לומר.

יצאנו מהמסעדה והוא התעקש לנסוע באוטובוס. הוא נשען על מקלו, וכשהגיע האוטובוס נופף בו כבדרך על בימת קאברט. צחקנו שנינו, כשעלה לאוטובוס כשהוא נזהר במדרגות הגבוהות. הדלת נסגרה אחריו, וכשגבו היה מופנה אלי, נזכרתי שלא נפרדתי ממנו לשלום.

יומיים אחר־כך, לפני הטיסה הביתה, ניסיתי להתקשר אליו ללא הצלחה. לאחר שחזרנו למיניאפוליס, קיבלנו שיחת טלפון מחברו של פרד. הוא נפטר. היה זה ה־27 בפברואר 1980.

על ה"קדיש" להאמר בציבור, ליד הקבר. לפרד אין מצבה או משפחה. אך תמיד היה לו מנין, לא המינימום של עשרה, הדרוש לתפילה בציבור, אלא במובן הרחב של המלה, קבוצת אנשים. המנינים שלו הוציאו לפועל את עבודת חייו - כשרקדו כאילו "קדיש" חשאי נאמר על־ידם. פרד הורה לחבריו שלא לתת את גופתו לטקס קבורה אלא לפזר את אפרו לים.

ברק סמך על כל מיני סוגים של אנשים, שימצאו דרך לזהות משותפת והבעה עצמית. הוא גילה כשרון מיוחד לנצח על הרגשות בתוך קבוצה, באמצעות המחול. בהזדמנויות רבות ושונות - בעצרות ופסטיבלים, עם רקדנים מקצועניים או צעירים וחובבים - הוא ידע להוציא מהם את איכויות השמחה וההתרגשות.

הוא כיוון את עבודתו לאפיקים קהילתיים,, בבתי־כנסת, מרכזים יהודיים, אוניברסיטאות, מכללות ומחנות־קיץ, דרך מוסדות מבוססים. אך מעבר לידיעתו כיצד לתפקד בתוך מערכות ממוסדות של ארגונים יהודיים, עמד לו כוחו לגעת בלב אנשים. אפילו יהודים אדוקים הצטרפו לאתיאיסטים ורפורמיים כדי לרקוד תחת הוראותיו של פרד. הוא ידע כיצד להדגיש את האנושיות שבכל אחד, ואת הרצון להביע זאת בריקוד. כשעמד במרכז הקבוצה, חש כל משתתף שברק מדבר אליו. יכולת זאת הפיקה מרקדניו את המיטב.

למרות זאת, מחוץ לעבודתו, הוא היה אדם סגור, פרטי מאוד. אם כי שפע הומור,

לעיתים רחוקות השמיע הערות על נסיונו האישי. רוב הדברים שעשה נותרו תעלומה עבור אלה שעבדו איתו, אלה שלימד ואלה שעימם התיידד. אך השמירה על הפרטיות שלו לא הצרה את חוג חבריו.

הוא נאלץ לבחור בין חיים ליאוש פעמים רבות. והוא בחר בחיים באמצע הדראמה האיומה ביותר של תקופתנו. הוא נאבק על קיומו פעמים רבות עם שומרי הגבול העוינים, עם הרופאים הקשוחים, הסוכנים חומדי הבצע, פקידי הממשלה האדישים, בהזדמנויות שונות, כשקיומו היה בסכנה. והוא ניצח בקרב הממושך של נכות ומחלות גופניות, ונעשה למורה אמן של תנועה, למרות המיגבלה הפיסית.

הוא המשיך בחיפושיו במסעותיו, עם חברים וזרים, תמיד בוחן, חושב ומהרהר. האתגר ששלט בחייו והעניק להם משמעות מיוחדת היה: מה הם חיים יהודיים? מה גורם להם להתקיים? מי הם הרקדנים היהודיים, ומהי עבודתם ומשמעותה?

אולי התשובה לכל השאלות האלו הם חייו של פריץ ברגר, הידוע עתה כפרד ברק. הוא רקד את דרכו בחיים, מאבק אחרי מאבק, בסידרה של ריקודי נצחון.